GENTLEMEN CAPITALISTS

GENTLEMEN CAPITALISTS

British Imperialism in South East Asia 1770–1890

Anthony Webster

Tauris Academic Studies

LONDON • NEW YORK

For Lesley and my father,
and in memory of my mother

Published in 1998 by Tauris Academic Studies
an imprint of I.B. Tauris & Co Ltd
Victoria House, Bloomsbury Square, London WC1B 4DZ
175 Fifth Avenue, New York NY 10010

In the United States and Canada distributed by St. Martin's Press
175 Fifth Avenue, New York NY 10010

ISBN 1 86064 171 7

A full CIP record for this book is available from the British Library
A full CIP record for this book is available from the Library of Congress

Library of Congress catalog card: available

Typeset in Garamond by Julia Hedley, Ormskirk
Printed and bound in Great Britain by C.P.D. (Wales), Ebbw Vale

CONTENTS

PREFACE AND ACKNOWLEDGEMENTS

I began this book at a time of great personal sadness. My mother died suddenly and tragically shortly before I launched the project, and in completing it my thoughts are very much with her. The work is an extension of my PhD thesis, completed many more years ago than I care to remember. It is an attempt to draw together a wide body of theoretical and historical work on a region which only now is beginning to attract the academic attention it merits. The book is based on both archival research and extensive reading of the secondary literature, and attempts to apply some of the latest theoretical insights into imperialism to the phenomenon of British expansion into south east Asia.

It would be impossible to list all the kind friends who have helped me along the way to producing my first book, but I would like to mention several whose assistance and support have been invaluable. I thank Professor Peter Cain and Dr Ian Brown for their friendship and intellectual inspiration; Chris Parker and my colleagues in the history department at Edge Hill University College for their encouragement, as well as the institution itself for essential financial support; Mrs Julia Hedley for her help in preparing the manuscript; Dr Lester Crook at Tauris for his patience and good humour. I am also indebted to Professor Peter Marshall for his helpful comments on the script. I also thank the Calcutta High Court Archives for access to their invaluable collection of legal cases dating back to the late eighteenth century, and the staff of the British Library for their help in consulting both private papers and the India Office Records. I would also like to acknowledge Lord Harewood's kind permission to consult and quote from the papers of George Canning held by the West Yorkshire Archives.

Lastly, but not least I must pay tribute to my family. My supportive but long suffering wife Lesley has tolerated shameful neglect of household duties on my part. I promise, very publicly, to make amends. I owe so much to her love and help over the years. I would also like to thank my father and brothers, whose encouragement and support have sustained me throughout my efforts. My only regret is that my mother did not live to see this book completed. May it serve as a modest tribute to a very fine woman.

1. BRITISH IMPERIALISM IN SOUTH EAST ASIA: A HISTORIOGRAPHICAL INTRODUCTION

The case for a general history of British imperial expansion in south east Asia between 1750 and 1914 is not as straightforward as it might appear at first sight. The delineation of south east Asia as a suitable geographical framework needs to be treated with caution because it is a recent definition of western origin. At least one historian notes that the term south east Asia was first used during world war two, as a convenient description of a major theatre of military activity.[1] Although some conflicting definitions of the limits of the region have arisen, most writers using the term have included Burma, Thailand, Malaysia, Singapore, Brunei, Laos, Cambodia, Vietnam, the Phillippines and Indonesia. Located in the tropics, the region incorporates the south eastern corner of the Asian continent and an extensive archipelago of islands lying between Asia and Australia. The mainland portion consists of a peninsula separating the Bay of Bengal from the south China sea, encompassing the modern states of Burma, Thailand, Vietnam, Cambodia and Malaysia. Insular south east Asia includes Sumatra, Java, Borneo, Sulawesi and a myriad of tiny islands, which now mainly constitute the state of Indonesia. Physically the region falls within the Monsoon belt, and is subject to the periodic extremes of rain, wind and storms associated with that climatic system.

In the middle of the eighteenth century south east Asia was a varied region in both a physical and a cultural sense. At the beginning of our period, the Monsoon, high mountain ranges on the mainland and dense, tropical rain forest in the Malay peninsula and the islands, made for difficult communications and transport. The river systems of the region were very important for transport and settlement. Population was sparse, and scattered across tiny rural settlements based around kinship or tribal groups. There was a high degree of geographical mobility, assisted by simple housing built quickly from local materials, and the shifting nature of economic activities, which included fishing and swidden agriculture. Fishing, trade and rice cultivation were the main staples of life. Cultural diversity was exemplified by the co-existence of Buddhism (principally on the mainland) and Islam (in the islands) with older animist religions. There was also considerable linguistic variation. From the earliest times, small states had emerged, mainly financed by revenues raised from trade. These were fragile polities, vulnerable to the vagaries of commerce, war and imperial incursions. Since the fifteenth century there had been a volatile cycle of state formation and deconstruction. Such was the environment into which the British began to move in the later eighteenth century.

In light of this extreme diversity, how can south east Asia be regarded as a distinct, coherent region? The enormous variety of language, religion and economic activity is striking. The Buddhist culture of Burma differs quite sharply from the Islamic traditions of Malaysia and Indonesia. The ethnic mix of the region does not immediately suggest a common heritage, with a wide range of Malay, Thai, Burmese, Indian and Chinese communities scattered across the various countries. Even the European influence lacks uniformity, with overlapping and successive phases of Portuguese, Dutch, Spanish and British influences. To some it might seem that the very term "south east Asia" is a western categorisation redolent of European imperialist assumptions likely to prove a barrier rather an aid to understanding.

In addition, there are difficulties in identifying British imperialism within a specifically "south east Asian" context. British expansion in south east Asia was intimately linked with wider British economic and other interests throughout Asia, and the danger in adopting a regional focus is that the significance of wider developments might be lost.[2] Even the administrative structure governing British policy in the region came to be characterised by division. By 1870, Burma remained the only territory monitored by the India office, while the Malay peninsula and Sarawak had become the responsibility of the Colonial office. Siamese affairs were the exclusive preserve of the Foreign office. Such administrative division could be taken to suggest a lack of coherence in British policy towards the region.

But in fact, the regional focus of this study is not hard to justify. Recent scholarship strongly suggests that south east Asia enjoyed a distinct cultural and geographical identity long before the period of European incursion. The region displays many common topographical and environmental features, such as the ubiquitous presence of tropical rain forest, which in turn created a distinctive general economic structure based on rice cultivation, fishing, trade and the gathering of forest products.[3] South east Asia was also separated from the rest of Asia by mountains, dense forest and the fierce monsoons, which made large scale incursion into the region hazardous. The shelter afforded by the many islands and bays permitted frequent commercial and social intercourse, facilitating the emergence of a south east Asian culture, which, though by no means uniform, was distinctive from other parts of the Asian continent. But this distinctiveness did not imply isolation. Trade between China and south east Asia had assisted the emergence of successive Malay states for nearly two thousand years.[4] The high demand for Malay commodities in China and India made south east Asia a particular focus of

Chinese and Indian commercial interest, and those coastal settlements in the region able to supply such produce became favourite ports of resort for Chinese and Indian traders. The wealth accumulated by these ports through trading monopolies, customs revenue and tribute from subsidiary ports, sustained military and political power. A distinctive, cyclical pattern of political relations emerged over time; with periods of single city-entrepot state domination giving way to phases in which competition and conflict for supremacy between city states would persist, until a new dominant port-state emerged. Examples were Srivijaya (seventh to fourteenth centuries) Melaka (fourteenth to sixteenth centuries) and Riau-Johore (sixteenth to eighteenth centuries).[5] This pattern of political development was peculiar to the region, and the rulers of emergent city states, such as Melaka, claimed legitimacy on the basis of descent from the ruling family of Srivijaya. There was clearly a durable and widespread Malay culture to which successive regimes could refer for ideological justification. All this points to the existence of a discrete identity for south east Asia before the period of European imperialism. That other Asian polities in the pre-European period regarded south east Asia as a distinct entity seems beyond doubt. To the Indians it was the "land beyond the winds", for the Chinese it was "Nanyang" (southern ocean).

Another reason for a regional study of British imperialism is that south east Asia came to make a specific and unique contribution to the empire in its own right. In particular, the raw material output of the region proved increasingly valuable; notably rubber, tin, teak, rice and a range of other commodities. Neither should the administrative divisions in British policy formation in the region be read as evidence of a lack of coherent strategy. The home correspondence between the various departments reveals a conscious and consistent attempt to co-ordinate policy. For example, British intervention in Burma in 1885, was preceded by intensive consultation between the India and Foreign Offices to gauge the impact of developments on Anglo-French and Anglo-Siamese relations. Before 1867 the suzerainty enjoyed by Siam over the Malay states necessitated regular consultation between the Foreign Office and the India Office, which dealt with Anglo-Siamese relations and Straits affairs respectively. After 1867 the Colonial Office inherited this particular task along with control of the Straits Settlements and relations with the Malay states. Although failures in communication and inter-departmental rivalries were not unknown, a generally consistent and coherent policy in the region was hammered out by this process of consultation. Taken together, these observations point to the existence of a regional culture and economic structure, and a specific, coherent role for the British possessions in south east Asia within the empire. These provide ample justification for the regional emphasis of the present study.

**

Any history of British imperialism in south east Asia must be constructed around a framework of key dates and events: the acquisition of Pinang by Francis Light in 1786; the seizure of Dutch possessions in 1795 and 1811 and their subsequent restoration; the three wars against Burma between 1824 and 1885; the Bowring treaty with Siam in 1855 are just a few examples. Many of these specific events have generated detailed studies in their own right, and the challenge is how to weld this array of detailed analyses into a coherent study. There are dangers here. Excessive preoccupation with these detailed controversies could easily produce a disjointed account which loses sight of wider themes running through the period. A clear theoretical framework is essential if one is not to lose sight of the intricacies of particular developments and debates.

The imperial historian has a surfeit of theoretical explanations of imperialism. Indeed, the variety and disagreement which has characterised the debate about the origins of British imperialism compels even the historian concerned with a limited geographical field of expansion to address these wider controversies. Past interpretations of British expansion in south east Asia have drawn heavily on some of these theoretical explanations, and therefore one is forced to consider the theoretical debate in constructing any general history. A brief review of the theoretical debate about British imperialism, with particular attention of its relevance to south east Asia, is therefore a good starting point in setting the context of this book.

Many contemporaries of the British empire saw it is a product of fortune and accident, secured in a fit of "absent-mindedness", although there were always critics of this view, from Richard Cobden to Karl Marx. However, with the exception of Marx, few of the earlier studies of imperialism seem to have survived intact into modern historical debate as viable explanations of imperialism. The modern historical debate about British imperialism can be traced back to the period before and during the first world war, when imperial rivalries dominated international relations and political debate. Of particular importance was the work of the liberal English journalist J.A. Hobson, writing in the 1890s and early 1900s.[6] He argued that two main factors propelled British imperial expansion. Firstly, inequality in income distribution in Britain stifled domestic investment opportunities by constraining home demand, a problem neatly summarised as "underconsumption". The effect was to drive investment overseas, particularly to those less developed parts of the world where an abundance of unexploited natural resources promised high returns. Secondly, the wealthy financiers engaged in this stampede to invest in the less developed world enjoyed great political influence through their entrenchment in the political establishment and high society. British imperial expansion was thus engineered by a financial class able to secure state protection for its overseas investments.

The author of the second influential theory was the Russian revolutionary, V.I. Lenin. Lenin saw imperialism as an international rather than a specifically British phenomenon.[7] Writing during the first world war, Lenin sought to explain the current world conflict as the consequence of the economic and social changes wrought by a century of world capitalist development. The early stages of capitalism, particularly in early nineteenth century Britain, were characterised by the prevalence of small scale industrial capitalist organisation. The process of ruthless competition which followed not only eliminated the majority of these small firms, but also allowed the emergence of larger, wealthier corporate capitalist organisations whose wealth and political influence were formidable. By the end of the nineteenth century, cartels of wealthy capitalist corporations had arisen within the emerging industrial nations, closely connected with banks and other financial institutions. The political systems of these leading capitalist nations served the needs of their respective bourgeois elites who owned and controlled these "monopoly capitalist" firms. Underconsumption at home, and the quest for markets and raw materials overseas, prompted these elites to employ state power in imperialist expansion. The international rivalries which ensued caused scrambles for colonies, escalating arms races, rival systems of military alliances and ultimately war. Unlike Hobson, Lenin regarded this process as the unavoidable destiny of capitalism, and also as a necessary precursor of international revolution. In contrast, Hobson believed that income redistribution by social reform offered a way to end the domestic underconsumption which drove investment overseas. Capitalism was thus not beyond redemption. In spite of these differences, both Hobson and Lenin offered economic interpretations of imperialism which seemed to account for the "high noon" of empire between 1870 and 1914. They promised to provide convenient explanations for numerous episodes of European colonial expansion, including those by the Dutch, French and British in south east Asia.

However, the identification of the late nineteenth century as a period of "high" imperialism raised new questions. If later imperialism was driven by the economic forces of capitalism, how were earlier phases of empire building in the seventeenth and eighteenth century to be explained? British historians of the 1920s identified two separate eighteenth century British empires: a first Atlantic empire based upon the Caribbean and American colonies, and a second Asian empire in India which was completed in the two decades after defeat in America.[8] They argued that the dominant mercantilist economic assumptions of the day drove the European powers towards imperial expansion. According to the tenets of mercantilism, wealth and trade were finite entities which had to be seized and protected from rivals. To ensure national prosperity and strength, territories rich in desirable resources had to be annexed and defended. National power and prestige depended upon amassing territory and commerce, and maintaining sufficient military prowess to deter aggression. These assumptions were manifested as imperial expansion, militarism and rigid monopolies of trade, as exemplified by the European chartered trading companies of the seventeenth and eighteenth centuries.

According to this interpretation, the preoccupation with territorial acquisition and commercial monopoly of the eighteenth century was dispelled only by the effects of industrialisation. The protectionism, commercial privilege and regressive taxation intrinsic to the mercantilist order were resented by the emergent new class of entrepreneurs associated with industry. Favourite targets for their ire were the chartered trading companies and their commercial monopolies, which were regarded as artificial barriers restricting access to markets and resources coveted by the new industrialists. Free trade offered expanding sales in the widest possible range of international markets, while cheap foreign raw materials and food promised to help keep the costs of production to a minimum. Ultimately, the rising political clout of the industrialists enabled them to break the protectionist edifices of the old colonial empires, ending, for example, the East India Company's monopolies of trade with India and China by 1833. In this interpretation of developing imperial policy, the aggressive expansionism of the first and second empires gave way by the mid-Victorian period to a new phase of "anti-imperialism", in which further territorial expansion was perceived as an expensive burden upon Britain's burgeoning industrial economy. Mid-Victorian Liberal governments, while unwilling to dismantle the empire, expressed profound opposition to further expansion, regarding it as expensive and hazardous to the peaceful international order so beneficial for British economic fortunes. The anti-imperialist and pro-free trade sentiments of Manchester, most eloquently expressed by Cobden and Bright, set the ideological agenda of this new phase of "reluctant imperialism". Economic developments later in the nineteenth century, coupled with intensifying great power rivalries, triggered the "New Imperialism" of the post 1870 period defined by Hobson and Lenin.

There were critics of this neat compartmentalisation of British imperial history and economic explanations of imperialism. Joseph Schumpeter argued that imperial expansion was driven not by economics, but by atavistic feudal notions of power and supremacy.[9] Schumpeter noted the persistence of feudal structures of political power in many European countries long after capitalism had transformed their economies. The traditional feudal elites of countries like pre-1914 imperial Germany, still nurtured pre-modern notions of the acquisition of territory and colonies as a source of political and economic power. Thus guilt for imperial adventures and war lay with decaying aristocratic elites, not the capitalist system.

But the most important attack upon the established economic interpretation of late nineteenth century imperialism, came from Gallagher and Robinson in the 1950s.[10] Gallagher and Robinson changed the terms of debate about British imperialism. They challenged an unstated assumption that imperialism was solely the assertion of direct, formal political control by the imperial power over a territory or state via structures of formal, governing administrations set up in place of, or subsuming, local political systems. This simple equation of imperial control with formal colonial rule was rejected. The expansion of British trade and foreign investment following industrialisation, brought the British economy into contact with all parts of the globe. Britain became the principal international supplier of manufactures and investment. As the most prosperous society in the world, Britain also became a vital market for foreign producers of raw materials and food. The British market therefore became important for the prosperity and survival of local ruling elites in many developing states. In this way many less developed countries outside the formal British empire became economically dependent upon Britain. Successive British governments were quick to exploit this dependence to procure advantages for British economic interests around the world. In many cases, economic dependence on the British amounted to a relationship of "informal imperialism" in which the governments of these less developed "client" states were compelled to shape their policies to accommodate the requirements of the British. The British preferred informal empire to direct colonial rule because it avoided the costs and risks of direct rule. Where infringement of the political sovereignty of less developed states was necessary, it was better achieved by cheap informal persuasion rather than expensive military coercion. In redefining the concept of imperialism to include informal empire, Gallagher and Robinson massively extended the recognised bounds of empire at a stroke. Whole continents never previously considered to be subject to British rule, such as Latin America, were now categorised as fields of informal British imperialism.

The implications of informal empire for the accepted chronological framework of British imperialism were profound. Far from representing an age of anti imperialism, the mid-Victorian period now appeared to be one of continuing imperial expansion via the extension of informal British influence. An age of informal imperialism in the middle decades of the nineteenth century thus joined in seamless continuity the first and second empires of the late eighteenth and early nineteenth centuries with the supposedly "new" imperial phase of the post 1870 period. After 1870 there was a widespread extension of formal empire by all the European powers, but this was not related to the evolving structure of capitalism as claimed by Hobson and Lenin. Rather it was the industrialisation of Germany and other European states which forced them to seek markets and resources in the less developed world, in the process infringing British areas of interest. Thus it was the spread of economic modernisation across Europe itself, not any change in the organisation of capitalism within those states, that triggered European imperial competition in the later nineteenth century. For Britain, this meant that pre-existing channels of informal rule were increasingly vulnerable, as client states in Africa, the far east and south east Asia were able to turn to alternative sources of capital and markets in continental Europe. Faced with this weakening of informal empire, the British had to resort increasingly to formal rule to defend their overseas interests. Global European imperial competition therefore tipped the balance in favour of formal, as opposed to informal, empire.

Building upon the Gallagher and Robinson thesis, Harlow's study of the second British empire contended that pressure for the removal of trade barriers was undermining the "old colonial" structure as early as the late eighteenth century.[11] Harlow argued that the industrial interests and forces of expansion associated with informal empire, were operating from the earliest stages of industrialisation. Harlow's interpretation suggested that the second empire was not an age of imperialism separate from the industrially driven expansionism of the nineteenth century, but rather the beginning of that later process. Harlow argued that the late eighteenth century was actually the beginning of a "long nineteenth century" of industrial, free trading imperialism.[12]

There followed various studies of British imperialism after 1870 which examined particular examples of transition from informal to formal control. There was much interest in the local circumstances which contributed to such developments. There was a shift of emphasis away from the "metropolitan" theatre of policy formation to the "periphery" of empire. It was argued that informal rule depended upon delicate collaborative relationships between British economic interests and local elites.[13] These relationships were vulnerable to a variety of destabilising influences, including the growth of rival social elites able to challenge local collaborators, attempts by rival imperial powers to woo collaborators away from loyalty to the British, and the efforts of British "sub-imperialists" at the frontier to provoke formal annexation. J.S. Galbraith stressed friction with local polities as a factor which precipitated forward movements by the British.[14] D.K. Fieldhouse's survey of British imperial expansion in the later nineteenth century, stressed a wide range of peripheral factors, including European rivalry and local initiatives by sub-imperialists, in explaining the "new imperialism" of the period.[15] Fieldhouse rejected the metropolitan economic explanations proferred by Hobson and Lenin. The conclusive argument was that most British investment overseas did not go to areas of imperial expansion. Levels of overseas investment in and trade with new colonial acquisitions in Africa and south east Asia were too low to lend credibility to economic explanations of imperial expansion in those regions.

Some studies emphasised the destabilising impact of imperial economic developments upon local political structures. Wealth accumulated by local traders or other subordinate social groups enabled them to challenge existing political elites. The internal conflicts which ensued endangered imperial trading interests and created an impression of local "chaos" in the eyes of British officials on the spot, which could only be remedied by the imposition of formal control. For example, Khoo Kay Kim argues that developing commercial relations between the British Straits Settlements and the western Malay states from the 1840s had profoundly destabilising consequences for local political structures.[16] Local chiefs in Perak, Selangor and Negri Sembilan, enriched by revenues levied on the lucrative tin trade of Chinese entrepeneurs, challenged the authority of their Sultans, and fought each other for control of the tin revenues. For Khoo, civil wars and the consequent disruption of trade were behind the British assertion of formal control in the form of the Residency system after 1874.

Marxist historians continued to argue the case for a link between capitalist development and imperial incursions into the less developed world. "New Left" sociologists such as Gunder Frank contended that both formal and informal imperialism "underdeveloped" the economies of the less developed countries.[17] The potential for local industrial and commercial development in the "third world" had been drowned by floods of cheap imports from the advanced capitalist economies, while local production was subordinated and shaped to meet the requirements of the imperial economies. While some local elites prospered as clients and collaborators of the imperial powers, poverty and chronic underdevelopment were the lot of the wider population and the local economy. These Marxist and neo-Marxist interpretations of imperialism maintained a significant rearguard defence of economic and metropolitan versions of imperial history.

Much of the writing about British expansion into south east Asia has coincided with this debate, especially from the 1950s to the 1970s, and has been distinctly influenced by the concepts of free trade imperialism and the importance of developments at the periphery. The last attempt at an overarching study of British imperialism in south east Asia before 1914 was by D.R. SarDesai in 1977.[18] Like previous studies, SarDesai was profoundly influenced by the Gallagher and Robinson "school". There is the familiar emphasis on free trade, the periphery and industrial capitalism. But the theoretical debate about imperialism has moved on since the 1970s, and there is a need to reconsider British imperialism in south east Asia in the light of new thinking about imperialism. These new interpretations will be explored, but first we must clarify the main arguments offered by previous accounts of British expansion in south east Asia.

***

The initial phase of British expansion in south east Asia between 1786 and 1824 has received considerable attention from historians. During this phase of expansion the British secured the Straits Settlements of Pinang, Melaka and Singapore, as well as temporarily occupying most of the Dutch possessions in south east Asia for much of the Napoleonic wars. By 1819 when Singapore was acquired, the British were the dominant power in the region. The Treaty of London in 1824 between the British and Dutch designated the Melaka straits and the Malay peninsula as a distinct sphere of British political and economic influence. The treaty defined the scope for further expansion by both the British and the Dutch for the rest of the nineteenth century, and so represented a milestone in the development of European influence in the region. Gallagher and Robinson's free trade imperialism and Harlow's concept of the "long nineteenth century" strongly influenced studies of these developments.

For example, Wright argued that between the acquisitions of Pinang in 1784 and Singapore in 1819 there was a dramatic change in the nature of British interest in south east Asia.[19] British economic interests in the region in the late eighteenth century were concerned with the "old colonial" trade between India, China and Britain. By that period, the East India Company's commercial viability rested upon profits from tea imports from China into Britain. Funds for the purchase of Chinese tea and other produce depended upon the export to China of commodities procured by British traders in India and south east Asia. Indian opium became the most important export to China, but a range of Malay products also made a significant contribution, including spices, areca nut, tin, rattan canes and various other commodities found in the tropical rain forests and islands of the region. These considerations, and the strategic importance and vulnerability of the trade routes through south east Asia to piracy and intervention by rival European powers, were the principal motives for the British presence in the region. But abolition of the East India Company's monopoly of trade with India and south east Asia in 1813, opened the latter to the export of British manufactures, especially cotton goods. Subsequently the emergence of south east Asia as a market for British produce surpassed the older imperialist motives for interest in the region. Wright argued that British priorities in negotiating the treaty of 1824 were dictated by British manufacturers and those engaged in the export of industrial produce. One recent account accepts Wright's analysis of older colonial economic interests being superseded by the needs of British manufacturers in dictating the priorities of British policy after 1813.[20]

The most comprehensive account of the negotiations leading to the Anglo-Dutch treaty of 1824 is also set firmly in the framework of "free trade imperialism".[21] Marks describes how the British government was persuaded by the East India Company and British manufacturing interests to retain Singapore, in spite of strong Dutch claims to legal sovereignty over the island. Seen initially in 1819 as an irritating obstacle to harmonious Anglo-Dutch relations, Singapore came to be regarded as an essential outlet into the markets of south east Asia for British manufactures. It is assumed that British manufacturers were responsible for this change of policy. SarDesai also accepts Wright's notion of a shift from "old colonial" to "new industrial" priorities in the formation of British policy. In this account, Thomas Stamford Raffles, the founder of Singapore, remains the central charismatic figure in the process of British expansion. Raffles is depicted as a far sighted colonial official, as attuned to the requirements of British manufacturing industry as to the needs of the colonial administration of the East India Company in Bengal. Raffles' role as a defender of British manufacturing interests, and the importance of manufactured exports in the impressive rise of Singapore's trade with south east Asia in the 1820s has also figured prominently in work on Singapore's commercial growth later in the nineteenth century.[22] Singapore is seen primarily as an outlet for British manufactured exports during the 1830s and 1840s.

Social and political developments in the Malay peninsula from the 1840s have also been considered by historians. Increasing immigration of Chinese labourers, organised by Chinese merchants in the Straits Settlements, accompanied the expansion of primary production on the peninsula, especially gambier, pepper and most importantly, tin. The rise of the Chinese communities has been identified as a factor contributing to the political instability which eventually triggered formal British intervention in the 1870s. Once again, the influence of free trade imperialism and developments on the periphery are strongly emphasised.

Much historical debate has surrounded the decision by the British to exert more formal control over the western Malay states in 1873/74, with the establishment of British advisers ("Residents") in the states of Perak, Selangor and Negri Sembilan. Here again, the influence of free trade imperialism has been marked. British concern about the intentions of other major European powers towards the Malay states has been mooted as the main reason for British intervention.[23] It is argued that the Residency arrangement was designed to deter any possible extension of foreign influence, without resorting to annexation. In this sense it was intended to minimise the extension of formal control as much as possible. This interpretation has attracted wide support.[24] In 1873, A British company formed in Singapore to exploit the tin reserves of Selangor, passed on to the Colonial Office rumours that at least one of the warring factions in the peninsula had been approached by agents of the German government, with a view to establishing a foothold in the western Malay states. British merchants and officials in the Straits Settlements had also been pressing the Colonial Office for more interventionist policies towards the Malay states since the late 1860s. Some have argued that the trend towards intervention in the Malay states was a more protracted process than the focus upon the 1870s suggests.[25] The emphasis upon the Residents as advisers for local rulers was not entirely new, with some British officials recognising the need to exert influence as early as the 1820s. Others have argued that intervention in the 1870s was motivated more by a desire to protect British commercial interests than any real fear of foreign imperial rivals.[26] But common to all these views is an emphasis upon free trade imperialism and events at the periphery shaping policy in the metropole.

Other examples of the influence of free trade imperialism and the importance of the periphery can be found in work on the three Burma wars of 1824-26, !852 and 1885, which resulted in the annexation of Burma.

Kitzan's work on the first Burma war strongly emphasises local territorial disputes and misunderstandings on both sides as the main reasons for expansion.[27] Ramachandra largely concurs on the primacy of local disagreements, as opposed to policy in London, as the driving force behind expansion, although his work focuses mainly on the motives of the Burmese and the British response to their actions.[28] Probably the most influential work on the second Anglo-Burmese war has been Pollak's detailed study of Anglo-Burmese relations between the 1830s and the 1870s.[29] For Pollak, this second phase of expansion was also a response by the British authorities in India to local difficulties between the Burmese authorities and British officials and traders. In this account, British traders in Rangoon and Moulmein were particularly influential in precipitating British military intervention. A strong theme is the role of the "turbulent frontier". Another issue which has received attention was the role of Lord Dalhousie in the decision to go to war, and Philips' essay on this subject remains perhaps the most significant contribution.[30] The final phase of annexation between 1880 and 1885 has been the subject of rather more debate among historians, but the influence of the Gallagher and Robinson thesis remains strong. Hall, Fieldhouse and Keeton all assert the importance of growing imperial rivalry between France and Britain as the principal reason for the British decision to annex Upper Burma in 1885.[31] Others have argued that it was the need to defend British commercial interests, rather than imperial rivalry, which spurred the British to intervene.[32] Recent work particularly stresses the effectiveness of the British commercial lobby in Burma, and the aggressive imperialism of Lord Randolph Churchill.[33] But once again, free trade imperialism and the primacy of the periphery remain the central themes.

Accounts of British and European relations with the Kingdom of Siam have also been shaped by free trade imperialism and its associated ideas. The rise of British political and commercial influence in Siam, and the fact that the Siamese monarchy managed to avoid British formal rule has been seen by historians as a classic instance of infomal imperialism at work.[34]

Siam has been seen as a beleaguered "buffer state" subject to a series of attempts by the British and French to bring the kingdom within their formal or informal empire.[35] But successive Siamese administrations proved themselves adept at playing off rival powers against each other in order to preserve at least formal political autonomy.[36] Conquest was avoided even if the kingdom's sovereignty was curtailed by the reality of greater foreign military and economic power. Some have argued that the success of Siamese efforts to exploit Anglo-French differences have been exaggerated, and that Siamese independence was essentially a product of agreement between the British and French over which the Siamese had little influence.[37]

These are a few examples of the influence of Gallagher and Robinson on the historiography of British imperialism in south east Asia. The purpose here is not to dismiss these studies as outdated or necessarily incorrect in some of their conclusions; rather it is to demonstrate the extent to which this earlier general interpretation of British imperialism has so completely held sway. A revised account of British expansion into south east Asia must take account of the considerable body of work which has emerged since the 1970s.

****

The last twenty years have seen the emergence of new approaches to British imperial history which offer the prospect of a new interpretation of British expansion into south east Asia. These have broadly pursued three lines of enquiry. Firstly, those which present a new general interpretation of British imperialism based upon new research into British economic and social history; secondly those which offer new insights into the British regime in India in the later eighteenth and early nineteenth centuries, from which initial incursions were launched into south east Asia; and finally new work on south east Asia itself, which has been concerned with the nature of political and economic organisation of local societies, and with major immigrant groups such as the Chinese.

Since the late 1970s, there has been a revolution in thinking about British economic, social and political history. The new ideas which have emerged may be summarised in several key assertions. Firstly, the pace and extent of industrial change is now thought to have been much less impressive than was once assumed. The persistence of traditional methods of production in many industries, ponderous improvements in industrial productivity and the continuing vitality of the agricultural sector, at least until the late nineteenth century, all suggest the gradual pace of British industrialisation.[38] The slow pace of modernisation had important political and social ramifications. Earlier assumptions that industrialisation dictated the development of political and social institutions during the first half of the nineteenth century have been challenged.[39] It has been argued that the nineteenth century saw the continuance of an English "Ancien Regime", in which landed wealth, established religion and traditional values still determined political and moral debates. The replacement of this ancien regime by the social formations of modern industrialism was a far slower process than previously believed. While accepting some aspects of this revisionist analysis, Rubinstein, Cain and Hopkins see the eighteenth and nineteenth centuries as a period distinct from the old post feudal society.[40] For them, the period saw the emergence of a dynamic new capitalist class in Britain, which eventually came to share power with the landed elite - but this was a class whose wealth was based upon trade and finance, rather than manufacturing industry.

The work of Cain and Hopkins is most relevant here, because it addresses directly the question of British imperial expansion and the principal motivations behind it. They reassert the view that the main forces shaping British imperial expansion and the empire were located within British society. But developments at the periphery are not dismissed as unimportant. It is conceded that events at the periphery triggered numerous forward movements in the empire. However, the developments which determined the direction of British imperial expansion were British in origin. To explain the evolution of empire, the development of British society is traced from 1688, when the "glorious revolution" and its aftermath necessitated a new political settlement between crown and aristocracy. The settlement of 1688 established the principle of parliamentary sovereignty, and represented a decisive shift of power in favour of the landed interest, who subsequently dominated politics until the early twentieth century. However, the perceived vulnerability of the new order and its supporters to foreign and domestic challenges necessitated a strong military arm of the state. The Jacobite rebellion of the 1740s and global international conflicts such as the seven years war were timely reminders that the Hanoverian dynasty needed strong martial defences. But a major problem was how to ensure the military security of the regime without inflicting excessive tax burdens on the general population and the landed elite, which might precipitate domestic revolt. In the eighteenth century this was achieved by a combination of regressive indirect taxation, particularly on trade, and the cultivation by the state of the emerging financial and commercial institutions of the City of London. The term "military fiscalism" has been used to summarise this predominance of military concerns in state policy formation and financial priorities. Institutions such as the Bank of England were created specifically to fund the national debt, incurred largely to sustain national military strength. London's merchants and bankers enthusiastically availed themselves of the profitable opportunities in lending to government, confident in the state's commitment of tax revenues to servicing the national debt. The corollary of this growing importance of financial institutions to the state, was greater political influence for the City. The political security of the regime came to depend increasingly upon an emergent "gentlemanly capitalist" class of merchants and financiers in London, whose proximity to the centre of power in the capital lent them considerable political influence. The upshot was an emerging alliance between the landed interest and this financial/commercial capitalist class, which bestowed considerable privileges upon the City.

Herein lay the roots of the "Old Corruption" condemned so roundly by commentators such as Cobbett. More importantly, state patronage and the co-operation of the landed elite provided a political framework which enabled London to develop into the major centre of European trade and finance by the end of the eighteenth century. According to this view, the eighteenth century was a period of economic and social revolution, but it was one based upon financial as much as industrial capital. Industry did contribute significantly to the rapid growth and economic supremacy which Britain came to enjoy by the early nineteenth century, but industrial entrepeneurs never achieved the political clout enjoyed by the City. The state's dependence upon London's financiers, and industry's social and geographical distance from the institutions of power in London, ensured the political hegemony of land and finance over industry. Within this context, overseas empire complimented military fiscalism at home. Overseas possessions in the Americas, and later India, were important sources of profit for London financiers, thus helping to secure funding of the national debt. Naval strength, reinforced by the Navigation Acts, was also a by product of empire. In addition, taxes on colonial entrepeneurs, notably in the American colonies, helped pay for empire and supplemented the revenues needed to fund government expenditure. To fulfill these roles, imperial administrations in India and the Americas came to reflect the military fiscalism of the metropolitan regime. Defence of empire required military strength in the colonies, which in turn necessitated high revenues to meet defence costs. In the case of India, the need for ever increasing revenues, combined with a politically powerful military machine under the auspices of the East India Company, were the main motivating factors behind British expansion in the latter half of the eighteenth century. Like Britain itself, many colonies were run by militaristic administrations drawn from the landed elite, working closely with local British commercial interests.

During the second half of the eighteenth century, the economic and political arrangements which had flowed from the 1688 settlement, came under increasing strain. Rivalry with other colonial powers, notably the French and the Dutch, caused major problems. International conflicts, particularly the seven years war, upset the delicate balance between politically acceptable levels of taxation and adequate expenditure on defence. The high levels of military expenditure generated during and after the conflict resulted in increased tax burdens not only in Britain but throughout the empire. Ultimately this was to be a decisive factor in the revolt of the American colonies in the 1770s, and a major cause of the East India Company's deepening financial difficulties in the 1770s and 1780s. Yet these difficulties were to seem mild when compared to the effects of revolution in France in 1789, and the global war which followed. The financial burdens of the Napoleonic wars pushed levels of taxation to alarmingly high levels, and contributed significantly to the landed elite's fear of instability and revolution. The end of the war provided little relief, as it ushered in a new period of economic difficulty and social unrest which continued intermittently until the 1850s. Of course, this coincided with a period of rapid industrialisation, the social consequences of which exacerbated the landed elite's fear of revolution. To alleviate these difficulties, and accommodate social and economic change, the regime responded with a series of piecemeal reforms from the 1770s onwards. These gradually transformed the economic and political principles which governed the regime. The protectionist and monopolistic framework which governed trade and finance was stripped away, partly in response to opposition from new economic interest groups linked with industry, and partly at the behest of the financial class themselves. The industrialists wanted unrestricted access to markets, particularly in the far east, which had previously been the monopoly of chartered trading firms such as the East India Company. The City, which had been one of the prime beneficiaries of protection and monopoly, gradually came to the view that there were larger profits to be made from the expansion of international trade likely to follow a general relaxation of protectionism. It was a view strengthened significantly after the victory of 1815, which underlined British political and economic supremacy. Manifestations of the new "liberal" policies included greater state control over the East India Company in the 1780s, in return for the financial rescue of the Company by the State. Administrative reform in India followed, and the East India Charter Acts of 1813 and 1833, opened first India and then China to free trade.[41] Responding to social unrest after 1815, Lord Liverpool's "liberal" Tory administrations reduced the burdens of taxation and public expenditure, and relaxed tariffs in the 1820s.[42] It became accepted that the stimulus to economic activity provided by lower taxes and fewer controls would produce higher tax returns in the long run, without the necessity of punitively high rates. By the 1850s, the alliance of landed and financial interests had transformed the protectionist and mercantilist edifice of the eighteenth century into a liberal regime of free trade, low taxation, sound government finance and the gold standard.

Although this more liberal environment benefited the new class of industrialists in northern Britain, it was not one created by them. Land, supported by the City, remained firmly in political control, even at such difficult moments as the repeal of the Corn Laws in 1846. The "enlightened Toryism" of the first half of the nineteenth century was a process of adjustment to economic and social changes at home, caused partly by industrialisation, and was designed to take advantage of the new opportunities opened to Britain by her growing economy and political dominance following victory in 1815. Inevitably these policies meant some concessions to new social classes, such as the industrialists. But the industrial interests were never incorporated into the alliance between finance and land, they remained political "outsiders" in the determination of policy. Indeed, the liberal policies of free trade and sound money benefitted the City much more than industry. In the second half of the nineteenth century, the City took spectacular advantage of the growth of international trade and Britain's reputation for financial security and sound management. Capital exports and the provision of shipping, insurance and a range of other financial services, established London as the capital of the international financial and trading system. Capital raised in London financed the economic development of many parts of the non European world, and the gentlemanly capitalists of the City rose to new heights of wealth and political influence. The nexus between the old landed elite and finance continued to dominate British politics and imperial policy well into the twentieth century, with finance increasingly the dominant partner, as land declined as a source of wealth. In addition, from the mid nineteenth century, the interests of gentlemanly capitalism gradually emerged as the principal determinant of imperial policy. British imperial influence followed British investment overseas. Both formal and informal rule were extended to defend and promote these financial interests. The period after 1870, far from seeing a shift from informal to formal rule as depicted by Gallagher and Robinson, in fact witnessed a massive extension of informal British influence as foreign governments and entrepeneurs became dependent upon British capital. Gentlemanly capitalists in London skillfully used their informal social links with parliament, the Bank of England and government departments to shape imperial and foreign policy to suit their needs.

Previous interpretations of imperial expansion into south east Asia in the early nineteenth century, place a strong emphasis upon the search for industrial export markets and the primacy of industrial interests in shaping such diplomatic settlements as the Anglo-Dutch treaty of 1824. Yet this earlier view runs contrary to the marginalised role accorded to industry in these later histories of British development and imperial expansion. How can these contrasting interpretations be reconciled? Can British expansion into south east Asia in the period 1780 to 1830 be explained within the context of political and imperial adjustment in Britain described by Cain and Hopkins? Did gentlemanly capitalists seek outlets in south east Asia? To what extent were forward movements in Malaya and Burma, and the colonial regimes which emerged from them, products of gentlemanly capitalism?

The second body of new work concerns developments in British India in the eighteenth century. It has been argued recently that military fiscalism within the colonial administration proved to be a motor for imperial expansion on the sub continent.[43] Whereas previous accounts of the disintegration of the Mughal empire stress poverty and economic stagnation as reasons for collapse, this new view attributes Mughal instability to a dynamic phase of rapid economic growth and development which began in the fifteenth century. Growth facilitated the emergence of regional political rulers, enriched and strengthened by revenues arising from expanding commerce. During the eighteenth century, these regional polities asserted independence from Delhi. Mughal authority had been weakened by successive military invasions by central Asian tribes attracted by the growing wealth of the empire. The process of fragmentation was characterised by military conflicts between central and local authority, and between new regional states battling for control of valuable trade routes and other sources of revenue. The survival and success of these regional states depended upon military strength, which in turn required revenue income. The European chartered companies operating in India were drawn into these conflicts, particularly the British East India Company, which was fast emerging as the most powerful of these bodies. A crucial development was the company's involvement in domestic politics in Bengal in the 1750s, which culminated in Clive's victory at Plassey in 1757 and the subsequent assertion of Company rule in Bengal. A process of British expansion began which had engulfed most of India by 1830. Two influences shaped the organisation and administrative ethos of the Company during this period. Firstly, in order to resist aggression from local regional powers such as the Mahrattas and the Sikhs, it had to adopt the same pattern of development as that followed by local regional states. The Company had to build military strength and were drawn into aggressive territorial expansion, which in turn depended upon and facilitated ever growing revenues from land and trade. Thus the military fiscalism of the East India Company resulted partly from the need to adjust to local conditions. A second influence was the pattern of domestic British development. The eighteenth century saw the consolidation of the United Kingdom, a process by which the landed elites of Wales, Scotland and Ireland were incorporated into the ruling establishment of the English dominated Hanoverian regime. A strong sense of British nationalism was necessary to weld together the disparate ethnic elements of the British isles and ensure unity in the face of continental aggression and rivalry. Imperialism was a vital component of this new nationalist ideology, and militarism and aggression became important manifestations of this British nationalism. Thus military fiscalism in India also had roots in the metropolitan emergence of a British national identity. An important feature of this was the growing numbers of Scottish and Irish officials and merchants active on the frontier of empire - particularly in India.

Other historians have developed this theme. Military fiscalism involved the emergence of the army as a powerful interest group, which could dictate policy to the civil administration and even influence decisions in London.[44] It is even suspected that military fiscalism in India may have been a major factor in British expansion into south east Asia.[45] The salient issue arising from all these studies is the extent to which British expansion into south east Asia in the period was driven by these developments in British India. To what extent did the impetus for expansion into Burma in 1852, for example, come from Calcutta rather than developments in Rangoon and Burma itself?

The third area of new research has focused upon developments within the societies of south east Asia. Here a rich variety of studies offer new insights into the process of imperial expansion. A principal area of interest has been the process of state formation within the region. Recent work on the emergence of the Burmese state in the seventeenth and eighteenth centuries, for example, raises numerous questions about the origins of the successive conflicts with the British in the nineteenth century.[46] Similarly, the political evolution of Siam has profound implications for any re-examination of British imperialism in the region. Brown, for example, explains how in the late nineteenth century the institutions of the Siamese state and their policies were shaped by the need to accommodate the demands and interests of European powers, particularly the British.[47] The Siamese elite were constantly aware that defiance of foreign interests, particularly in areas such as foreign trade and economic policy, might precipitate European aggression and absorption of Siam into either or both of the neighbouring British and French empires. One recent interpretation of Siamese state formation in the nineteenth century argues that consolidation of the state's authority over the frontier regions of the country, and the emergence of a centralised state bureaucracy, were facilitated by growing British influence in Siam.[48] Increased British trade and investment in the country helped to furnish growing state revenues, which in turn financed the exertion of Bangkok's authority over border territories and ensured the security of the regime. According to this view, Siamese state formation was thus inextricably linked with the extension of British informal empire in the region. Once again, there is a clear need to evaluate and incorporate these approaches into a wider reassessment of British expansion into the region.

In a similar vein, Reid's masterly analysis of south east Asian societies in the period of initial European expansion between the fifteenth and seventeenth centuries, requires comment.[49] It provides an invaluable account of the prevailing economic and political structures upon which the Europeans imposed themselves. South east Asia was a region experiencing severe political and economic crisis in the seventeenth century, raising the question of how far this turmoil facilitated and encouraged British expansion in the eighteenth century.

Another important focus of recent research has been the emergence of the Chinese as a distinct ethnic and economic interest group within the "Nanyang". While the Chinese presence in south east Asia preceded the Europeans, they became integral to the development of European economic interests in south east Asia during the nineteenth century. As early as the eighteenth century, Dutch Melaka depended heavily for its prosperity upon its local Chinese mercantile community, while in both Pinang and Singapore large Chinese immigrant populations played a central role in developing the local economy, providing the Straits Settlements with a reservoir of labour and active mercantile intermediaries between European traders and the south east Asian population. In the second half of the nineteenth century, Chinese entrepeneurs and labour developed tin mining in south east Asia, particularly in the western Malay states of Perak, Selangor and Negri Sembilan.[50] Ethnic and secret society loyalties enabled the Chinese to mobilise capital and labour to impressive effect. More recent studies have focused upon Chinese social and mercantile structures and have produced analyses of Chinese society which have profound implications for understanding the dynamics of British imperialism in the region. Trocki's study of Chinese society in the Straits Settlements and Johore describes how economic relations with the British and Europeans shaped Chinese social relationships, and paved the way for the emergence of a commercial elite within the confines of Chinese society, whose fortunes lay inextricably with the global trade upon which the Straits Settlements depended.[51] The central role of opium retailing by the Chinese to their own labourers, which ensured high profits and a compliant workforce, are also highlighted. In particular the continuing importance for much of the nineteenth century of the trade in opium from India is now widely recognised. This has stimulated new debate about the role of Chinese enterprise in the later development of the south east Asian economy, particularly in Singapore.[52] One recent study illustrates the extreme dependence of British merchants and administrators upon Chinese merchants and leaders, as both a medium through which the economic resources and trade of the region were utilised, and a source of order within the expatriate Chinese community itself.[53]

Numerous questions arise from this body of work on the Chinese. What was the role of the Chinese in the process of British imperial expansion in the Malay states? What does the importance of opium in facilitating Chinese entrepeneurial activity suggest about the importance of trade between south east Asia and India in the nineteenth century? How did the dependence of British merchants in the Straits upon Chinese middlemen affect attempts by "gentlemanly capitalists" in London to secure profitable investments in the Malay states? To what extent was Chinese society shaped by the experience of British rule in the nineteenth century, and how did this contribute to the fortunes of the various post colonial states?

Plainly this book draws upon a wide range of primary and secondary sources, and is revisionist in intent, seeking as it does to synthesise recent innovations in the theoretical explanation of imperialism with new research on south east Asia. It is worth setting out the main arguments which permeate the book and which distinguish it from earlier histories of British imperialism in the region. Firstly, it will be argued that the spread of British formal rule in the region stemmed partly from the destabilising impact of British commerce upon the political structures of south east Asian states. The emerging British commitment to free trade, a trend bolstered by the reluctance of British merchants to pay prices for south east Asian produce inflated by local trade monopolies, ensured that profits and revenues which flowed from trade tended to enrich indigenous merchants, local chiefs and other rivals to the central authority of the local state. Consequently, trade with the British brought internal conflict and unrest to the states of the region. The influx of British merchants, and in Malaya their Chinese compradors, served to exacerbate local instability. When these fragile polities were threatened by political collapse, the ensuing disruption of British commerce equipped British merchants with powerful arguments with which to persuade London of the necessity for intervention and conquest. This pattern was repeated several times; in Northern Sumatra in the early nineteenth century, Burma in the early 1850s and 1880s, and in the Western Malay states from the 1870s. It was a pattern which largely determined the timing and character of British intervention.

Secondly, this book will challenge prevailing assumptions about the nature of British economic interest in south east Asia, which place too much emphasis upon the importance of the region as a market for British manufactured exports. There has been a tendency to identify British industrialism as the engine of imperial expansion. It will be argued that at least until the 1860s, commercial interests connected with traditional Asian networks of commerce were far more important, both as a source of profits for the British, and in shaping imperial policy. These networks displayed various characteristics, such as the prevalence of trade in Asian products like opium; the enduring importance of trade links within the Asian world, notably between south east Asia, India and China; and the prominence of Asian mercantile organisations such as those of the Chinese. These longstanding Asian niches of commerce remained the mainstay of the British imperial economy in south east Asia well into the second half of the nineteenth century. British industrial exports played a significant but supplementary role. Some historians have implied that these older Asian networks of commerce were contingent upon the East India Company's monopoly of trade between Britain and the east, and that as this protectionist system gave way to free trade, they faded in importance as the export trade in manufactures from Britain to south east Asia grew in volume and value. The contention here is that these Asian markets and networks remained central to the British imperial economy in the region well into the second half of the century. Indeed it will be seen that traditional eastern economic structures were instrumental in the initial development of production of tin, gambier, sugar and other commodities in demand on the world market; a process which gradually incorporated the region into the emergent global economy.

Thirdly, it is the view here that gentlemanly capitalists in the City of London became prominent in British imperial expansion in south east Asia. The main thrust of their influence was felt in the second half of the nineteenth century, but they also made an impact before 1850, most notably in the consolidation of Singapore as a British possession during the Anglo-Dutch negotiations of 1819 to 1824. It will be seen that in the late nineteenth century British gentlemanly capitalists developed close links with British commercial enterprises in the east, alliances which were to play a crucial role in expansion of British imperial power and influence into Malaya, Borneo, Burma and Siam.

NOTES

1. D.R. SarDesai, South East Asia: Past and Present (Basingstoke, Macmillan 1989), p.3.
2. See C.A. Bayly, Imperial Meridian: The British Empire and the World 1780-1830 (London, Longman 1989).
3. A. Reid, Southeast Asia in the Age of Commerce Volume One: The Lands Below the Winds (New Haven, Yale University Press 1988).
4. B.W. Andaya and L.Y. Andaya, A History of Malaysia (Basingstoke, Macmillan 1982) chs 1 and 2.
5. Ibid.: 31-34
6. J. Hobson, "Capitalism and Imperialism in South Africa" Contemporary Review LXIII (1890).
    J. Hobson, Imperialism: A Study (London, Unwin Hyam 1902).
7. V.I. Lenin, Imperialism: The Highest Stage of Capitalism (Moscow, Progress Publishers 1978).
8. J. Holland Rose, A.P. Newton and E.A. Benians (eds.), The Old Empire from Beginnings to 1783 (Cambridge 1930).
    Sir R. Coupland, The British Empire after the American Revolution (London, Longmans, Green and Co. 1930)
9. J. Schumpeter (1919), "The Sociology of Imperialism" reprinted in J. Schumpeter, Imperialism and Social Classes (New York, Augustus M. Kelley, 1951).
10. J. Gallagher and R. Robinson, "The Imperialism of Free Trade" Economic History Review 2nd series, 6 (1953) 1-13.
    J. Gallagher and R. Robinson, Africa and the Victorians: The Official Mind of Imperialism (London, Macmillan 1961).
11. V.T. Harlow, The Founding of the Second British Empire 2 vols. (London, Longman 1952, 1964).
12. P.J. Cain and A.G. Hopkins, British Imperialism: Innovation and Expansion 1688-1914 Vol. 1 (London, Longman 1993).
13. R. Robinson, "Non European Foundations of European Imperialism: Sketch for a Theory of Collaboration" in R. Owen and R. Sutcliffe (eds.), Studies in the Theory of Imperialism (London 1972)
14. J.S. Galbraith, "The Turbulent Frontier as a Factor in British Expansion" Comparative Studies in Society and History 2 (1960) pp150-168.
15. D.K. Fieldhouse, Economics and Empire 1880-1914 (Ithaca New York, Cornell University Press 1973).

16. Khoo Kay Kim, The Western Malay States 1850-1873: The Effects of Commercial Development on Malay Politics (Oxford University Press, Kuala Lumpur 1972).

17. Andre Gunder Frank, Capitalism and Underdevelopment in Latin America (Hamondsworth, Penguin 1971)

18. D.R. SarDesai, British Trade and Expansion in Southeast Asia 1830-1914 (New Delhi, Allied Publishers 1977).

19. H.R.C. Wright, "The Anglo-Dutch Dispute in the East 1814-24" Economic History Review 3: 2, (1950-51) 229-239.

20. N. Tarling, Anglo-Dutch Rivalry in the Malay World 1780-1824 (Queensland, University of Queensland Press 1962).
    N. Tarling, The Fall of Imperial Britain in Southeast Asia (Singapore, Oxford University Press 1993).

21. H. Marks, The First Contest for Singapore (Gravenhage, Nijhoff 1959).

22. Wong Lin Ken, "The Trade of Singapore 1819-69" Journal of the Malaysian Branch of the Royal Asiatic Society 33: 4 (1960) 11-301. See pp.27-30 and 160-161.

23. C.D. Cowan, Nineteenth Century Malaya: The Origins of British Political Control (London, Oxford University Press 1961).

24. D. McIntyre, "Britain's Intervention in Malaya: The Origin of Lord Kimberley's Instructions to Sir Andrew Clarke in 1873" Journal of Southeast Asian History 11: 3 (1961) 47-69.
    D. McIntyre, The Imperial Frontier in the Tropics 1865-75 (London, Macmillan 1967) Chs 5 and 6.

25. N. Tarling, "Intervention and Non Intervention in Malaya" Journal of Asian Studies 11: 4 (1962) 523-527.

26. D.R. SarDesai, British Trade and Expansion

27. L. Kitzan, "Lord Amherst and the Declaration of War on Burma 1824" Journal of Asian History 9: 2 (1975) 101-127.
    L. Kitzan, "Lord Amherst and Pegu: The Annexation Issue 1824-26" Journal of Southeast Asian Studies 8 (1977) 176-194.

28. G.P. Ramachandra, "The Outbreak of the First Anglo-Burmese War" Journal of the Malaysian Branch of the Royal Asiatic Society 51 (1978) 69-100.

29. O.B. Pollak, Empires in Collision: Anglo-Burmese Relations in the Mid-Nineteenth Century (Greenwood, Westport 1979).

30. Sir C. Philips, "Dalhousie and the Burma War of 1852" in C.D. Cowan and O.W. Wolters (eds), Southeast Asia and Historiography (Ithaca, Cornell University Press 1976).

31. J. Furnivall, Colonial Policy and Practice: A Comparative Study of Burma and Netherlands India (Cambridge, Cambridge University Press 1948).
    D.G.E. Hall, A History of Southeast Asia (London, Macmillan 1955)
    D.K. Fieldhouse, Economics and Empire
    C.L. Keeton, King Thebaw and the Ecological Rape of Burma (Delhi, Manohar 1974).

32. D.P. Singhal, The Annexation of Upper Burma (Singapore, South Asian publishers, 2nd edn 1981).
    D. Woodman, The Making of Burma (London, Cresset 1962).

33. Maung Htin Aung, Lord Randolph Churchill and the Dancing Peacock: British Conquest of Burma 1885 (New Delhi, Manohar 1990).

34. SarDesai, British Trade and Expansion p.270.

35. C. Jesharun, The Contest for Siam, 1889-1902: A Study in Diplomatic Rivalry (Kuala Lumpur, University of Malaya 1977).

36. I.G. Brown, The Ministry of Finance and the Early Development of Modern Financial Administration in Siam 1885-1910 (Unpublished PhD thesis, University of London 1975)

37. M.F. Goldman, "Franco-British Rivalry over Siam 1896-1904" Journal of Southeast Asian Studies 3 (1972) 2,

38. N. Crafts, British Economic Growth during the Industrial Revolution (Oxford 1985).

39. J.C.D. Clark, English Society 1688-1832 (Cambridge University Press 1985).

40. W.D. Rubinstein, Capitalism, Culture and Decline in Britain 1750-1990 (London, Routledge 1993).
Cain and Hopkins, British Imperialism: Innovation and Expansion

41. A. Webster, "The Political Economy of Trade Liberalisation: The East India Charter act of 1813" Economic History Review 2nd series, XLIII: 3 (1990) 404-419.
P.J. Marshall, Bengal: The British Bridgehead, Eastern India 1740-1820 (Cambridge, Cambridge University Press 1987).
C.A. Bayly, Indian Society and the Making of the British Empire (Cambridge University Press 1988).

42. B. Hilton, Corn, Cash and Commerce; The Economic Policies of the Tory Governments 1815-1830 (Oxford, Oxford University Press 1977).
J.E. Cookson, "British Society and the French Wars, 1793-1815" Australian Journal of Politics and History 31 (1985) 192-203.

43. See Marshall, Bengal; the British Bridgehead and Bayly, Indian Society.

44. D. Peers, "Between Mars and Mammon; the East India Company and efforts to Reform its Army, 1796-1832" Historical Journal 33: 2 (1990) 385-401.
D.Peers, "The Duke of Wellington and British India during the Liverpool Administration, 1819-27" Journal of Imperial and Commonwealth History 17: 1 (1988) 1-25.

45. D. Washbrook, Paper to the Annual conference of the Economic History Society, April 1994.

46. V. Lieberman, "Local Integration and Eurasian Analogies: Structuring Southeast Asian History 1350-1830" Modern Asian Studies 27: 3 (1993) 475-572.
V. Lieberman, "Secular Trends in Burmese Economic History, c.1350-1830, and their Implications for State Formation" Modern Asian Studies 25: 1 (1991) 1-31.
V. Lieberman, Burmese Administrative Cycles: Anarchy and Conquest: c. 1580-1760 (Princeton, Princeton University Press 1984).

47. I.G. Brown The Elite and the Economy in Siam 1890-1920 (Singapore, Oxford University Press 1988).

48. C. Rajchagool, The Rise and Fall of the Thai Absolute Monarchy (Bangkok, White Lotus 1995).

49. A. Reid, Southeast Asia in the Age of Commerce 1450-1680: Volume Two: Expansion and Crisis (New Haven, Yale University Press 1993).

50. Wong Lin Ken, The Malayan Tin Industry to 1914 (University of Arizona 1965).
Cowan, Nineteenth Century Malaya
Khoo Kay Kim, The Western Malay States

51. C. Trocki, Opium and Empire: Chinese Society in Colonial Singapore 1800-1910 (Ithaca, Cornell University Press 1990).

52. C.F. Yong, Chinese Leadership and Power in Colonial Singapore (Singapore, Times Academic Press 1992).

R.A. Brown, *Capital and Entrepeneurship in South-East Asia* (Basingstoke, Macmillan 1994).

53. R.K. Ray, "Asian Capital in the Age of European Domination: the Rise of the Bazaar 1800-1914" *Modern Asian Studies* 29: 3 (1995) 449-554.

2. EARLY BRITISH EXPANSION INTO SOUTH EAST ASIA: 1750-1795

British interest in south east Asia can be traced back to the early seventeenth century, when the newly formed English East India Company began to compete with the Dutch East India Company for the trade in spices and other produce of the islands of the Indonesian archipelago. These beginnings were inauspicious, because the wealthy Dutch Company, supported by its government, outmatched the English in resources and military strength. The torture and massacre by the Dutch of ten English Company servants at Amboina in 1623 convinced the English of the overwhelming power of their rivals. It was a lesson which was repeated when the Dutch seized Banten in Java in 1682 and expelled British traders. Subsequently, the English Company's attentions were concentrated on the Indian sub continent, and in spite of the acquisition of Benkulen on the west coast of Sumatra in 1685, English interest remained subdued for the rest of the seventeenth century. It was not until the later eighteenth century that British commercial interest revived.

By the mid eighteenth century, the states and societies of south east Asia were complex but fragile social formations created by several centuries of turbulent economic and political development. Between the fourteenth and seventeenth centuries there had been a frenetic period of state formation, which has been described famously as "the Age of Commerce".[1] The produce of the region, including spices, tin, benzoin and other commodities, had long attracted traders from India and China, and by the fifteenth and sixteenth centuries they were joined by Portuguese and Dutch adventurers. Rapid expansion of trade brought larger tax revenues to the emergent polities of the region, particularly Aceh in northern Sumatra, Melaka, Ayudhaya (Siam), Banten and Mataram in Java, and Burma. These states were heavily dependent upon revenues drawn from trade, either through taxes levied on commerce, or state monopolies imposed upon the trade in certain articles. Dependence upon trade determined the coastal locations of many of these states and facilitated spectacular growth. Contemporary European visitors estimated the population of Ayudhaya as 200,000 in the seventeenth century, Aceh over 100,000, and Melaka and Banten of roughly similar proportions.[2]

These were absolutist states, in which local rulers secured scarce labour power by conquest, enslavement and a complex system of debt bondage. Retaining local population was often a major problem. The people of south east Asia were noted for the portability of their dwellings, their adaptibility to new environments and their maritime skills, all attributes which made for an itinerant population. Absolutism was an attempt to curb these tendencies by means of ideology and intimidation. Elaborate religous justifications for royal power were devised and celebrated, with some Malay rulers such as Iskandar of Melaka claiming direct descent from Alexander the Great.[3] Brutal means were sometimes employed to crush resistance. Smugglers, local chiefs or even wealthy merchants were targets for persecution. For example, Iskandar Muda of Aceh (1607-36) massacred a large number of his Orang Kaya (merchants) out of fear that they were conspiring to challenge his authority.[4]

Absolutism went hand in hand with political instability. The main cause was the fluidity of south east Asian societies. Extreme population mobility was one reason for this, another was the wealth which commercial expansion brought to local merchants, enabling them to challenge existing rulers. Many of the ruling dynasties of the "Age of Commerce" owed their rise to recent commercial success rather than ancient birthright, regardless of spurious claims to the contrary. The fragility of south east Asian polities was demonstrated dramatically during the international economic downturn of the seventeenth century, when the collapsing trade revenues precipitated widespread political disintegration across the region.[5] The commercial depression was not the only cause of turmoil. It was the brittleness of local societies and political structures which made the impact of the global crisis upon Melaka, Aceh, Ayudhaya and other states, so devastating.[6] The appearance of predatory European powers in the form of the Portuguese and Dutch also contributed to instability, as demonstrated by the successive Portuguese and Dutch conquests of Melaka in 1511 and 1641. The Dutch in particular made their presence felt by local alliances and intrigues which set local rulers against each other. But the impact of the European presence cannot disguise the importance of local reasons for political instability. Neither Portuguese nor Dutch power were boundless. At the end of the seventeenth century the Dutch authorities acknowledged that their ability to enforce their will in the region was constrained by the limits of their naval power. Subsequently they concentrated their resources in the Indian Ocean and western Indonesian archipelago, abandoning earlier efforts to dominate the eastern sea routes to China.[7]

Conditions in south east Asia during the eighteenth century, on the eve of British expansion, have recently attracted the renewed interest of historians. First, it is plain that the internal instability which characterised many states in the seventeenth century was still apparent after 1750.[8] In

Burma the Toungoo rulers were overthrown in 1752, and their successors destroyed Ayudhaya fifteen years later. Political weakness remained the overwhelming characteristic of Acehnese Sultans throughout the eighteenth century, a fact which at different times enticed and frustrated British interest.[9] Events in Johore in 1699, which culminated in the murder of the Sultan there, destabilised the Malay peninsula, as states such as Perak, Selangor, Trengganu and Kedah emerged from Johore's shadow to compete for territorial dominance. Within these states, internal instability was also a debilitating problem. In 1743, the ruler of Perak was deposed by local chiefs operating in alliance with elements from nearby Selangor.[10] Similarly, an internal rebellion in Kedah in 1771 attracted the involvement of Selangor, a development which prompted the Sultan of Kedah to seek assistance from the English East India Company.[11]

But political instability coincided with an economic recovery which brought, for some parts of the region at least, the prospect of greater social and political cohesion. Global economic recovery resulted in a general upturn in trade to south east Asia after 1750. The British involvement in this recovery is well recorded. The numbers of British trading vessels calling at the port of Melaka, for example, rose from 24 in 1764 to 85 in 1776.[12] Non European commerce also flourished. The growth of Chinese trade to Nanyang was accompanied by substantial levels of migration into the region. Among groups indigenous to south east Asia, the Bugis of Sulawesi were particularly instrumental in the commercial recovery after 1750. Bugis commercial expansion had been accompanied by migration to the Malay peninsula, where their political influence grew significantly.[13]

Commercial recovery brought political renewal to parts of the region. Following the Konbaung rebellion in Burma, expanding commerce brought larger revenues for the state, increased prosperity and social cohesion; developments which promoted both the consolidation and expansion of the new Burmese regime.[14] Burmese rulers were assisted by the growth of an extensive peasant agricultural sector absent from most of the island regimes of the region. Extensive rice cultivation in upper as well as lower Burma, assisted by experimentation with new crops and irrigation schemes, provided a cushion against the worst effects of commercial depression; enabling the local elite to retreat into exploitation of the peasantry to sustain the regime. Indeed, agricultural growth combined with administrative reform designed to promote exports, were strategies common to the three mainland states of Burma, Vietnam and Siam between the fifteenth and nineteenth centuries.[15] These policies enabled the mainland states to weather the difficult period of crisis more successfully than the regimes of island south east Asia. While some historians believe that in the case of Siam it was international commerce rather than domestic agriculture which was central to political revival in the late eighteenth century, there is a broad consensus that the late eighteenth century saw stronger political revival and social cohesion on the mainland than in peninsular and island south east Asia.[16]

British interest in south east Asia was directed first towards the islands of Indonesia and the Malay peninsula. For various reasons, the turbulence of the seventeenth century crisis was not dispelled by commercial recovery. The prevalence of tropical rain forest limited food production, overland communications and population, thereby denying this part of the region the more extensive peasant agricultural base enjoyed by the mainland regimes. It has been estimated that the population of the western Malay states at the turn of the nineteenth century was probably less than 20-30,000.[17] Consequently, for these states revival from the consequences of depression was much more fragile. The mobility of shifting cultivators, coupled with poor communications made it very difficult for the rulers of states on Sumatra and the Malay peninsula to reassert their authority over their local populations, even when trade recovered after 1750. Much power had devolved to local chiefs, who exercised more effective authority in their localities than could a remote Sultan. Some wealthier merchants also grew in power because of their involvement in foreign trade, making them indispensable for the collection of trade taxes. In Aceh royal authority was diminished by the rising power of the ulubalang (territorial chiefs), who exercised local authority and tax raising powers in their respective mukim (administrative districts), and the Orang Kaya (merchants) who occupied key tax collecting positions such as Syabandar (harbour master/controller of imports and exports).[18]

Another factor which promoted instability was the presence of immigrant groups within local Malay societies and the efforts of some European powers, notably the Dutch, to assert monopolistic control over local trade. Wealthy Bugis migrants to the Malay peninsula and the islands of the Indonesian archipelago, emerged as contenders for power, particularly in Aceh and Johore. By the 1770s they controlled Riau, and exerted considerable power over the Sultan of Johore.[19] As expert sailors, traders, and formidable warriors, the Bugis populations of the Malay states became embroiled in local conflicts. It was a Bugis attack from Selangor in 1771 which sent the Sultan of Kedah scurrying for British assistance. Another migrant group in the Malay peninsula, the Minangkabau from eastern Sumatra, clashed consistently with both Bugis and Malays in Negri Sembilan, their main area of settlement.[20] Even the Dutch experienced Bugis power. In 1784 they finally swept the Bugis from Riau, after only narrowly surviving a five month siege of Melaka by Raja Haji, the formidable Bugis ruler of Riau-Johore.[21]

Of course, incursions by European powers also destabilised the Malay states. Dutch efforts to enforce monopolistic treaties with Malay states brought them into conflict with local rulers anxious to take full advantage of the commercial opportunities before them, as well as the Bugis and rival Europeans. War broke out between the British and Dutch in south east Asia, lasting from 1780 to 1784. Trade was disrupted, and severe tension, suspicion and emnity long outlived the cessation of fighting.[22] Following their defeat of the Bugis in 1784, the Dutch sought to consolidate and assert political authority over Selangor. After initial setbacks, the Dutch enforced a rigorous blockade of the state.[23] But it was not only Europeans who threatened the sovereignty of Malay rulers. Following the revival of Siam, the Chakri kings tried to reassert their authority over the Malay peninsula.[24] The question of Siamese authority had always been viewed differently by the Malays and the Siamese. The traditional symbol of Malay submission was the delivery to the Siamese court of the Bunga Mas, the golden flowers; but the two sides interpreted the gesture differently. While the Siamese viewed it as a clear acknowledgement of the tributary status of the Malay states, the Malays construed it as a gift, suggesting a less subordinate relationship than the Siamese desired.

These then were the volatile circumstances which prevailed in the Malay peninsula and the Indonesian archipelago in the later eighteenth century. Renewed trade and economic activity brought wealth for many local rulers and their subordinates, but not the political stability which by the end of the century was apparent in the mainland states. Strong governments there had been able to ensure that trade and its revenues would strengthen central state authority, but in the Malay peninsula and the Indonesian islands few local rulers had the military or administrative means to ensure that central authority would reap its due benefits. Instead, local chiefs and powerful merchants were able to accumulate sufficient wealth and power to defy their rulers. One consequence of weak state power, intermittent warfare on land and sea, and increased maritime traffic was an alarming increase in piracy on the high seas, a serious hazard for European and local traders alike. The severity of this problem is illustrated by the effect of piracy upon tin production on the island of Bangka, a particularly important source of this commodity for the Dutch. Piratical raids on the island and its trade, particularly by the feared Ilanun pirates of the Sulu archipelago, resulted in a steady decline in tin production from the mid 1770s.[25] In this way, commercial growth actually exacerbated instability in the late eighteenth century. This unpredictable political climate had implications for the expansion of British imperial power into the region.

In particular, the British came to be seen as a powerful potential ally against either external or internal enemies. In Aceh, Sultan Mahmud Syah (1760-1781) wanted to grant British merchants trading and revenue collection rights in the mid 1760s, in exchange for support against the the more powerful merchants in the kingdom.[26] The Sultan of Kedah's approach to the East India Company for help against Selangor in return for a factory in 1771 has already been noted; and Sultan Abdullah's decision to grant Pinang to the British in 1786 was motivated by a need for powerful allies in the face of possible Siamese aggression.[27] In 1783, the Bugis ruler of Riau Johore, Raja Haji, offered Thomas Forrest, the British merchant, the opportunity to establish an East India Company base on the island of Riau, then heavily frequented by British merchantmen.[28] Raja Haji hoped to enlist the help of the British against the Dutch, but he was defeated and killed by the Dutch in

1784 before his plans came to fruition. In this way British territorial expansion was encouraged by local rulers struggling to cope with their turbulent political environment.

Turmoil in the Malay archipelago reinforced British opinions of local societies. Internal struggles for power were often construed by the British as evidence of weakness, moral cowardice and corruption. Mahmud Syah of Aceh, for example found his efforts to make a deal with Desvoeux of the East India Company by granting to the British the right to collect trade duties at the port of Aceh, thwarted by resistance from Chuliah merchants with influence at court. Sultan Mahmud was forced to abandon an initial agreement with Desvoeux, who displayed little appreciation of the internal difficulties in the regime which made it so difficult for Mahmud to deliver his promises. Desvoeux's perspective on events was typical of so many British officials. To him, Mahmud's volte face was attributable solely to the Sultan's indecisive nature, weakness and his susceptibility to Court flatterers.[29] There were numerous such encounters with Malay rulers which reinforced British racial and ethnic stereotypes. Malay rulers were labelled as capricious, untrustworthy, weak, degenerate and incompetent. Generally, the British did not appreciate the strictures, pressures and local cultural expectations bearing down on local rulers. From this perspective, it was easy to construct moral justifications for the arbitrary application of British power at the expense of local states.

Piracy was seen as yet further proof of the immorality and weakness of local societies. From the earliest years of British expansion into south east Asia, a strong military presence was regarded as essential to provide the protection which local political leaders could not be trusted to deliver. Yet before the global war of 1793 to 1815, British administrations in India were anxious to curb the imperialist inclinations of officials and merchants in south east Asia. This restraint was not borne of any sympathy for the integrity of local states, but rather to avoid the heavy costs which expansion would incur, particularly through obligations to help allies of dubious character in local disputes. Then of course there was the question of the Dutch. East India Company officials in London and Calcutta were reluctant to inflame Dutch opposition in a region considered by the Dutch to be their own sphere of influence. Such a course could encourage military rivalry, prompting conflict and crippling financial committments. Thus, in the period before 1795, the imperialist instincts of British officers and traders in south east Asia were reined in, and acquisitions and committments restricted to the bare essentials deemed necessary to protect the national interest. But this was to change.

**

The growth of British interest in south east Asia culminated in the East India Company's acquisition of Pinang in 1786. British involvement in the region was related to the spread of British rule in India. Following the conquest of Bengal in 1757, the East India Company extended its domain through successive wars with the princely states, in the process transforming itself from a purely commercial organisation into a military and administrative bureaucracy.[30] The importance of imperial expansion in India for state formation in Britain itself has already been mentioned.[31] Within the East India Company, territorial expansion created a culture of "military fiscalism", which promoted aggression and further acquisitions of territory. There emerged a self perpetuating cycle of militarism and imperial expansion. In order to defeat local Indian states, the Company had to expand its miliary forces. To pay for this, the Company had to acquire an ever wider revenue base, which meant further territorial conquests.

The culture of military fiscalism within the Company, which elevated soldiers to positions of authority, inevitably coloured British attitudes towards the societies and states of south east Asia. Company officials viewed the polities of the region with the same contempt, aggression and suspicion which pervaded their view of Indian states. But developments in India were to propel the British towards south east Asia for economic as well as cultural reasons. Initially, the Company's quest for revenue and profit to offset the expense of militarism was not successful. Inefficiency and corruption within the Company's administrative structure, the sheer scale of military costs incurred, and the inability of the Company to generate sufficient trading profits all contributed to a deepening crisis. So serious were these financial difficulties that the Company in London was forced to seek assistance from the British state. Although help was forthcoming, the price was high. The Company was required to undertake far reaching reforms, which were incorporated into the Regulating Act of 1778, the India Act of 1784, and the Charter Act of 1793.[32] These included the establishment of the Board of Control, a government department empowered to supervise the Company's affairs, and the elimination of private commercial interests among Company employees.[33] For a time, these reforms helped the Company ease its financial problems. Another development also helped postpone financial oblivion. In the last decades of the eighteenth century there was a rapid expansion of trade between India and China. The Company discovered that the teas, silks and ceramics of China commanded a ready market in Britain and Europe, promising the high returns needed to restore solvency and profitability. Since the Company enjoyed a monopoly of trade between Britain and China, it was the main beneficiary of the China trade. A system of trade between India, China and Britain emerged which was to prolong the existence of the Company as a viable commercial organisation and enable it, for a time, to meet its swelling political and administrative costs.

The rise of British power in India in the eighteenth century was accompanied by the growing success of their merchants in securing the lion's share of trade between the ports of southern and eastern India and south east Asia.[34] They gradually displaced the southern Indian merchants as the most important traders to that region. By the 1740s, British traders from Madras had developed extensive trade links with Pegu and Aceh.[35] In spite of some difficulties, Aceh was the port most frequented by British traders before 1786. A longstanding trade agreement between the East India Company and Aceh had been signed as early as 1602, when the Company's representative, James Lancaster, signed a treaty of friendship with Sultan Ala'ad-din Riayat Shah (1588-1604), granting to the Company extra-territorial rights, exemption from certain customs duties and free trade.[36] In fact the Company did not avail itself of these privileges, leaving the conduct of trade with Aceh and south east Asia largely to individuals trading on their own account. In the eighteenth century, this trade began to grow. Before the reforms of the 1780s, Company officials were permitted to supplement their remuneration with their own private trading adventures. Many of the trade initiatives pursued by individual free merchants into south east Asia were backed by Company servants on private account. These arrangements meant that senior Company officials in India were inclined to take great interest in private trade to the region, even when attending to East India Company business.

British trade with Aceh and other ports of the Malay archipelago was based upon the exchange of Indian produce, mainly rice and textiles, for south east Asian produce such as pepper, spices, betelnut, benzoin, dammer and tin.[37] But in the long run, trade with south east Asia became connected with the growing British trade between India and China. A problem for both the Company and private merchants was the indifference of Chinese consumers to Indian produce, a difficulty only remedied by the large scale development of Indian opium production after the 1780s. Before then, British traders had to pay for Chinese goods in gold or silver specie if their exports were unable to match the value of Chinese commodities purchased. The consequent drain of specie was viewed with alarm by senior Company officials, who saw this as a potential cause of economic depression for the Indian economy. It was in this context that south east Asian commodities became valuable in the China trade. Tin, betelnut, spices and a vast array of south east Asian produce had long found a market in China, a fact demonstrated by the historic trade between China and the Nanyang. Thus trade with south east Asia promised to furnish British traders with the exports they so badly required for the Chinese market. Increasingly, British traders with south east Asia sold their produce to their peers engaged in the China trade; transactions which were often completed in the south east Asian ports by traders en route to China. This branch of commerce became more important as the latter half of the eighteenth century progressed, and by the first decades of the nineteenth century was the principal function of British trade to south east Asia. Earlier historians have tended to see this as almost the sole reason for the expansion of British commerce with the region in the 1750s and 1760s.[38] In part, this was because the China trade was seen by some as already having acquired an enhanced significance in the decades of the mid eighteenth century. In the early eighteenth century trade between eastern

India and the ports of the Indian west coast, the gulf and the Red sea had been the main trade networks of the sub continent. Some historians have argued that these trade links began to decline in the 1740s, but were fortuitously replaced by a rapid increase in the volume of trade with China in the 1750s and 1760s.[39] Therefore, the post 1750 expansion of British trade with south east Asia was promoted by the greater significance of the Chinese market.

However, more recent research has rejected this analysis. Even in its heyday in the 1740s, the trade with western India and the middle east was insufficient to provide employment for all of the ambitious private merchants of Calcutta and Madras, and even then, trade between India and south east Asia was of significant value to British interests.[40] Moreover, nearly thirty years elapsed before the China trade had developed sufficiently to replace the western branch of commerce.[41] Far from interest in south east Asia resulting solely from the growth of the China trade, the region offered markets which became needed urgently not only to absorb some of the Bengal and eastern Indian exports previously directed to the Gulf and middle east ports, but also to help accommodate the rise in production which followed the British conquest of Bengal. Thus the expansion of trade to south east Asia after 1750 was not just to use that region as a medium of commodity exchange to service the China trade. It was a market for Indian produce in its own right. It is true that by the 1770s China vastly outstripped south east Asia as a market for Indian exports, but the region remained an important if lesser outlet. At times of difficulty for the China trade, south east Asia tended to assume an enhanced importance for British commercial interests, both as a marginal market to absorb Indian produce unable to reach the China market, and as a clandestine route for Indian goods into China, via the Chinese junk trade with south east Asia.

The new British interest in south east Asia began to be manifested officially in the 1760s, although East India Company officials were uncertain of the best strategy to secure markets in the region. At first it was hoped that Benkulen might provide access to the Malay archipelago. Benkulen also controlled several smaller outposts on the coast of Sumatra, and it was hoped that through these, the produce and markets of Sumatra could be exploited fully.[42] However, Benkulen suffered formidable problems. Situated on the west coast of Sumatra, it was poorly placed to exploit the richest centres of trade, which were to the east of the island. Few Malay or Bugis merchants came to Benkulen. The port possessed poor harbour facilities and was burdened with an infamous reputation for disease. Only Benkulen's annual pepper investment for the East India Company contributed to the high costs of the settlement, while its proximity to Batavia, and its dependence on that Dutch port for many of its vital supplies of timber and food, made the port strategically vulnerable.[43]

In spite of these difficulties, the Court of Directors in London tried in the early 1760s to improve British prospects in Sumatra. After a brief two year period under French control during the seven years war, Benkulen had been restored to the British in 1762. Various schemes were then attempted to improve trading prospects. In 1762, the Court of Directors suggested the removal of the seat of British power to a new station at Semangka Bay on the Sunda Straits.[44] Fears that a British base so close to Batavia would inflame Dutch hostility delayed activity until 1764, when an engineer, Captain Tolley, led an expedition to explore the possibility of a station at Semangka Bay. But Tolley's equivocal report, and continuing reluctance to antagonise the Dutch meant that the plan came to nothing.[45]

Other attempts to attract the Malay and Bugis trade to Benkulen were made by Roger Carter, Governor of the settlement between 1762 and 1767. Through such schemes as the reduction of trade duties and the purchase of spices from Malay traders on Company account, Carter tried to establish regular and reliable trade links with other parts of the region.[46] These were not successful, and Carter was ordered in 1766 to cease spice purchases on Company account. Among Carter's schemes, the opium society established in 1763, perhaps best illustrates the problems which the Benkulen administration found so intractable. Indian based British country traders proved too competitive for the Benkulen opium society in supplying the growing south east Asian market. The society consisted exclusively of members of the Benkulen Council, and was severely hampered by its arrangements and close connections with the East India Company. They had promised the Company a profit of $100 on each chest of opium sold, an arrangement made in return for the society enjoying a monopoly of the sale of the drug at Benkulen.[47] British traders from India, unhampered by such obligations easily undercut the Benkulen society, who consequently found great difficulty in attracting local traders to the port. Ultimately all of these attempts to enhance Benkulen's position failed. British traders found that more centrally situated entrepots, such as Riau, were much more successful in attracting the Malay and Bugis traders so important for British trade in the region. By 1770, the Company authorities in India and the country traders had focused their attention on the Straits of Melaka and other more central locations for a new British station in the region.[48]

In fact, interest in these areas emerged as early as the 1760s. In 1763, a prominent Madras civil servant, Alexander Dalrymple, pressed for expansion into those parts of south east Asia not under Spanish or Dutch control. He was particularly attracted to the Sulu archipelago, the east coast of Borneo and the northern coast of Sulawesi. Between 1759 and 1764, Dalrymple was authorised by the Madras presidency to undertake a series of expeditions to the Sulu archipelago with a view to establishing friendly contacts with local rulers. In September 1762, Dalrymple obtained the cession of Balambangan from Sultan Bantilan of Sulu.[49] Concern about inflaming Anglo-Dutch rivalry made the Court of Directors hesitant, and Dalrymple's acceptance of the grant was only ratified in 1768.[50] A British settlement on Balambangan was only established in 1773, and proved to be a commercial failure. The

British officer appointed to oversee the new settlement, John Herbert, has been criticised for overambition and lack of judgement. Dalrymple had advocated the sale of arms to the most powerful local polity, the Taosug, as the fastest way to establish the settlement's commercial viability, a strategy also designed to enlist Taosug assistance against rival European powers. Herbert was guilty of excessive zeal in pursuit of this strategy, selling arms and opium in huge quantities, with damaging consequences for Taosug society. Taosug merchants engaged in trade with the British used their new found wealth to challenge the authority of the traditional aristocratic elite, while the proliferating use of opium by local chiefs undermined the quality of governance and judgement they provided. In early 1775, the Taosug Sultan, Mahommed Israel, captured and destroyed Balambangan, having correctly identified it as a major cause of local instability. Heavy costs and disappointing returns at the settlement discouraged the Company from any immediate attempt to restore their position.

The experience of Balambangan is illuminating, because it was to be repeated elsewhere in south east Asia. Trade with the British brought dangers as well as advantages for local rulers. While growing trade brought larger revenues, it also increased the wealth and power of local merchants and chiefs, enabling them to resist central authority. The ability of central authority to sustain its position depended largely upon the acquisition of sufficient resources to fund military power, arrangements for which could be easily undermined by downturns in trading activity. Conversely, however, expanding trade was only beneficial to central authority if the state could assert its revenue and monopoly rights to secure its share of wealth. Failure to do this usually resulted in the enrichment and empowerment of local chiefs and merchants, who could then challenge the power of the ruler. British commerce in the period from 1750 was usually conducted by individual merchants and adventurers with little respect for the monopolies and revenue prerogatives of local rulers, which in British eyes often served to increase the price of local produce and suppress the prices of exports into the region. British merchants favoured a liberal trade environment, in which they could sell to and buy from whoever they liked. They lobbied the East India Company to use its political clout in dealings with local states to reduce local duties and monopolies. Consequently, the growth of commerce between the British and south east Asian states often served to destabilise rather than strengthen the local political order. This was one reason why the expansion of trade after the mid eighteenth century did not produce the powerful centralised states of the fifteenth and sixteenth centuries. It was the relatively unfettered nature of the British country trade between India and south east Asia, and the willingness of the East India Company to protect the rights of private British merchants, which made it difficult for south east Asian rulers to turn the growth of trade to their political advantage.

By the 1770s, these British country traders had established firm commercial links in south east Asia. As early as 1766, the Madras house of

Jourdan, Sulivan and De Souza sent Gowan Harrop to Aceh to develop trade.[51] In 1770, the renowned free merchant Francis Light also visited the Sultanate.[52] By February 1772 the Madras Association had exported goods worth £120,000 to Aceh, and had purchased Straits produce of equivalent value.[53] The apparent success of the Madras firm prompted the interest of the East India Company in London, which, in the wake of conflict with the French and Dutch had become more amenable to the idea of a permanent base in south east Asia.[54] In February 1772, on orders from London, the East India Company authorities in Madras despatched Charles Desvoeux to Aceh to explore the potential value of Aceh as a source of exports to China. Desvoeux was unable to reach any agreement with the Sultan and the mission came to nothing. In the following fifty years interest in Aceh as a possible location for a British commercial or military base waxed sporadically, as trading links were built up with the pepper and betelnut ports of west and eastern Sumatra. Severe political instability, caused partly by the strengthening of local chiefs through direct trade with British merchants in contravention of the Sultan's trading and revenue collection rights, ultimately dissuaded the British from establishing themselves there, from fear of expensive entanglements in local disputes.

Other free merchants, notably Francis Light, cultivated connections with the western Malay states. Territorial conflicts between these states, and their growing fear of Siamese and Dutch aggression, made the Malay Sultans amenable to closer ties with other major European powers as a counterweight. In January 1772 Light recommended to Warren Hastings, recently appointed Governor General in Bengal, the establishment of a British station in Kedah. Grossly exaggerating the value of Kedah's external trade, Light claimed that a British base there would prove an ideal port of refreshment for the China trade, also furnishing East Indiamen with plentiful supplies of Malay produce for the China market.[55] In February 1772, the Company sent a mission to Kedah from Madras, under the authority of Edward Monckton. But when he reported that the Sultan of Kedah saw the British as potential allies in his aggressive plans against Selangor, the proposal for a Kedah settlement was dropped instantly.[56]

Light remained at the forefront of attempts to secure a Malay port for the British. After resigning from the Madras association in 1772, he spent most of the next sixteen years on the island of Phuket, trading in arms and becoming acquainted with successive Siamese governors of the island. In 1778 Light advised Thomas Rumbold, Governor of Madras, to seize Phuket for the East India Company, or for a consortium of private British entrepeneurs.[57] Once again, the Company's reluctance to embroil itself in local conflicts and incur heavy expenditure, led to outright rejection of these overtures.

Changing strategic circumstances in the early 1780s eventually persuaded the Company to adopt a bolder stance on the question of a new British settlement in the region. Until then, commercial considerations had dominated British interest in south east Asia, and setbacks, such as the failure of Balambangan and the successive missions to Aceh and Kedah, had discouraged efforts by the Company in this direction.[58] In 1780, the outbreak of war with the French and Dutch in India rekindled strategic interest in a base in south east Asia.[59] Such a base might provide much needed protection for British shipping. Lawrence Sulivan and William James, prominent East India Company Directors, pressed strongly for a base in Aceh in anticipation of seizure of Benkulen by the Dutch. In September 1782, Henry Botham was sent from Calcutta to Aceh to negotiate for a British base.[60] The mission failed due to the opposition of the local Syabandar, Poh Salleh. In 1784 Thomas Forrest suggested a naval station on St Matthew's Island off the Isthmus of Kra, but the sparseness of local population and distance from the principal trade routes of the Malay archipelago prompted rejection by the Bengal administration. Even though strategic concerns predominated in the early 1780s, commercial considerations remained important in determining British policy.[61]

Indeed, a combination of commercial and strategic priorities prompted the acquisition of Pinang in 1786. In 1783, Raja Haji, powerful ruler of the Bugis Johore empire, contacted Forrest through the Sultan of Selangor. At the time, Johore was embroiled in hostilities with the Dutch, and Raja Haji viewed the British as a powerful potential ally. Raja Haji offered the British a base on Riau, to the south of the Malay peninsula, and ideally placed to exploit the trade routes which converged in the area. Forrest told the Bengal administration of the offer on his return to Calcutta in April 1784. Riau had developed into the most important commercial port in south east Asia for the British during the 1770s and 1780s. Abundant supplies of Malay produce, especially tin, could be procured at the port, which was also situated conveniently on the route to China.[62] Strong government under the Bugis had ensured a stable environment for trade, and the prospect of a British base seemed too good to forego. Nevertheless, the Anglo-Dutch treaty of 1784 had very recently established a fragile peace which London was eager to consolidate.[63] Any moves by Bengal to court the Johore empire, which was at war with the Dutch, held profound dangers for this uneasy peace. The Indian government hesitated. Forrest was instructed to negotiate for a base dedicated exclusively to trade, without the slightest hint of military intent. Commercial priorities had clearly reasserted themselves at this stage.

Events overtook the British plan. Forrest was unable to sail from Calcutta until June 1784, days after the Dutch had defeated and killed Raja Haji. By the end of the year the Dutch had occupied Riau and asserted their authority over Selangor and Siak. The British were alarmed by the new Dutch stranglehold on the Straits of Melaka, and the acquisition of a base to counteract the potential Dutch threat became an urgent priority. In 1786, with full support of the East India Company, Francis Light negotiated an agreement with the Sultan of Kedah for the establishment of a British base on the island of Pinang. For his part, the Sultan was looking for British protection from the Siamese. He believed wrongly that cession of Pinang to the British would draw them into a protective alliance with Kedah. The British had no intention to meet these expectations, but it suited them not to disabuse the Sultan of his illusions. Thus Pinang was founded as a result of the contrasting and pressing strategic imperatives of both parties. It was only a matter of time before the British made plain their aversion to engagements in local disputes, souring relations with the Sultan. Nevertheless it is important to recognise that local dynamics of rivalry between the Malay states and Siam played an important role in drawing the British into Pinang; British strategic priorities were not the only forces at work. Also, the commercial considerations which had long influenced British policy in the region were to shape Bengal's subsequent policy towards Pinang. While Anglo-Dutch rivalry had been predominant in the final decision to acquire Pinang, in the long run Bengal and London were determined to turn their new possession into a profitable as well as a protective utility.

***

The foundation of Pinang in 1786 began a new phase of British imperial involvement in south east Asia, in which the British tried to use the new settlement to develop trade links within the region. It was believed that the settlement would attract Bugis and Malay traders from all parts of the Malay archipelago, who would come to the island to supply the China trade with Malay produce. Thus although initial acquisition of the island had been motivated primarily by defensive strategic considerations, commercial expectations for the settlement in Bengal and London were very high.

There were other reasons why the 1780s were a turning point in the development of British trade and influence in south east Asia. During the 1780s there were major changes in the administrative and economic structure of British rule in India. The financial difficulties of the 1770s and early 1780s had forced the East India Company to seek help from the British government. Assistance was conditional upon far reaching reform of the Company's structure. The most important aspect of these reforms was Pitt's India act of 1784 which created a government ministry, the Board of Control, to supervise the Company's administration, but other reforms in the 1780s were directed at the Company administration in India. It was Governor General Cornwallis who set out to reform the Company administration following his appointment in 1785. Cornwallis aimed to modernise and professionalise the Company bureaucracy. In future, Company servants were debarred from involvement in private commerce on their own account, a sacrifice for which they would be compensated by appointments on merit and more generous salaries.[64] The exclusion of Company men from private enterprise was designed to eliminate the corruption and conflict of interest blamed for the earlier financial crises. Free merchants, those entrepeneurs not employed by the Company, were presented with many new opportunities for enterprise, as Company servants retreated from private commercial dealings. New commercial opportunities were also created by the continuing expansion of the China trade in the 1780s, which increased demand for shipping and the procurement of commodities for the Chinese market. The development of opium production furnished the British with a commodity readily in demand in China, in spite of its illegality there. While the main phase of expansion of production and export of the commodity occurred after the late 1790s, increased exports were already beginning to boost British trade in the 1780s.[65]

While these new opportunities were welcome, they posed problems for entrepeneurs which could only be overcome by their own organisational reforms. The growing demand for shipping and the acquisition of commodities for the burgeoning Chinese market, required the input of large sums of capital which few individual merchants possessed. During the 1780s, merchants overcame this by pooling their resources with other merchants, and by collectively spreading their risks across a wide range of commercial activities. The new organisations which emerged were called agency houses, and their operations included overseas trade, shipbuilding and ownership, investment in agricultural production, banking and insurance. These last two activities were particularly important not only in opening supplies of capital in the form of bank deposits and insurance premiums, but also in enhancing their reputation and political influence. The agency houses were attractive to European investors in India, because they offered secure and regular returns. An army of 1300 Company servants excluded by the Cornwallis reforms from private enterprise deposited their salaries with the agency houses, who were able to utilise this large reservoir of capital for commercial expansion. From the mid 1780s, the agency houses became extremely valuable to the East India Company. The houses financed and directed much of the country trade between India and China, facilitating the growing export of Indian and Malay produce to China. In China, the private merchants paid the receipts of their trade into the East India Company's coffers, in return for bills of exchange payable in London or Calcutta.[66] The houses also became major creditors to the Company administration in India, financing warfare and the general costs of territorial expansion. Although excluded from direct trade with Europe by the East India Company's monopoly, the agency houses were able to remit wealth to London via Company bills of exchange and the limited quota of trade goods they were allowed to send to Britain on East India Company ships. Consequently, from the 1780s there emerged London based "sister" houses to those in India, which engaged in a range of commercial activities and built up considerable influence within the East India Company's London administrative structure. By 1790, some fifteen leading houses in Bengal had come to dominate the non-Company European commercial sector. The most prominent were the houses of Fairlie, Fergusson and Co.; Paxton, Cockerell and Delisle; Lambert and Ross; Colvins and Bazett; and Joseph Baretto. They financed the production of silk, indigo, sugar and opium, and ran three banks and four insurance companies. They were instrumental in the revival in the Company's economic fortunes after the 1790s and during the first two decades of the nineteenth century. The agency houses underwrote military fiscalism and imperial expansion. They provided the economic means which enabled the aggressive and expansionist culture which pervaded the Company's institutions in India to realise its aspirations. Inevitably this role brought influence and power to the houses, both in India and in London. The expansion of trade into south east Asia from the 1780s was largely facilitated by the agency houses, whose symbiotic relationship with the East India Company afforded them considerable influence over its policy in the region. Moreover, these Indian based interests, rather than industrial interests located in Britain, were the main determinants of British policy in south east Asia.

Thus the acquisition of Pinang coincided with economic and administrative changes in Bengal, and a new phase of growth in the China trade, which marked the subsequent four or five decades as a distinctive phase in British imperial expansion into south east Asia. Pinang was expected by the East India Company to establish itself quickly as the main entrepot of south east Asia, attracting local traders who would supply East Indiamen bound for China with tin, benzoin, pepper, spices, betelnut and other Malay produce. In return these traders would take away opium, cotton and other produce of India, steadily enhancing the value of the region as a market for Indian exports. Ultimately these expectations proved overambitious, because Pinang was situated too far north to be visited conveniently by the traders of the southern archipelago. Lying 400 miles north of the southern tip of the Malay peninsula, it was too distant from the most lucrative markets south east Asia, and journeys there ran excessively high risks from piracy and the monsoon. What is intriguing is that the authorities in Bengal and London only became aware of these limitations in 1808, when Thomas Stamford Raffles exposed them in a report on Melaka and trade in the Straits. Up till then, British policy in south east Asia was premised on an erroneously optimistic assessment of Pinang's ability to service British trade with the region.

The reasons for this are not difficult to identify. The settlement's founder, Francis Light, habitually exaggerated the potential and performance of his new command. For example, Light repeatedly told his Bengal superiors that Pinang conducted a regular annual trade with Bugis traders from Sulawesi, and in November 1792 he submitted a request to Bengal for 200 chests of opium to supply Bugis traders together with $300,000 in cash and commodities for trading purposes.[67] Yet a report on annual imports into Pinang by indigenous vessels, submitted in 1793 show that Light's expectations were not fulfilled.[68] In 1792 the total value of all imports on local vessels was only $224,533, significantly lower than Light's estimate for the Bugis fleet alone. Light referred repeatedly to a consistent and flourishing trade to the settlement from all parts of south east Asia, a claim which is flatly contradicted by analysis of the few statistical records available for trade to Pinang by local vessels.[69] These show that between March 1789 and January 1790, some six hundred prows visited Pinang from Malay ports north of Melaka, compared with only thirteen from south of Melaka.[70] Between 1 May and 31 October 1796, the figures were 421 and 8, respectively.[71] In his 1808 memorandum, Raffles referred specifically to the inability of Pinang to regularly attract Bugis traders, which normally went no further north than Melaka.[72] Records of European shipping arrivals at Pinang reinforce this point about the weakness of the port's connections with the southern archipelago, and reveal another significant feature. Between 1786 and 1794, there were 365 recorded arrivals of vessels from ports north of Melaka, compared with only 40 from ports south of Melaka.[73] Even more interesting was a regular shipping connection between Pinang and Melaka; with some 120 ships arriving from Melaka between 1786 and 1794.[74] European traders based at Pinang regularly sailed south to Melaka to secure supplies of local produce which Pinang could not obtain from visiting local traders. Given that Melaka was a Dutch port until seized by the British in 1795, and that the Dutch viewed the British with suspicious hostility, the relationship between the two ports might seem unexpected - especially as the Dutch apparently made no effort to impede the trade. Perhaps they were reluctant to suppress a channel of commerce in which their own merchants had a vested interest. It is fascinating to observe that at the frontier of two hostile empires, commercial relations which benefitted merchants from both, flourished so quickly after 1786. Following the British conquest of Melaka in 1795, the trade between the two ports increased even more rapidly, and with it Pinang's dependence upon its erstwhile southern rival.

Yet none of this came to the notice of the Bengal authorities until Raffles' 1808 memorandum. Light appears to have deliberately withheld any information which might suggest Pinang's commercial limitations. From the outset, Light had exaggerated the island's potential when initially promoting it as a possible British base. Once embarked upon this course, Light found it impossible to admit the inaccuracy of his earlier assessments without damaging his own reputation. This was not merely a matter of pride. Light had subsequently built up a significant body of personal interests on the island which might be jeopardised by a retraction of the Company's commitment to the settlement. As time went on, it became inconvenient for later governors to expose Light's deceit. Their own status and power rested upon the prestige of their command, which could only be damaged by a more realistic assessment of its commercial potential.

In fact, this exaggerated view of Pinang's value was itself an obstacle to improvement of the settlement's fortunes. Cornwallis' determination to impose discipline upon Indian finances made him reluctant to commit monies to Pinang, or allow the local administration to engage in any political initiatives which might make demands on Indian finances. This effectively ruled out treaties or agreements with local states, or any activities which might provoke Dutch resentment and possibly trigger expensive and unpredictable conflict. In view of Light's glowing assessments of Pinang's potential, this was not unreasonable. If local traders were so enthusiastic to use the port, there would be no need to actively stimulate them by means of treaties with local Sultans, who, in the turbulent environment which prevailed, invariably saw the British as possible military allies. Pinang's relations with Kedah demonstrated the problems this could cause. The treaty of 1786 with the Sultan which secured the island for the British, stipulated a payment of $10,000 to him, an obligation which neither Light nor the Bengal administration apparently had any intention of honouring.[75] Impatience led the Sultan to first threaten to disrupt trade with Pinang, and then in 1791 to threaten invasion of the island.[76] Light's anxious pleas to Bengal for either permission to pay the Sultan, or resources to defend the settlement, were initially rejected by the Bengal administration, who only reluctantly allowed Light to pay the Sultan when invasion was imminent.[77] Attempts by Light to consolidate Pinang's commerce by diplomacy were also blocked. Bengal refused to support Light's attempts in the late 1780s to negotiate commercial treaties with Selangor, Perak and Trengganu because they seemed to entail some measure of British support for these states against the Siamese.[78]

In fact, Bengal's assumption that conflict and expense could be avoided simply by vetoing formal political agreements with Malay states revealed a lack of understanding of the pressures on local rulers. State power in the Malay archipelago rested upon trade revenues and monopolies, arrangements which compelled local rulers to seek regulation of commerce via political agreements. In the case of Aceh, Light was only too happy to observe Bengal warnings against local political entanglements. British and other merchants based on Pinang were able, by trading freely with local chiefs and merchants within Aceh, to obtain supplies of betelnut and pepper at prices kept low by competition among Acehnese traders. Light rejected overtures from Sultan Muhammed Syah to regulate trade between Aceh and Pinang by an agreement which would recognise the Sultan's right to regulate trade, raise taxes on it and compel Pinang merchants to trade only at the the capital, Banda Aceh.[79] Relations between Pinang and Aceh subsequently deteriorated as Muhammed Syah tried to impose his regulations on Pinang shipping through the employment of European mercenaries.[80] Inevitably there were clashes between Pinang merchants and Acehnese officials. In this context, Bengal's embargo on diplomatic agreement with Aceh actually exacerbated tensions with Pinang and contributed to local political instability. When Light's successor, Forbes Ross Macdonald, tried in September 1797 to take up Acehnese proposals for a commercial treaty which would restrict Pinang traders to Banda Aceh, he was prevented from doing so by the Bengal administration.[81] Macdonald recognised that unfettered trade was the main source of conflict between the British and Acehnese, and that an agreement might serve to both improve relations and strengthen the Acehnese state, thereby ensuring a stable and peaceful political environment in which British trade could thrive. The Bengal administration failed to recognise these advantages, and an opportunity to avoid further difficulties was lost.

The Bengal administration's vigilant restriction of Pinang's external relations was not matched by equal supervision of commercial development of the island itself, which was left to Light and the Pinang administration's control. The reasons for this apparent lack of interest are unclear, and seems odd in light of the sweeping tide of reform and parsimony associated with Cornwallis' Governor-Generalship. Earlier historians have suggested that this stemmed from a general satisfaction with the commercial performance of the settlement during its first decade, rendering detailed scrutiny unnecessary.[82] Certainly Company servants in south east Asia continued to enjoy the right to conduct trade on their own account for some time after it had ceased in Bengal. For example, John Prince, Resident of Natal, then of Tapanuli from 1798, was permitted to continue as a major shareholder in a private firm, the Natal concern. It seems that he also used his East India Company office to further his private interests.[83] Similarly, Light was permitted to engage in commercial speculation, regardless of his Company duties as governor of Pinang. The reasons for Bengal's initial liberality in its dealings Company officials in south east Asia probably stemmed from pressure of work in India itself, making effective supervision of geographically distant officials impractical. What is clear is that earlier optimistic assessment of Bengal's satisfaction with Pinang's performance can be easily dismissed. Disappointed with the performance of the settlement, the Bengal administration sent one Major Alexander Kyd to the island in July 1794 to report on commercial progress.[84] Kyd remained on the island for over a year, during which time Light died, and was succeeded by a subordinate, Philip Mannington. Kyd's report to Bengal submitted in September 1795 was sensational both in its damning assessment of the settlement's commercial performance to date, and its sweeping condemnation of Light's governorship.[85]

Kyd dismissed any notion that Pinang had met expectations as an entrepot and supply port for the China trade, but he did not blame the island's geographical location. Instead, Kyd argued that Light's pursuit of his own commercial interests were responsible for failure. Soon after the settlement had been established, a commercial partnership had been formed between Light and James Scott, the principal European merchant on the island. Kyd alleged that Light had used his power as governor to advance the interests of Scott and Co. at the expense of other firms on the island. In his dealings with local Malay traders, Light had consciously directed them to deal only with Scott and Co. These allegations was given substance by other reports. Forbes Ross Macdonald, sent to govern the island in 1796, claimed that Scott and Co. were so dominant over other traders that the firm was even able to exclude the wealthy Bengal agency houses from involvement in the island's trade.[86] Indeed, Macdonald contended that Scott and Co. were the only firm on the island "which merits the epithet commercial".[87] The implication was that Light and Scott were operating an effective monopoly which impeded development of the island and prevented an influx of much needed capital from Bengal.

Some historians have dismissed Macdonald as an overbearing disciplinarian, jealous of Light's reputation and success.[88] It is claimed that Light was only a sleeping partner in Scott and Co. and that he interfered little in the island's commercial affairs. Indeed, when other Pinang traders grumbled to Bengal about the success of Scott and Co. in 1790, Light offered to sever all of his personal contacts with the firm, an offer which Cornwallis did not deem necessary to accept. One historian cites this as evidence of Light's "high minded and earnest nature".[89] But others have been more critical, accepting Macdonald's central allegation that the Scott-Light partnership was a misuse of power by Light.[90] On balance, the weight of evidence supports this latter view. The fact that Kyd as well as Macdonald criticised Light, suggests that Macdonald was not motivated by jealousy. There is other evidence of Scott and Co.'s disproportionate commercial power. Light's successor, Mannington, reported in May 1795 that Scott and Co. had declined to purchase opium from the East India Company. This refusal was a direct response to complaints from other Pinang merchants that Scott had previously exerted a virtual monopoly of all opium purchases from the Company on the island.[91] Scott recommended that the opium be put up for public sale, allowing other merchants to bid for it without having to compete with Scott. When Mannington did this, he was shocked to discover that he could not secure a satisfactory price, indicating either the relative poverty of other merchants compared to Scott, or their unwillingness to act against Scott's interests. Whichever was the case, there is no doubt about the considerable harm which the firm could inflict upon East India Company interests at the settlement. Commenting upon the affair, Macdonald argued that Scott had used his influence to prevent opium purchases by other merchants in order to browbeat Mannington into accepting Scott and Co.'s position of privilege. Certainly receipts from Company opium sales under Mannington fell to one third of their previous level under Light.[92]

Land policy and development were also subject to manipulation by Scott and Light. Light consistently emphasised the island's agricultural progress in his letters to Bengal, yet by 1796 most of the land granted remained undeveloped. In that year 1477 acres were held by Europeans, yet 1300 acres were yet to be worked.[93] Only the Chinese appear to have expanded cultivation. Light encouraged concentration of land ownership into a few European hands, in contradiction to instructions from Bengal. In 1794, Bengal ordered Light not to issue land leases exceeding five years in duration, a policy which Bengal insisted be publicised throughout the island.[94] Light was also instructed to account for all allottments of land on the island, and to specify the size and productive capacity of each allottment. The Bengal administration was concerned lest uncontrolled grants of land might be amassed by a few Europeans without the capital or inclination to bring them into cultivation quickly. The five year limit on leases was intended to prevent speculative abuses. But initial costs involved in the development of pepper plantations were high, and several years usually elapsed before production was forthcoming. Restricting leases to five years duration introduced an unwelcome element of uncertainty, since it was theoretically possible for a planter to have his lease terminated just as he was beginning to recoup a return on his initial investment. Light took this view, and neither enforced nor publicised the restriction. G.W. Young, a trader, landowner and close associate of Scott and Light, had embarked upon development of his lands for pepper production, and had been assured by Light that the five year lease restriction would not be applied, a reassurance which Macdonald bluntly refused to confirm in 1796.[95] One is inclined to question whether the uncertainty introduced by the five year limit on leases was as serious a problem as Light and Young suggested, because the clear intention was that successful and industrious plantation owners had little to fear from the restriction. A more likely reason for Light's non compliance was his desire to help his friends and associates. It is interesting to note that Light does not appear to have submitted the detailed account of land allocations requested by Bengal.

In addition, Scott used the land question to extend further his power and influence over other merchants. As the wealthiest trader on the island, Scott was one of the few people to whom prospective plantation farmers could turn for the large sums required to bring their land into production. Loans were granted on a land mortgage basis, whereby defaulting farmers could lose their land to Scott, their creditor. Macdonald was suspicious of the fact that Scott refused to reveal the extent of his mortgage agreements. He warned Bengal of the urgent need to control Scott's mortgaging activities, and of the need for a detailed survey of land ownership and cultivation.[96]

Thus, Pinang appears to have suffered in its first decade from an overbearing domination of its commerce and administration by a handful of merchants, with the knowing complicity of Light. In many respects, this was reminiscent of arrangements in India before the Cornwallis reforms, when private interest distorted the execution of East India Company duties by the organisation's employees. The effect was to create a highly lucrative business for Scott, Light and a handful of their associates, which enabled them to prevent the fast emerging Bengal agency houses from establishing strong links with merchants on the island. The arrangements also appear to have contributed to the disappointing performance of the settlement, although trade with the Malay states, Aceh and other parts of the east coast of Sumatra appear to have grown considerably. Certainly Chuliah merchants, Arabs and Chinese appear to have been attracted to the settlement, suggesting that commercial achievements were not neglible. What is interesting is that Bengal was encouraged by the reports of Kyd and Macdonald to attribute the disappointing progress of the settlement solely to the depredations of the Light-Scott partnership. Consequently, the geographical limitations of the settlement's commerce were overlooked, only to be revealed fully by Raffles in 1808. This explains why the Bengal administration and London continued to harbour high hopes for Pinang for so long, and were prepared, even after almost twenty years of unfulfilled expectations, to elevate it to full Presidency status in 1805. In the process, the search for a more effective base from which to pursue British commercial interests was postponed.

The end of Light's superintendency of the island in 1795 coincided with several other developments which ushered in a new phase of British expansion into south east Asia, and which were to extend and consolidate the British presence on a permanent basis. Following revolution and the outbreak of war in Europe in 1793, the low countries were overrun by the French. British fear that Dutch possessions in south east Asia would fall into French hands, enabling them to threaten the fast growing trade between India and China, prompted a more aggressive and interventionist policy. In 1795 the Dutch port of Melaka was seized by the British, and a successful invasion of Dutch possessions in the Molucca spice islands followed. At the same time the trade between India and China, especially the export of opium, grew rapidly, benefitting both the East India Company and the Bengal agency houses. The exposure of Light and Scott on Pinang, and the temporary elimination of the Dutch from the Straits of Melaka, opened up new opportunities for trade and enterprise in south east Asia which the increasingly wealthy Bengal agency houses and merchants could not resist. A new era of British commercial expansion from India into south east Asia was just beginning.

NOTES

1. A. Reid, South East Asia in the Age of Commerce Vols 1 & 2 (New Haven, Yale University Press 1988 and 1993).
2. Ibid.: Vol 2, pp69-72.
3. B.W. Andaya and L.Y. Andaya, A History of Malaysia p33.
4. Lee Kam Hing, The Sultanate of Aceh: Relations with the British 1760-1824 (Kuala Lumpur, Oxford University Press 1995).
5. Perhaps the best summary of the seventeenth century crisis is to be found in: A. Reid, "The Seventeenth Century Crisis in Southeast Asia" Modern Asian Studies 24:4 (1990) 639-659.
6. Ibid.: pp652-653
7. L. Bluss,, "No Boats to China. The Dutch East India Company and the Changing Pattern of the China Sea Trade, 1635-1690" Modern Asian Studies 30:1 (1996) 51-76.
8. A. Reid and C. Trocki, "The Last Stand of Autonomous States in Southeast Asia and Korea, 1750-1870: Problems, Possibilities, and a Project" Asian Studies Review 17:2 (1993) 103-120.
9. Lee, The Sultanate of Aceh
10. Andaya and Andaya, A History of Malaysia pp86-87.
11. Lee, The Sultanate of Aceh p42.
12. Reid and Trocki, "The Last Stand of Autonomous States" p111.
13. Andaya and Andaya, A History of Malaysia pp97-99.
14. V. Lieberman, "Secular Trends in Burmese Economic History, c.1350-1830 and their Implications for State Formation" Modern Asian Studies 25:1 (1991) 1-31. pp15-17.
15. V. Lieberman, "Local Integration and Eurasian Analogies: Structuring South East Asian History c. 1350-1830" Modern Asian Studies 27:3 (1993) 475-572.
16. Hans-Dieter Evers, "Trade and State Formation: Siam in the Early Bangkok Period" Modern Asian Studies 21:4 (1987) 751-771.
17. Khoo Kay Kim, The Western Malay States
18. Lee, The Sultanate of Aceh pp7-12.
19. Andaya and Andaya, A History of Malaysia pp98-99.
20. Ibid.: pp94-97.
21. Ibid.: pp102-106.
22. Ibid.: p104.
23. Ibid.: p105.

24. An excellent study of the difficulties this relationship would generate in the case of Kedah is: R. Bonney, Kedah 1771-1821: The Search for Security and Independence (Kuala Lumpur, Oxford University Press 1971).
25. M.F. Somers Heidhues, Bangka Tin and Mentok Pepper: Chinese Settlement on an Indonesian Island (Singapore, Institute of South East Asian Studies 1992).
26. Lee, The Sultanate of Aceh p32.
27. Bonney, Kedah 1771-1821 ch 3.
28. D. Lewis, "The Growth of the Country Trade to the Straits of Malacca 1760-1777" Journal of the Malaysian Branch of the Royal Asiatic Society 43:2 (1970) 114-129.
29. Lee, The Sultanate of Aceh p50.
30. C. Bayly, Imperial Meridian: The British Empire and the World 1780-1830 (London, Longman 1989).
    C. Bayly, Indian Society and the Making of the British Empire (Cambridge, Cambridge University Press 1988).
31. See Bayly, Imperial Meridian Chs 3 and 4.
32. Bayly, Indian Society pp76-77.
33. See P.J. Marshall, East Indian Fortunes (Oxford, Oxford University Press 1976).
34. K.N. Chaudhuri, The Trading World of Asia and the English East India Company 1660-1760 (Cambridge, Cambridge University Press 1978) pp198-199.
35. D.K. Bassett, "The British Country Trade and Local Trade Networks in the Thai and Malay States c.1680-1770" Modern Asian Studies 23:4 (1989) 625-643, p625.
36. Lee, The Sultanate of Aceh p.13.
37. Bassett, "The British Country Trade and Local trade Networks" p.630.
38. D.K. Bassett, "British Trade and Policy in Indonesia 1760 to 1772" Bijdragen 120:2 (1964) 197-223; republished in D.K. Bassett, British Trade and Policy in Indonesia and Malaysia in the Late Eighteenth Century (Hull, Centre for South East Asian Studies 1971) pp1-29 (all references cite this source)..
39. H. Furber, John Company at Work (Harvard University Press 1948).
40. P.J. Marshall, East Indian Fortunes p76.
41. Ibid.: p104.
42.. These outposts were Tapanuli, Natal, Moko Moko, Lais, Manna, and Krui.
43. Bassett, "British Trade and Policy in Indonesia" p3.
44. Ibid.: pp5-6.
45. Ibid.: p9.
46. Ibid.: pp10-11.
47. Ibid.: p13.
48. Ibid.: pp26-27.
49. J. Warren, "Balambangan and the Rise of the Sulu Sultanate 1772-1775" Journal of the Malaysian Branch of the Royal Asiatic Society 50:1 (1977) 73-93.
50. Bassett, "British Trade and Policy in Indonesia
51. Lee, The Sultanate of Aceh p29.
52. D.K. Bassett, "British Commercial and Strategic Interest in the Malay Peninsula during the late eighteenth century" in J. Bastin and R. Roolvink, Malaysian and Indonesian Studies: Essays Presented to Sir Richard Winstedt on his Eighty Fifth Birthday (Oxford 1964); also in D.K. Bassett, British Trade and Policy in Indonesia and Malaysia in the Eighteenth Century pp50-71 (All references cite this source).
53. Ibid.: p52.
54. Lee, The Sultanate of Aceh

55. Bassett, "British Commercial and Strategic Interest" p54.
56. Ibid.: p55.
57. Ibid.: pp64-65.
58. Ibid.: p66.
59. B.E. Kennedy, "Anglo-French Rivalry in South East Asia 1763-1793" Journal of Southeast Asian History 4:2 (1973) 199-213.
60. Lee, The Sultanate of Aceh pp64-66.
61. Bassett, "British Commercial and Strategic Interests" p66.
62. D. Lewis, "The Growth of the Country Trade".
63. N. Tarling, Anglo-Dutch Rivalry in the Malay World (Queensland 1962).
64. P. Lawson, The East India Company: A History (London, Longman 1993) pp128-131.
65. J.F. Richards, "The Indian Empire and Peasant Production of Opium in the Nineteenth Century" Modern Asian Studies 15:1 (1981) 59-83.
66. For explanations of this process see: A. Tripathi, Trade and Finance in the Bengal Presidency 1793-1833 (Calcutta, Oxford University Press, 1979 2nd edn).
    P.J. Marshall, East Indian Fortunes
    S. B. Singh, European Agency Houses in Bengal (Calcutta, Firma K.L. Mukhopadhyay 1966).
67. Light to Bengal Council, 12 November 1792, SSR G/34/5, IOR, London.
68. Report on Annual Prow Imports at Pinang, January 1790-March 1793 (Fort William 5 April 1793) SSR G/34/5, IOR, London..
69. D.K. Bassett, "Anglo-Malay Relations 1786 to 1795" Journal of the Malaysian Branch of the Royal Asiatic Society 38:2 (1965) 183-212 (All references cite this source); and in D.K. Bassett, British Trade and Policy in Indonesia and Malaysia pp108-123.
70. Compiled from shipping lists contained in SSR G/34/1 to G/34/7, and BPC 1796, 4/39 to 4/46, IOR, London.
71. Ibid.
72. C.E. Wurtzburg, Raffles of the Eastern Isles (London, Hodder and Stoughton 1954) pp66-72.
73. Compiled from shipping lists for 1788-1794, in SSR G/34/3 to G/34/7, and BPC 3/32 to 4/46, IOR, London. Also see A. Webster, The Origins of the Straits Settlements: British Trade and Policy in the Malay Archipelago 1786 to 1824 (Birmingham University, unpublished PhD thesis 1984) pp51-52.
74. Webster, Ibid. :p52.
75. Bonney, Kedah 1771 to 1821 p85 and pp98-99.
76. Light to the Bengal Council, 22 December 1790, (Fort William 12 January 1791), SSR G/34/4, IOR, London.
77. For details of Light's pleas and Bengal's initial rejection, see Light to Bengal Council, 19 March 1791, (Fort William 20 April 1791), SSR G/34/4, and Bengal Council to Light, 29 April 1791, (Fort William 29 April 1791), SSR G/34/4, IOR, London.
78. Bassett, "Anglo-Malay Relations" pp194-200.
79. Sultan Muhammed Syah's overtures to Light were reported by Light to Bengal, 20 June 1788, (Fort William 25 August 1788), SSR G/34/3, IOR, London.
80. Lee, The Sultanate of Aceh pp76-83.
81. Ibid.: p91, and Macdonald to the Bengal Council, 20 September 1797, (Fort William 5 March 1798), BPC 4/52, IOR, London.

82. H.P. Clodd, Malaya's First Pioneer: The Life of Francis Light (London, Luzac and Co. 1948) p67.
83. Lee, The Sultanate of Aceh pp99-100.
84. Governor General to Light, 10 July 1794, (Fort William 10 July 1794), SSR G/34/6, IOR, London.
85. Kyd to the Bengal Council, 2 August 1795, (Fort William 28 September 1795) SSR G/34/6, IOR, London.
86. Macdonald to the Bengal Council, 20 July 1796, (Fort William 28 August 1797), BPC 4/52, IOR, London.
87. Ibid.
88. Clodd, Malaya's First Pioneer pp68-69.
89. Ibid.
90. F.G. Stevens, "A Contribution to the Early History of Prince of Wales Island" Journal of the Malaysian Branch of the Royal Asiatic Society 7:2 (1929) 377-414.
91. Mannington to the Bengal Council, 13 May 1795, (Fort William 8 June 1795) SSR G/34/7, IOR, London.
92. Macdonald to the Bengal Council, 20 July 1796.
93. Ibid.
94. Bengal Council to Light, 1 August 1794, (Fort William 1 August 1794), SSR G/34/1, IOR, London.
95. Macdonald to Bengal Council, 20 July 1796.
96. George Caunter to Bengal Council, 16 July 1799, (Fort William 5 September 1799) BPC 5/6, IOR, London.

3. THE ORIGINS OF SINGAPORE 1795-1819

The period between 1795 and 1819 saw a dramatic extension of British political control and commercial involvement in the Malay archipelago. War in Europe forced the East India Company to pay special attention to the defence of the trade routes to China through south east Asia. The immediate fear was that Dutch possessions in the region would fall into French hands, and to prevent this Dutch Melaka was seized in 1795, together with the Dutch Moluccas. A temporary peace was established in 1803, but renewed hostilities heightened fears sufficiently for the British to seize the island of Java in 1811, establishing complete, though temporary, British control of the trade and much of the territory in the region. At the end of the war in 1815, the priorities of European politics continued to determine British policy in the region, but now these dictated a rapid return of Java, Melaka and all the wartime confiscations back to Dutch control. Anxious to prevent a repeat of French continental expansionism, the British government wanted a revitalised and strengthened Dutch kingdom to become a buffer against French aggression and territorial ambitions. It was believed that Dutch economic revival was necessary for this to be accomplished, and a return of the Dutch colonies was seen as a prerequisite of recovery. Merchants and officials in the east were dismayed, because during the period of British rule, trade had expanded considerably, encouraging expectations that the temporary acquisitions might be made permanent. Following the restoration of Dutch authority, this anxiety contributed to the acquisition of Singapore in 1819.

The British seizures of Dutch colonies in south east Asia between 1795 and 1815 were motivated by fear that these possessions might fall under French control, posing a threat to British shipping in south east Asia, and on the route to China. Some of the Company officials placed in charge of these temporary possessions became fervent lobbyists for the permanent annexation of their commands. Their enthusiasm arose from the rapid growth of British trade to these former Dutch possessions, following the removal of Dutch protectionism. These Company officials were charged to run their commands as efficiently as possible, minimising costs at a time of financial stringency. The higher revenues which expanding trade with India and other parts of the region brought, made many keenly aware of the commercial potential of these temporary additions to empire. From here it was only a short step for officials to seek the permanent annexation of the Dutch territories, as a way of consolidating the gains achieved by private commerce, and a way of making their own insecure commands permanent.

Probably the best example of this was the governorship of Thomas Stamford Raffles in Java between 1811 and 1815. Raffles wanted to ensure a stable revenue base for Java, which he believed would help persuade his superiors to keep the island British. Raffles wanted to integrate the Javanese peasant cultivators into the international economy, and so he introduced policies encouraging them to produce for the market.[1] Raffles was strongly influenced by the Cornwallis Indian reforms of the 1790s. There, the permanent settlement of 1793 had attempted to create market-responsive landowners and peasants, who would earn cash with which to pay the taxes necessary to fund Company rule. Raffles believed that a similar policy in Java would provide resources to meet the costs of government, and would encourage Bengal and London to annex the island. This was not a policy of simple liberalisation, sweeping away the old system of monopolistic control by the Dutch. Raffles was almost as ruthless as the Dutch in quelling local Muslim nobles in their attempts to restore some degree of their status and power.[2] Not all forced labour was dispensed with, and certain Dutch monopolistic controls were retained. Raffles' disregard for traditional political forms and customs almost equalled his predecessors. His land policy in Java was a curious blend of mercantilist and free trade ideas; in which monopolies, limited forced labour and suppression of traditional political practices sustained imperial control. Encouragement of British trade and enterprise in Java, Sumatra and other local islands, combined with progressive marketisation of peasant agricultural production, were policies designed to generate the revenues necessary to finance the colonial administration of the island, rather than to fulfil any ideological commitment to the virtues of the market. Raffles calculated that a successful class of peasant producers, flourishing through direct commerce with British traders, would be loyal to British rule, thereby minimising the possibility of local resistance. In this respect, the objective in promoting a more "liberal" land policy was the establishment of British colonial rule on a permanent basis.

Raffles also used his temporary administration to promote and extend British trade throughout the Malay archipelago. In Java itself, a new European trading community linked with British India quickly grew up, establishing itself as an intermediary between the Bengal agency houses and Javanese producers and traders. Many of these European merchants flocked to Java from other British settlements in south east Asia, such as Pinang, Melaka and Benkulen. For example, John Deans and Robert Scott came from Pinang to establish a trading partnership with the Bengal agency house of

John Palmer, the wealthiest and most influential firm in British India.[3] They became involved in opium retailing and agriculture. Raffles also sought to revitalise the island of Bangka as a centre of tin production for the China market, appointing an East India Company Resident and four agents to make advances to Chinese tin mining concerns and collect tin ready for export.[4] To ensure adequate labour supplies, the Java administration allowed the immigration into Bangka of some 1600 Chinese coolies in 1813, an increase in the island's Chinese population of about 80 per cent.[5] So successful did Raffles' Bangka reforms prove that they were continued under Dutch rule after 1816. However, Raffles' determination to secure permanent advantage from the occupation of Java is illustrated even more clearly in his conduct of relations with local rulers in the southern islands of south east Asia, particularly in Borneo. Raffles believed that British trade needed to be fostered by the development of close political links between the Java administration and local states. Recognising that Dutch political claims in Borneo were particularly weak, he despatched emissaries to the rulers of Pontianak, Banjermassin and Sambas in pursuit of agreements providing permanent access for British trade.[6] Raffles instructed his agents to promise political recognition to the respective rulers in exchange for commercial agreements. By 1814, he was seeking assurances from Bengal and London that these agreements would stand even after the return of Java to Dutch control. But he was overruled, because of the British government's determination to enlist Dutch co-operation in post war Europe.

The significance of the Raffles administration in Java is twofold for the expansion of British commercial and imperial interest in the region. Firstly, the replacement of Dutch authority by the British undoubtedly made it easier for British traders to penetrate the markets south east Asia, because it removed the possibility of Dutch obstruction. Commercial expeditions were more predictable, less hazardous and more profitable. Secondly, the Raffles administration demonstrated the ambitions of East India Company officials in south east Asia. They became strident in their pleas for the permanent annexation of the Dutch colonies. While the more ambitious demands were rejected by the authorities in Bengal and London, some did strike a chord. For example, Robert Townsend Farquhar, British Resident for the Moluccas between 1798 and 1802, persuaded the Indian government of the need for a more permanent presence in the eastern islands of south east Asia, leading to the decision in 1803 to re-establish the long abandoned British base at Balambangan.[7] Farquhar then tried to use his position as leader of the expedition to Balambangan to shape wider British imperial policy in the region. Farquhar continued with this project after his appointment to the Governorship of Pinang in 1804, and although he was ultimately unsuccessful in securing Balambangan on a permanent basis, for a time he managed to influence British policy in a number of important ways.[8] On a less grand scale, East India Company officials were quick to exploit temporary control of the Moluccas for more permanent British advantage. Dr Roxburgh, the

East India Company's botanist in Calcutta, and C. Smith his subordinate, transplanted nutmeg and clove plants to Calcutta and Pinang.[9] In these ways, the temporary assertion of British power in the region nurtured an imperialist mentality among a new generation of Company officials.

While temporary expansion of British control helped foster an imperialistic mentality and opened new opportunities for British trade, simultaneous commercial developments in India generated expansion of British trade to south east Asia and China. By the late 1790s, the administrative reforms of Cornwallis, and the reorganisation of private enterprise which stemmed from them had promoted the emergence of the Bengal agency houses, which used the savings of Company servants to finance, a wide range of commercial activities, including agriculture and the country trade with China and south east Asia. At the turn of the century there were fifteen main firms, and by 1830 six main firms dominated commercial activity, particularly the house of John Palmer.[10] The pivotal role of the houses in the China trade brought growing political influence in the councils of the East India Company both in India and London.

The agency houses became heavily involved in organising the export of Indian and Malay commodities to Canton in China; where a mutually beneficial arrangement with the East India Company's officials operated. The agency house merchants paid their trade receipts into the East India Company treasury in Canton in return for bills of exchange payable in either London or Calcutta, an arrangement which facilitated safe transmission of agency house profits to India or Britain.[11] The Company used these funds to buy tea, silks and other Chinese produce for export to Britain and the European market. For the agency houses, remittance by bills to Britain was particularly valuable, because of the restrictions imposed on private trade with Britain by the East India Company's monopoly of trade between Britain and India. As the agency houses and individual merchants used bills to remit wealth in this way, there grew up in London, sister houses which corresponded and worked with the Indian agency houses. Usually these London houses were run by individuals who had retired to Britain after a long stint in the east, working as a partner in the Indian house. They helped to organise imports from and exports to India, via the limited space allocated for private trade on Company ships, and engaged in commodity dealing, bill broking and investment in the East India Company. By the 1820s the agency houses constituted a formidable interest group among the Company shareholders, with substantial representation in the Court of Directors.[12]

The China trade became more important during the 1790s because of several other developments. Firstly, the economic and social changes wrought by industrialisation in Britain contributed significantly to the growing profitability of Chinese imports into Britain. The fast growing urban industrial centres of Britain were also the most rapidly expanding markets for Chinese tea, especially after the Commutation Act of 1784 drastically reduced the import duty on tea, and therefore its retail price.[13] Secondly, opium proved to be most popular in the Chinese market. Opium exports increased significantly in both volume and value between 1797 and 1815, substantially inflating the revenues of the East India Company.[14] In India the Company enjoyed a monopoly of the procurement and sale of the drug.[15] They sold the drug to private merchants at auction in Calcutta, who exported the commodity to China and south east Asia. This lucrative source of funds for the Company overcame the old problem of excessive export of gold and silver to finance the purchase of Chinese goods. The value of opium exports increased very rapidly. In 1796/97, opium worth 539,325 Rupees was exported to China. By 1802/3 the figure was Rs2,710,470; rising to Rs4,689,248 by 1809/10, then Rs7,117,764 by 1814/15, and remaining over Rs6 million for every year thereafter until 1819/20.[16] The trade ensured both the high profitability of the agency houses and the commercial viability of the East India Company.

In addition to servicing the passing trade to China, south east Asia was also a market for Indian opium. Though smaller than the Chinese market, the region's consumption of the drug was significant. Up till the last quarter of the eighteenth century it had been the most important market for Indian opium, which was a major article in the Dutch East India Company's trade with India.[17] In the initial period of rapid growth of opium exports, between 1796 and 1802, south east Asia continued to absorb a significant quantity of the drug, helping to maintain high prices and profits in a crucial phase of expansion. In 1796/97, for example, the Malay archipelago absorbed opium to the value of Rs604,800, or 45 per cent of total opium exports from Bengal.[18] Until 1813/14, the Malay archipelago absorbed at least 20 per cent of all Bengal opium exports, and in some years the figure rose to almost 30 per cent. In fact, south east Asia was to remain an important market for Indian opium well into the second half of the nineteenth century. While the Chinese market became the principal outlet for Indian opium, south east Asia became an important secondary "marginal" market, providing a vital alternative when the Chinese market was depressed, or an alternative route into the Chinese market at times of resistance to opium imports by the Chinese state. Historians have paid too little attention to this marginal market function. There has been a tendency to see British interest in the region before 1815 as purely strategic, with a secondary aim to procure Malay produce for export to China. More emphasis has been placed upon the value of south east Asia as a market for British industrial exports after the East India Company Charter Act of 1813, which permitted direct commerce from Britain.[19]

The agency houses quickly recognised the opportunities opened by temporary British control of the Dutch colonies during the Napoleonic wars. As early as 1795, David Scott, a former partner in the Bombay agency house Scott, Tate and Adamson, and from 1786 the head of its sister agency house in London, was adamant that the Dutch colonies should be opened permanently to British trade.[20] As trade with the Malay archipelago grew, the

Bengal agency houses established a network of commercial contacts throughout the region. John Palmer was closely associated with the merchant David Brown on Pinang, also a prominent pepper planter.[21] Another contact there was Syed Hussein, an Acehnese merchant who emerged as a contender for power in the Acehnese civil war of 1814 to 1819.[22] Palmer, who had developed extensive trading interests with Aceh, and felt threatened by the efforts of the reigning Sultan to regulate and tax overseas trade, became involved in intrigues to place Syed Hussein's son on the throne. Elsewhere, Palmer sought to cultivate links with local political rulers, particularly the Sultan of Pontianak.[23] He also owned several plantations at Tjikandi on Java.[24] In 1820 he even contemplated raising a loan in Calcutta for the Dutch administration of the East Indies, though he did not follow this through.[25] Fairlie, Fergusson and Co. of Calcutta had close contacts with Carnegy and Co. on Pinang, and Clark and Hare at Melaka.[26] There is evidence that they too were becoming involved in the export trade with Borneo.[27] The house of Joseph Barretto also traded extensively in gold dust with Melaka.[28]

British trade confidently followed the flag. During the years of British rule in Java, some 78 ships with a total tonnage of 25,024 cleared Bengal for the island.[29] Opium to the value of Rs2,103,392 and Rs1,371,720 of cotton and silk goods were exported there between 1811 and 1816.[30] While this was excellent for commercial interests in Bengal, the merchants of Pinang were alarmed by the preference among Bengal country traders for direct trade with the ports of the Malay archipelago, rather than using Pinang as an entrepot. By 1815, when London ordered the restoration of Dutch authority to their former possessions, the influential Bengal agency houses and merchants had built networks of trade and investment which were alarmingly vulnerable, should the Dutch decide to return to their monopolistic practices of the past. But the Bengal merchants were determined to protect their interests.

❊❊

The fortunes of Pinang fluctuated dramatically after the British conquests of 1795. Although the commerce and status of the settlement grew in the years up to 1808, there was already a drift among Bengal-based traders towards more direct commercial links with the ports of the Malay archipelago. In 1808, however, Raffles' memorandum from Melaka shattered many illusions about the commercial potential of Pinang. Thereafter, the status of the settlement began to slide, and the dispatch of Raffles' expedition to establish a new British outpost to the south of Melaka in 1818 signalled a loss of faith in Pinang's commercial potential. Following the establishment of Singapore, Pinang inevitably suffered a loss of prestige. What were the most significant developments in this process of decline?

By 1795, reports of the Light-Scott monopoly of commerce were beginning to cause serious worries in Bengal. The Bengal administration was concerned that existing arrangements were stifling enterprise, agriculture and commerce. In 1796 a new superintendent was appointed with instructions to implement reform.

Forbes Ross Macdonald took charge of Pinang in February 1796. He was one of the new breed of Company official created by the Cornwallis reforms. Well paid and free of conflicting private commercial interests, Macdonald was a loyal, skilled and disciplined man who enjoyed the full confidence of his superiors.[31] Earlier portrayals of him as a martinet embittered by his exclusion from private commerce, seem to have little foundation.[32] Within months of his appointment, Macdonald clashed with Scott and his entourage, and revealed his misgivings about Scott's power in a lengthy memorandum to Bengal.[33] From this time on, the Bengal administration accepted the need to curb Scott's power and cleanse the Pinang administration. Scott tried to refute Macdonald's allegations with complaints about the intolerant and repressive inclinations of the new superintendent.[34] Macdonald responded with his own complaints about Scott's hostility.[35] Accusation and counter accusation flew thick and fast. Macdonald voiced suspicions that Scott was engaged in disloyal clandestine correspondence with the Sultan of Kedah through a close associate, Mr G.W. Young. While the Bengal administration concluded that there was insufficient evidence for them to act against Young, they were disturbed by Scott's obvious disrespect for the Company's authority.[36] Then in December 1797 George Caunter, the acting superintendent of the settlement during Macdonald's absence, voiced his own suspicions of clandestine plots between Scott's supporters and the Sultan.[37] In the following April, Caunter reported unrest among the Chinese population, rumoured to have been instigated by Scott and his friends.[38] A subsequent governor of the settlement, George Leith, complained of Scott's defiance of authority and overbearing influence, especially through his loan arrangements with other merchants. In May 1801, Leith also reported that Scott had broken his land contract by constructing certain buildings.[39] In addition, Scott had defied Leith's orders to pay an outstanding debt to another merchant, John Cornelius.[40] When Scott appealed against Leith's directive, the Bengal administration backed Leith fully, forcing Scott to pay.[41]

In response to these reports, Bengal insisted on reform. When in 1796 it became known that Light's allocation of land did not comply with instructions, Bengal ordered that all future land grants be restricted to twenty five acres, until the whole land question could be considered in depth.[42] This was followed in 1800 by the Bengal administration asserting direct supervision of all land allocations. Bengal sought thereafter to ensure that no individual received too generous a land grant, and that no second grants would be issued until the first was brought fully into production.[43] Leith attributed a significant increase in the number of pepper vines in production in 1801 to this more interventionist policy from Calcutta.[44] In September 1804, Bengal instructed the then governor, Robert Townsend Farquhar, to establish a special Board of Plantations to monitor and encourage agricultural development.[45] The Board was to be empowered to make financial advances to individuals out of the public treasury, thus breaking Scott's near monopoly of loan finance. In addition, officials appointed to Pinang after Light were to be of the new type created by the Cornwallis reforms, committed exclusively to the Company's welfare and devoid of conflicting private interests. These cumulative reforms persuaded the Bengal administration that obstacles to the commercial success of Pinang had been removed, and that the settlement would now fulfill expectations. The gradual diminution of Scott's power also meant that other merchants could prosper, and in the process, develop close links with the Bengal agency houses. Increasingly the fortunes of the island's mercantile community became interwoven with those of Calcutta.

The East India Company demonstrated its confidence in Pinang by granting the settlement Presidency status following the breakdown of the uneasy peace established at Amiens in 1803.[46] Faced with the prospect of a lengthy war which might damage trade in the east, Bengal and London wanted to fortify the island, transforming it into a formidable naval base. Together with the planned re-establishment of Balambangan, this strengthening of Pinang would ensure adequate protection for the China trade. Robert Townsend Farquhar, head of the expedition which re-established Balambangan in late 1803, and Governor of Pinang from January 1804, was entrusted with accomplishing these objectives.[47] Farquhar's enthusiasm for his brief arose from his own strategy for the long term development and protection of British interests in south east Asia. He wanted the permanent establishment of British hegemony in the Malay world. Farquhar believed that Pinang and Balambangan together could provide the commercial facilities for a dramatic and permanent expansion of British trade, and the military prowess to defeat any challenge. Balambangan, because of its location, would attract the lucrative spice of trade of the Moluccas, Borneo and the Philippines, while Pinang would remain an effective entrepot for the Straits of Melaka and the western islands of south east Asia.[48] Balambangan flourished very quickly after its establishment, mainly due to the rapidly expanding country trade from Bengal. In October 1803 alone, some one hundred and fifty traders had visited the new settlement.[49] To prevent Melaka threatening this new order following its possible return to Dutch possession, Farquhar strongly urged Bengal to destroy the port, relocating its population and resources to Pinang. Bengal and London agreed to this in 1805.[50] British supremacy was to be underpinned by a series of commercial treaties with local Malay states, based on a common model, which would ensure trade with the British on a most favoured nation basis, and exclude the Dutch.[51] Only Sumatra was excluded from Farquhar's strategy, on the grounds that Pinang traders had already captured the island's markets. Instead, Farquhar proposed an agreement with the Dutch which would prohibit all political commitments and possessions on the island by either side, while preserving free access for traders from both countries. The superiority of British merchants would then ensure that they benefitted most from the arrangement.[52] Farquhar was even prepared to abandon Benkulen as part of his policy of mutual political exclusion from Sumatra.[53] With the exception of the suggested abandonment of Benkulen, and reaffirming the prohibition on British intervention in local political disputes, Bengal approved Farquhar's plans in principle. Ultimately however, Farquhar's tenure ended before his plans could be realised.

Farquhar's Pinang administration launched an extensive programme of public works to improve roads, water supply and the fortifications of the settlement.[54] In 1805 a customs collector was appointed for the first time. Unfortunately for Farquhar the heavy costs involved, and certain improprieties in financial record keeping, brought criticism upon him from Bengal and Pinang's incoming Presidential administration headed by Philip Dundas.[55] Early historians accepted these damning assessments of Farquhar's governorship, depicting Farquhar as a corrupt, impulsive and disreputable official.[56] But there is little evidence of corruption. Furthermore, high inflation and labour shortages, coupled with unrealistic budget limitations imposed from Bengal, made it impossible for Farquhar to satisfy Bengal's financial expectations.[57]

Farquhar, like his Bengal superiors, accepted unquestioningly the earlier optimistic assessments of Pinang's commercial potential. He assumed that after the destruction of Melaka, Pinang could successfully attract trade from islands situated to the south of the Malay peninsula. Indeed his faith in Pinang was further demonstrated by his continuing determination to destroy Melaka after the decision in London in 1805 to abandon Balambangan once again.[58] At a time of difficulty in Europe, the British were reluctant to provoke the Spanish, who were uneasy at the proximity of a British base to their possessions in the Philippines.

But of course, Farquhar's trust in Pinang's attractiveness to the Malay and Bugis traders of the southern archipelago was misplaced. Pinang depended upon Melaka for those few reliable commercial links which had been established with the southern islands. Substantial amounts of produce, particularly tin, were ferried northwards by European ships trading between the two ports. Malay traders brought tin to Melaka from southern Sumatra and Bangka, from whence it was shipped to Pinang by European traders.[59] The link supplied some 10,000 piculs of tin worth $130,000 to Pinang in 1802 alone.[60] Only two commodities, pepper ($400,000 per annum) and betelnut ($240,000) exceeded tin in value. Together all three commodities accounted for over two thirds of the value of imports into Pinang from the Malay world. Such was the value of the Melaka connection to Pinang's trading position. In addition, after Melaka was acquired by the British in 1795, it became increasingly popular with British traders from India, because it provided better direct contact with the Bugis and other traders from the southern islands of the Malay archipelago. In 1796 alone, some one hundred and thirty chests of opium were exported to Melaka.[61] But this latter development only fuelled enthusiasm on Pinang for the destruction of

Melaka, which after 1795 began to be seen by some as a dangerous rival. The Pinang pepper planter, David Brown was a particularly strong supporter of the plan to destroy Melaka.[62] Ignorance of the value of Melaka stemmed partly from Pinang's lack of a permanent customs collector, who could gather accurate information of the true state of the island's commerce.[63]

But the years before the granting of Presidency status do seem to have witnessed an improvement in the commercial performance of Pinang, a development which also curbed the monopolistic tendencies of Scott and Co. Enhanced prosperity brought new merchants to the fore who were not so dependent upon the patronage of Scott. Among these were Syed Hussein, the Acehnese merchant who was to play such an important role in the Acehnese civil war after 1815. James Carnegy, a sea captain in Light's time, had also established a successful trading house by 1805 and was destined for wealth and influence. Perhaps the most interesting and best known of the new men was the pepper planter David Brown, who estimated in 1803 that the island's pepper output had risen to 1200 tons annually.[64] These improvements undoubtedly helped persuade London and Bengal to grant Presidency status, and helped sustain the overoptimistic assessments of Pinang's potential as an entrepot. Certainly the new Presidential administration, which was significantly larger than its predecessor, continued the strategy of reducing Melaka. But shipping statistics for the period 1806 to 1811 demonstrate Pinang's continuing dependence upon Melaka for supplies of produce from the southern archipelago.[65] Plainly Pinang's trade in fact stood to lose considerably from the policy of destroying Melaka, even though this was not recognised.

The enthusiam for destroying Melaka after 1806 grew out of a creeping awareness of the growth of direct trade between Bengal and the Malay archipelago and dissatisfaction with Pinang's effectiveness as an entrepot. Philip Dundas, first head of the new presidency, lamented a lack of capital on the island which meant that Bengal based British traders could often obtain a better price for opium at other Malay ports.[66] Dundas' preferred solution, a resumption of opium sales on East India Company account, a practice abandoned in 1798, was rejected.[67] But Dundas had a point. The Pinang merchants were financially overstretched in a wide range of activities, making them poor customers for Bengal merchants and agency houses looking to offload large and expensive cargoes.[68] After 1806, renewed hostilities in Europe hindered trade. Pepper prices fell, cutting the profits of the island's pepper planters, and the merchants engaged in the pepper trade with Aceh.[69] In February 1807, the Collector at Pinang, W.E. Phillips, advocated that the Bengal administration should purchase the island's pepper output to prevent widespread bankruptcies.[70] By December 1808, distress was so acute that the Pinang Council desperately sought financial aid from Bengal.[71] The request was refused.[72] There was mounting desperation at the reluctance of Bengal merchants to visit Pinang. In January 1803 Governor Macalister of Pinang had even suggested to the Court of Directors that the East India Company should compel Bengal traders to sell their opium at Pinang. But this was rejected because the Company's fortunes depended in no small way upon the ability of the Bengal country traders to pursue their business with minimal interference.[73] Such was the climate of deepening worry which made the destruction of Melaka so attractive.

The first step in the suppression of Melaka was the implementation of heavy trade duties there, shortly after Pinang received presidency status. The aim was to discourage the Bengal traders from using the port instead of Pinang, and to compel Malay traders to travel north to Pinang.[74] The long term aim of physical destruction could not be implemented immediately, because substantial amounts of wealth and property were tied up in the settlement. The inhabitants of Melaka had to be persuaded to relocate with their businesses to Pinang. Any sudden move towards destruction would have most damaging consequences for the reputation of the British as peaceful defenders of trade, and would probably scatter the Malay and Chinese traders of Melaka across the archipelago, rather than draw them north to Pinang. The wealth and population of Melaka had to be cajoled or enticed to Pinang, and this subtly coercive process took time. One attempt to drain Melaka's resources involved the funds of the Trustees of the Orphan College of Melaka, a wealthy charitable organisation which also provided banking facilities for the Melaka community. The Pinang administration wanted to "borrow" the capital resources of the college to finance agricultural development on Pinang.[75] The trustees were advised that investments in Melaka could not be guaranteed immunity from the consequences of the settlement's destruction.

These plans for Melaka were dramatically overturned by a memorandum to the Bengal administration from Thomas Stamford Raffles, Secretary to the Pinang administration, who was convalescing at Melaka.[76] Raffles urged his superiors to drop plans to destroy Melaka. The memorandum argued that Chinese or Malay traders could not be enticed to Pinang, which was simply too far north for even the most intrepid Bugis traders. Raffles demonstrated the dependence of Europeans at Melaka upon Chinese middlemen, who bartered with the Malay merchants visiting the port. The Chinese community had amassed over several hundred years an unrivalled expertise in trade. Melaka was simply better placed than Pinang to take advantage of the trade of the southern Malay archipelago, a fact illustrated by the popularity of the port with the Bengal traders, who regularly brought 100 to 150 chests of opium to Melaka each year. Raffles described how the trade between Pinang and Melaka supplied the former with produce from the southern archipelago, particularly Bangka tin, which would not have been delivered by indigenous traders. Raffles wanted Melaka to be retained permanently by the British, for to return it to the Dutch would be disastrous for Pinang. The Dutch could easily destroy Pinang's commerce by refusing to allow the trade with Pinang to continue. As it was, Pinang could only be protected from the damaging consequences of competition with its more attractive neighbour, by heavy duties on trade between the Indian ports and Melaka. Best then to make Melaka a permanent satellite of Pinang, which would augment its trade.

Raffles' memorandum persuaded Bengal and London to abandon the plan to destroy Melaka. Moreover, Raffles' exposure of the limitations of Pinang as an entrepot diminished Pinang's prestige in Calcutta and London. The memorandum thus marked the beginning of Pinang's decline as a major British possession. The Pinang administration tried to make the best of its new situation. The Pinang authorities maintained heavy duties at Melaka to stop it eclipsing Pinang. A heavy duty was imposed on opium imports, which entered Pinang free of tax, and an import duty of 6 per cent was imposed on British ships sailing to Melaka from west of the Arakan river in Burma.[77] The object was to persuade traders to use Pinang rather than Melaka, thereby preserving Pinang's commercial supremacy, whilst allowing merchants at the presidency to utilise the entrepot facilities of Melaka. There were complaints from merchants at Melaka against the heavy duties, but these received little sympathy from the Pinang administration, who conceded only minor adjustments.[78] In spite of these measures, Melaka remained attractive for Bengal traders. It was reported that better prices could be obtained for Bengal produce at Melaka.[79] Also, after 1808, at least two prominent Pinang merchants, Patrick Clark and Edward Capes moved to Melaka, preferring opportunities there to those available at Pinang.[80]

By the time Java was seized by the British in 1811, Pinang's reputation had already suffered greatly. There was by now a creeping awareness among Bengal merchants that a more centrally located British base was really required in the Malay archipelago. In the meantime, the acquisition of Java had devastating consequences for the trade of Pinang. Bengal traders now chose to trade directly with Java, and Pinang, located so far from the lucrative ports of the southern archipelago seemed less attractive than ever. Bangka, the main source of tin imports into Pinang, via Melaka, was placed under the authority of the British administration on Java, which quickly ensured that the island's trade would come to Javanese ports. After 1811, this resulted in a severe slump in Pinang's trade.[81] In addition, disruption of international trade was intensified by the outbreak of war between Britain and the United States in 1812. The collapse of pepper and other commodity prices was devastating not only for pepper cultivators on the island, but also those engaged in the vital trade in pepper with Aceh.[82] Attacks on British shipping by American privateers, and deepening instability in Aceh itself, further disrupted this branch of commerce. By 1815, there was serious concern about the deterioration of order in Aceh, and the general state of Pinang's commerce. The illusions upon which the high status of the settlement had been built were being cruelly exposed.

The Napoleonic wars had seen some relaxation of Bengal's restrictions on Pinang's diplomatic and commercial dealings with neighbouring Malay states. For example, in 1800 the Pinang administration were permitted to negotiate with the Sultan of Kedah for a strip of land on the adjacent coast, to help provide food and greater security for the island.[83] Bengal had also allowed Robert Farquhar considerable leeway in negotiating commercial treaties with the Malay states, although his governorship ended before he could turn these into reality. In 1809, fear that Aceh might become a base for the French from where they could threaten British trade, led to David Campbell's mission from Bengal to explore the possibility of a British base in the Sultanate. The mission proved fruitless, principally because seizure of Java diminished British fears of the French.[84] But there were still limits. Bengal prohibited any treaties or agreements which might embroil the Company in local disputes or wars. This prohibition of political commitments to local rulers allowed the Pinang administration little room for manouevre. But it did not stop individual European, Chinese or local merchants based on Pinang cultivating close ties with local rulers, or their rivals, where this might offer commercial advantages. Sometimes members of the Pinang administration lent informal support to local rulers or their enemies. This was most evident in Aceh after 1812, where Sultan Jauhar was desperately trying to assert his authority over defiant local chiefs, enriched and empowered by trade with the merchants of Pinang. Ultimately Jauhar's power depended upon his ability to raise revenue from trade. By 1815 there was bitter division within the Pinang commercial community between those who supported and opposed Jauhar.[85] Jauhar's supporters included Dunbar and McGee, Pinang merchants who had been granted a monopoly of the lucrative betelnut trade by Jauhar in 1814. His enemies included Carnegy and Co., Scott and Co. and of course Syed Hussein, who emerged briefly as a contender for power in 1815. These merchants were strong supporters of free trade with Aceh, and opposed the regulations on trade imposed by the Sultan. Both cliques gave financial support and arms to their respective sides in the dispute. Members of the Pinang administration even became involved, some giving informal support for Syed Hussein, while a minority favoured Jauhar. William Petrie, Governor of Pinang between September 1812 and October 1816, was notoriously partisan in his opposition to Jauhar.[86] Clearly Bengal's strictures against formal political or military commitments did not prevent informal involvement in local politics by merchants or officials. Nevertheless, Bengal and London made every effort to curb such tendencies out of fear of where they might lead. At a time of financial stringency, costly involvement in local wars was most unwelcome. That this did not always prevent informal and sometimes covert actions by Company servants on the spot, was a consequence of distance, poor communications and an unavoidable need to trust officials with greater knowledge of local circumstances. The case of Aceh was an example of how informal and unofficial involvement in local politics could have as far reaching an impact on local polities as formal diplomatic commitments.

***

The end of war in Europe brought dramatic change to the position of the British in south east Asia. The British government were determined to avoid any repeat of French expansionism. It was believed that a strengthened Dutch state would provide an effective buffer against French ambitions. To achieve this, the Dutch economy needed to be bolstered by the return of all conquered Dutch colonies in south east Asia. The Convention of 1814 set out this strategy, and incorporated Belgium into the Dutch state, together with the prosperous Flanders textile industry.[87] The post war settlement reflected the new international order in which the British had emerged as the dominant European power. The Dutch were effectively recruited as junior partners in an international settlement designed to suit British needs.[88] But in return, the British now had to subordinate their trading interests in south east Asia to this new policy of friendship with the Dutch.

British commercial interests in the east could not be sacrificed completely, even though the termination of the Company's monopoly of trade with India in 1813 demonstrated its unpopularity in governing circles.[89] It was significant that even Buckinghamshire, one of the most hostile Presidents of the Board of Control ever to confront the Court of Directors, was unprepared to end the Company's monopoly of trade with China. The China monopoly was still seen as essential for the financial solvency of the Company, and therefore a crucial bulwark against financial crisis at home, and foreign rivalry in the east.[90] In this context, the British policy of Dutch restoration held many pitfalls. If the Dutch were permitted to revert to the protectionism and commercial monopolies of the past British trade with south east Asia and China would undoubtedly suffer. Alternatively, a complete subjugation of Dutch commercial policy and interests in favour of British interests might delay or even prevent the revival of Dutch power which was integral to Britain's post war European strategy. A delicate balance needed to be struck.

British Company officials and merchants in the east were understandably anxious, and this was shared by the East India Company and its associated trading and shipping interests in London. The revival of Dutch power in the Malay archipelago threatened the networks of trade in the region built up in the long period of British hegemony.[91] It has also been argued that industrial interest groups in Britain actively opposed any measures which might close overseas markets.[92] To British industrialists, south east Asia was a promising market for British manufactured textiles and other produce. War and its aftermath had left many problems, particularly for the British textile industry.[93] New markets were desperately needed, and it was partly pressure from these industrial and associated mercantile interests which had persuaded government to abolish the East India Company's monopoly of the trade to India and south east Asia in 1813. After 1815, south east Asia and China (even under monopoly) were stable markets, at a time when British exports generally were experiencing severe recession.[94] Together these arguments form a wider interpretation of British expansion in south east Asia, which sees it as being driven by the need for new markets for British manufactures.

But there are problems with this interpretation. British industrialists displayed little interest in the Dutch threat in south east Asia after 1815. Those who argue for the primacy of industrial interests are forced to base their views on a particular interpretation of the motives of Thomas Stamford Raffles in his efforts to organise opposition in Bengal against the Dutch. It is argued that Raffles was made aware of the potential market for British manufactures in south east Asia by his experience as Lt Governor of Java. Raffles' plans to integrate Java into the British empire, and develop the island as a market oriented centre of agricultural production, were designed to provide a growing market for British manufactures, especially cotton goods.[95] Also, Singapore was established in 1819 principally to secure an effective · entrepot which would open the whole region for British industrial exports.

But this view of Raffles is open to question. Firstly, it suggests that Raffles was mainly preoccupied with protecting the interests of Britain's manufacturers. While he probably knew of Britain's post war industrial problems, it is important to remember that Raffles was a career East India Company servant whose skill, knowledge and priorities were directed exclusively to meet the needs of his employers. He was acutely aware of the problems confronting British commercial interests in India, particularly those concerning defence of the China trade and trade with the Malay archipelago. Secondly, Raffles' role in shaping British policy in south east Asia has been exaggerated. Other individuals, notably Hastings, the Governor General, were crucial in supporting resistance against the Dutch, and sanctioning the foundation of a new British base. In the calculations of men like Hastings, and influential British merchants like John Palmer, the welfare of British industry was not a priority. For them, the interests of British commercial and political interests in India were paramount. It is the contention here that such concerns were far more important in determining the East India Company's policy towards south east Asia.

Recent economic developments in India served to heighten concern in Bengal at the prospect of Dutch resurgence. The opening of trade between Britain, India and south east Asia to non East India Company merchants by the Charter act of 1813, had far reaching consequences. The Act of 1813 was the product of a complex process of accommodation of industrial interests, adjustment to the pressures of war and a changing world economy.[96] Fear of uncontrolled inflation at home, combined with looming raw material and food shortages, persuaded Lord Liverpool's government to liberalise trade with India. Unfortunately for supporters of continued monopoly, the East India Company came under attack just when some of its allies, especially in the City of London, were being tempted by the opportunities offered by a more liberal international trading environment.[97] In total, the Charter is best understood as part of the process of adjustment made by the military fiscalist British state, and its privileged allies in trade and finance, to accommodate not only the growing commercial requirements of industrialists, but also the urgent needs of a turbulent urban population who inspired fear of revolution among the elite.

But the termination of the India monopoly posed severe problems for the colonial administration in India. Under the monopoly, the Company and the Bengal agency houses had developed a complimentary relationship, based upon agency house involvement in the country trade, and the provision by them of loan finance to the Company.[98] In return, the agency houses enjoyed a near monopoly of European, non Company commercial activity within the East India Company's empire. By 1815, most of the country trade, banking, shipbuilding, indigo-planting and insurance were in the hands of six leading firms. They also controlled distribution of British manufactures imported by the East India Company under the conditions of the monopoly. The monopoly restricted the volume of British manufactured imports, thereby preventing overstocking, while the Company controlled licences permitting individuals to engage in the country trade, preventing excessive competition which might reduce agency house profits. It was a highly regulated system which worked to the mutual advantage of agency houses and the East India Company alike.

Even within this framework of regulated monopoly, crises were not entirely avoidable. Agency houses were volatile instruments, generally dependent upon a few individual partners' expertise and ability to work together harmoniously.[99] Partners often left agency houses, either to establish their own independent firms or to return to Britain. They remitted their wealth to London and established "sister" houses in the City. Occasionally such remittances by departing partners exacerbated shortages of capital in Bengal, forcing up East India Company debt-servicing costs. In addition, by 1813, heavy military expenditure in India and the cessation of bullion imports from Europe and America caused severe recession, and much worry in governing circles.

The opening of the Indian and south east Asian markets by the Charter Act deepened these economic difficulties. The careful regulation of British trade with India, which on the one hand ensured healthy profits for the agency houses, and on the other guaranteed regular loan finance for the East India Company's activities, was ended at a stroke. In 1813/14, there was frantic speculation in Bengal goods for the British market by British based private traders. The value of the rupee rose significantly against sterling, at a time when the Bengal administration needed to borrow large sums from the agency houses to pay for the Investment. The Company bills and securities normally issued to fund these activities offered a far lower rate of exchange for the rupee than could be obtained in private transactions.[100] Also, the burgeoning demand for Bengal produce by private traders from Britain stimulated the agency houses to invest in production of these commodities, diminishing further the capital available for the East India Company's needs.

The opening of trade thus threatened to destabilise the relationship between private capital and the East India Company in India.

Between 1813 and 1817, the East India Company's financial position deteriorated still further because of war in India against the Mahrattas and Nepalese, as high military spending reduced funds for the Investment.[101] Only final victory over the Marathas in 1817 averted financial disaster, and the Marquis of Hastings was savagely criticised by the Court of Directors for his belligerence and financial profligacy. The situation worsened as the problems bequeathed by the Charter Act began to change in nature. The speculative boom in Bengal produce of 1813/14 quickly receded, to be followed by a catastrophic fall in demand. Raw cotton, a commodity which attracted great enthusiasm from British private traders in 1813/14, when war with the United States had curtailed supplies from that quarter, soon fell out of favour when American supplies were restored on cessation of hostilities. Demand for other commodities, notably silk and indigo also declined, while the rapid increase in British cotton manufactures exported to India began to challenge Bengal cotton piece goods in their home market.[102] These difficulties were made worse by the heavy investment of funds in these Indian products following the speculative boom of 1813/14. The sequence of events which occurred then, now went into reverse. The rupee fell in value against sterling, and money for loans was once again plentiful, but the fall in demand for Indian produce in Britain meant that there was no way for surpluses of funds in India to be remitted to Britain.[103]

These highly unstable circumstances were made even more unpredictable by the effect of the influx of British manufactures on the agency houses. New merchants flocked to India from Britain, while some partners in existing houses set up their own firms, to engage in distribution of British imports. There was a proliferation of the number of agency houses from about 20 in 1815 to 32 in 1829, many with contacts in the provincial ports of Britain. The six main Bengal firms now faced unwelcome competition, which spread quickly from the distribution of British manufactures into the country trade and other activities, hitherto the exclusive preserve of the Bengal agency houses. Excessive competition, oversupply and falling prices ensued, precipitating a downturn in the China trade.[104]

By August 1818, Hastings was aware of a looming economic crisis in the colonial economy.[105] The collapse of several merchant firms in Calcutta, and a glut in Bengal of both British manufactures and Indian produce, caused falling prices and the danger of more widespread bankruptcies. Shipping was also seriously affected, a point noted by John Adam, Hastings' private political secretary.[106] Fierce competition between Indian based British shipowners and newcomers from Britain drove down freight rates, and widespread depression was the result. Unstable interest rates also made business ventures difficult to predict.[107] By 1818 there was both a glut of commodities in Bengal which required markets, and excess capital seeking profitable investment opportunities. One contemporary observed that the paucity of such opportunities tempted many of the agency houses into unsound investments, such as housing in Calcutta, shipbuilding, spice and coffee plantations, few of which proved successful in the long term.[108] The writer, John Crawfurd, regarded these unwise investment decisions as a major factor contributing to the eventual demise of the agency houses in the financial crisis of 1832/33.

By 1818, Bengal merchants and administrators were acutely aware of the need to expand Indian exports to diminish the glut of Indian produce which was depressing prices and profits and threatening to undermine the economic basis of the colonial system. Exclusion from overseas markets at such a time would be most unwelcome. In this context, developments in south east Asia were causing great anxiety in Bengal by 1818. The Malay archipelago, long an important market for Indian opium and cotton goods, acquired a new importance in light of these economic difficulties. There was alarm at the prospect of restoration of the Dutch colonies and the protectionism for which their earlier colonial regime had been noted. Following the return of Java to the Dutch, Hastings was informed of Dutch attempts to curb British trade with the island. The importance of trade to Java for Bengal commercial interests was stressed in the Bengal commercial reports of 1817 and 1818, which described the growth of exports from British India to Java and the surrounding islands, during the period of British control of the island.[109] The Board of Trade lamented the return of Java to Dutch rule as possibly "the greatest error against sound policy that ever was committed".[110] They warned of the dire consequences for British trade likely to follow an extension of Dutch authority in Sumatra. Adam concurred in this high estimation of Java as a market for Bengal commodities.[111] Members of the Bengal mercantile community repeated these sentiments. John Palmer, a fierce opponent of Dutch revival, strongly advocated the retention of Melaka, and the establishment of a new British port in south east Asia, which could protect free access to the markets of the region.[112] Such fears of the consequences of Dutch revival were also expressed by merchants and officials on Pinang.

Following the return of Java in 1816, the Dutch authorities tried to restore former treaties which excluded the trade of other European powers. Dutch agents were sent to Pontianak in Borneo, the Lampongs area of southern Sumatra and the southern Malay states, with instructions to re-establish Dutch monopolies of trade. Melaka was also returned to the Dutch in 1818, an almost catastrophic move for British merchants on Pinang. Raffles led the resistance against the Dutch, and he articulated views held widely throughout the British communities in the east. The loss of Java was a bitter blow for Raffles, ending his plans for a permanent extension of British authority and divesting him of a position of high status and power. In 1816, he returned despondently to Britain for a brief visit, where he continued to press for his ideas, most notably in a long paper to George Canning, then President of the Board of Control. Raffles contended that the treaties he had concluded with local states as Lt Governor of Java, morally and legally obliged the Dutch to protect the rights of British traders. Should the Dutch fail to honour this duty, Raffles argued that the British should occupy an island south of Melaka, either Bangka or Riau, to ensure British access to these important markets. This new station would provide naval protection for British trade, and also evolve as a central entrepot, enabling British traders to conduct business with local merchants without the obstacle of Dutch protectionism. In this way an outlet for British and Indian exports would be secured. Raffles also wanted a clear demarcation between British and Dutch zones of political and commercial influence, with the Malay peninsula and Sumatra clearly falling within the British sphere. The Dutch would be excluded from Sumatra, just at a time when they were actively seeking to establish their presence. Raffles also wanted a base in Aceh. His strategy implied greater importance for Benkulen and its satellites, as important strategic defences against Dutch expansion. Raffles also suggested another British base at the southern tip of Sumatra to ensure British access to south east Asia via the Straits of Sunda, and which could also attract Javanese and other traders, enabling them to defy any monopolistic restrictions imposed by the Dutch. Thus Raffles envisaged British political control of the northern part of the region through a new agreement with the Dutch and several new settlements on Sumatra, combined with commercial access to all the markets of the region via a new central entrepot. British interests would be secured by a chain of bases, a strategy guided by principles similar to those which shaped Farquhar's plan of 1804/05.

What motivated Raffles in this expansionist strategy? The view that he was driven by a desire to secure markets for British manufactures is questionable. While Raffles certainly appreciated that south east Asia was valuable for British exports, the interests of the East India Company were always paramount. He was motivated primarily by the commercial needs of British India. Raffles wanted British expansion in south east Asia to protect access for Indian commodities at a time when they were losing ground in Europe:

> "To ensure a market for the manufactures of India, and thus promote its industry and prosperity, and give an advantage beneficial to the energy of its people becomes an object of great and increasing importance. The extraordinary advance of British manufactures having in a great measure excluded those of India from the European market, it is to the populous and less civilised countries of the further east that we can alone look to for a permanent demand.......The consequences that would attend the loss of this trade, limited as it now is, are too obvious to require explanation, and the security and improvement of it are in consequence most intimately connected with the prosperity of our Indian empire."[113]

Following his appointment as Governor of Benkulen in March 1818, Raffles tried to implement his ideas. He immediately sent officers to investigate the possibility of a new base at Semangka bay at the southern tip of the island, and in July followed this up with energetic resistance against the Dutch in Palembang and the Sumatran interior. Raffles also pressed his own views about how to deal with the deepening crisis in Aceh. Although the Bengal administration ultimately rejected Raffles' plans for Sumatra, by late 1818 he had established himself as a major influence over policy formation. In November, he was summoned by Hastings to Calcutta to discuss the wider question of how to deal with Dutch resurgence. From Calcutta, Hastings sent him on a mission to Aceh and to establish a new base in the southern Malay archipelago. It was in pursuit of these instructions that Raffles founded Singapore in January 1819.

But others also had a crucial hand in events. Hastings was much more instrumental in shaping British policy and in the foundation of Singapore than has been suggested.[114] He refused to accept Raffles' proposals uncritically, rejecting in particular Raffles' aggressive plan for a base at Semangka bay, chiding him for his lack of caution in his dealings with the Dutch.[115] Hastings' motives in sanctioning the acquisition of a new port were made clear in his minute of November 1818. It is clear that Hastings wanted a new port to protect and extend the established trade between India and south east Asia, particularly the export of Indian commodities. British manufactures were not identified as a priority by Hastings, whose overwhelming concern was to ensure economic stability in India at a time of change and uncertainty, which threatened to overturn the delicate relationships between Company and private interests, and Indian producers and British merchants.

Raffles was thus despatched to Pinang to establish a new southern port and to help resolve the Acehnese succession dispute. After reaching Pinang, Raffles learnt that Riau, his and Hastings preferred location for a southern port, had been secured by the Dutch through a treaty with the Sultan of Johore, Abdul Rahman. Hastings, fearing that continuation of the mission would provoke a confrontation with the Dutch which the British government would refuse to support, ordered Raffles to abandon the quest for a southern port. Raffles had already encountered resistance to a new British acquisition in Pinang, where merchants and officials feared loss of trade.[116] Defying both the Pinang interests and Hastings, Raffles went south and reached Singapore on 19 January 1819. There, Raffles discovered that the Sultan of Johore's brother, Tunku Hussein, also claimed the throne. In return for British support, the Temmengong, a senior official in the Johore empire and an ardent supporter of Tunku Hussein, ceded Singapore to Raffles. Once again, the instability of local politics and the perceived advantages of close co-operation with a European power had led local rulers to surrender important territorial concessions. For the British the quest for a southern port had been accomplished. Hastings, initially anxious lest Raffles actions cause conflict with the Dutch, eventually threw his support behind the new acquisition.[117] For this, he received the fulsome support of the Calcutta mercantile community.[118] It had been the need to protect the China trade and the markets for Indian produce in south east Asia itself which prompted Hastings to disobey London's directives to avoid conflict with the Dutch, and sanction the acquisition of Singapore.

The second aspect of Raffles' mission was also significant. Since his accession in 1814, Sultan Jauhar, had been trying to assert his authority over the kingdom. He had tried desperately to enforce royal monopolies on commerce and to force trade to Banda Aceh, the capital. But these efforts had brought Jauhar into a series of major conflicts with his own local regional chiefs. Many Pinang merchants were also strongly opposed to these attempts by Jauhar to regulate commerce. They wanted free access to the ports of Aceh and low duties to maximise profits. They regarded Jauhar's attempts to assert his rights as a threat to Pinang's commercial interests. Inevitably, there were incidents in which Pinang ships were harassed and even seized by the Sultan's police. In 1815 Saif-Al-Alam, son of Syed Hussein, the prominent Pinang merchant had emerged as a contender for the Acehnese throne. Both the Pinang administration and the mercantile community were divided over the contest for the throne. On the one hand, Syed Hussein and merchant firms such as Carnegy and Co. strongly supported Saif-Al-Alam, while a faction including a significant portion of the Chinese merchant community, and Dunbar and McGee, who had been granted a monopoly of the betelnut trade by Jauhar, supported the reigning Sultan. Bengal traders were also drawn into supporting one or other of the two contenders.[119] John Palmer supported Saif-Al-Alam, mainly as a consequence of close commercial connections with Syed Hussein, while Fergusson, Fairlie and Co. wanted victory for Jauhar. In spite of hopes that the dispute could be resolved quickly, intermittent warfare dragged on for several years, disrupting trade in the process.[120] The re-emergence of the Dutch as a force in Sumatra after 1816 worried Pinang and Bengal, who feared Dutch intervention in Aceh. Late in 1817, the newly appointed Governor of Pinang, J. Bannerman, a former Director of the East India company, sent Captain John Coombs to Aceh to assess the legitimacy of the competing claims.[121] Coombs was influenced by the Saif-Al-Alam faction on Pinang, and his report, submitted to Bengal in February 1818, advocated recognition of Saif, and a treaty with him to establish a British Resident and factory in Aceh.[122]

The Bengal administration were too preoccupied with other matters to act upon Coombs' recommendations immediately, allowing Raffles time to voice support for Jauhar. In his capacities as Secretary at Pinang, and Lt Governor of Java, Raffles had conducted a long correspondence with Jauhar. Jauhar regarded Raffles as the only British official sympathetic to his position, and had bestowed upon him the Order of the Golden Sword, an honour awarded to few Europeans.[123] Raffles argued that to support any dubious contender for power in the Malay world would undermine British interests in the long run. It would encourage potential usurpers throughout south east Asia to challenge existing political regimes. The outcome would be a general wave of unrest and conflict, bringing chronic instability and disorder which would harm British trade and provide opportunities for Dutch expansion. The damage to British trade caused by the Acehnese civil war, and the inability of the British to resolve it quickly and satisfactorily, was clear evidence of where support for an illegitimate contender could lead. Raffles believed that British commercial and political interests would be best served by consistently supporting legitimate and established regimes, even if occasionally this meant accepting regulations and restrictions on commerce which were unpalatable for British merchants. In the long run, such a policy would win the trust of local rulers and dispose them to seek British rather than Dutch assistance, thus strengthening British influence and commerce throughout the region. Support for Jauhar was the only logical position from this perspective. Raffles wanted the British to clearly recognise Jauhar, rebuild mutual trust and friendship, and cement this new relationship with a permanent British Residency at Aceh, which would exclude all foreign influences and provide another link in Raffles' "chain of ports" strategy.[124]

Hastings was aware of British divisions over Aceh, and he was careful not to be misled by either faction. He was indifferent as to who should emerge as Sultan. What mattered was that order and commerce be restored, and all foreign rivals excluded from political influence in the Sultanate. When Raffles came to Calcutta in November 1818, Hastings listened to his arguments, but felt that Raffles was too ambitious and confrontational in Sumatra. In the end Hastings agreed to Raffles leading a new mission to Aceh, but insisted that it be carried out jointly with Coombs, a strong opponent of Jauhar. Hastings believed that Coombs would provide a balance against Raffles' preference for Jauhar, tempering the latter's zealous ambitions. Raffles and Coombs went first to Pinang, where Raffles briefly left Coombs while he went south to establish Singapore. Raffles was unpopular on Pinang, especially among Saif-Al-Alam's supporters, and his relations with Coombs were also very frosty. Eventually, on 8 March 1819, the two men proceeded to Banda Aceh, where talks were stalled by the unwillingness of the senior officials, the Panglima Sagis, to allow the British commissioners to disembark.[125] For the rest of March, the two commissioners spent their time debating which of the contenders had the most convincing case. Raffles, the senior official, got the best of these exchanges, and by 5 April the mission had agreed to support Jauhar. A treaty was signed which recognised Jauhar as Sultan, his right to regulate trade, and promised British military aid. Effectively this ended Saif-Al-Alam's challenge for the throne, although internal dissent against Jauhar continued after the 1819 treaty, fuelled by clandestine support from Pinang merchants dissatisfied with the terms of the treaty.[126] No Resident was appointed, mainly because Raffles no longer felt one to be necessary in the wake of the foundation of Singapore. The Bengal administration, though pleased to have brought matters closer to a conclusion in Aceh, were correctly pessimistic about the chances of a permanent end to unrest there, and were rather critical of Raffles for engaging in private correspondence with Jauhar whilst at Pinang, without informing Coombs. Nevertheless, the Treaty of Aceh of 1819 at least seemed to prevent Dutch opportunism in northern Sumatra. Ultimately, these efforts were rendered futile by the Anglo-Dutch treaty of 1824.

The years after 1815 had proven to be disappointing and ultimately very damaging for Pinang. The return of Melaka to the Dutch severed links via that settlement with the southern archipelago, while the surrender of Bangka terminated an important supply of tin. Trade in the northern archipelago had been severely disrupted by the Acehnese civil war, and Bengal's support for Raffles' mission to establish a new base to the south was a clear indication of disillusionment with Pinang's commercial performance. Once established, Singapore emerged quickly as the main focus for British trade in south east Asia. Attempts were made to improve Pinang's commerce, but with limited success. The failed effort to replace Jauhar had been partly motivated by a desire to create more favourable conditions for trade. Another initiative was Governor Bannerman's tin scheme, launched in September 1818.[127] Under this, Bannerman entered the tin trade on the East India Company's account, through Anderson, Pinang's tin agent. By the time of Bannerman's death in August 1819, some 650 bahars of tin had been secured from Perak and Selangor, but the general state of unrest in the Malay states, caused by the increasingly assertive policies of the Siamese, led to the failure and abandonment of the scheme.[128] Nevertheless, Bannerman had negotiated treaties with the Malay tin states of Perak and Selangor, which invalidated older treaties made by these states which excluded British trade. William Farquhar, former British Resident at Melaka had secured similar treaties with Riau, Lingga and Siak, before his replacement by the Dutch. In the long run it was to the west coast states of the Malay peninsula that Pinang's merchants would look for entrepeneurial opportunities, particularly in the fields of pepper and sugar production, and tin mining. In the 1820s, however, the limited local population of these states and difficulties of communications and transport, made for very slow progress.

Furthermore, the political condition of these states also retarded the progress of economic development. These states were in a gradual process of recovery from the long period of economic and political stagnation which had characterised the seventeenth and much of the eighteenth centuries. That process was accompanied by conflict, as rival Sultans and local chiefs competed for control of the revenues derived from the trade and river traffic of the west coast of the Malay peninsula. These conflicts were aggravated further in the late eighteenth century, as a resurgent Siam began to reassert its authority over the Malay states, sometimes inciting warfare between them, and occasionally intervening directly. In 1821, Kedah was invaded by the Siamese, and the Sultan compelled to seek asylum with the British. It was very difficult for British traders to make rapid headway in such an uncertain and unstable political environment, and considerable efforts were made by successive Pinang administrations in the 1820s to improve and stabilise political relations on the peninsula. One important aspect of this after the early 1820s were the initiatives to improve relations and trade with Siam. The establishment of Singapore ended Pinang's pretensions to be a successful entrepot for the whole region, but reoriented its trade towards the Malay peninsula, a trend which was to have important consequences in the long run. Meanwhile, in the immediate aftermath of the foundation of Singapore, a central question hung over British officials and merchants in south east Asia and Bengal: What would be the reaction of the British government to this latest, unsolicited addition to empire?

NOTES

1. H.R.C. Wright, East Indian Economic Problems: The Age of Cornwallis and Raffles (London, Luzac and Co. 1961).
2. Bayly, Imperial Meridian pp211-212.
3. G.R. Knight, "John Palmer and Plantation Development in Western Java in the early nineteenth century" Bijdragen 131:2/3 (1975) 309-337.
4. Somers Heidhues, Bangka Tin and Mentok Pepper pp30-31.
5. Ibid.: p32.
6. J. Bastin, "Raffles and British Policy in the Indian archipelago" Journal of the Malaysian Branch of the Royal Asiatic Society 27;1 (1954) 84-119.
7. W.G. Miller, "Robert Farquhar in the Malay World" Journal of the Malaysian Branch of the Royal Asiatic Society 51:2 (1978) 123-138, pp135-136.
8. A. Webster, "British Expansion in South East Asia and the Role of Robert Farquhar, Lt-Governor of Penang 1804-5" Journal of Imperial and Commonwealth History 23:1 (1995) 1-25.
9. Farquhar's Report, September 1805, Appendix 4, SSR G/34/12, IOR, London.
10. S. Bhattacharya, "Eastern India" in D. Kumar and M. Desai (eds), The Cambridge Economic History of India Volume Two (Cambridge, Cambridge University Press 1983) p293.
11. Tan Chung, "The British-China-India Trade Triangle 1771-1840" Indian Economic and Social History Review 11:4 (1974) 411-431.
12. C.H. Philips, The East India Company 1784-1834 (Manchester, Manchester University Press 1961) Ch 9.
13. J.R. Ward, "The Industrial Revolution and British Imperialism 1750-1850" Economic History Review 157:1 (1994) 44-65, pp51-55.
14. Richards, "The Indian Empire and Peasant Production of Opium".
15. O. Prakash, "Opium Monopoly in India and Indonesia in the Eighteenth century" Indian Economic and Social History Review 24:1 (1987) 63-80, p66.
16. Figures taken from the Bengal Commercial Reports 1796-1826, 174/13 to 174/37, IOR, London.
17. O. Prakash, "Opium Monopoly in India and Indonesia" p64.
18. For a full analysis of opium exports see: A. Webster, "British Export Interests in Bengal and Imperial Expansion into south east Asia: The Origins of the Straits Settlements" in B. Ingham and C. Simmons (eds), Development Studies and Colonial Policy (London, Frank Cass 1987) 138-174, see appendix 2, p172 for

figures for opium exports to the Malay archilpelago, and appendix 3, p173 for opium exports to China.

19. A view found in: H. Marks, The First Contest for Singapore (Nijhoff, Gravenhage 1959).
D.R. SarDesai, British Trade and Expansion in South East Asia 1830-1914.
Wong Lin Ken, "The Trade of Singapore 1819-69" úJournal of the Malaysian Branch of the Royal Asiatic Society 33:4 (1960) 11-301.
H.R.C. Wright, "The Anglo-Dutch Dispute in the East 1814-24" Economic History Review 3:2 (1950/51) 229-239.

20. David Scott to Fairlie, M.P. for Leominster, 20 February 1795, in C.H. Philips, The Correspondence of David Scott (London Camden Third Series 1951) p18.

21. An extensive correspondence between the two men is to be found in the Palmer Papers, Eng Lett c.86, Bodleian Library, Oxford.

22. Lee, The Sultanate of Aceh p224.

23. Details of this connection are found in papers relating to the case of Edward Swale Portbury vs George Charles Lindsay, Records of the Supreme Court, CHCA (Calcutta High Court Archives), Calcutta, West Bengal.

24. See G.R. Knight, "John Palmer and Plantation Development".

25. N. Tarling, "The Palmer Loans" Bijdragen 119:2 (1963) 161-168.

26. Minute of Governor Bannerman of Pinang (undated), Dutch Records, 1/2/29, IOR, London.

27. Case of Portbuty vs Lindsay.

28. Deposition of Luis Barretto, partner in the agency house of Joseph Barretto, 16 November 1803, in the case of Thomas Asken vs Gavin Hamilton and Alexander Aberdein 1803, CHCA, Calcutta, West Bengal.

29. Select Committee of the House of Commons on the Affairs of the East India Company, 1832. Parliamentary Papers 10:735, II.

30. Webster, "British Export Interests in Bengal" pp171-174.

31. An indication of the high esteem in which Macdonald was held was his entrustment with the supervision of the military force which seized Melaka in 1795. Bassett particularly depicts Macdonald as a trusted and talented diplomat. See: D.K. Bassett, "The Surrender of Dutch Malacca, 1795" Bijdragen 117:3 (1961) 344-358.
G.W. Irwin, "Governor Couperus and the Surrender of Malacca" Journal of the Malaysian Branch of the Royal Asiatic Society 29:3 (1956) 86-134.

32. H.P. Clodd, Malaya's First Pioneer pp68-69.

33. Macdonald to Bengal Council, 20 July 1796, (Fort William 2 August 1797) BPC 4/52, IOR, London.

34. Macdonald to Bengal Council, 28 August 1796, (Fort William 19 December 1796) BPC 4/46, IOR, London.

35. Macdonald to Bengal Council, 15 September 1796, (Fort William 19 December 1796) BPC 4/46, IOR, London.

36. Governor General John Shore's minute, 5 March 1798, (Fort William 5 March 1798) BPC 4/59, IOR, London.

37. Caunter to Bengal Council, 23 December 1797, (Fort William 5 March 1798) BPC 4/59, IOR, London.

38. Caunter to Bengal Council, 26 April 1798, (Fort William 4 January 1799) BPC 5/2, IOR, London.

39. Leith to Bengal Council, 26 May 1801, (Fort William 23 July 1801) BPC 5/23, IOR, London.

40. Leith to Bengal Council, 9 June 1801, (Fort William 23 July 1801) BPC 5/23, IOR, London.
41. Scott to W.E. Phillips, 17 May 1801, (Fort William 23 July 1801) BPC 5/23, and Bengal Council to Leith, 31 March 1803, (Fort William 31 March 1803) BPC 5/43, IOR, London.
42. Bengal Council to Macdonald, 22 August 1796, SSR G/34/1, IOR, London.
43. Bengal Council to Leith, 20 March 1800, SSR G/34/1, IOR, London.
44. George Leith's Book, SSR G/34/1.
45. Governor General Wellesley to Farquhar, 27 September 1804, SSR G/34/11, p90, IOR, London.
46. Webster, "British Expansion in South East Asia and the Role of Robert Farquhar" pp4-5.
47. W.G. Miller, "Robert Farquhar in the Malay World" pp136-137.
48. Webster, "British Expansion in South East Asia" pp18-19.
49. Farquhar to Bengal Council, 26 November 1803, BSC (Bengal Secret Consultations) 166, IOR, London.
50. Webster, "British Expansion" pp16-17.
51. Ibid.: pp17-18.
52. Ibid.; p18.
53. Farquhar to Wellesley, 16 May 1805, (Fort William 30 September 1805) Misc documents, SSR G/34/9, IOR, London.
54. Webster "British Expansion" pp7-8.
55. Ibid.: pp13-14.
56. T. Braddell, "Notices of Pinang" Journal of the Indian Archipelago and Eastern Asia (Singapore, 1851) p414.
    Clodd, Malaya's First Pioneer pp142-143.
57. This is the central argument presented in my article "British Expansion in South East Asia".
58. Udny and Lumsden in Bengal to the Court of Directors, 25 January 1806, Add Ms 13870, BL, London, and George Holford on behalf of the Board of Control to Wellesley, 18 February 1805, L/PS/5/541, Board's drafts of secret letters to India, IOR, London.
59. Webster, The Origins of the Straits Settlements (Unpublished PhD thesis, University of Birmingham 1984) p85.
60. Extract from George Leith's book 1802, SSR G/34/1.
61. Webster, The Origins of the Straits Settlements p111.
62. Brown to Cockburn, 31 December 1803, Papers of David Brown, Royal Commonwealth Society Library, London.
63. Undated memorandum from Farquhar to Wellesley, Add Ms 13870, p13, BL, London.
64. Brown to Cockburn, 31 December 1803.
65. Taken from the Prince of Wales Island Gazette, 1806-1811, on microfilm, IOR, London; also Webster, The Origins of the Straits Settlements pp109-110.
66. Dundas to Court of Directors, 12 November 1805, in C.D. Cowan, "Early Penang and the Rise of Singapore 1805 to 1832" Journal of the Malaysian Branch of the Royal Asiatic Society 23:2 (1950) 1-210.
67. Dundas to Court of Directors, 31 July 1806, in Cowan, ibid.
68. Webster, The Origins of the Straits Settlements pp118-120.
69. Dundas to Court of Directors, 20 March 1806, in Cowan, "Early Penang".

70. W.E. Phillips to T.S. Raffles (Secretary to the Pinang Administration), February 1807, (Fort Cornwallis 24 February 1807) SSR G/34/17.
71. Pinang Council minutes, 15 December 1808, in Cowan, "Early Penang".
72. Pinang Council Minutes, 25 May 1809, in Cowan, ibid.
73. Macalister to Court of Directors, 29 January 1808, in Cowan, ibid.
74. Pinang Council Minutes, (Fort Cornwallis 17 January 1806) SSR G/34/13.
75. W. Farquhar to Pinang Council (Fort Cornwallis 15 March 1810) SSR G/34/26.
76. For the full text of the memorandum, see: C.E. Wurtzburg, Raffles of the Eastern Isles (London, Hodder and Stoughton 1954) pp68-80.
77. Record of duties on commodities imported at Melaka in 1812, W. Farquhar at Melaka to Pinang Council, 26 March 1812, (Fort Cornwallis 2 April 1812) SSR G/34/34, IOR, London.
78. Melaka merchants to W. Farquhar, 26 March 1812, and Collector J. Macalister to Pinang Council 25 March 1812, (Fort Cornwallis 2 April 1812) SSR G/34/34, IOR, London.
79. Collector' reports at Melaka, 25 March 1812, (Fort Cornwallis 2 April 1812) SSR G/34/34, IOR, London.
80. eg Patrick Clark and Edward Capes. Capes was a merchant at Pinang from before 1805 until August 1807. During that time one of his major activities was the auctioneering house of Capes and Carroll. The partnership was dissolved in August 1807 (Prince of Wales Island Gazette 8 August 1807) and presumably Capes moved to Melaka after this date, although it seems improbable that he would have decided to move until after Raffles' memorandun of August 1808, and the resultant change in attitude to Melaka.
Clark had been a partner in the firm of Carnegy and Co., which he left in February 1808 (Prince of Wales Island Gazette 20 February 1808). Clark was no penniless adventurer. He had been a respected partner in Carnegy and Co. and had been active on the committee of landowners. Whether he moved to Melaka after the Raffles memorandum is also unclear. Both Capes and Clark were active merchants at Melaka in 1812, and signed the emrchants petition against heavy duties at that port (Melaka merchants to W. Farquhar, 2 March 1812, SSR G/34/34, IOR, London.
81. M. Lee (Stubbs Brown), "Trade and Shipping in Early Penang" Malaysia in History 21, 17-35 (1978) pp20-21.
82. Lee, The Sultanate of Aceh pp198-200.
83. Bengal Council to Caunter, 5 September 1799, (Fort William 5 September 1799) BPC 5/6, IOR, London.
84. Lee, The Sultanate of Aceh pp134-140.
85. Ibid.: pp201-203.
86. Ibid.: pp202-203.
87. Marks, The First Contest for Singapore Ch. 1.
88. N. Tarling, The Fall of Imperial Britain in South East Asia (Singapore, Oxford University Press 1993) pp26-27.
89. A. Webster, "The Political Economy of Trade Liberalisation: the East India Company Charter Act of 1813" Economic History Review 43:3 (1990) 404-419.
90. Philips, The East India Company p186.
91. SarDesai, British Trade and Policy in South East Asia
92. Wright, "The Anglo-Dutch Dispute in the East"

93. A useful brief summary of these problems is to be found in P.J. Cain and A.G. Hopkins, "The Political Economy of British Expansion Overseas 1750 to 1914" Economic History Review 33:4 (1980) 463-490.

94. Marks, The First Contest for Singapore p11.

95. An argument presented most forcibly in Wright, East Indian Economic Problems.

96. Webster, "The Political Economy of Trade Liberalisation".

97. Ibid.: pp416-418.

98. For a fuller description of these arrangements, see: Philips, The East India Company p46, and Tripathi, Trade and Finance in the Bengal Presidency p123.

99. An excellent insight into the day to day operation of agency houses, and the dependence on the commitment of a few men, may be found in the memoirs of William Prinsep, an employee and then partner in several agency houses between 1817 and 1842, including the firm of John Palmer. Mss Eur D. 1160/1-3, IOR, London, and A.C. Staples, "Memoirs of William Prinsep: Calcutta Years 1817-1842" Indian Economic and Social History Review 26:1 (1989) 61-79.

100. Tripathi, Trade and Finance in the Bengal Presidency pp122-123.

101. Ibid.: pp126-127 and 132-133.

102. Ibid.: p137.

103. Ibid.: p137.

104. Greenberg, British Trade and the Opening of China p85.

105. Import Warehousekeeper, J. Trotter to George Udny, Acting President of the Board of Trade, 19 July 1818, Board of Trade Proceedings, Vol. 346, August 1818, West Bengal Archives, Calcutta. A copy was sent to Governor General Hastings.

106. Papers of John Adam, Eur Mss F/109/34, Notebook on the Trade of Bengal, p6, IOR, London.

107. Ibid.: p4.

108. J. Crawfurd (1837), "A Sketch of the Commercial Resources and Monetary and Mercantile System of British India with Suggestions for their Improvement by means of Banking Establishments" in K.N. Chaudhuri, The Economic Development of India under the East India Company 1814-1858 (Cambridge, Cambridge University Press 1971) pp217-316.

109. Bengal Commercial Reports, 1817/1818, Range 174, Volume 29, IOR, London.

110. Ibid.: Vol 30, IOR, London.

111. Papers of John Adam, Notebook on Trade of Bengal, pp50-51.

112. Palmer to David Brown (between March and June 1818), Palmer papers, Eng Lett c.86, p289, Bodleian Library, Oxford. Also, for more details of Palmer's involvement in the quest for a southern port, see N. Tarling, "The Prince of Merchants and the Lion's City" Journal of the Malaysian Branch of the Royal Asiatic Society 37:1 (1964) 20-40.

113. "Substance of a Memoir on the Administration of the Eastern Islands by Sir Stamford Raffles", Raffles Papers, Eur Mss D/742/39, IOR, London.

114. Marks, The First Contest for Singapore p69, SarDesai, British Trade and Policy in South East Asia p34.

115. Hastings' minute, November 1818, Dutch Records I/2/29, IOR, London.

116. Lee, The Sultanate of Aceh pp282-285.

117. Webster, "British Export Interests in Bengal" p165.

118. C.M. Turnbull, A History of Singapore 1819 to 1975 (Oxford, Oxford University Press 1977) p11.

119. Lee, The Sultanate of Aceh pp219-270.
120. Ibid.: pp248-249.
121. Ibid.: pp263-269.
122. Ibid.: p269.
123. J. Gibson-Hill, "Raffles, Acheen and the Order of the Golden Sword" Journal of the Malaysian Branch of the Royal Asiatic Society 29:1 (1956) 1-20.
124. J.S. Tay, "The Attempts of Raffles to Establish a Base in South east Asia" Journal of Southeast Asian History 1:2 (1960) 30-46.
125. Lee, The Sultanate of Aceh pp290-291.
126. Ibid.: pp305-306.
127. C.D. Cowan, "Governor Bannerman and the Penang Tin Scheme, 1818-1819" Journal of the Malaysian Branch of the Royal Asiatic Society 23:1 (1950) 52-84.
128. Lee (Stubbs-Brown), "Trade and Shipping in Early Penang" pp32-33.

4. ANGLO-DUTCH RELATIONS AND THE TREATY OF LONDON: 1819-1824

The foundation of Singapore in 1819 represented a major extension of British imperial power in south east Asia, a fact underlined by the meteoric rise of the new settlement in the 1820s. Commercial success brought great political and imperial influence in the region, at the expense of the Dutch. British foreign policy in Europe since 1815 had sought to establish the Netherlands as a strong buffer against French expansion in Europe. To strengthen the Dutch, their colonies in south east Asia had been returned in the early years of peace, and they had been permitted to re-establish the treaties and agreements with south east Asian states which had characterised Dutch policy before 1795. There was always a delicate balance of interests for the British government. Dutch revival was not intended to undermine British economic interests in south east Asia. The stability of British colonial rule in India depended upon the success of trade with China and south east Asia, and Dutch recovery was not to be at the expense of these crucial interests.

In pursuit of this balance, the British government had to rely upon the East India Company colonial administrations in Calcutta and Pinang. Knowledge of south east Asia in London was limited, and execution of the policy of assisting Dutch colonial revival without impairing British economic interests, fell to East India Company officials on the spot, who knew local conditions and could negotiate with their Dutch counterparts in the region. The problem with this was that most officials in the east harboured bitter misgivings about the restoration of Dutch power. These stemmed from experience of Dutch methods in the past, prejudice, xenophobia and recognition of the great expansion of British trade with the Dutch colonies which had occurred under British rule. These factors alone were bound to make the British authorities in the east unreliable executors of the British policy of Dutch revival.

Moreover, there were other reasons for resisting London's policy towards the Dutch. The opening of the India market to British manufactures and merchants in 1813, threatened to undermine the colonial economic system which had evolved in Bengal since the 1780s. Cheap British cotton manufactures threatened to undercut Indian producers, thereby reducing the value of the substantial investments made by the agency houses. The influx of new British merchants and shipowners brought unwelcome competition, which in the long run might undermine the profitability of the agency houses upon which the East India company had come to depend for the successful operation of the China trade. Dutch revival compounded these fears, threatening as it did to cut off access to south east Asian markets, just as their value as an outlet for Indian cotton goods was at a premium. By 1815 so much Anglo-Indian capital and shipping was engaged in the trade to south east Asia, that any loss of commercial opportunities there could have the most disastrous consequences for the agency houses of Bengal, who were already feeling the ruinous effects of unfettered competition with the newcomers from Britain. It was the severity of this looming economic crisis in India which was decisive in persuading Hastings and his administration to act in defence of British commercial interests in south east Asia, even though this ran the danger of defying the whole direction of London's pro-Dutch foreign policy. It was the need to stabilise and protect the old colonial economic order which had grown up under monopoly, and which was now threatened by the consequences of its abolition, which prompted the acquisition of Singapore and the Aceh treaty of 1819.

The acquisition of Singapore thus needs to be seen in a wider context. The period from the 1780s to the 1820s had been a difficult period of adaptation and accommodation for the alliance of landed and mercantile interests which had dominated British society in the eighteenth century. The rise of industry in the later eighteenth century was accompanied by the emergence of manufacturing pressure groups determined to gain access to foreign markets by breaking down the trading monopolies and privileges bestowed upon the great chartered companies. Although these industrial interests never achieved the political clout enjoyed by the financiers and merchants of the City of London, the potential for revolutionary unrest in a growing urban population of alienated and impoverished industrial workers, meant that the needs of industry could not be simply ignored. Concessions had to be made to preserve the power of the existing landed elite and its London based mercantile allies. Revolution in France in 1789, and the European war which ensued, made the threat of revolution seem even more immediate, as the disruption of international trade and wartime shortages caused unemployment and inflation in Britain. By the time of the outbreak of war with the United States in 1812, Liverpool's government feared that unrest at home might bring defeat in war and revolutionary upheaval. In this context, concessions to and accommodation of the needs of industry became the landed elite's strategy for political survival. In response, Liverpool's administration developed its "liberal Tory" economic policies between 1812 and the late 1820s. These gradually reduced state restrictions on international trade to promote new export markets for industry. Fear of domestic unrest did not disappear with victory in 1815, for trade depression, unemployment and civil disorder continued throughout the following two decades. There was a gradual shift towards a liberal, free trade environment which accommodated the needs of industry, while preserving the political dominance of the landed elite and their allies in the City.

Two particular aspects of this strategy of adjustment and accommodation are of particular importance when considering the British position in south east Asia. Firstly, the ending of the East India Company's India trade monopoly in 1813 was a product of this process of adjustment, opening as it did new markets for industrial produce in India, and new sources of cotton and other commodities for the British market. Unfortunately, it also threatened to destabilise the existing colonial economic system, and as a consequence markets for Indian produce in south east Asia acquired a new importance. Secondly, military victory in 1815 removed the immediate threat to Britain's international position, establishing her as the dominant European power. But the problem was how to prevent a resurgence of French power and preserve Britain's hard won dominance, without incurring excessively high levels of military expenditure and taxation. Such an onerous financial burden would contradict the low spending and tax policies of new liberal Toryism. This is why the policy of maintaining a strong Netherlands as a client state for the British, was so attractive to the Liverpool government. It appeared to offer security for British interests in Europe without the heavy costs of maintaining a large standing army.

But these two policies, ending the East India Company trade monopoly, and promoting Dutch strength and economic recovery via its south east Asian colonies, were contradictory. The increased importance of south east Asia for Bengal merchants and administrators in the aftermath of the 1813 Charter Act, ran contrary to the objective of resurgent Dutch power and monopolistic commerce in that region. It was left to East India Company officials in the east to find a way to overcome this incompatibility. Thus the Liverpool government's accommodation of the new forces of industrialism, forced colonial officials in India to make adjustments of their own to adapt to the changed circumstances brought about by the policy changes in London. In this respect, the Liverpool government's concessions to industry had a "ripple" effect, forcing the colonial administration in India to revise its policies to protect the old colonial economic system from the destabilising forces unleashed by trade liberalisation. The foundation of Singapore was such an adjustment. It was designed to preserve access to south east Asian markets at a time when their importance for British India had been heightened by new competition from Britain, but without undermining London's policy of promoting Dutch resurgence. The Dutch colonies were not threatened by the new British acquisition, whose intended function was solely commercial. From this perspective the significance of the British acquisition of Singapore is best understood as part of the wider process of accommodation and policy adjustment necessitated by the rise of industry and British victory in global war.

The Bengal administration were not, however, the final arbiters of their efforts to adjust to changes thrust upon them by London. The Dutch authorities in the east questioned the legality of Raffles' acquisition of Singapore. Inevitably, this issue was referred to the respective Dutch and British governments in Europe, and as the argument over Singapore unfolded, the need for clarification of British and Dutch interests in south east Asia became apparent. Out of the ensuing negotiations, the Treaty of London of 1824 defined the respective geographical limits of Dutch and British influence in the region for the rest of the century. A permanent British imperial presence in the region was formally recognised, and the basis for later expansion of British power was laid. Various questions arise in relation to the negotiations. How confident were British politicians about the legality of their claim to Singapore? Who in Britain supported the retention of Singapore in the face of Dutch protests and why? What is the significance of these questions for wider theories about British imperialism and the nature of the British political system?

**

The British government reacted to news of the foundation of Singapore with surprise and embarrassment. The need to strengthen the Netherlands, inclined ministers to be critical of the Bengal administration. There was an immediate suspicion that Hastings had been unnecessarily belligerent towards the Dutch. But soon after the news reached London in August 1819, it quickly became apparent that British acquisition of Singapore had its supporters in Britain as well as in India. Who were these supporters? What were their reasons for publicly speaking out in favour of retention of the settlement?

Firstly, there were many in the East India Company's bureaucracy in London who recognised the importance of British trade between India and the Malay archipelago. Charles Grant, the influential East India Company director, testified to select committees of both houses of parliament that defence of the trade to China and south east Asia was essential for the economic stability of British India.[1] He also specifically supported retention of Singapore, even though he had always opposed territorial expansion on principle.[2] Against him were others who were more sceptical of the value of the new settlement. There was a general consensus that defence of the China trade was essential, but this was slow to be articulated. In July 1820, the Company formed a Secret Select Committee of four directors to advise the British team involved in negotiations with the Dutch. It was influential in persuading the British negotiators of the value of Singapore.

A second source of influence was the manufacturing and mercantile communities of provincial Britain, mainly connected with the country's emergent industrial sector. Based in towns and ports like Liverpool, Manchester, Leeds and Glasgow, pressure groups had existed since the 1790s which lobbied and petitioned parliament on questions concerned with trade to the far east. These provincial groups were independent of London interests and lobbied parliament and government ministers separately. They had been particularly active in campaigning for the abolition of the East India Company's monopoly in 1813, using the press, pamphlets, parliamentary contacts, and interviews with ministers to secure their aims.[3] The loss of markets during the war, and the continuation of economic difficulties after 1815, meant that these industrial pressure groups continued to be active, especially on questions related to the export trade. In June 1820, two Manchester newspapers carried petitions from industrialists and merchants for the retention of Singapore.[4] Some historians have argued that these industrial interests were very important in persuading Liverpool's government to retain Singapore.[5]

The third group interested in the Singapore question and the future of commerce in south east Asia were the London based East India agency houses, which had been established by retired partners of the Indian agency houses. These included such firms as Alexander and Co., Forbes and Co. and Paxton, Cockerell and Trail. These houses acted as correspondents for the Indian agency houses, conducting business with them and protecting their interests in the capital. They took responsibility for handling the considerable wealth remitted by East India Company servants and agency house partners in India, which they usually chose to invest in East India Company stock. Such investments gave the London agency houses votes in the Court of Proprietors, the principal body representing shareholders in the East India Company, entrenching their influence within the Company's decision making structures. This private agency house lobby grew markedly after 1813.[6] The London houses were also part of the powerful amalgam of financial and mercantile interests which made up the City of London, and which played such an important role in British political life.[7] City merchants and financiers funded the Hanoverian regime's considerable defence expenditure, necessary in face of international hostility and the possibility of internal revolt. Members of the landed gentry also availed themselves of the financial resources of City bankers, whose growing wealth and usefulness to the elite gained them admittance into the ranks of high society. This was early "gentlemanly capitalism", in which financial and mercantile capitalists secured for themselves political influence and privilege by providing financial support for the landed regime. In the eighteenth century, this position of privilege was manifested as restrictive trade monopolies such as that enjoyed by the East India Company. During the first half of the nineteenth century, such legal privileges were gradually stripped away, as the landed elite was forced to accommodate the demands and requirements of a new class of industrialists and their volatile urban workers. This did not, however, represent a loss of influence or status for the interests of the City. City merchant bankers and merchants quickly discovered that the emerging environment of free trade was one even better suited to their needs than restrictive monopolies. As the century proceeded, the merchant banks accumulated vast wealth by accepting and discounting the bills of exchange of British and foreign merchants. London became the centre of shipping and insurance for the expanding trade of the world. In the difficult years after 1815, the Liverpool governments were very attentive to financiers' needs.[8] Prominent merchant bankers such as Nathan M. Rothschild and Alexander Baring wielded powerful influence over key government economic decisions, especially the return to the bullion standard after the war.[9]

The position of the London East India agency houses in this shifting pattern of City influence requires comment. The opening of the trade to India in 1813 had damaged the interests of some of the Indian based agency houses, bringing fierce competition which contributed to the ultimate collapse of the Bengal agency houses in the early 1830s.[10] But their sister agency houses in London survived this collapse of the old colonial economic order in India, and adapted successfully to the changing international economic order in which the City had to operate. Far from being swept aside by the emergent industrial interests and their mercantile allies in the outports, the London houses accommodated these new interests through their control of finance and knowledge of the eastern markets. Many of the London agency houses became successful commission agents for provincial industrialists, arranging the export of manufactures to overseas markets.[11] The commissions earned from this enabled the London houses to develop their business and political influence. The efforts of the London houses to keep Singapore in British hands was an example of that political influence in action.

But historians have tended to confuse the London East India agency houses with the provincial and industrial pressure groups lobbying for retention of Singapore. For example, the East India Trade Committee, a London based pressure group which consisted exclusively of agency house merchants has been described as representing the outport merchants and industrialists.[12] This is misleading. No industrialists or provincial merchants appeared on the numerous petitions presented by the committee; and the London agency houses were involved in a far wider range of commercial activities than just the export of cotton manufactures. In fact the London agency houses, as emergent members of the "gentlemanly capitalist" financial elite of London, were far more influential and important than provincial industrial interests in persuading the government to keep Singapore. If the port was initially acquired to help prop up a destabilised colonial economic system in India, it was consolidated as a permanent British possession by London based gentlemanly capitalists.

**

The convention of 1814 had not ended the problems which had beset Anglo-Dutch relations in the east. Both sides recognised the need for further negotiation to iron out numerous problems. These included the extent to which the British were prepared to tolerate a restoration of Dutch authority in south east Asia, and the issue of how Dutch possessions in India, seized by the British, were to be dealt with in the future. The Indian settlements of Chinsura, Sadras and Birnipatnam had all previously supplied the Dutch with Indian commodities such as opium. But this trade had declined, and the Dutch were now prepared to surrender them to the British, in exchange for British recognition of Dutch supremacy in Sumatra. Falck, the Dutch colonial minister, envisaged a direct exchange of the Dutch Indian settlements for Benkulen and its subsidiary Sumatran outposts.[13] There would also be a division of south east Asia into separate British and Dutch spheres of influence. Certain ideas which were eventually incorporated into the treaty of London of 1824 were thus being mooted as early as 1818.

From the British point of view, the expectation that a restoration of Dutch power would present no serious difficulties, gave way to new worries about the likely consequences for British commerce in the east. Continuing depression in Britain heightened this concern, and in February 1819, the British Foreign Secretary, Castlereagh, complained to Fagel, the Dutch ambassador in London, about the high levels of Dutch duties in Java.[14] Castlereagh was responding to complaints from the London Ship Owners' Society, a body which included members of the London East India agency houses. There was a failure by both sides to appreciate fully the concerns of the other. Just as the Dutch underestimated the value of the Malay archipelago for British commerce, the British failed to appreciate the strength of Dutch determination to return to protectionism and monopoly.

News of Singapore's foundation injected these discussions with a new urgency. The President of the Board of Control at the time the news was received, George Canning, was unprepared to pass judgement on the Singapore question until more information was forthcoming from the east. Castlereagh arranged for formal discussions with the Dutch to begin in November 1819, hoping that further intelligence would arrive before these talks began. Castlereagh instructed the British ambassador in the Hague, Lord Clancarty, to arrange the conference. Clancarty was ordered to inform the Dutch that there were two principles which the British would stoutly defend. First, the British would refuse to accept any exclusion "or mere passive toleration" of British commerce in south east Asia. Secondly they would not allow "the military and naval keys to the China trade", namely the Straits of Melaka, to fall under Dutch control.[15]

This opening statement of the British position has been attributed to George Canning, who as President of the Board and a Liverpool M.P., was well acquainted with the trade to south east Asia. However, it is clear from Castlereagh's correspondence with Clancarty that the Foreign Secretary himself had a firm grasp of the importance of this branch of commerce. Castlereagh urged Clancarty specifically to defend the right of British merchants to establish their own agents throughout the region.[16]

Castlereagh's contacts with the London shipowners and representatives of the London agency houses guided him on which British rights needed to be defended. Agency house influence in the negotiations thus began rather earlier than some historians have suggested. The staff of the India Board also liaised closely with the London firms, particularly those engaged in the trade to Java.[17] It is plain that the London houses had contributed to the formulation by the British of their two guiding principles right at the beginning of the negotiations.

When Clancarty conveyed Castlereagh's wishes for a November conference to Falck and Van Nagell (the Dutch Foreign Minister), he was able to glean some insight into Dutch thinking on south east Asia. They welcomed the proposal for an early conference. While denying any intention to exclude British commerce, the Dutch strongly defended their revived treaties with local states. Clancarty also detected a degree of alarm at the actions of Raffles at Singapore, which to some Dutch officials presaged further British expansion in the region.[18] Van Nagell argued that Dutch actions had been entirely consistent with the 1814 convention, and in no way breached Castlereagh's cherished two principles.[19] While agreeing in principle to an early conference, however, the Dutch requested a postponement of talks until the delivery of a report from their Commissoners General in the east. Like the British, they were reluctant to engage too hastily in discussion, at least until further information could be obtained from the men on the spot. The report of one of the returning Commissioners, Theodorus Elout, compounded Falck's underestimation of the importance of the Malay archipelago to British trade. Like Falck, Elout proposed that the Dutch should leave India in return for a similar British abandonment of possessions in south east Asia. The British right to navigation through and trade in the eastern seas would be guaranteed by the Dutch, but all territorial rights and possessions would be abrogated.

In fact, the proposed conference was delayed substantially; November was ruled out because the Dutch needed time to consider Elout's report, and then in January 1820 King George III died. Further delay followed as the scandal of George IV's divorce occupied senior politicians. But these delays were not unwelcome to the British. It gave British negotiators time to assess the value of Singapore. Pressure groups interested in the trade to south east Asia reminded parliament of the importance of south east Asian commerce. On 17 August, only days after news of Singapore had reached Britain, the Society of Shipowners petitioned government for the abolition of all remaining restrictions on commerce with India and the Malay archipelago.[20] The merchants and manufacturers of Liverpool, Manchester, Glasgow, Edinburgh and Leeds all repeated these demands, emphasising the need for new export markets for industry.[21]

Two petitions, however, did not conform to the demands of the majority.[22] The petitions presented by the provincial industrial interests demanded an end to the East India Company's China trade monopoly, as well as preservation of access to south east Asia. But ending the China monopoly was unacceptable to the government of the day, and the demand did little to impress ministers. In contrast, a petition from the London East India agency houses was treated far more seriously, because it displayed a pragmatic understanding of the government's commitment to defend most of the East India Company's trade privileges. Their petition suggested a limited liberalisation of the China monopoly, permitting both London and Indian based agency houses to engage in the export trade from China to Europe. The monopoly of trade between China and Britain would remain intact. Canning took the suggestion very seriously, perceiving in it advantages for both British commerce in general, and the reputation of the East India Company. Canning put it to the Court of Directors, suggesting that opening exports from China to Europe would:-

> "give relief and satisfaction to the merchants and create a favourable impression of the liberal motives by which the Company is activated"[23]

Canning emphasised that the Indian export trade to China, necessary to finance an intended expansion of Chinese exports to Europe, would be conducted through the existing channels of the country trade, and that most of the Company's trading privileges between Britain and China would stand. Although the directors refused to accept the proposal, here again is evidence of the growing influence of the London houses.[24] Also, two Parliamentary Select Committees were established in 1821 and 1822 to assess the effects of the 1813 Charter Act upon British political and commercial interests in the east. The coincidence of their deliberations with the renewed Anglo-Dutch discussions on south east Asia and the Singapore question, provided an opportunity for the various pressure groups interested in trade to south east Asia to gain the attention of the government. It enabled some of them to have a significant influence on the outcome of the negotiations.

In preparing for the forthcoming negotiations with the Dutch, Canning had requested that the Court of Directors appoint a Secret Select Committee to advise him on south east Asian affairs. The committee consisted of four senior directors; James Pattison, Campbell Marjoribanks, William Fullerton Elphinstone, and the influential Charles Grant. The committee recommended the retention of Singapore, but strongly urged that an alternative port be established should Singapore have to be abandoned.[25] Grant emerged as a fervent supporter of Singapore, both in his role on this Secret Committee, and in his testimonies to the parliamentary committees.[26] Grant openly supported the foundation of Singapore to Raffles himself.[27] Grant's motives were indeed very similar to Raffles'. Both recognised that the efficient functioning of the Calcutta agency houses was vital for the East India Company, and that the Charter Act of 1813 had disrupted the colonial economic system so essential for British rule. The opening of the Malay archipelago to an expansion of Indian exports offered some relief.[28] Support for Singapore spread from London to the provinces in due course. Testimonies to the parliamentary committees from London and provincial interests alike, though revealing differences over the question of the East India Company's China monopoly, were united in their support for Singapore or a similar port in south east Asia.

While this growing support for Singapore undoubtedly had an effect on the views of the British government, it would be a mistake to assume that they secured an unshakable commitment to keep Singapore as early as 1820. It was by no means clear to ministers then that Singapore was either successful or the best site for a new British acquisition in the region. Neither was it clear that Raffles' acquisition of the island was achieved by acceptable diplomatic or legal means. The central difficulty was that information filtered back from the east very slowly. The consequence was that when formal discussions between the British and Dutch finally began in July 1820, the British negotiators found themselves in the uncomfortable position of being urged by a growing body of British based pressure groups to defend and uphold a territorial acquisition of uncertain legality or value.

Negotiations eventually began on 20 July 1820. The opening positions taken by the two sides set the terms of debate. For the Dutch, Fagel and Elout asserted their right to trade freely with their Indian possessions, and to occupy Melaka, Padang, Palembang, Bangka and Billiton. They also rejected any British claim to Singapore, arguing that Raffles' agreement had been made with a false pretender to the throne, and infringed not only the rights of the true Sultan, but also those of the Dutch, who enjoyed exclusive rights in Johore by virtue of their longstanding alliance with the legitimate ruler. The Dutch representatives did not present Fagel's plan for a clear division of spheres of influence, probably fearing a negative and angry response which might sour discussions. For the British, George Canning put some fourteen points before the Dutch, most concerned with wartime debts for military stores owed by the Dutch to the British. The Dutch did not contest these. Canning asserted the British right to trade and navigation through south east Asia, but questioned the Dutch claim to Billiton, denying that this island was a dependency of Bangka, as contended by the Dutch, and arguing that there was no authority for its acquisition under the 1814 convention. On the question of Singapore, Canning conceded that while the Dutch position might be valid, a final decision could only be made on receipt of further information from the east. Canning also mentioned the growing interest in the settlement by the British public.[29]

At the end of the 20 July meeting, both sides agreed, on Canning's suggestion, to prepare written drafts of their respective positions, with some suggestions as to how differences might be resolved. These drafts could then be discussed privately by both sides in preparation for a second meeting. Canning's doubts about the British right to Singapore became evident, but so also did his growing conviction of the necessity of a new British settlement at the heart of south east Asia. He proposed that in return for Bangka and the Indian settlement of Fultah, the British would abandon Singapore and waive all Dutch debts. Even though Canning doubted the British right to Singapore, he still wanted to use it for bargaining purposes in the negotiations. Other concessions offered by Canning were unrestricted Dutch export of opium and saltpetre from their Indian factories in return for a general opening of trade in south east Asia, and mutual communication of all treaties and agreements made with local states. The Dutch paper restated their demand for the evacuation of Singapore, and offered to surrender Fultah to the British, in return for British recognition of their right to Billiton.[30]

The next meeting took place on 26 July, and progress was made only on non-controversial issues. Both sides agreed to co-operate in the elimination of piracy and to guarantee free navigation through south east Asia. But the contentious questions remained unresolved. Canning now stated that he was unwilling to reach a conclusion on the Singapore question until further information was received from the British authorities in the east. This has been seen as a hardening of the British position, instigated by the Secret Select Committee of the East India Company, who warned Canning that Bangka could not provide adequate protection for the China trade. But the committee was not as committed to Singapore as this interpretation suggests. Grant spoke for the committee when he expressed a willingness to accept an alternative to Singapore, in his testimony to the Lords committee on 6 July.[31] A more likely explanation for Canning's reluctance to settle the Singapore question was the one he gave to the Dutch, that he was genuinely uncertain about the legality of the British claim, and needed more details from the east. Even though it does seem that Canning harboured doubts about the validity of the British claim, to surrender to the Dutch without first considering the Governor General's views would be judged very harshly by a public already voicing support for Singapore.[32] It was this wider expression of opinion, rather than just the Secret Select Committee's advice, which appears to have made Canning cautious. The provincial and London newspapers all called for the retention of Singapore, and the London papers, particularly the Times, were especially vociferous.[33] Without doubt, the London papers spoke for the City and its associated financial and mercantile interests, and Canning was later to admit to Charles Bragge Bathurst, his successor at the India Board, that he saw the newspapers as the great instigators of public support for Singapore.[34]

By the morning of 27 July it became apparent that an impasse had been reached in the negotiations. The Dutch insisted upon the illegitimacy of Singapore, and were suspicious of Canning's reluctance to clarify the British position. When pressed again, Canning appeared to concede the likelihood of the Dutch claims being verified, but stuck to his refusal to commit himself until further information was forthcoming. In the afternoon, Canning suggested that a way forward might be for the Dutch to concede that the British had a right to a new settlement, even if it was not to be

Singapore. Canning suggested Billiton as a possible site for such an alternative British base. But the Dutch were committed to their own possession of Billiton as strategically essential for the defence of nearby Bangka. When negotiations were resumed on the 29 July, Castlereagh appeared alongside Canning, and repeated the British refusal to surrender Singapore until either further information was forthcoming, or a suitable alternative base was agreed upon. He also argued that representatives of British agency houses should be allowed to settle at, and conduct their business from Dutch possessions throughout south east Asia. The Dutch retorted that there was a history of such British agents being used by East India Company officials to undermine Dutch influence, an accusation not entirely unfounded in light of Raffles' policies as Lt Governor of Java. Attempts to reach a compromise failed, and on 5 August, further discussions were suspended pending further information from Bengal. Both sides agreed not to impede the traders of the other, except in respect of the Dutch Moluccas, considered by both sides as essential for Dutch economic recovery. It was agreed that trade between British and Dutch colonies would be on a "most favoured nation" basis, and that details of new or existing treaties with local states would be exchanged. Both sides promised not to make any treaties which excluded the commerce of the other. There were, however, some ten points, including the Singapore question, which remained to be resolved.[35]

Of the two sides, the Dutch emerged from this first round of negotiations with greater confidence. Canning had all but conceded the illegality of Singapore, and it was hard to see how the Bengal administration could now concoct a convincing argument for the port's retention. In contrast, the British negotiators found themselves being pressed by domestic public opinion to retain an acquisition which they strongly suspected was illegal, and potentially damaging for diplomatic relations with a neighbouring power whose friendship was crucial for British policy in Europe. It was not clear how public opinion could be reconciled with the wider strategic imperatives governing British foreign policy. Only a brief interlude was anticipated before discussions were resumed, and a British climbdown on the Singapore question appeared to both sides to be the most likely outcome. However, the expected early resumption of talks did not happen. It was not until late 1823 that negotiations were reopened - with very different results to those anticipated in August 1820.

*****

The three year delay in the resumption of talks was caused by a variety of factors. One view attributes the delay to internal political problems within the British government, a dispute between the Dutch and British governments over the slave trade and continuing delays in communications from the east.[36] An earlier view held by Dutch historians, that the three year delay was a deliberate British ruse to prevent the loss of Singapore, has been rejected by most British historians.[37] The unintended effect of the delay was to allow Singapore to acquire such commercial importance, that by the time negotiations were resumed abandonment had become unthinkable. But this belief that there was no deliberate policy of delay does not stand examination. While delay on the British side was probably unintentional for the rest of 1820 and most of 1821, by 1822 a deliberate strategy of delay was being pursued.

Domestic problems in 1820 made early resumption of discussions difficult for the British side. The divorce trial of Queen Caroline continued until November 1820, and involved most of the cabinet. By late November, Fagel was impatiently pressing for renewed talks, and passed on to Castlereagh copies of correspondence between Governor General Hastings and Van Der Capellen on the Singapore question.[38] These documents were disturbing and confusing for the British side. Hastings admitted that Raffles had disobeyed orders by proceeding to Singapore after he had been instructed to abandon the mission and to avoid confrontation with the Dutch. But at the same time the British Governor General refused to abandon Singapore on the grounds that the Dutch had no legal claim to the island. Hastings claimed that neither the treaty of 1784 between the Dutch and the Johore empire, nor the subsequent Dutch treaty with Riau in 1818, gave the Dutch authority over Singapore. Neither was British possession of the island precluded. But Hastings presented little argument or evidence to support his claims.[39] Taken alone, the correspondence was most damaging for the British case, revealing as it did the questionable character of Hastings' arguments. Castlereagh responded by sticking to the British position of August, that further discussions could only be resumed when further reports were received from Hastings. Domestic developments caused further delay. In December, Canning resigned from the cabinet over the question of the royal divorce, and was replaced at the India Board by Charles Bragge Bathurst, who held the Presidency until February 1822.

Despatches were eventually received from Hastings in late January 1821, but were to prove as inconclusive and confusing as the Governor General's correspondence with Van Der Capellen.[40] In these new despatches Hastings argued that the succession dispute in Johore complicated the Singapore question. Hastings admitted that Tunku Hussein, with whom Raffles' agreement to establish a British base on Singapore had been made, had not established himself as the rightful Sultan. However Raffles had conducted his negotiations with the Temmenggong, a senior official whose authority was not disputed. Furthermore, Hastings pointed out that when the British seized Melaka in 1795, the Dutch had denied that Johore was bound in any way to treaties with Melaka. Yet the Dutch treaty of 1784, now invoked to exert Dutch control over Johore, had been made by the Dutch administration at Melaka. But Hastings could not be confident in these arguments. He had already questioned the legitimacy of Tunku Hussein's claim to the throne, and produced little evidence of the Temmenggong's alleged supremacy in the Johore empire or his legal right to act independently from the sovereign. Limply, Hastings had to concede:-

> "We confess that we require more perfect information before we can make up our minds on the rights of the two princes."[41]

In truth, Hastings' position was difficult. He enjoyed the near unanimous support of the Bengal administration and merchants for a new central port in the southern archipelago, but he was also aware of the dubious basis of Raffles' acquisition of Singapore. As he was under strict orders from London to avoid confrontation with the Dutch, Hastings had to tread carefully if he was to hold onto Singapore, and not incur the wrath of his London superiors. The best course was one of apparent indecision and delay, allowing the new settlement to acquire a commercial value which would render abandonment politically impractical. The contention of an earlier historian, that Hastings was a passive conveyor of confusing indecision, without any hidden expansionist motives, is supported only by an isolated testimony from James Stuart, a member of the Bengal Council.[42] But the argument of some Dutch historians, that London was the instigator of Hastings' apparent indecision and deliberate delay, is no more convincing. Hastings' relations with his superiors were tainted with mutual distrust; it is difficult to see such an intimate conspiracy being struck up - especially as Hastings stood to carry the blame if events took an unwelcome turn.[43] The initiative to keep Singapore came solely from Calcutta.

The inconclusive nature of these despatches delayed still further the reopening of negotiations. The British negotiators had little choice but to await further communications from Hastings to clarify matters. Other developments compounded this delay. Throughout 1821, Dutch refusal to abandon their involvement in the slave trade soured relations, and occupied both sides to the exclusion of other issues. The 1814 convention included an article designed to suppress slave trading, and in 1818 an Anglo-Dutch treaty had been signed which sought to eliminate the slave trade completely. In May 1821, Castlereagh indicated that it would be difficult to make progress on the question of the East Indies until this issue had been finally resolved. Not until January 1822 did the Dutch submit documents and information related to the slave trade requested by the British. But even then the British refused to resume negotiations on south east Asia, on the grounds that the long awaited Bengal despatches had not yet arrived.

Historians are silent on these awaited dispatches. In fact, Hastings submitted his response in a letter to Charles Bragge Bathurst dated 21 August 1821.[44] Hastings now dismissed as irrelevant legal arguments pertaining to agreements made with Malay rulers. He argued that such treaties were a facade, not to be treated seriously by Europeans. On the machinations of the rivals for the throne of Johore and their respective agreements with the Dutch and the British, Hastings was witheringly contemptuous:-

"Towards both us and the Dutch the Malay authorities played the same game. Uncertain of which of the two nations might preponderate in that quarter, when they formed a compact with one party, they by secret letters, represented it to the other party as having been unjustly imposed upon them by compulsion. It was the silly artifice of ignorant and frightened people, from which no legitimate inferences could be drawn."

Contradicting his assertion that legal argument was irrelevant, Hastings finished his letter by reiterating his earlier repudiation of Dutch legal rights in Johore, citing the Dutch governor of Melaka's denial of them in 1795. Hastings was also acidic about Canning's acceptance of Dutch remonstrances:-

"I have regretted to perceive that Mr Canning has been in some degree won upon by the dexterity of Mr Elout, who is a capital simulator and a virulent enemy of England."

Hastings' reply reached Bathurst in January 1822, who immediately sent the letter on to Canning, via John Backhouse, his own private secretary and a close acquaintance of Canning.[45] Canning was displeased with Hastings' failure to provide convincing legal argument for the retention of Singapore. Moreover, Canning suspected that Hastings was trying to create circumstances in which the British government would be forced by public opinion to ratify the Bengal administration's illegal actions.[46]

By now Canning was almost convinced that Singapore should be abandoned. But he noted the strong public support for retention. Canning speculated that so much time had passed since the negotiations, that Dutch expectations of a British surrender of Singapore might have receded. But if not, Canning was clear that Singapore must be abandoned.[47]

Charles Wynn, who replaced Bathurst as President of the Board in January 1822, knew of Hastings' letter and the absence of a convincing legal defence for the retention of Singapore.[48] Yet neither Wynn nor Castlereagh made any move to re-open talks with the Dutch. In March 1822 an official at the Board of Control, Thomas Courtenay, tried to construct a legal defence for Singapore in a lengthy minute, which made no reference to Hastings' letter of August 1821.[49] He pointed out that in August 1818 William Farquhar, the last British commandant of Melaka, had signed a treaty with Abdul Rahman, the rival of Tunku Hussein for the throne of Johore, which provided for trade between Johore and Britain as most favoured nation. The treaty was signed before the return of Melaka to Dutch control. Courtenay argued that Dutch treaties with, and alleged sovereignty over Johore had been suspended during the years of British occupation of Melaka between 1795 and 1818. He cited the fact that the new Dutch administration at Melaka had seen fit to sign a new treaty with Johore in November 1818, as evidence that no Dutch rights or authority were in force when Farquhar's treaty had been signed in August. As a consequence, argued Courtenay, Farquhar's treaty took precedence over the Dutch treaty signed in the following November. Even Courtenay admitted that this in itself did not justify the establishment of Singapore, which was based upon a treaty with Abdul Rahman's bitter rival. Nevertheless, it would ensure that even if Singapore were surrendered by the British, the port would not automatically pass into Dutch possession. Since Farquhar's treaty predated the Dutch renewal treaty of November of 1818, British rights took precedence over Dutch rights. As Johore's "most favoured" trading partner, the British could not tolerate a Dutch settlement within the territories of Johore - indeed, the British alone were diplomatically placed to acquire such favours from the Sultan of Johore.

But this convoluted argument was defensive and open to challenge. Courtenay was unable to put forward a convincing legal argument for retention on the basis of Raffles' agreement with the Temmenggong and Tunku Hussein; so he opted for an argument which would frustrate Dutch hopes that they would benefit from abandonment of Singapore; and which might pave the way for a legitimate British acquisition within the limits of the Johore empire. Moreover, a different reading of Courtenay's argument weakens still further the basis for Raffles' actions in January 1819. Farquhar's treaty had been with Abdul Rahman, implicitly recognising that contender as true sovereign. According to Courtenay's own logic, the Bengal authorities themselves should have disowned Singapore, on discovering the terms of Raffles' agreement. Conversely, if the British wished to argue that Raffles' agreement superceded Farquhar's treaty with Abdul Rahman, it could be argued that the effect was to invalidate Farquhar's earlier treaty, thus establishing the Dutch treaty with Johore of November 1818 as the oldest and therefore the most authoritative international agreement. Also, of course, the British would still be left with the difficult task of justifying legally their recognition of Tunku Hussein as the true sovereign, when less than a year earlier they had accorded that status to his rival. In either case, defence of the British position was problematic. Even more interesting is the fact that Courtenay's minute makes no reference anywhere to Hastings' own views as expressed in his letter of 21 August 1821. It is not even certain that Courtenay knew of its contents. Nevertheless, Courtenay's memorandum became the basis for British legal and diplomatic argument for the rest of the negotiations leading to the treaty of 1824. In fact, not even the chief negotiator on the British side, George Canning, was convinced of the validity of the British position.

Hastings' letter of 21 August 1821 has not been considered by earlier historians, yet it reveals much about the British attitude towards Singapore and the negotiations with the Dutch. There is strong evidence that by the spring of 1822, senior officials on the British side doubted the British right to Singapore, and that they had adopted a policy of deliberately delaying the resumption of negotiations until the new acquisition had become so conspicuously important for British commercial interests that the Dutch would be discouraged from pursuing demands for abandonment. Canning's inclination to abandon Singapore was reversed by new information. Early in 1822, John Backhouse informed Canning of a recent dinner engagement with the Dutch ambassador, Fagel, and his secretary which had taken place at the end of January.[50] Through careful questioning of Fagel's secretary, Backhouse detected a lack of resolve on the Dutch side over the Singapore question, suggesting that continued delay would persuade the Dutch to capitulate. The effect of these revelations on Canning was dramatic. From the pessimism of his letter to Bathurst on 5 February 1822, by April Canning was sufficiently confident to advise Wynn that:

> "Indeed our best chance of retaining Singapore appears to me to
> be the protraction of the negotiation; and the growing up there
> in the meantime of a British interest too valuable and too firmly
> settled for the Netherlanders to expect that we can consent to
> remove it"[51]

Backhouse's role as secretary to the Liverpool Parliamentary Office, a prominent mouthpiece for Liverpool mercantile opinion, might lead one to suspect that he was acting on behalf of interests in that city, and nearby industrial centres such as Manchester. But the Liverpool Parliamentary Office papers, containing an extensive correspondence with the Liverpool merchants, show no reference to Singapore, let alone clear evidence of effective lobbying.[52] Backhouse, it seems, was acting purely in his capacity as Bathurst's secretary.

Wynn's muted response to Hastings' letter of August 1821 suggested a strategy of deliberately delaying the negotiations, even before Canning's advocacy of this policy in April 1822. The suicide of Castlereagh in August 1822 brought Canning to the Foreign Office, and entrenched this strategy. In October, Canning's excuse for continuing delay was the awaited return of Lord Hastings from Bengal, and only in January 1823 did Canning express a willingness to resume talks.[53] In March 1823, the Secret Committee of the East India Company instructed the Bengal administration to ignore all protests against Singapore either from the Dutch or their local allies, a move clearly paving the way for the settlement's incorporation into the British empire.[54]

There were further differences over where the negotiations should take place. Eventually, in September 1823 it was agreed that the venue should be London, after a major concession had been conceded by the Dutch. Fagel hinted to Canning that Dutch claims for Singapore would be dropped. Negotiations were scheduled to resume in November. The British had effectively won the Singapore question even before the resumption of formal talks. The policy of calculated delay and obstruction had succeeded. For his part, Canning was never convinced of the British legal argument for Singapore. During the ensuing negotiations, Canning wrote to Wynn of "clinching the success of our grand injustice at Singapore".[55] The remark brought forth an uncomfortable assertion of the validity of the British case from Wynn.[56] But a senior British negotiator had acknowledged privately that the retention of Singapore was a victory for British duplicity.

*****

Thus by early 1822, the British were committed to retaining Singapore, because of its commercial value and the enormous public support which it enjoyed. The public clamour to keep the port merits further explanation. Previous historians cite the importance of mercantile testimonies before the parliamentary committees, inferring that the East India Company and its associated interest groups, and the provincial manufacturing and merchant groups, were all represented before these committees.[57] The Lords committee has been identified as particularly important, but there has been little examination of the evidence presented at its hearings. Only the testimony of Charles Grant has attracted comment.[58] The testimonies from members of the London East India agency houses, who were overwhelmingly represented at the hearings of the committee have been largely overlooked. Yet it was the London East India houses who were the main advocates of retention of Singapore before both committees.[59] All six of the main London agency houses were also represented on the highly influential East India Trade Committee which lobbied the British negotiators during the negotiations of 1823/24.[60] Senior India Board officials, such as Thomas Courtenay, also advised his superiors that the London private merchants were probably better informed about matters in south east Asia than even the East India Company's own officials.[61]

It has been implied that the provincial manufacturers and merchants were central in persuading the government and public opinion of the value of Singapore for British commerce. Although they certainly wanted to keep Singapore, and advertised their views in articles to the provincial press, the argument that they played a major role is not convincing.[62] They certainly did not obtain the access to the higher circles of government enjoyed by the London East India agency houses. East India agency house merchants with interests in Java had been able to persuade Castlereagh to take up their case with the Dutch ambassador in 1819. Their claim to open the trade between China and Europe had been considered seriously by Canning, while the demands of the provincial industrial and outport merchants for an immediate termination of the China monopoly had been ignored. The testimonies of the London East India agency houses dominated the evidence of the two parliamentary committees, while few outport merchants or manufacturers were interviewed by these two bodies. In any case, the principal concern of industrialists and outport merchants was to break down the remaining vestiges of the East India Company's monopoly, rather than the consolidation of Singapore.[63] It was the London houses, not the manufacturers who argued most effectively for Singapore to the parliamentary committees, and it was to them that Courtenay directed the politicians for advice. They were to organise and co-ordinate their efforts most effectively during the 1823/24 negotiations, but they had already persuaded Canning of the importance of keeping Singapore as early as the spring of 1822, and in so doing had already effectively accomplished their main objective.

The fact that the agency houses were well represented as shareholders of the East India Company by the 1820s, also opened channels of political influence closed to the provincial interests.[64] For example, during the early stages of the renewed negotiations, the agency houses used contacts in the East India Company directorate to voice their opinion to the British negotiators. One of the directors dependent upon support from the private trade interest within the Company, W.T. Money, was approached by a number of London merchants with financial interests in Java.[65] These merchants complained of attempts by the local Dutch authorities to force them to sell Javanese coffee to the Dutch government of Batavia at a fixed price. According to the London petitioners, this was only half the price obtainable on the free market. The merchants also wrote directly to Falck, one of the Dutch negotiators. Several of the merchants who wrote to Money and Falck were also involved in the East India Trade Committee.

The East India Trade Committee, formed at the end of 1823, is perhaps the clearest indication that, as far as negotiations in Europe were concerned, it was London based agency houses who played the leading role, not only in the Singapore question, but also on the wider issue of defending British commercial interests in south east Asia. The committee represented exclusively the London East India agency houses and merchants. Although by the end of 1823 Singapore's retention was almost a formality, the committee was determined to prevent strangulation of Singapore's commerce. The Dutch authorities in the east had already introduced prohibitively high tariffs in Java, and threatened to stifle British trade elsewhere in the region. The secretary of the East India Trade Committee (E.I.T.C), John Begbie, advised J. Wilmot-Horton, Undersecretary for War and the Colonies, of the need for an additional new settlement, this time on the northern coast of Australia, to preserve British access to the markets of south east Asia.[66] Begbie's letter was signed by nineteen London East India agency houses. On 18 December, one of the officials of the E.I.T.C, George Larpent, repeated to Thomas Courtenay both the committee's fears of Dutch curtailment of British trade, and Begbie's recommendation for a northern Australian port.[67] A deputation from the E.I.T.C. then met Bathurst, Secretary for War and Colonies in late December, to argue for a British port on the Cobourg peninsula of northern Australia, and for the

British negotiators to resist Dutch efforts to exclude British commerce. In late January 1824, Begbie also supplied Bathurst with details of Dutch duties at Java.[68] Courtenay then approached the E.I.T.C. for more information about Dutch obstructions of British trade, a request to which Larpent quickly responded.[69] But Canning rejected these overtures for a new Australian settlement because of the need to secure a wider agreement with the Dutch in south east Asia. Nevertheless, the ease with which the London interests gained access to the British negotiators is significant, and underlines their role as the main domestic pressure group influencing government policy in the region.

******

The negotiations eventually resumed on 15 December 1823, when Canning and Wynn, negotiators for the British, met their Dutch counterparts Falck and Fagel. At this first meeting, the Dutch representatives pressed for a territorial demarcation of spheres of influence in south east Asia, and this became the basis for subsequent discussions. Three meetings took place between 15 December and Christmas, all of them concerned predominantly with this question of demarcation. The Dutch pressed for a line of demarcation running down the Straits of Melaka, then due east south of Singapore. Territories north of this would fall within the British sphere of influence, and those to the south within the Dutch sphere. The British would have to surrender Benkulen, together with its satellite settlements, and the Dutch would hand over to the British their remaining settlements in India and the port of Melaka. The British had to consult with the East India Company's Secret Select Committee, who were initially hesitant about the surrender of Benkulen, until they were overruled by Canning in January 1824.[70] In February and early March, the negotiations focused upon trade duties and financial issues. The articles agreed to in 1820, promising free trade and mutual communication of treaties with local states, were incorporated into the draft treaty. In addition it was agreed that neither side would impose import or export duties on the nationals of the other which were more than double those paid by their own merchants. Eventually, the final draft was signed by both sides on 23 March 1824. It was a historic document, because it proved to be the foundation of Anglo-Dutch relations for the rest of the century.

The treaty consisted of seventeen articles. The first seven set out to regulate trade in south east Asia. British and Dutch traders were to be admitted to the ports of the other power to trade on a "most favoured nation" basis. Tariffs imposed upon traders of the other nation were not to exceed double the amount charged to the traders of the revenue collecting power. Free access to all ports of south east Asia for British, Dutch and local traders was to be respected by both powers. No treaties were to be made by either side with local states which excluded the commerce of the other, and all agreements made with local rulers were to be communicated to the other power. The establishment of new settlements, or the conquest of new territories by maverick local officials was strictly forbidden. New acquisitions could only be made with the express permission of the respective European government. This was an attempt to tighten the grip of the European governments on their subordinates in the east. There was also a commitment from both sides to suppress piracy and maintain peaceful commercial relations throughout the region. There was one exception to the provisions ensuring free commerce; this was the Moluccas, where the Dutch monopoly of the spice trade would be allowed to continue to promote Dutch economic recovery. But a provision was included which stated that should the Dutch ever relax or relinquish their monopoly by opening up the spice trade to another power, the British would be admitted to the spice trade on the same terms as that other power. The object of these commercial provisions was to reconcile the two contradictory elements of Anglo-Dutch political relations; the need to provide for British commercial access and expansion in south east Asia, while simultaneously maintaining Dutch political power and economic activity in the region. British traders were to be allowed free rein in their pursuit of new markets, but the most vital area for Dutch trade was to be ruled out of bounds to the British.

The other articles addressed the new arrangement of two separate spheres of influence. Benkulen and its satellites were ceded by the British, in return for Dutch surrender of their Indian possessions and Melaka. Under the treaty, all Dutch objections to Singapore were dropped, and the port was clearly established as a permanent British possession. All territories to the north of the Straits of Melaka were designated as the British sphere of interest, everything to the south, but also including Sumatra, was defined as the Dutch sphere. Inhabitants of the settlements and territories changing hands were given until March 1830 to dispose of their property and arrange to move, if they so wished. The exchange was to take place no later than 1 March 1825. It was also a specific condition that neither side was allowed to surrender any of its possessions to a third foreign power.

In total, the treaty heralded a new order of European authority in south east Asia. No longer were the Dutch undisputed masters of the region. They had been forced to accommodate British power and interests, and British superiority in economic and military terms meant that they had become junior partners in a joint enterprise of imperial domination, which blatantly favoured the British. It was a situation which was hard to accept for the Dutch, and the years immediately following the treaty saw numerous attempts by local Dutch officials to frustrate British commerce in the region. This was not simply pique arising from injured national pride. There was a genuine fear that the competitiveness of British merchants might undermine markets for Dutch produce in the region, thereby preventing the effective recovery of the colonial economy upon which Dutch strength was to be rebuilt. Ultimately, none of these   attempts were successful, but they underline the fact that the 1824 treaty contained rather than ended Anglo-Dutch conflict.

The British were much more satisfied with the new arrangements. The British had effectively recruited the Dutch as collaborators in their own imperial strategy in south east Asia.[71] As long as the Dutch governed the islands of the Indonesian archipelago, there was little or no danger to British commerce or navigation through that region. As a minor European power, the Dutch were ill placed to challenge the British in a way that could cause really serious concern in London. A formidable European power, such as France, would cause much more serious worry if it established a presence in the region. From the British view, the Dutch were valuable for what their presence prevented.

Considered from a wider historical perspective, the establishment of Singapore and the 1824 treaty were products of the adjustment by the existing political and economic order in Britain to new demands placed upon it by war, international dominance in the wake of victory, and the need to accommodate new social forces at home created by industrialisation. The eighteenth century political and economic order had been based upon close co-operation between the landed interest and an emergent financial and mercantile middle class, based in the City London. In return for financial support for the state and monarchy, which were institutions embodying the power of land, the City and its associated commercial interests were accorded a wide range of privileges, including trading monopolies, lucrative profits from financing the national debt, and acceptance into high society. The alliance between the landed elite and this emergent "gentlemanly capitalist" class, which dominated the institutions of state and political decision making, survived by accommodating the demands and needs of social groups created by provincial industrialisation. A new class of wealthy industrialists wanted a share of political power to help their own business interests, and a burgeoning, impoverished and unruly industrial urban working class threatened social disorder at a time when fear of revolution was rife. War between 1793 and 1815, with its associated problems of inflation, food shortages and depression, brought matters to a head, compelling the old order to surrender concessions. Continuing economic and political difficulties after the war resulted in a string of policies favouring the industrialists, including political reform and a steady drift towards free trade. The wartime crisis and shortages, crucially for the question of policy in the east, resulted in the termination of the East India Company monopoly of trade to India and south east Asia in 1813.

The effects of this limited trade liberalisation, however, were not foreseen in London. Under the auspices of the old trading privileges accorded to the East India Company, a commercial order had emerged in Bengal and India, which involved co-operation between private agency house capitalists and the East India Company's Indian administration. The influx into India of British cotton imports and free booting provincial traders threatened to destabilise this "old colonial" edifice, and created a deepening sense of crisis within the British colonial community in the east. At the same time, the post-war decision to instate the Dutch as the principal buffer against renewed French ambitions, had the unfortunate effect of threatening these old colonial British interests with the loss of vital south east Asian markets. Under these circumstances, the Bengal administration, private merchants and officials in south east Asia took matters into their own hands, and the acquisition of Singapore was the result. The willingness to take a course of action independent of London should not be surprising. Over half a century of territorial expansion in British India had sprung from the ability and willingness of British administrations in India to use force unilaterally in defence of what they saw as their essential interests. The emergence of a "military-fiscalist" culture within the East India Company's organisation in India, in which territorial conquest became the preferred method of securing the revenues necessary to support a growing military machine, meant that responses to crises were often aggressive and acquisitive. Hastings' and Raffles' interventionist and expansionist responses to the revival of Dutch power in south east Asia were consistent with this tradition. Thus the initial acquisition of Singapore is best understood as the response of a semi-autonomous and militaristic colonial regime in India, to changes forced upon it by a British ruling elite seeking to accommodate the demands and needs of an emerging industrial constituency, while establishing a post war European political order which provided the maximum political security for Britain at the lowest possible cost.

The ensuing negotiations in Europe, which culminated in the permanent incorporation of Singapore into the empire, were strongly influenced by London based interests which had grown out of the old colonial commercial arrangements of the East India Company. In this sense, they were part of the gentlemanly capitalist community of London at once so important to, and favoured by, the landed regime. Singapore and the treaty of 1824 were thus mainly the result of their efforts to bolster an established colonial system placed under growing pressure from political and economic changes and accommodations made by the elite. Ultimately, these attempts to save the old colonial structures in India and the east did not succeed. In the early 1830s a major financial crisis in India swept away the agency houses and the East India Company's remaining monopoly of trade to China. It did not mean the demise of the London agency houses, merchant banks and other financial institutions associated with gentlemanly capitalism, who skilfully adapted to a new, liberalising environment of international trade. From the early 1820s onwards the London East India agency houses turned increasingly to export agency, using their contacts in the east to find markets for British industrial produce - for handsome commissions, of course. Thus the retention of Singapore and the creation of a British sphere of influence in south east Asia were to a very large extent the work of early gentlemanly capitalists. From this foundation, British territorial   control in the region was to grow.

NOTES

1. See Grant's testimonies to the Lords and Commons Select Committees on trade to the East India and China, Parliamentary Papers c.476 and c.746.
2. See A.T. Embree, Charles Grant and British Rule in India (London, Allen and Unwin 1962) pp278-281.
3. See, for example, D.J. Moss, "Birmingham and the Campaigns against the Orders in Council and the East India Charter, 1812-13" Canadian Journal of History 11 (1976) 173-188.
4. Manchester Mercury and Manchester Chronicle 27 June 1820, Local History Section, Manchester Central Library, Manchester.
5. SarDesai, British Trade and Expansion p41.
6. Philips, The East India Company p243.
7. Cain and Hopkins, British Imperialism: Innovation and Expansion 1688-1914 pp58-71.
8. B. Hilton, Corn Cash and Commerce: The Economic Policies of the Tory Governments 1815 to 1830 (Oxford, Oxford University Press 1977) see chapter 2.
9. Ibid.: pp35-36, and L. Jenks, The Migration of British Capital to 1875 (New York 1927) pp42-44.
10. J. Crawfurd, "A Sketch of the Commercial Resources and Monetary and Mercantile System of British India".
11. S.D. Chapman, "Business Marketing Enterprise: The Changing Role of Merchants, Manufacturers and Financiers 1700 to 1860" Business History Review 53 (1979) 205-233.
12. SarDesai, British Trade and Expansion p41.
13. Marks, The First Contest for Singapore Ch. 3, Falck proposed this to the Dutch king in December 1818.
14. Castlereagh to Fagel, 10 February 1819, FO 37/109, PRO, London.
15. Castlereagh to Clancarty, 13 August 1819, FO 37/107, PRO, London.
16. Ibid.
17. Minute by an unidentified member of the India Board (undated), Dutch Records, I/2/31, Vol. 30, p85, IOR, London. The minute discusses forthcoming negotiations with the Dutch "in November". This, and a reference to the two principles set out by Castlereagh to Clancarty, dates the minute at some time between August and November 1819.
18. Marks, The First Contest for Singapore Ch. 3.
19. Ibid.: Note from Van Nagell to Castlereagh through Fagel, 7 September 1819.

20. Appendix (U) to the Lords Select Committee on Foreign Trade (East Indies and China) May 1821, Parliamentary Papers c.476.

21. Ibid.

22. Petition to the Privy Council from the merchants of London, 1 November 1819, and petition from London East India Agents, 26 November 1819, Parliamentary Papers c.476.

23. Canning to the Chairs of the East India Company, 17 May 1820, Appendix (U), Parliamentary Papers c.476.

24. C.A. Robinson and T. Reid (East India Company chairs) to Canning, 7 June 1820, Appendix (U), Parliamentary Papers c.476.

25. Philips, The East India Company p232, and the memorandum of Thomas Courtenay (Secretary to the India Board), March 1822, Dutch Records, I/2/31, IOR, London.

26. Grant's Testimonies, Parliamentary Papers c.476 and c.746.

27. Grant to Raffles, 19 July 1820, Raffles Papers, Eur Mss D/742/3, IOR, London.

28. Grant to Lansdowne, 6 July 1820, Parliamentary Papers c.476.

29. Marks, The First Contest for Singapore p87.

30. Ibid.: see Ch. 3.

31. Grant to Lansdowne, 6 July 1820.

32. Marks, The First Contest for Singapore p102.

33. Ibid.: pp102-103.

34. Canning to C.B. Bathurst, 3 February 1822, Stapleton Mss, 31/3, West Yorkshire Archives, Sheepscar, Leeds.

35. These ten points were:
    (1) Singapore
    (2) Billiton
    (3) Dutch Possessions in India
    (4) Reciprocal equality in import/export duties
    (5) Repression of Piracy
    (6), (7) and (8) Financial debts, and the question of disputed properties near Padang
    (9) British establishment in the archipelago
    (10) Question of the appointment of British Consuls (commercial agents in Java).

36. Marks, The First Contest for Singapore pp112-113.

37. P.H. Van Der Kemp, De Singapoorsche Papierlog (The Hague 1898).

38. Marks, The First Contest for Singapore Ch 4, Hastings to Van Der Capellen, 14 January 1820.

39. Ibid.: Ch. 4.

40. Ibid.: Ch. 4.

41. Ibid.: Hastings 22 April 1820.

42. Ibid.: p118.

43. For example, there were growing disagreements between Hastings and the Court of Directors on questions related to the Bengal army. see D. Peers, "Between Mars and Mammon: The East India Company and Efforts to Reform its Army, 1796-1832" Historical Journal 33;2 (1990) 385-401, see pp393-394.

44. Hastings to Bathurst, 21 August 1821, Canning Papers, Harewood Mss, 99a, West Yorkshire Archives, Sheepscar, Leeds.

45. J. Backhouse to Canning, 28 January 1822, Canning Papers, Harewood Mss 76a, West Yorkshire Archives, Sheepscar, Leeds. Backhouse had been

Canning's private secretary from 1816 to 1821. Backhouse was also secretary to the Liverpool Parliamentary Office from 1812 to 1823. See W.O. Henderson, "The Liverpool Office in London" Economica 13 (1933) 473-479.

46. Canning to Backhouse, 5 February 1822, Stapleton Mss 31/3, West Yorkshire Archives, Sheepscar, Leeds.

47. Ibid.

48. Wynn to Canning, 11 February 1822, Canning Papers, Harewood Mss 78a, West Yorkshire Archives, Sheepscar, Leeds.

49. T. Courtenay, "Observations upon the State of the Negotiations between the British and the Netherlands" March 1822, Dutch Records, I/2/31, IOR, London.

50. Backhouse to Canning, 5 February 1822, Canning Papers, Harewood Mss 76a, West Yorkshire Archives, Sheepscar, Leeds.

51. Canning to Wynn, 18 May 1822, Canning Papers, Harewood Mss 78a, West Yorkshire Archives, Sheepscar, Leeds.

52. Liverpool Parliamentary Office Papers, PAR/328, Local History Library, Central Libraries, Liverpool.

53. Hastings was replaced by Lord Amherst. He left India for Britain in January 1823.

54. Marks, The First Contest for Singapore p153.

55. Canning to Wynn, 18 December 1823, Canning Papers, Harewood Mss 78a, West Yorkshire Archives, Sheepscar, Leeds.

56. Wynn to Canning, 21 December 1823, Canning Papers, Harewood Mss 78a, West Yorkshire Archives, Sheepscar, Leeds.

57. Lords and Commons Committees, Parliamentary Papers c.476 and c.746.

58. Marks, The First Contest for Singapore p143.

59. Minutes of Evidence, Parliamentary Papers c.476 and c.746. The representatives were:

    (1) George Larpent of Paxton, Cockerill and Trail.
    (2) Robert Rickards of Rickards, Mackintosh, Law and Co.
    (3) Henry Blanshard, a shipowner and merchant.
    (4) Patrick Maclachlan, Shipowner, merchant and head of his own agency house.
    (5) John Forbes Inglis of Smith, Inglis and Co.
    (6) William Fairlie of Fairlie, Bonham and Co.

60. Begbie and Larpent for the East India Trade Committee to Bathurst, Principal Secretary of State for the Colonial Department, 13 December 1823, signed by 19 agency houses, Dutch Records I/2/32, IOR, London.

61. Courtenay, "Observations upon the State of the Negotiations".

62. Manchester Chronicle 9 June 1821, Local History Section, Central Library, Manchester.

63. A. Redford, Manchester Merchants and Foreign Trade (Manchester, Manchester University Press 1934) pp111-117.

64. Philips, The East India Company pp335-337.

65. W.T. Money to Canning, 30 December 1823, Canning Papers, Harewood Mss 99a, West Yorkshire Archives, Sheepscar, Leeds.

66. Marks, The First Contest for Singapore p214, Begbie to Wilmot Horton, 13 December 1823.

67. Ibid.: p215, Larpent to Courtenay, 18 December 1823.

68. Ibid.: p216.

69. Ibid.: p217.

70. Ibid.: Ch. 4.
71. N. Tarling, The Fall of Imperial Britain in South East Asia pp29-30.

5. THE BRITISH IN BORNEO AND THE MALAY STATES: 1824 - 1850

The treaty of 1824 delineated the British and Dutch spheres of interest in maritime south east Asia, secured the Straits Settlements, and set the limits of further British commercial expansion into the region for the rest of the nineteenth century. The division of spoils was the result of efforts by the British to shore up an older colonial economic and political system in the east, in the face of economic and social change in Britain. Singapore had been established to protect the interests of the East India Company and the Bengal agency houses, and the terms of the treaty of 1824 had been shaped by London commercial groups closely related to these old colonial interests.

What followed in the Malay world was thirty years of consolidation and commercial development. Singapore became, as Raffles had predicted, the fulcrum upon which British fortunes were balanced in the region. The growth of British trade to maritime south east Asia accelerated spectacularly in the 1820s. In 1823/24, the value of British exports to Singapore alone was $1,109,994.[1] By 1830/31 they had risen to over $3 million, although they were to fall back to just over $1,000,000 annually for most years in the 1830s and 1840s.[2] Earlier historians have seen British cotton manufactures as the most significant component of this export drive, with Singapore rapidly becoming the centre of this thriving export trade in the region.[3] This is, of course, consistent with the wider interpretation of British imperial expansion, which identifies free trade and the search for markets for industrial produce as its defining features. The export of Malay produce to China was also important in the new settlement's trade, and in that respect Singapore was always regarded as a most valuable accessory for the East India Company's trade network in the far east. But the monopoly was abolished in 1833, and thereafter Singapore became predominantly an outlet for British cotton manufactures into the modest but significant markets of south east Asia. However, it will be argued here that other branches of Singapore's commerce, most notably with India, have been underestimated in their importance for the development of British economic interests in south east Asia.

Very quickly after its foundation, Singapore attracted the lion's share of British trade with the region, whether it originated in Britain itself, or in British India. The new settlement's central position, just south of the Malay peninsula, enabled it to become the most successful entrepot in the region, attracting traders from all over south east Asia, who brought local produce to exchange for British and Indian manufactures, opium and local produce. The effect was to rationalise the trade carried on British shipping. Instead of having to visit a myriad of tiny ports in the region, British shipowners could offload their outward cargoes and take on south east Asian produce at Singapore. Singapore rapidly eclipsed its sister Straits Settlements. Pinang's trade links with the southern Malay archipelago, always tenuous and dependent upon intermediate trade with Melaka, withered as local traders flooded to Singapore. Melaka suffered in a similar way. The two northern settlements had to depend heavily upon trade with the Malay peninsula and northern Sumatra, a factor which promoted British political involvement in the Malay peninsula. British commerce brought steady growth in the populations of all three settlements. Singapore's population spiralled to just under 11,000 by January 1824, even before permanent British possession had been firmly established.[4] Within ten years the population had doubled to over 20,000.[5] By 1850, it was just under 60,000.[6] Pinang's population was just under 40,000 in 1821.[7] By the end of the 1850s it had risen to 97,000.[8] Melaka's population rose from 22,000 in 1821 to 54,000 by 1859.[9]

Between the 1820s and the 1850s, Singapore's trade was directed to four main global regions. Approximately a fifth to one quarter of the port's trade was with Britain and Europe. British textiles and other manufactures dominated the export branch of this trade. Between 15 per cent and 23 per cent of trade was with eastern Asia, predominantly China. British and European traders conducted this commerce, together with Chinese traders on their junks. Chinese pottery, silks and tea, were exchanged for Malay produce and Indian opium. About a fifth of Singapore's trade up to 1850 was with India, and consisted largely of Indian cotton piece goods and opium, which generated a steady flow of silver and gold specie to Calcutta and Madras from south east Asia. This branch of the port's commerce was far more important for the development of British economic interests in the region than has been recognised. Finally, the vast bulk and value of Singapore's commerce, between two fifths and one half, was with ports in south east Asia.[10] It was this last branch of trade which made Singapore so successful, because the port proved to be ideally situated to attract seafarers from all over the region. They brought to Singapore a wide range of local products and exchanged them for Indian opium, piece goods and British manufactures, which they sold on their return journeys from Singapore. Two groups of traders were particularly important. The Bugis traders were adept seafaring merchants who conducted a wide ranging commerce throughout the islands of maritime south east Asia. They furnished Singapore with supplies of Malay produce, even from territories under the control of the Dutch, who made strenuous efforts to stifle Singapore's commerce with their possessions. Because of the monsoon winds the Bugis trade was seasonal, the traders arriving in Singapore between September and November each year.[11] The other important group were the Chinese who conducted trade with Singapore from various ports in China, arriving in Singapore aboard their junks usually between January and April. They brought Chinese goods and Chinese migrants (sinkeh) seeking employment opportunities in south east Asia, and took back Malay produce and Indian opium to sell in the Chinese market.[12] They also brought rice and other commodities taken aboard en route to Singapore, usually in Siam. They often traded illegally, defying regulations and restrictions imposed by the Chinese empire. At times of conflict between the British and Chinese, this proved to be very useful for the British. The junks provided access to the Chinese market for British and Indian produce, especially opium, and provided an invaluable source of Chinese tea. During the war of 1839 to 1842, for example, there was a sharp increase in the volume of junk traffic to Singapore, bringing some 10,000 chests of tea in the early months of 1840 alone.[13] There was also a huge increase in opium exports to the Straits Settlements, particularly Singapore, which were then redirected to China via the junks. Opium exports from Bengal to the Straits had averaged between one and two thousand chests per annum throughout the 1830s, rising marginally above 3,000 chests in 1837/38 and 1838/39. Then in 1839/40, opium exports to the Straits leapt to 14,000 chests, and were 11,000 and 8,000 chests for the next two years, before declining back to levels which were significantly higher than the 1830s.[14] Of course, traders from other parts of south east Asia also contributed to Singapore's success. From the outset, a policy of free trade was adopted, with no duties or customs levied on trade. There was a stark contrast with the punitive taxes imposed at Dutch or local ports. The policy caused irritation in Calcutta because of the high levels of subsidy required to fund the Straits administration, which after 1832 was located in Singapore. There were attempts by the Bengal administration, most notably in 1836, to impose duties at Singapore, which were always successfully resisted by merchants at Singapore, who appealed with consummate skill and energy to the British government and parliament.[15]

Up till the late 1840s, Singapore's thriving commerce with the Malay archipelago was a source of considerable tension in Anglo-Dutch relations. The Dutch feared that Singapore would develop an extensive illicit trade with the Dutch possessions, flooding them with cheap British and Indian manufactures, thereby undermining attempts to establish a strong Dutch colonial economy in the east. The Dutch response contravened the spirit, and in some cases the letter, of the 1824 treaty. In February 1824, almost at the time when the treaty was being signed, the Dutch authorities in the east imposed an additional 10 per cent duty on British textiles imported into their territories from Singapore.[16] The British government initially ignored the complaints of Singapore merchants. The Dutch were encouraged by the apparent lack of interest in London, and when these initial attempts to curtail British trade proved unsuccessful, they resorted to even tougher measures. In 1836 and 1837, even more swingeing tariffs on trade from Singapore were imposed, and in spite of protests from both the Singapore mercantile community and the British government, they remained in force until the 1860s.[17] British reluctance to challenge these restrictions stemmed from the wider strategy of promoting Dutch economic and political strength in Europe. In any case, the tariffs did not appear to damage Singapore's trade with the Dutch possessions, which was largely conducted by local traders who successfully avoided Dutch tariffs and regulations.[18] The Dutch also sought to stimy Singapore's trade by establishing a string of rival Dutch free ports throughout the archipelago.[19] Between 1829 and 1853, Riau, Pontianak, Sambas, Succanda, Macassar, Menado, Kemar, Amboina and Ternate were all declared free ports. But the policy did not succeed. Singapore's trade to the islands of the southern archipelago continued to flourish, although at least one commentator in the 1860s believed that growth was not as great as it would have been had Dutch obstructionism been curbed.[20] The British government felt they could afford to tolerate Dutch infringements of the treaty of 1824, because of the larger issue of European co-operation and the relative ineffectiveness of the Dutch measures. The collaborative relationship between the two powers was too important for the wider British strategy to be overturned merely to defend local interests. Nevertheless, in the 1830s and 1840s, the British Foreign office did complain about protectionism, and this probably contributed to the British government's acquiescence in the expansion of Brooke rule in Sarawak in the latter decade.[21]

Although earlier historians have tended to emphasise the importance of Singapore and south east Asia as an outlet for British manufactures, up to at least 1850 they were also important markets for Indian produce, and a useful source of specie and bullion for the Bengal economy. This has tended to be underestimated, partly because of an apparent decline in the Bengal administration's interest in south east Asia, following the end of the East India Company's China monopoly in 1833.[22] According to this view, Singapore was valued by the East India Company's officials in London and Bengal principally as a provider of Malay produce for the China market, and when the Company's privileged position in trade to China was swept away, its interest in south east Asia was severely curtailed. Certainly after 1833, the merchants and officials of the Straits Settlements found it difficult to secure policies in Bengal which suited their interests, and there was continual frustration at the apparent ignorance of south east Asian problems among Bengal officials. The Straits merchants' dispute with Bengal in 1836 over trade duties was a manifestation of this, as was the dispute over currency in the 1850s, when the Indian authorities tried to impose the Indian Rupee as exclusive legal tender in the Straits.[23] The India Office put up little resistance when in 1867 the British government decided that supervision of the Straits Settlements should be transferred to the Colonial Office.

But while Bengal administrators lost interest in Straits affairs after the 1830s, this did not mean that south east Asia held no value for the Indian empire. Lack of interest and attention merely reflected the fact that Singapore and the other Straits Settlements appeared to be providing adequate opportunities for Anglo-Indian commerce, and so did not require constant interference from Calcutta. The Bengal Commercial reports reveal that up to the 1850s, south east Asia provided significant markets for Bengal cotton piece goods and Indian opium, contributing considerably to Indian revenues and prosperity during a period of some hardship for the Indian colonial economy. During the 1830s and 1840s, for example, the markets of south east Asia, including Burma, the Straits and Java, regularly absorbed between 1,000 and 2,000 chests of opium, or between 11 per cent and 20 per cent of total Bengal exports of the drug.[24] The surge of opium exports to the Straits during the Anglo-Chinese war of 1839-42 underlined the value of Singapore as a "back door" into the Chinese market during times of crisis in Anglo-Chinese relations. In absolute terms, exports to the Straits Settlements in the 1840s were consistently higher than in the 1830s, averaging above 4,000 chests per annum compared with the 1-2,000 chests of the 1830s.[25] By then, the rapidly growing Chinese population of the Straits Settlements and nearby states constituted a significant market in their own right. The fact that south east Asia, particularly the Straits Settlements and the Malay archipelago, regularly absorbed approximately 15 per cent of all Bengal opium exports helped sustain the price of the commodity and boost the Indian government's revenues. South east Asia was an even more important market for Indian cotton piece goods. In the 1830s and 1840s between 30 per cent and 40 per cent of all Bengal piece goods exports went to south east Asian markets.[26] At the end of the 1820s, the value of south east Asia for Indian piece goods exports was emphasised by Robert Fullerton, the Governor of the Straits Settlements, in a minute to his superiors in Calcutta.[27] According to Fullerton, imports of Indian piece goods were double the quantity of British piece goods, which were regarded by Malay consumers as inferior in quality to the Indian product. The whole thrust of Fullerton's minute was that the Straits Settlements were invaluable for British India.

Imports into India of specie and precious metals were also significant. According to the Bengal Commercial Reports, in the 1830s and 1840s approximately a third of net imports of specie and bullion into Bengal on private account came from south east Asia.[28] In 1847/48, total imports of specie into Bengal from south east Asia amounted to Rs2825211 out of total imports of Rs7830609, or 36 per cent.[29] The importance of the south east Asian supplies for this year are even clearer if net imports from south east Asia (ie imports minus exports of specie to south east Asia) are measured as a proportion of total net imports into Bengal. Net imports from south east Asia on private account amounted to Rs2647111, out of total net imports on private account of Rs4776749, or 55 per cent.[30]

Statistics such as these should eradicate finally any notion that before 1850 south east Asia was valuable to the British only as a market for British manufactures. South east Asia was an important branch of what was essentially an Asian system of trade, incorporating India and China, which was very important in maintaining the economic viability of the British Indian empire. After 1850, as India grew progressively into a primary producing economy serving the markets of the industrial world, the south east Asian markets did recede in their importance for Indian exports, but this was a slower process than is sometimes suggested. Certainly in the first half of the century the evidence suggests a continuing prominence for south east Asia in the trade and economy of India. That this did not translate into greater political clout for Straits administrators and merchants stemmed partly from financial restraints imposed by Bengal administrations seeking to ease their own budgetary difficulties, policy restrictions imposed by the Foreign Office and encompassed by the treaty of 1824, and the fact that existing arrangements appeared to serve the commercial needs of Bengal quite adequately. Moreover, one particular branch of commerce between India and south east Asia, namely the opium trade, was to play a vital role in the development of the Malay peninsula as a source of such primary produce as sugar, gambier, pepper and tin. To appreciate this fully, the evolution of British commercial interests in the Straits Settlements and their relationship with key ethnic groups such as the Chinese, must be understood.

**

As Singapore grew, the structure of British political authority came under close scrutiny. The Straits government was initially situated in Pinang, but the rapid growth of Singapore resulted in a shift of the Straits capital to that port in 1832.[31] In 1829, the Straits Settlements were defined as a single administrative command subject to the authority of the Bengal administration, sweeping away the quasi-independence enjoyed by the Presidency of Pinang.[32] The restructuring was in response to a severe financial crisis, and to cut costs the senior administrative establishment for the Straits was reduced from nineteen posts to eight.[33] The difficulties caused by this inadequate administrative provision contributed to dissatisfaction in the Straits Settlements with Bengal's direction of affairs.[34] The Bengal administration's abortive attempt to introduce trade duties in 1836, prompted the European merchants at Singapore to create their own Chamber of Commerce in 1837.[35] The Singapore chamber rapidly became part of a wider movement throughout the east of merchants establishing such bodies to represent their views.[36] These chambers established links with their counterparts in Britain, and there emerged in 1836 an East India and China Association, which spoke up for British south east Asian interests in London.[37] Interestingly, the Chair of the association until 1848 was Sir George Larpent of the London East India Agency house of Cockerell and

Larpent. He had been active in the East India Trade Committee which had influenced the treaty negotiations of 1823/24. The City thus remained vigilant of any political developments which affected their interests in the far east. By the 1830s, the London East India houses offered services as commission agents in the export of British manufactures to the east, a fact reflected by the emergence of East India associations in Liverpool (1839) and Glasgow (1830).[38] British manufacturing interests connected with south east Asia thus found a political voice, but the London association, with its City connections, remained the principal mouthpiece for those trading with the region. In 1836 the London association represented Singapore merchants' grievances against Dutch protectionism to the Foreign Office, though with little tangible success.[39] The links between merchants in the east and City firms involved in trade to south east Asia remained active, although the British diplomatic settlement with the Dutch and the tight finances of Bengal administrations following the financial collapse in Calcutta of 1833, prohibited any measures to defend their interests which might require territorial expansion or high levels of Company expenditure. Nevertheless, it is possible to trace connections between the mercantile communities in the Straits and interested parties in the City from the 1820s up to the formation in London of the Straits Settlements Association in 1868.[40]

The structure and methods of British firms in the Straits strongly influenced economic development there and in the Malay peninsula. By the end of the Napoleonic wars, Pinang's mercantile community was dominated by agency houses engaged in a wide variety of activities, notably Carnegy and Co, Dunbar and McGee, and Forbes and Brown.[41] These firms established close links with the wealthy agency houses of Calcutta, to gain access to their vast financial resources. The early European settlers on Singapore also sought connections with the Calcutta houses. Some early Singapore firms were mere branches of the Calcutta firms.[42] Prominent Bengal merchant firms, notably John Palmer and Barretto and Co., were major owners of land on Singapore as early as 1823.[43] In the 1820s, Singapore merchants believed that the East India Company's monopoly would continue indefinitely, and they organised their activities accordingly. They exchanged opium, Indian and British cotton manufactures for Malay produce which could be sold to country traders en route to China. Profits were also made by exploiting a legal loophole in the monopoly. While the direct export of produce from China to Britain by non East India Company vessels was specifically prohibited by the 1813 Act, the export of Chinese goods to Singapore was not. Neither was the export of goods from Singapore to Britain. If goods were unloaded at Singapore, reloaded with new documentation onto the same vessel which then sailed for Britain, the monopoly could be technically avoided. For a 1 per cent commission, some Singapore firms were prepared to supervise such operations, and they expected the Company monopoly to continue for the forseeable future.[44]

But between the mid 1820s and the 1840s the commercial environment deteriorated severely for British and European commercial firms in the Straits. The obstructive trade policies of the Dutch have already been described, but a second problem arose from two consecutive and related developments in the early 1830s. A major financial crisis in Bengal had been looming throughout the 1820s, as the disruptive consequences of the 1813 Charter Act, the heavy costs of the Burmese war of 1824-26 and questionable commercial judgements by the houses themselves, undermined the financial structures which underpinned Company rule in Bengal.[45] The leading agency houses collapsed, and in the ensuing political crisis, the remaining trading privileges enjoyed by the Company were removed by the Charter Act of 1833. Trade to China was thrown open, and at a stroke the transhipment ploy ceased to be a profitable line of business. The collapse of the Calcutta houses swept away a body of mercantile wealth and political influence which had been a powerful ally for the smaller and poorer firms of the Straits Settlements. While the Straits interests were quick to develop new channels of influence through Chambers of Commerce and contacts with the East India associations in Britain, the Calcutta houses and their powerful influence in the councils of British administration in India, were resources of financial support and political clout not easily replaced. The Straits Settlements and their commercial communities, after all, had been products of the old colonial economic system in India which had emerged in the later eighteenth century. The demise of that system cut off essential channels of political influence in Calcutta. After the mid 1830s, merchants in the Straits complained incessantly about the indifference of the Bengal authorities, and the eventual transfer of the Straits Settlements to the authority of the Colonial Office in the 1860s was welcomed enthusiastically in Singapore, Pinang and Melaka. The financial crises of the 1830s were marked by price instability and violent fluctuations in trade which caused considerable hardship in the Straits.[46] Thirdly, the Treaty of Nanking which concluded the Anglo-Chinese war of 1839 to 1842, delivered into British possession the port of Hong Kong, which presented Singapore with unwelcome competition for the trade of China and south east Asia. The effect was to "shrink the circle" of Singapore's range of trade to the Malay peninsula, Sumatra, Borneo and Siam.[47] By 1845, some 34 per cent of Singapore's trade was with the Malay peninsula, compared to only 15 per cent in 1825.[48] In the same period, trade share with the islands of the archipelago shrank from 74 per cent to 53 per cent. Although these unexpected and unwelcome changes did not present insurmountable obstacles to the long term commercial progress of Singapore and the other Straits Settlements, as shown by the subsequent growth of all three ports, there is no doubt that the 1830s and 1840s were a period of hardship, uncertainty and anxiety for the British mercantile communities in south east Asia.

The period was also to prove formative in the evolution of British mercantile capitalism in the region. The merchant firms of the settlements were engaged mainly in trade, and also earned commisssions from their involvement in transhipment work. The Straits firms exploited their commercial connections with Britain and India. They imported British and Indian manufactures and exchanged them for south east Asian produce in demand in Europe and China. The Straits merchants themselves possessed little capital, and they depended heavily upon trade credit extended by the London based East India houses, who exported British produce on a commission basis. These arrangements were assisted by informal links between the Singapore firms and "sister" organisations set up in Britain, usually by partners retiring to the home country. For example, in 1846, William Paterson and Co. had sister organisations in Glasgow, Manila and Batavia.[49] The international system of credit enabled the Singapore and other Straits firms to conduct a much larger volume of business than their immediate financial resources would have allowed.[50]

But other, local relationships were even more important to British capital in the Straits. Straits merchants rarely physically conducted the trade in which they were engaged. Instead, they relied upon London and Indian based shipping firms to conduct trade with India and Britain, and a range of local middlemen who controlled the entrepot trade. This latter group was particularly important. Consignments of British and Indian goods purchased by the British merchant firms on credit were advanced in small amounts to Chinese and other Asian merchants, who undertook the task of selling them to the south east Asian and Chinese seafaring merchants who visited Singapore. Just as the British merchant firms themselves relied upon credit extended to them from Britain, so they in turn were required to allow credit to their Chinese middlemen. It was a relationship which often excluded the need for cash transactions. Rather than paying in cash for the British and Indian manufactures advanced to them, the Chinese merchants usually settled their debts in south east Asian produce purchased from visiting local traders. The produce would then be re-exported by the British merchant to India, China or Britain. These were precarious arrangements which resulted in many instances of unpaid debts triggering default.[51] Problems arose particularly when British merchants miscalculated the extent of the market for their imports from Britain and India, and flooded the local market with produce which could not be sold by the Chinese middlemen, who were then unable to settle their debts to the British merchants.[52] In 1835, attempts were made to enforce a stricter system of enforced cash payments, but with little success.[53] The credit system continued, as did the high numbers of defaults. For much of the first half of the nineteenth century the heavy dependence upon Chinese middlemen, meant that they often held the whiphand in commercial relations with their European "superiors". At times, the Chinese demanded that credit be extended to them for their purchase of goods from the European merchants, while insisting on cash payment for their own sales to the same men.[54] These difficult circumstances for the British firms were exacerbated by the influx of a steady stream of new European speculators, who intensified competition and swelled the ranks of failed entrepeneurs. In this Darwinian environment, only the most shrewd and innovative businessmen survived. Of the thirty firms affiliated to the Chamber of Commerce in 1859, only six survived until the 1920s.[55] But this fierce environment did promote an adaptability and resourcefulness in the surviving firms, which enabled them to flourish and prosper into the twentieth century.

**

The dependence of British enterprise upon Asian middlemen has only recently begun to receive the attention it deserves. In fact it was a widespread phenomenon throughout Asia.[56] Sophisticated Asian trade and credit networks, many predating European imperial expansion in the seventeenth and eighteenth centuries, enabled European capitalists to gain access to the markets and produce of Asia. Asian ethnic groups involved in south east Asian networks included the Chuliah merchants who originated from India's Coromandel coast, the Chinese and the Bugis. These Asian entrepeneurs exploited the commercial opportunities brought by the spread of European commerce in the eighteenth and nineteenth centuries. The Europeans looked to the Chinese for administrative as well as commercial assistance, particularly in the collection of taxes.[57] The British dependence on Chinese merchants took various forms. The Chinese conducted direct commercial relations with the local traders of south east Asia, a specialised activity about which most British merchants understood very little. Singapore rapidly emerged as the centre of a Chinese commercial network which extended throughout the Nanyang. This network channelled Chinese capital and labour to Chinese controlled centres of production throughout the region; including the tin mines of Bangka and the Malay peninsula, the gold mines of Borneo and the pepper and gambier plantations of Riau and Johore.[58] An expanding supply of local produce was thus provided for British merchants to export to China and elsewhere.

Before 1880, the development of primary production in the Malay peninsula was almost exclusively the work of Chinese entrepeneurs and Chinese labour. British merchants in the Straits Settlements were the main market for Chinese produce, but control of production remained mostly in Chinese hands. Their activities included sugar plantations in Province Wellesley and Kedah, which were pioneered by prominent Pinang Chinese families such as that of Lee Ghe-ang.[59] Untypically, European planters did establish themselves in sugar by the 1850s.[60] In the immediate proximity of Singapore, particularly in mainland Johore, the Chinese developed gambier and pepper plantations, two compatible crops grown together under what became known as the "Kangchu" system.[61] The Chinese had pioneered gambier and pepper cultivation on Riau before the acquisition of Singapore, but in the late 1830s there was a rapid expansion of production in Singapore, which spread to mainland Johore as the pressure on land intensified. The number of gambier and pepper plantations on Singapore island grew from 250 in 1836 to 477 by 1840.[62] Such growth was all the more impressive in light of difficulties such as price instability and shortages of land.[63] Both gambier and pepper found a ready market in Britain, India and China.[64]

In the long run, however, probably the most important Chinese activity proved to be tin mining in the states of the Malay peninsula. Although the main phase of expansion came after the 1840s, Straits Chinese merchants had already been engaged in the tin trade for several decades. At first the Chinese merchants restricted themselves to merely trading with Malay chiefs, exchanging rice, opium and other commodities for Malay tin. The tin was extracted by Malay miners who were required by local custom to sell their produce at a fixed price to the local chief, who in turn sold it on to Chinese or European merchants. Some Chinese merchants rose to prominence in this field, notably Chee Yam Chuan of Melaka, Lim Leack of Singapore and the Koh family of Pinang.[65] European merchants also became involved in the tin trade, notably George Stuart and Lawrence Nairne of Pinang, and the Velge and Neubronner families of Melaka.[66] Supplies of tin were modest, but yielded considerable revenues. In 1835/36, for example, over 7,000 piculs of tin worth $313,368 were imported into Singapore, and as an item of trade was second in value only to European and Indian piece goods.[67] In the late 1830s production grew rapidly, particularly in the western Malay state of Perak, where the most accessible and richest lodes were located. Later, in the 1850s, production was expanded in Selangor and Negri Sembilan. Expansion of the tin trade was assisted by the gradual breakdown in the late 1830s of the monopolies exercised by Malay chiefs over the tin trade, which interposed them as intermediaries between the Malay miners and the Chinese and European traders. Malay miners were subsequently permitted to trade directly with the foreign merchants, and Malay chiefs adopted other strategies to maximise benefits from the tin trade. Most important was the imposition of taxes on the river traffic in tin, which was the principal means of transport out of the Malay peninsula.[68] The opening of the Malay states to direct commerce paved the way for direct involvement in mining by the Chinese themselves.

Chinese dominance of export production was reflected in the ethnic complexion of the Straits population. Between 1843 and 1853, 8,000 to 10,000 Chinese immigrants arrived annually in Singapore, and by the early 1850s the total Chinese population of all three Straits Settlements was over 62,000.[69] Out of a total Singapore population of just under 60,000 in 1850, almost 25,000 were Chinese.[70] Chinese migration was fuelled by the growing demand for Chinese labour. Why was it that the Chinese were such successful entrepeneurs, and why did they become so important as compradors and partners for British enterprise?

Chinese enterprise enjoyed a number of crucial advantages. Firstly, Chinese trading organisations had long been based upon a principle of co-operation between capital and labour. This was exemplified by the Kongsi (syndicate) form of organisation in the early pepper and gambier plantations on Riau, among the tin miners of Bangka, and gold miners in Borneo. Under the Kongsi arrangement, all members of the syndicate were effectively partners in a joint enterprise, and were entitled to a share of profits. In the earliest days, there was an assumption of equality of status among those engaged in a particular Kongsi enterprise, which engendered strong ties of loyalty and co-operation invaluable for survival in often turbulent political circumstances.[71] But equality of status did not mean material equality. There were always wealthier Taukehs (merchants/entrepeneurs) who provided the lion's share of investment capital and took most of the profits. As the nineteenth century progressed and Chinese entrepeneurs developed their trade and investment activities, this material inequality became more marked, and a distinctive Chinese merchant class arose, which rubbed shoulders with their European counterparts in the commercial and social life of the Straits. Eventually they emerged as a separate class from the swelling ranks of the impoverished Chinese labourers, who flooded to the Straits in search of work. The Kongsis became increasingly hierarchical, asserting the authority of the wealthy merchants over the poor labourers, and establishing a culture of obedience. In short, a class system emerged within Chinese society.[72]

But Kongsi allegiances remained strong. Chinese merchants and their labourers shared loyalties to a particular Kongsi, identifying and elevating common interests above any divisions between entrepeneur and labourer. The basis of a system of class collaboration thus emerged, which helped to ensure stable labour relations and high profits for the Chinese merchants. Various factors contributed to the durability of the Kongsis. Among the Chinese settlers in the Straits there were troublesome ethnic tensions. Kongsis tended to reflect these ethnic divisions, uniting men from a particular region, regardless of social status, against those from other parts of China. In the nineteenth century some Kongsis evolved into "secret societies", dedicated to the clandestine furtherance of clan interests at the expense of rival organisations. The largest secret society in the Straits Settlements, the Ghee Hin, was overwhelmingly Cantonese in its membership, while the Hai San came to represent the Hakka community and the Toa Peh Kong consisted primarily of Hokkien.[73] The British regarded them as sinister institutions which imported feuds and rivalries from China. But in fact, the secret societies helped to impose order upon a fast growing Chinese population, which at times threatened serious public disorder. The longstanding Chinese official positions for liaising with local Malay authorities and European interests, the Kapitans China (Captains China), came to be filled by leaders of the secret societies, whose clandestine positions of power enabled them to enforce agreements within the Chinese community. Later in the century, when unrest and rebellion swept the Chinese empire, the secret societies indeed came to reflect political differences which originated in the homeland, and as rivalries among the Chinese themselves intensified, the secret societies did resort sometimes to violent action. However, the origins of the Kongsis of south east Asia were essentially economic, and it was the economic advantages which they bestowed upon Chinese entrepeneurs, such as the control and discipline of labour, which were the core of their activities and objectives.[74] Nevertheless, the secret societies which emerged from them contributed to the destabilisation of Malay societies on the peninsula.

The system for supplying Chinese labour was a second reason for Chinese success. The expansion of gambier, pepper and sugar production in the 1830s increased the demand for Chinese labour, and poor Chinese peasants began to flood into the Nanyang to escape the poverty of their homeland. Extreme poverty delivered an endless stream of young men into the hands of wealthy Chinese merchants and junk captains, who alone had the resources to provide transport to the region. Unable even to afford the passage, most Chinese migrants depended upon a credit arrangement with the Junk captain who brought them to the Straits. Less frequently, credit for the fare to Singapore might be arranged with the China based agent of a Straits Chinese entrepeneur. On arrival in the Straits Settlements, the Chinese migrant (referred to as a "sinkeh") would be confined to the junk which brought him until Chinese entrepeneurs requiring coolie labourers approached the junk captain with offers to settle the migrant's debt. The migrant's debt then shifted to the entrepeneur, who insisted upon settlement of the debt through the provision of free labour services by the sinkeh, at an agreed rate for an agreed period of time. The entrepeneur thereby obtained a continuous supply of cheap labour, insulating his business against short run fluctuations in the labour market which might bring periods of labour scarcity. In practice, it took most sinkeh far longer to settle their debts than the stipulated period; chiefly because most sinkeh ran up further debts for supplies of food, clothing and opium which were usually provided by his new employer. In such circumstances, Chinese coolies were inexorably drawn into the web of Kongsi and secret society loyalties. This system of indentured labour ensured that Chinese entrepeneurs were best placed to develop the agricultural resources and mines of the region. What emerged was a Chinese society in south east Asia divided increasingly along lines of social class, in which the Chinese coolie enjoyed few opportunities for social advancement.[75] The rise from obscurity and poverty of such men as Yap Ah Loy, who eventually became the most prominent Chinese merchant and political leader in Selangor in the late nineteenth century, was a notable but rare exception.[76] Although stratified rigidly by these economic arrangements, the Chinese class system largely avoided class conflict between coolie and entrepeneur. Ethnic and Kongsi allegiances were effective barriers against the emergence of horizontal social loyalties. Also, the tight hold enjoyed by the entrepreneurial class over the coolies, through the sinkeh and Kongsi employment systems, deterred resistance from below.

A third factor which contributed to Chinese success, but which also tied them into the imperial economic system of the British, was the importance of opium in Chinese economic activity. Opium became very popular among Chinese labourers, providing temporary relief from their miseries and hardships. Chinese merchants quickly realised that by selling opium to their own labourers, the meagre wages paid to them could be recouped. Also, the relationship of indebtedness which maintained a pool of tied labour could be prolonged, because the poorest sinkehs had to buy their opium on credit from their employers. Opium therefore provided a way of maximising profit from the Chinese labourers, enticing them to pay back their wages to Chinese entrepeneurs for the drug, thereby enabling the substantial accumulation of capital needed to finance commercial expansion.[77] Opium contributed very significantly to the leading role of Chinese capital in the development of primary production throughout the region. In the Straits Settlements, it generated income for the European merchants who imported the raw product, while the system of official opium farms provided the revenues necessary to pay for British administration. The British were therefore able to avoid the imposition of trade tariffs, which helped to attract local traders, and contributed greatly to the success of the ports.

An opium farm was an exclusive right to process raw opium into smokable chandu, and sell it to the inhabitants of the Straits Settlements. Chinese labourers working the pepper and gambier plantations on Singapore and in Johore were a lucrative market. Sale of the farm, of the exclusive right to sell opium for a fixed period of time, was a vital source of revenue for the Straits Settlements administration. The prospective opium farmer, or opium farming kongsi, had to bid for a lease which bestowed the farm upon them, usually for a period of three years. Income received by the Straits government from the sale of the opium farm constituted about a half of total revenues. The system did cause problems. Competition among the Chinese Kongsis for the opium farm occasionally caused violent conflict. Between the 1840s and the 1870s, sporadic rioting disturbed the peace, generating anxiety within the small European community.[78] In the 1860s, an uneasy peace was restored by an emerging syndicate of powerful taukehs, which controlled the opium farm.[79] From the 1840s, as Chinese miners moved into the western Malay states, opium also helped Chinese tin merchants to maximise their profits. The right to sell opium to mineworkers was written into most agreements between wealthy Straits taukehs and the Chinese mineowners.[80] Chinese mining entrepeneurs often lacked the capital to meet the initial costs of opening new mines, and so were forced to borrow from the wealthy taukehs who resided in the Straits Settlements. As a condition of such loans, the taukeh secured the exclusive right to supply the mining settlements with food, tools and opium, at prices fixed by them. In this way, mining, like other Chinese ventures, secured a very high return for the taukehs, ensuring high levels of capital accumulation. Opium thus played a crucial role in the initial development of the Malay peninsula as an exporter of primary produce. It also furnished the European merchants with new sources of income through the re-export of raw opium to the archipelago, and sale of the drug to the Chinese opium farmer for local retail. In addition, the British administration in the Straits received revenue income to cover the costs of government. It also entrenched Chinese capital and enterprise as indispensable partners for European entrepeneurs, who generally lacked sufficient capital to develop the local economy. Plainly the older imperial trade networks in Asia were instrumental in developing the Malay peninsula as an international supplier of primary produce. The opium trade, originally a key component of the trading system of the old East India Company monopoly was central in providing the capital to finance this process. Once again, the enduring significance of trade between south east Asia and India is apparent. Moreover, the identification of British rule with principles of free trade and competition so frequently made by earlier historians, sits uneasily with the British promotion of monopolistic opium farms designed to maximise state revenues.[81] Clearly, the shift towards a prevailing ideology of free trade was far more gradual, selective and pragmatic than has sometimes been suggested.

Several conclusions may be drawn from this analysis of commercial enterprise in the Straits Settlements. Firstly, the European merchant houses were essentially products of the old colonial system which had prevailed under the East India Company monopoly. In the late 1820s, when many new merchants established themselves in Singapore, there was a general expectation that the monopoly of trade with China would continue indefinitely. But this optimism was false. The collapse of the Calcutta agency houses and the China monopoly in the 1830s created problems for the European community in the Straits Settlements. These were compounded by continuing Dutch protectionism and the foundation of Hong Kong in 1842. European merchants were forced to adapt their activities in order to survive. It was the evolving relationship between European and Chinese merchants which was the key to such adaptation. It was the Chinese middlemen who facilitated the expansion of trade with the islands of the Malay archipelago, and it was the Chinese who developed the Malay peninsula as a source of export commodities. British and European merchants then profited from the export of Malay produce to Europe and China. The commercial relationship between European merchants and Chinese compradors had been evolving since the eighteenth century or even earlier, particularly in Pinang and Melaka. But on Singapore there was a considerable expansion of Chinese activity, and their involvement in pepper, gambier, sugar and eventually tin production represented an entirely new phase of economic activity.

Relations with the Chinese, and Chinese success, were cemented by the continuing importance of branches of the country trade within Asia, which had developed originally under the old colonial system. Of these, the opium trade was crucial for both European and Chinese fortunes, providing high rates of profit for the European merchants who imported the raw commodity into the Straits, and also for the Chinese, for whom the drug provided the means of intense exploitation of their own labourers. While exports of British manufactures undoubtedly generated handsome profits for the British merchants in the Straits Settlements, the continuing value of the traditional Asian trade network has been underestimated. In total, the British imperial economy in south east Asia in the first half of the nineteenth century was an old colonial system adjusting to the end of monopoly and the collapse of key financial and mercantile interests in India, rather than as a new system created by British manufacturing and export interests committed to free trade.

****

What were the consequences of the expansion of British commerce for the Malay states? How did the growing British presence in the region affect them? In the 1820s the Malay states were sparsely populated and undeveloped economically. It has been estimated, for example, that the total population of Perak, the most populous state, was only 35,000 in the 1830s, rising to 60,000 by 1879, after a prolonged period of economic development.[82] In the 1820s, the population of Selangor was estimated by one contemporary to be about 6,000 and grew little before the 1870s.[83] Dense tropical rain forest and mountainous terrain made transport very difficult. The river systems, especially on the west coast, were the main centres of population and the only means of communication. These were the main arteries of trade, through which tin and forest produce were exported and Indian and British goods imported. Control of the rivers provided local rulers with the tax revenues needed to finance their military and ceremonial requirements. These Malay societies were hierarchical, with a Sultan at the apex who theoretically enjoyed supreme power, surrounded by families of aristocratic descent. From these ranks were drawn men to occupy the senior administrative positions such as the Laxsamana (head of military affairs) and Bendahara (foreign minister). The origins of these titled positions lay in antiquity, and their practical functions were often more varied and far reaching than the formal titles suggested. Below these elevated administrative offices, the Malay states were sub divided into districts, each of which was governed by a local chief, usually a member of the aristocracy who enjoyed a degree of authority constrained only by the Sultan's power. Below the chief, each village was presided over by a Penghulu (headman) who enforced local laws and customs, and was directly answerable to his district chief.

Although the position of Sultan was usually hereditary, Malay custom did vary across the peninsula. In Negri Sembilan succession to the throne was theoretically subject to ratification by assemblies of the whole people.[84] The polygamous nature of Malay families sometimes complicated succession to the throne. The royal families constituted a separate stratum (the anak raja) over and above the aristocracy. The emergence of several possible contenders for the throne, often from different queens, frequently led to conflict. In practice, a reigning Sultan and his chosen successor had to build alliances with powerful chiefs to ensure stability during the process of succession, and indeed throughout the whole reign of the Sultan. The Malay custom of the reigning Sultan designating an heir apparent (Raja Muda) and bestowing upon him administrative duties and authority, usually served to ensure a smooth transition of authority from the Sultan to his chosen successor. But the system did not always work. Later in the nineteenth century, there were succession disputes in several western Malay states which erupted into civil war.

The nature of peasant society exacerbated this political volatility. The subsistence peasant economy was based upon a mixture of shifting cultivation, fishing and hunting, and was oriented towards subsistence rather than the market. The few market oriented activities such as tin mining and smelting were limited by proximity to suitable mining land, difficulties of transport and the need to concentrate most time and energy on food production. The skill of many Malays at boat building, the portability and ease of construction of their dwellings, and the shifting nature of their farming, made for a highly mobile population which could flee quickly in response to any perceived threat. Thus war between the Malay states was accompanied by destabilising population movements which served to add internal social dislocation to the threat of external conquest. In the context of such a scarce and mobile population, political power rested with those able to control large numbers of people for the purposes of warfare, labour and revenue collection. The visible ability to command large numbers of followers, servants and slaves, was the most potent symbol of authority and power, and the higher the status of the Malay chief, the more people he was expected to command. Debt bondage provided a means of securing a large following. Financial debts owed to members of the elite were paid in labour services and conspicuous submission, rather than cash. It was, in total, a precarious structure of power and authority. War quickly undermined the fragile basis of political authority. Defeat in battle was often followed by the immediate desertion of bands of followers, or even their wholesale defection to the victorious side.

Trade contributed greatly to the rise of central state authority in the Malay world, as illustrated by the emergence of large centres of population such as Melaka in the fifteenth century.[85] During that earlier period, Malay polities thrived on trade revenues, and achieved size and pre-eminence unparallelled by any of the Malay states of the nineteenth century. Yet the period between the mid eighteenth and nineteenth centuries was one of almost continuous growth in international trade throughout the region. Why did this not provide the means of state formation in the Malay peninsula on the same scale as a few centuries earlier? Why did the Malay states continue to be sparsely populated, poor and in conflict with each other?

An important factor was the European dominance of trade during the latter half of the eighteenth century. Whereas in the "Age of Commerce", the fruits of expanding trade accrued directly to local Malay rulers, it was the

Dutch and British East India Companies and their coteries of private merchants who were the main beneficiaries of economic revival in this later period. Where local rulers did try to secure a share of the new wealth by the traditional customs of royal monopoly and taxes on trade, they quickly encountered European resistance. The British particularly resented obstacles to free trade erected by local rulers, even where state monopolies and trade taxes were essential for preserving political authority and order. Probably the best example of this was the stubborn refusal of both the Bengal and Pinang administrations to tolerate the efforts of the Acehnese monarch, Jauhar al-Alam, to assert his traditional rights over the trade of his kingdom, in the period between 1800 and 1819. Some British officials were even willing to depose the Sultan to preserve free access to the markets and resources of his kingdom. The lesson could not have been lost on other Malay rulers who might have been inclined to assert their traditional rights. In Aceh and elsewhere, the British preferred to deal with local chiefs rather than the Sultan. Their superior local knowledge and authority made the local chiefs much more useful for British traders. Through trade with the British, these local chiefs grew in wealth and power, to the detriment of the Sultan's authority. This was why Jauhar found himself confronted by a factionalised kingdom of truculent vassals. It was an experience which was to be repeated in the western Malay states after the mid nineteenth century, as tin mining brought considerable revenue wealth to local chiefs, enabling them to defy the Sultan. One example was Long Jaafar, chief of Larut in Perak, who from the 1840s invited Chinese immigration and tin mining to improve his financial position.[86] Similarly, in Selangor, Raja Jumaat of Lukut, and Raja Abdullah of Klang, promoted mining and were enriched by trade revenues.[87] Although by 1840 the monopolies of trade which had been the right of local chiefs and Sultans were broken down, the ability of local chiefs to levy taxes on trade ensured their continuing rise to power. After 1850, these wealthy local chiefs became major participants in the civil unrest which swept the Malay peninsula in the decades before British intervention. Thus British commerce and the Chinese involvement in the local economies of the Malay states forestalled the emergence of strong polities, and helped to precipitate the crises in local political systems which attracted British intervention.

Other developments also contributed to instability. From the north, the peninsula attracted Siamese interest. By the early nineteenth century, Siam was recovering from earlier political crises, and began to reassert claims of suzerainty over the Malay states. In particular, ambitious Siamese governors of Ligore wanted to extend their authority over the Malay states.[88] Siamese aggression intensified with their deepening suspicions about British intentions in the Malay peninsula. Kedah proved to be a flashpoint. In 1821, allegations that Sultan Ahmad of Kedah was conspiring with the Burmese against Siam, provided the excuse for Siamese invasion. Sultan Ahmad fled to Pinang, fuelling British concern that the question of Kedah might ignite war between Britain and Siam. It was feared that the Siamese might also conquer Perak and

Selangor, threatening British trade there, but an alliance of the two states successfully repelled an invasion. Perak requested assistance from the British administration in Pinang, and in 1826, the military secretary there, Henry Burney, was sent to Bangkok to negotiate a settlement of Anglo-Siamese relations in the peninsula. Under the treaty which resulted, Siam agreed not to attack either Perak or Selangor, although provision was made for the voluntary submission by those states to Siamese authority. Kedah was acknowledged as a vassal state of Siam, although the status of other northern states such as Trengganu and Kelantan remained ambiguous. Also in 1826, a delegation led by Captain James Low went from Pinang to Perak, and signed a treaty guaranteeing Perak's sovereignty, with British military help if necessary. Although Calcutta did not ratify the treaty, the Siamese were reluctant to test the British will on the question of Perak. Nevertheless, even though the Siamese eventually permitted the restoration of Sultan Ahmad in Kedah in 1842, the Malay states remained subject to the influence of Bangkok throughout the first half of the nineteenth century, a factor which helped prevent the re-emergence of strong states on the peninsula.

Even before 1850 there were already tangible signs of local instability drawing the British into a more active role in local politics. As early as 1831, the British became embroiled in a local dispute in Naning, near Melaka, winning a small, brief but bloody war. Then there was piracy. Seafarers such as the Orang Laut had traditionally assisted state formation in south east Asia by forcibly extracting tribute from maritime traders for local Malay rulers.[89] With the collapse of so many Malay states after the seventeenth century, these groups were left to their own devices as state supervision and control over their activities slackened. Some resorted to plundering local and European vessels, occasionally with the covert support of local chiefs who would receive a share of the spoils. From the late eighteenth century until the 1870s the British authorities were engaged in a continuous battle against what they regarded as naked piracy. By the 1870s, the problem was brought under control, but only following strenuous and expensive efforts to police the waters of the archipelago, and after local Malay rulers had been successfully persuaded to co-operate in the suppression of their erstwhile allies.

During the 1840s, the fragility of local states stimulated British expansion in northern Borneo, at the expense of the Sultanate of Brunei. In the early nineteenth century the Sultanate had begun to exploit the resources of Sarawak, especially coal and antimony deposits which could find a ready market with the British traders en route to China. The coercive efforts of the Sultan's emissary, Pengiran Makhota, to compel the local populace to engage in mining, inspired rebellion. By the late 1830s trade was seriously disrupted by the uprising, and the Sultan sent his uncle and Prime Minister, Pengiran Muda Hashim to replace Makhota.[90] Significantly Brunei, like other states in the region, had to face vassals strengthened considerably by trade with the British and other Europeans.[91] In 1839, a British adventurer, James Brooke was sent by the Governor of the Straits Settlements to discuss the difficulties in Sarawak with Hashim. Brooke became embroiled in Hashim's campaign to restore order, and was so effective that in 1841, in return for an annual payment of £500, he was appointed as Raja of Sarawak, with full personal authority over a fiefdom referred to as the "First Division". In the following decades Brooke extended the territory under his rule, and established a monopoly over trade, mining and related activities.[92] Expediency dictated the official British view of Brooke rule in Sarawak. Singapore's commerce benefitted considerably from the expansion of Brooke rule, although the Straits merchants were displeased by Brooke's monopolisation of Sarawak's resources. Brooke rule also offered greater security for British trade to China and with the markets of Borneo at a time when the Dutch were trying to exclude British commerce from their sphere of influence. When the Dutch complained about Brooke's expansionism, his independent status enabled the British authorities to deny that Brooke was acting in any way on their behalf.

The true nature of the British position in Borneo became clear by 1846, when the British government officially informed the Netherlands that northern Borneo fell within the British sphere of influence. This position was consolidated in the following year, when under a treaty with Brunei, the island of Labuan was ceded to the British, who also gained the right to veto any future concessions of territory by the Sultan. Significantly, the first governor of Labuan was none other than James Brooke, now granted a knighthood and an official British government position to add to his status as the first "White Raja". The reward was intended to strengthen and extend Brooke's control over Sarawak. In his battles against the Ibans, a seafaring people well equipped to resist Brooke's efforts to control their territories, Brooke was assisted by the Royal Navy, under the pretext of suppressing Iban "piracy" on the high seas. While British strictures on free trade and against monopoly generally prevented the revival of local state power in south east Asia, the White Raja was treated very differently from his Malay peers. In addition to British military support against the opponents to his rule, Brooke was also indulged by the British authorities on economic matters. The Sarawak state's monopoly over mining enterprise in his territories would never have been tolerated by the British had it been implemented by a local ruler. Brooke's nationality unsurprisingly secured preferential treatment from his countrymen.

Thus British policies towards states on the peninsula and Borneo were designed to open opportunities for British trade, and Chinese enterprise. But there was never a conscious desire by the British to undermine local political systems. British policy makers, both in London and Bengal, were anxious to avoid an expensive extension of British formal rule in the region. They recognised that the political collapse of local states could easily drag the British into territorial expansion of incalculable duration and expense. Local instability might also prompt unwanted interest from powerful European or local rivals. In their negotiations with Siam and the Malay states the British tried to establish clearly defined frontiers and spheres of interest. Peace, stability and local rule over the Malay states were seen by the British as essential prerequisites for successful commerce, as was free and unrestricted trade by British and Chinese merchants. But the British failed to recognise that their quest for free trade was effectively undermining the revenue collection and wealth accumulation systems which financed state power in the Malay world. Furthermore, in permitting and encouraging Chinese commercial expansion into the Malay states at a time when the political structures there were being weakened, the British were unleashing forces which would further destabilise local societies. The scene was set for several decades of instability, unrest and eventually civil war, which in the 1870s would compel the British to intervene and assert direct political control.

NOTES

1. Wong Lin Ken, "The Trade of Singapore 1819-69" Journal of the Malaysian Branch of the Royal Asiatic Society 33:4 (1960) 11-301, p209.
2. Ibid.: p209.
3. SarDesai, British Trade and Expansion p43.
4. C. Buckley, An Anecdotal History of Old Times in Singapore 2 vols (Singapore, Fraser and Neave 1902) p74.
5. Ibid.: p226.
6. Ibid.: p533.
7. This was Crawfurd's estimate in 1821, J. Crawford, Journal of an Embassy from the Governor General of India to the Courts of Siam and Cochin China (London, Henry Colbourn 1828) p19.
8. Lord Stanley to Governor General of India in Council, 1 March 1859, CO/273/3, p93, PRO, London.
9. Ibid.: p93, Crawford, Journal of an Embassy p36.
10. Wong Lin Ken, "Singapore: Its Growth as an Entrepot 1819-1941" Journal of Southeast Asian Studies 9:1 (1978) 50-84, p53.
11. Wong Lin Ken, "The Trade of Singapore" pp74-75.
12. Ibid.: pp106-113.
13. Ibid.: p118.
14. These figures are taken from the Bengal Commercial Reports, P/174/42 to P/174/53, IOR, London.
15. Buckley, An Anecdotal History pp301-306.
16. Wong Lin Ken, "The Trade of Singapore" p41.
17. Ibid.; pp47-51.
18. Ibid.: p52. Wong shows that the value of Singapore's trade rose consistently, from $1,609,145 in 1823/24 to $6,649,534 in 1869.
19. Ibid.: p69.
20. J. Cameron (1865), Our Tropical Possessions in Malayan India, being a Descriptive Account of Singapore, Province Wellesley and Malacca: Their People, Products and Government (London, Elder and Co. 1865).
21. Tarling, The Fall of Imperial Britain p129.
22. SarDesai, British Trade and Expansion p46.
23. Buckley, An Anecdotal History pp596-599.
24. Figures taken from Bengal Commercial Reports, P/174/44 to P/174/61, IOR, London.

25. Ibid.; P/174/51 to P/174/61.
26. Ibid.: P/174/44 to P/174/61.
27. Minute by Robert Fullerton on the Trade of the Straits Settlements 1829-30, Boards Collections F/4/1271, No. 51022, pp118-120, IOR, London.
28. Bengal Commercial Reports, P/174/44 to P/174/61, IOR, London.
29. Ibid.: P/174/59.
30. Ibid.
31. Andaya and Andaya, A History of Malaysia pp122-123.
32. Wong Lin Ken, "The Trade of Singapore" p182.
33. C.M. Turnbull, A History of Singapore pp35-36.
34. Ibid.
35. Buckley, An Anecdotal History pp313-314.
36. I. Nish, "British Mercantile Co-operation in the Indo-China Trade from the End of the East India Company's Trading Monopoly" Journal of Southeast Asian History 3:2 (1962) 74-91.
37. Ibid.: pp84-85.
38. S.D. Chapman, "Financial Restraints on the Growth of Firms in the Cotton Industry 1790-1850" Economic History Review 32:1 (1979) 50-69.
39. Wong Lin Ken, "The Trade of Singapore" p49.
40. Letter from the Straits Settlements Association to the Colonial Office, 7 February 1868, CO/273/24, p185, PRO, London.
41. M. Lee (Stubbs Brown), "Trade and Shipping in Early Penang" pp29-30.
42. J.H. Drabble and P.J. Drake, "The British Agency Houses in Malaysia: Survival ina Changing World" Journal of Southeast Asian Studies 12:2 (1981) 297-328, p300.
43. Buckley, An Anecdotal History p166.
44. M. Greenberg, British Trade and the Opening of China 1800-42 (Cambridge, Cambridge University Press 1951) pp96-97.
45. A good account and explanation of the crisis is to be found in: A. Tripathi, Trade and Finance in the Bengal Presidency 1793-1833 (Calcutta, Oxford University Press 1979) Ch. 5.
46. C. Trocki, Opium and Empire: Chinese Society in Colonial Singapore 1800-1910 (Ithaca, Cornell University Press 1990) pp59-63.
47. Ibid.: p51.
48. Wong Lin Ken, "Singapore: Its Growth as an Entrepot" p54.
49. Buckley, An Anecdotal History p380.
50. Drabble and Drake, "The British Agency Houses in Malaysia" p302.
51. Ibid.: 303.
52. W. Makepeace, One Hundred Years of Singapore 2 Vols, (London, John Murray 1921), Vol 2 p32.
53. Drake and Drabble, "The British Agency Houses in Malaysia" p303.
54. Ibid.: p304.
55. Makepeace, One Hundred Years of Singapore Vol. 2, p35.
56. Rajat Kanta Ray, "Asian Capital in the Age of European Domination: The Rise of the Bazaar 1800-1914" Modern Asian Studies 29:3 (1995) 449-554.
57. Ibid.: p466.
58. Ibid.: p504.
59. Tan Kim Heng, "Chinese Sugar Planting and Social Mobility in Nineteenth Century Province Wellesley" Malaysia in History 24 (1981) 24-38, p30.
60. Ibid.; p29.

61. An excellent explanation of the Kangchu system is to be found in; C. Trocki, "The Origins of the Kangchu System 1740-1860" Journal of the Malaysian Branch of the Royal Asiatic Society 49:2 (1976) 132-155.
62. Buckley, An Anecdotal History p350.
63. Trocki, "The Origins of the Kangchu System" p143.
64. Ibid.: p140.
65. Khoo Kay Kim, The Western Malay States 1850-1873: The Effects of Commercial Development on Malay Politics (Kuala Lumpur, Oxford University Press 1972), p62 and p67.
66. Ibid.: pp60-67.
67. Ibid.: p56.
68. Ibid.: p77.
69. J.R. Logan, "Notes on the Chinese in the Straits" Journal of the Indian Archipelago and Eastern Asia 9 (1855) 109-124, p113 and p118.
70. Buckley, An Anecdotal History p533.
71. Trocki, Opium and Empire pp12-15.
72. The main features of the Chinese class system are described in: Yen Ching Hwang, "Class Structure and Social Mobility in the Chinese Community in Singapore and Malaya 1800-1911" Modern Asian Studies 21:3 (1987) 417-445, pp417-429.
73. Khoo Kay Kim, The Western Malay States pp111-112.
74. Trocki, Opium and Empire p13.
75. Lee Poh Ping, Chinese Society in Nineteenth Century Singapore: A Socio-economic Analysis (Kuala Lumpur, Oxford University Press 1978); Trocki, Opium and Empire; Yen Chin Hwang, "Class Structure and Social Mobility".
76. For Details on the life of Yap Ah Loy, see: S.M. Middlebrook, "Yap Ah Loy 1837-1885" Journal of the Malaysian Branch of the Royal Asiatic Society 24:2 (1951) 1-119.
77. C. Trocki, "The Rise of Singapore's Great Opium Syndicate 1840-86" Journal of Southeast Asian Studies 18:1 (1987) 58-80, p79.
78. Trocki, Opium and Empire pp82-116.
79. Ibid.: pp117-148.
80. Wong Lin Ken, The Malayan Tin Industry to 1914 (Tucson,University of Arizona 1965) pp60-64.
81. Trocki, "The Rise of Singapore's Great Opium Syndicate" p79.
82. E. Sadka, The Protected Malay States 1874-1895 (Kuala Lumpur, University of Malaya 1968) pp1-5.
83. Ibid.: 1-5.
84. Khoo Kay Kim, The Western Malay States p16.
85. Reid, South East Asia in the Age of Commerce Vol. 2, p69.
86. Khoo Kay Kim, The Western Malay States pp68-70.
87. Ibid.: pp70-75.
88. Andaya and Andaya, A History of Malaysia pp116-117.
89. Ibid.: pp130-133. E. Chew, "The Naning War, 1831-1832: Colonial Authority and Malay Resistance in the Early Period of British Expansion" Modern Asian Studies 32:2 (1998) pp351-387.
90. Amarjit Kaur, "The Babbling Brookes: Economic Change in Sarawak 1841-1941" Modern Asian Studies 29:1 (1995) 65-109, pp65-67.
91. Andaya and Andaya, A History of Malaysia pp124-125.
92. Kaur, "The Babbling Brookes" pp72-73.

6. BRITISH IMPERIALISM IN BURMA AND SIAM: 1820-1850

If British relations with the Malay states during the first half of the nineteenth century were characterised by extreme caution the same was not true of British relations with Burma. There were two wars, the first between 1824 and 1826, and the second in 1852 which resulted in the annexation of a substantial portion of Burmese territory, including the whole of the country's seaboard. These two wars proved to be a prelude to a third and final conflict in 1885, which resulted in the annexation of Upper Burma and the complete obliteration of the Burmese state. What were the reasons for these dramatic events?

The proximity of the Burmese state to the British empire in India shaped relations between them in the period leading to the outbreak of war in 1824. By 1820, the western edge of the Burmese empire bordered upon British Bengal, the political and commercial centre of British rule. Calcutta was inclined to see Burma as yet another Indian land power, similar to the various Indian states with whom the British had been in conflict for several decades. As an expanding empire, Burma was regarded with some apprehension, an attitude strengthened by the assertion of Burmese power over the frontier states of Assam, Manipur and Arakan in the early nineteenth century. Continuing westward expansion threatened the possibility of conflict.

Like other parts of south east Asia, Burma had experienced upheaval during the economic and political crises of the seventeenth and early eighteenth centuries. However, these were not so acute on mainland south east Asia as in the islands. Consequently, the Burmese kingdom recovered during the later eighteenth century.[1] Of particular importance was the emergence of the Konbaung dynasty in 1752. Under Alaungpaya and his successors, the Burmese kingdom grew from strength to strength, defeating first the Mons of Pegu and securing for the kingdom the rich lands and ports of Lower Burma by 1755. There were several conflicts with Siam, one of which, in the 1760s, effectively destroyed the old regime of Ayudhaya. By the early nineteenth century, Siamese revival forced the Burmese to look westward for further acquisitions of territory.[2] This change of direction was reinforced by the resurgence of Chinese strength to the north. Chinese imperial control over Yunnan province was established by about 1750 and the Burmese had to repel several attempted Chinese invasions later in the century. Although these were successful, the presence of the Chinese ended any possibility of northward expansion. The only way to expand was to the west, towards the frontiers of British India.

Recent work on the Burmese regime has revealed some of the reasons for its expansionist tendencies.[3] The availability of plentiful cultivable land along the Irrawaddy facilitated high levels of food production (particularly rice) which could sustain an increasing population. Consequently, the early Burmese kings enjoyed the benefits of a increasing population and revenues, providing significant military and economic advantages over neighbouring polities. A series of wars in the eighteenth century led to territorial expansion. By the end of the eighteenth century Burma had absorbed the Irrawaddy delta, and the border Shan states. The process strengthened the Burmese state and created a distinctive Burmese cultural identity, which at least one recent historian has described as "proto-nationalist".[4] Several factors served to strengthen the central state apparatus. The growth of external trade both with China and the wider world provided new sources of revenue in addition to those arising from land and agriculture.[5] The collection of trade duties was particularly amenable to control by central government, which also imposed monopolistic control over the trade in certain commodities, such as teak wood and gemstones. The state either engaged in exclusive commerce itself, or sold concessions to the highest bidder. Expanding international commerce increased imports of bullion and specie, while trade itself encouraged cash cropping (especially cotton for the Chinese market) and specialisation in non agricultural activities such as mining. Together these stimulated internal trade and the wider ubiquity of money and exchange relationships within the economy. Widespread monetisation made it easier for the state to collect taxes, which were increasingly in cash rather than kind, providing funds to pay for a strong army, able to sustain the crown's authority within the kingdom as well as wage war externally. The proportion of state revenues collected in kind fell from approximately 58 per cent under the Toungoo dynasty (1600-1752) to about 30 per cent under the early Konbaung monarchs (1752-1804).[6] During the eighteenth century, state authority over the countryside was tightened. Traditionally, the main source of authority at the local level was the village headman (athi), who enjoyed far reaching powers and independence as the main collector of revenues, dispenser of justice and lands, and conduit for the central state's edicts in the countryside. In practice, before the eighteenth century, the athis were an effective counterweight to the authority of the King and the central state, because of their control over tax collection and assessment. During the course of the eighteenth century, this independence was checked in several ways. As trade, monetary exchange and specialised production spread, many peasant producers, including the athis themselves, turned from subsistence farming to market-oriented production of rice, cotton and other commodities. A strong central state was essential to provide a peaceful framework for commerce, a fact recognised by the athis, who were consequently less inclined to resist central authority.

Commercialisation of the economy was accompanied by a thriving market in land, as athis became tempted to sell land to outsiders. The main beneficiaries were wealthy civil and military servants of central government. As the Burmese army grew, so the state saw fit to reward its leaders and their followers with special grants of land (Ahmudan), thus ensuring their continuing loyalty to the regime. In civil administration this was mirrored by the rise of centrally appointed provincial governors (Myowuns) who were also awarded land grants which could be supplemented by their own land purchases. The emerging picture was therefore of an increasingly militaristic state, successfully exerting its authority over the country by means of an expanding military and civil bureaucracy, paid for by the accumulating revenues arising from economic growth. Of course, the state played its role in this cycle of economic growth and ascending state power. In Upper Burma, for example, state patronage of extensive irrigation works was instrumental in helping to bring about higher levels of food production.[7] Successive waves of territorial expansion also assisted the centralisation of power, providing the King with new sources of agricultural wealth, such as the huge rice production of Lower Burma, and tracts of land to satisfy the appetite for it within the expanding state bureaucracy and war machine. Growing trade, population movements and the far reaching compass of state patronage, facilitated the emergence of a wider consciousness of, and affinity to, a specifically Burmese culture. Religous institutions closely allied to the state played a very important role here. The Sangha, the main institution of Theravada Buddhism, the dominant Burmese religion, oversaw a complex system of monasteries which spread the word and established common religous belief throughout Burmese territories. The Sangha was close to the throne, and as the power of the state grew, it became increasingly subject to state authority. It became a very powerful tool of state control, providing a pervasive ideological justification for state power. As the main agency of education, the Sangha was instrumental in spreading not only common moral assumptions and beliefs, but also the Burmese language. Burmese quickly became the lingua franca of the empire.[8] Literacy also became widespread, reaching an astonishing 50 per cent of the male population by the early nineteenth century.[9]

Thus Burma was a hierarchical society, in which a ruling elite of state bureaucrats and soldiers, created by the patronage of state power, prospered at the expense of traditional, local centres of authority. The prominent role of the military and the continual need for land and revenues to reward the swelling ranks of the civil and military elite, drove the regime towards continual territorial expansion. The central institutions of the state concentrated power into very few hands; ultimately into those of the monarch. But there were opportunities for the elite to influence developments through those state institutions in which they were strongly represented, namely the Hluttaw (State council) and the Byedaik (Palace secretariat). Religion provided a unifying ideology and moral justification for expansion. Burmese state formation and expansion accelerated during the eighteenth century, as the growth of trade and the commercial economy strengthened the central state. By the early nineteenth century, it was pushing the frontiers of the Burmese empire north westwards towards the British Indian empire.

One historian has described the second Anglo-Burmese war in 1851 as a "collision of empires", but this title is a better description of the origins of the first conflict.[10] In the decades following the Burmese conquest of Arakan in 1784, relations with the British became tense. Arakanese resistance leaders sought refuge in Bengal, and launched periodic raids from there into Burmese held Arakan. The most notorious was the infamous "Kingbering" (Chin Byan), whose activities prompted Burmese demands that the British authorities forcibly surrender all Arakanese refugees residing in British territory.[11] The Burmese became suspicious when the British refused to check the activities of the Arakanese rebels, or tolerate Burmese incursions into British territory to punish them.[12] Tensions were heightened by further Burmese expansion on the frontier with the British. In 1812, Manipur was conquered, and between 1817 and 1822, Assam fell to the Burmese. The problems of Arakan for the Burmese were repeated, as local leaders from both Manipur and Assam fled into British territory, from where they undertook retaliatory raids into territory recently conquered by the Burmese. By the end of 1822, relations between the Burmese and the British were icy, not least because of the situation in Cachar, where the reigning monarch, Govind Chandra, had been driven out by three contenders for his throne from Manipur. The British were concerned that the Burmese, who had long claimed suzerainty over Cachar, would use the dispute to invade and conquer that state.

What were the factors which shaped British attitudes towards Burmese expansion? By the early nineteenth century, the British East India Company had undertaken over half a century of territorial expansion in India. There had been almost continual warfare with the regional polities which emerged from the disintegration of the Mughal empire, wars which had been paid for by the acquisition of new sources of revenue.[13] "Military fiscalism" in India, or the pursuit and acquisition of territory for revenue to fund military power, was the result of several complex factors, particularly a strong sense of British nationalism with militaristic overtones. Such was the legacy of conflict with continental rivals and domestic opponents of British unification.[14] Also, the Company's need to be constantly ready for war in India, necessitated the maintenance of a large Indian army, led by British officers. The officers in the East India Company's army constituted the largest body of Europeans in India.[15] The continual fear of war meant that senior East India Company administrators had to be closely acquainted with military needs and perspectives, and tended to accord them the highest priority. One historian argues that the hierarchical structure of the East India Company's civil bureaucracy in India, closely resembled that of the organisation's military wing, and was imbued with a culture of authoritarianism, militarism and aggression.[16]

A succession of senior administrators in India were keenly influenced by military priorities, including John Malcolm, Thomas Munro, Mountstuart Elphinstone, John Adam, and most prominently, the Marquess of Hastings, Governor General from 1814 to 1822. Also, many officers in the service of the East India Company's army, were motivated by personal profit rather than loyalty to Company, King and country. Battles raged between the Court of Directors in London, and the Indian administration in Calcutta, over the question of officers' allowances and perquisites; specifically Batta (field pay). Between 1790 and the late 1820s, successive attempts were made by London to reduce the levels of Batta payable to the officers of the Company's regiments in Bengal, with little or no success. Even Governor General Cornwallis, the architect of the administrative reforms of the 1780s and 1790s, was stopped in his tracks on this issue by the threat of mutiny in 1796.[17] After 1814, the Bengal army found a powerful and zealous ally in Governor General Hastings, who flatly refused to implement instructions from London in 1817 and the early 1820s to reduce Batta payments.[18] Initially Hastings had been able to use the outbreak of wars with the Nepalese and the Mahrattas in 1817 as an excuse for not following the instructions, but when hostilities ceased and London's instructions were repeated, Hastings asserted that the question of military pay was one which only the Indian administration itself was fit to resolve. This act of open defiance and insubordination was instrumental in prompting London's removal of Hastings in 1823, and his replacement by the more compliant and less experienced Lord Amherst. Amherst was duly instructed to carry out the Court's orders to reduce expenditure on Batta, and was also warned against continuing Hastings' expensive policies of imperial expansion. Such was the context of political relations between London and Calcutta when the question of Burmese expansionism became prominent in the early 1820s. It was not lost upon senior military officers and their many sympathisers within the Company's Indian bureaucracy, that a new war would stop or delay the reforms, because of the need to maintain military morale.

On the eve of Amherst's arrival in August 1823, senior military figures in India argued that tensions on the eastern frontier necessitated an increase in the numbers of troops and European officers. J. Nicol, Adjutant-General of the army, pressed the acting Governor General John Adam for an increase in the size of the army, and he emphasised particularly the shortage of European officers.[19] Senior Company administrators responded sympathetically.[20] After Amherst's installation, these concerns were continually repeated to the new Governor General, not least by Sir Edward Paget, Commander in Chief of the armed forces.[21] Within days of Amherst's arrival, Paget directed Amherst to Adam for advice on the dire situation in the army.[22] The deepening crisis on the eastern frontier also persuaded Amherst to abandon reform of Batta.[23]

Whilst it would be simplistic to attribute the tough British response to Burmese expansion solely to the internal politics of the Bengal administration and the East India Company over the issue of army pay, there is no doubt that those resisting the policy of Batta reform found it politic to stimulate fear of Burmese aggression. The inexperience of the new Governor General, and his dependence upon senior Company officials who opposed military reform at a time when conflict with the Burmese seemed imminent, also ensured that a belligerent line would be taken by Calcutta in response to even minor Burmese provocations. The Bengal administration was also determined not to lose face in dealings with the Burmese, lest this encourage other "native" powers to take advantage of British "weakness".[24] In addition, there were elements in the Bengal administration which had long harboured aggressive intentions towards the rapidly growing Burmese empire in the east. One contemporary with experience as a soldier on the Arakanese frontier was Captain William White. His account of the origins of the first Ango-Burmese war, was deeply critical of the aggressive role played by some British officials in Bengal in the years before the conflict.[25] It seems that the British policy of harbouring rebels against Burmese rule from Arakan and Assam in the early 1820s, may have been calculated to undermine Burmese authority in the border states, in preparation for a more aggressive policy when time and circumstances were more convenient.[26] Even Amherst, for all his protests of pacific intent on the part of the British, argued that war with Burma would have come earlier had it not been for conflicts elsewhere.[27]

The immediate causes of the first Anglo-Burmese war were events on the Arakan and Assam borders during 1823. In Arakan there was disagreement about which side had rightful possession of the island of Shapuri in the River Naaf, the frontier between British and Burmese territory. The Burmese had long claimed jurisdiction over the whole river, including the right to collect customs duties, but this was disputed by the local British official, E. Lee Warner, Magistrate of Chittagong. An incident early in the year in which Burmese troops attacked a small band of local traders travelling on the river, resulted in the death of one of the traders and a heated exchange of letters between Warner and his Burmese counterpart.[28] In May 1823, the Bengal administration sanctioned the occupation of Shapuri by a small detachment of troops. The ensuing diplomatic row was in full swing when Amherst took over in August. Then on 24 September, Burmese forces attacked and overran the island, killing three sepoys and driving the rest away. This was an intolerable humiliation in Amherst's eyes. A policy of severe retaliation was urged upon him by the officials in his administration. Personal experience made Amherst receptive to these calls. Amherst's earlier career, particularly his experience as a British envoy to imperial China, had impressed upon him the importance of taking a firm stand when dealing in "oriental diplomacy".[29]

Although initially keen to engage in a limited response to Burmese aggression, Amherst received information from British sources at the frontier and in Arakan, some of it gross exaggeration, which suggested that a serious Burmese challenge to the British might be afoot. Warner, for example, wildly estimated that a force of 15,000 Burmese was being amassed across the border in Arakan.[30] It was also reported that the Burmese king, Bagyidaw, had given full backing to the assault on Shapuri.[31] In late November, British sepoys were sent to recapture Shapuri, only to discover on landing that the island had been abandoned. In the latter months of 1823, Amherst was compelled to make hurried plans for the possibility of a full scale war with the Burmese, including reinforcement of the north eastern frontier, together with contingency plans for a seaborne assault on Rangoon, should widescale hostilities commence. Then, almost at the end of the year, a Burmese assault on Cachar from Manipur and Assam, set in train the final descent into war. In January 1824, British troops were sent into Cachar to resist the Burmese advance. Fighting soon began, and when in February, two British officers were seized by Burmese forces while attacking and retaking Shapuri, the die was cast. Lord Amherst formally declared war on 5 March 1824.

While the British had quickly shifted from a position of cautious defence to belligerent confrontation, the Burmese misread British intentions. The Burmese failed to understand British anxieties over Burmese actions on the north east frontier, since they regarded their claims to Assam, Manipur and Cachar as uncontroversial, easily justifiable, and in no way directed against the British.[32] Similarly, they believed their claims to Shapuri to be based upon unchallengeable precedent and legal right. They suspected that the British had been deliberately misled by the various rebels and dissident elements in exile in British territory, and were motivated either by some misplaced sense of justice or a desire to make mischief, rather than concern about defensive security. In this the Burmese underestimated the extent of British alarm and suspicion at the gradual Burmese expansion during the previous few decades. The fierce diplomatic threats which were issued by the Governor of Arakan, in response to British resistance on the Shapuri question, were mere bluff, unsupported by real aggressive purpose.[33] The Burmese believed that a mere display of strength would suffice, because they did not appreciate the deadly seriousness of British intent. As a result, the Burmese were taken aback by the ferocity of the British response.

The war continued for almost two years, and the scale of casualties and financial costs shocked both sides. Hostilities began auspiciously enough for the British, who launched an offensive in Cachar in March, followed by a seaborne invasion of Lower Burma in May 1824, led by Sir Archibald Campbell. About a hundred ships and over 10,000 British and Indian troops were involved in the invasion, which took Rangoon very quickly on 11 May.[34] The invasion ensured that most of the conflict would be fought on Burmese soil rather than on the eastern frontier where the British were more vulnerable. Burmese forces on the Arakan frontier had defeated a British force of 1,000 men at Ramu in May, and the British invasion of Lower Burma was welcome relief for the British in Chittagong. But British optimism following the success of the invasion was short lived.[35] Burmese tactics were to retreat, harry and avoid the kind of set piece confrontation the British were used to in Europe and India. Rangoon had been left to the British as a deserted town, since most of the inhabitants had fled on hearing of the British invasion. From here it was very heavy going for the British. It took Campbell's forces nearly two months to secure control of the river immediately above Rangoon, before the folly of the timing of the British assault was fully exposed. The British had invaded during the rainy season, and quickly discovered the extreme difficulties of moving, not to say fighting, in a country where roads were few and river transport depended upon stable climatic conditions. Disease took a terrible toll on the British forces, who were continually harried by Burmese guerilla raids. Malaria, dysentery and leeches had a devastating impact upon the morale and fighting capacity of Campbell's men. The Burmese position was strengthened by 60,000 reinforcements brought south from Arakan under their charismatic general, Maha Bandula. For most of 1824, the two sides were locked in stalemate near Kemmendine, on the river north of Rangoon. The British were unable to advance because of sickness, Bandula's superior forces, and the weather. When the monsoon ended, the British had lost the initiative, and in December Bandula led a series of counter attacks. But after some initial successes, Bandula's forces were defeated.[36] Thereafter, the Burmese were in almost constant retreat, and British success was reinforced by victories in Arakan and Assam in the latter months of 1824.[37] Bandula's forces were eventually defeated at Danubyu on the Irrawaddy in March 1825, during which Bandula himself was killed. Thereafter, Campbell's forces moved on to Prome, but the onset of the rainy season, once again halted the British advance, and stalemate prevailed once more. This time however, Burmese efforts to regroup and put an effective army into the field were unsuccessful. When fighting resumed in January 1826, the British advance began again, this time with little resistance. The Burmese were forced to sue for peace, and there followed a month of fevered negotiation before the Treaty of Yandabo was eventually signed on 26 February 1826. British victory, against the numerically superior Burmese and appalling conditions was a product of superior weaponry, organisation and discipline. But the financial and human costs made it seem a rather pyrrhic victory.

The British position in the negotiations was strongly influenced by the heavy cost in lives and money which the war had entailed. Some 40,000 British and Indian troops had been involved, of whom 15,000 had been killed by fighting and disease. The cost to Indian finances had been almost ruinous, amounting to approximately £13 million.[38] The cost of the war contributed to a severe economic crisis in India, which by 1833 had bankrupted the Bengal agency houses and cost the East India Company its remaining privileges, including the monopoly of trade to China.[39] In the immediate aftermath of the war, there were loud voices on the British side for the most severe retribution against the Burmese. Thomas Munro, Governor of Madras, argued that the British would be best served by the dismemberment of the Burmese state, either through annexation of territory, or the granting of independence to states and territories which had been previously absorbed into the Burmese empire.[40] That an extreme version of this hawkish aggression was not allowed to prevail was due to a newly found resistance on the part of Amherst to the expansionist tendencies within the Bengal administration, discovered at last after over two years of succumbing to militaristic advisers and officials.[41] Amherst was conscious of his spectacular failure to cut expenditure and curb expansion, the two main objectives set for him by the Court of Directors. There had been moves for his recall in disgrace in 1825, which had only been defeated by the efforts of Amherst's friend, George Canning, and the Duke of Wellington.[42] Amherst could no longer afford to be seen to be in thrall to the hawks within his administration and the army. Standing firm against the more extreme demands for dismemberment and annexation was a way of rescuing his reputation. London saw him as incompetent, profligate and the feeble prisoner of warlike elements. Amherst also feared that disintegration of the Burmese empire might strengthen China or Siam, who would profit from the elimination of Burmese power. These powers might then be tempted into imperialist adventures of their own, creating new threats to the stability of the region. What was required was the maintenance of a delicate balance of power, even when punishing the Burmese for their misdeeds.[43] Thus Amherst resisted demands for the removal of Lower Burma (Pegu) from the Burmese empire by annexation or "liberation".

In spite of this element of restraint, the terms of the treaty were severe. The territories of Arakan, Tenasserim and Assam were all ceded to the British. But the Burmese nurtured hopes that their lost territories might be returned when relations improved, a misconception which contributed greatly to the subsequent difficulties between the two powers. An indemnity of Rs 10 million was set, and Rangoon was to remain in British hands until at least a quarter of this sum was paid. There was to be a permanent British Resident at the Burmese capital, with access to the Burmese court. His main task was to defuse tensions, and the post was taken first by John Crawfurd, the eminent oriental scholar and administrator. His first job was to negotiate a commercial treaty between the two powers, a task which was completed with great difficulty by November 1826. It was a vague document, which left intact virtually all of the restrictions imposed on trade by the Burmese. The Burmese continued to enforce state monopolies and high tariffs, and ultimately the treaty delivered few meaningful concessions to British traders.[44]

For the Burmese, the treaty was a disastrous humiliation. The loss of Tenasserim, Arakan and Assam was never really accepted, and strenuous, but unsuccessful efforts were made to persuade the British to return them. There was deep resentment at the foisting upon the Burmese capital of an uninvited British Resident, an encumbrance which was a daily reminder of the humiliation of defeat. It was more than either Bagyidaw, or his successor, Tharrawaddy, could bear. From the outset, the succession of British Residents, including Crawfurd, Burney, Benson and McLeod, all suffered slights and indignities from the Burmese court.[45] But the defeat posed more serious problems for the Burmese than just loss of face. The Burmese state had previously been a dynamic entity in which a growing elite had built its wealth and power upon territorial expansion and military conquest. An expanding empire yielded growing revenues as new lands became subject to taxation, facilitating the growth and enrichment of the military and civil elites. Defeat and loss of territory brought this cycle of expansion and state formation to a halt. The loss of Arakan, Tenasserim and Assam represented a loss of lands and revenues which could be dispersed by the crown to key interests in the military and civil elites. In future, rewards for these would have to be extracted from the remaining territories, and from trade, placing greater burdens on the peasantry and mercantile classes. Certainly the decades which followed the defeat of 1826 were characterised by greater tension and conflict within the Burmese elite, particularly at times of royal succession, and it is likely that a contributory factor was dissatisfaction within elite groups around the king. Certainly at least one historian has shown that such conflicts later in the century were closely related to deepening economic difficulties and an erosion of the state's revenue base.[46] British victory in 1826 and the harsh peace terms represented a turning point in the process of Bumese state formation from which the kingdom never really recovered.

Most accounts of the Anglo-Burmese war of 1824-26 have tended to blame Burmese expansionism and belligerence for the conflict. One account contrasts the East India Company's "patient and forbearing" attitude with the "confrontation policy" of the Burmese.[47] Another compliments but chides the British for their "very civilised" policy of negotiation in the face of aggression from the "warlike" Burmese.[48] But it is clear that British responsibility for the conflict has been underestimated. The militaristic nature of the administration was decisive in generating a ferocious British response. The belligerence which characterised British attitudes prevented any really concerted attempt to resolve by diplomacy the differences over Cachar and Shapuri. This is not to deny the expansionist nature of the Burmese regime, which created the circumstances of tension between the two powers, but the Burmese had little appetite for war with such a powerful neighbour as the British.[49] The Burmese were reacting to what they saw as provocation from the British, and there was a complete breakdown of understanding and communication between the two sides. British motives for war and expansion were obscure. Economic and commercial considerations played little part in promoting expansion, although once the war was won, the British were eager to maximise any economic benefits which might accrue to them - hence the provision for a commercial treaty with the Burmese in the treaty of Yandabo. The first Burmese war and the subsequent British annexations are best understood within the wider context of British expansion in India, because the preoccupations and fears shaping British actions were largely the same as those which prevailed there. Concern about frontier security, the primacy of military priorities, an authoritarian culture of government and contempt for local polities, were the principal factors shaping the British response to Burmese expansion. In this respect, the first Burmese war was yet another example of the sub-imperialism of British rule in India. Of course it was only the first phase in a process which would eventually destroy the Burmese state and absorb it into the British empire. It shall be seen that in the later phases, additional factors arose to push the British forward.

**

British diplomatic relations with the Burmese never recovered from the bitterness and humiliation felt by the Burmese as a result of the first war. This was epitomised by the disastrous relations between the British Residents and the two Burmese kings, Bagyidaw and his successor Tharrawaddy. The vague and unsatisfactory commercial treaty signed in the aftermath of Yandabo caused rather than diminished conflict. When Henry Burney became Resident in 1830, he tried to clarify interpretation of the treaty, but with little success.[50] When Bagyidaw was deposed by his brother Tharrawaddy in 1837, matters deteriorated further. So obstructive was the new king, in his refusal to meet Burney or observe diplomatic etiquette, that Burney took it upon himself to withdraw the Residency, thereby incurring the wrath of Lord Auckland, the Governor General.[51] Burney's replacement, Captain Richard Benson, was unfortunate enough to take up his position just at the time when Tharrawaddy was relocating his capital from Ava to Amarapura, a move which necessitated new accommodation for the British Resident. The Burmese deliberately allocated an unhealthy piece of swampland to the hapless Benson, who within months was forced to withdraw from the city due to illness. His assistant, Captain William McLeod struggled gamely on until March 1839, when he too decided that his position was impossible and left the city. While these discourtesies infuriated the Bengal administration, military commitments elsewhere, and the generally poor state of the East India Company's finances, meant that military action was out of the question. In 1840, Auckland, with the support of London, formally withdrew the Residency.[52] It has been argued that the withdrawal was fatal for Anglo-Burmese relations, virtually ensuring that when tensions intensified in the early 1850s, war would be the outcome.[53] Mutual suspicions and misunderstandings were intensified by the closure of this sole if imperfect channel of regular diplomatic contact. Various factors contributed to the failure of the Residency arrangements. Residual Burmese bitterness was intensified by political struggles within the ruling elite, especially during the successions of Tharrawaddy and Pagan Min in 1837 and 1845 respectively. Taking a strong line against the detested British was a way of securing support within the elite, and of displaying strength and resolution. Also, it was becoming clear by the late 1830s that the British had no intention of returning Arakan or Tenasserim, much to the fury of the Burmese.

In the 1830s Burma began to acquire a new economic significance for the British. Arakan began to export rice to India. The British Indian administration also became interested in developing an overland route into Yunnan, the south eastern province of China. Burney approached the Burmese authorities about this in the 1830s, but the hostile political climate in Burma and in China prevented progress.[54] The most important commercial development was forestry. The rich teak forests of Lower Burma and Tenasserim attracted numerous British and Asian entrepeneurs to the port of Moulmein in British held Tenasserim, and Rangoon in Lower Burma. Timber provided the raw material for the shipbuilding industry in Moulmein and Calcutta. By 1852, the Moulmein shipyards had built over a hundred ships with a tonnage of 30,000.[55] With the teak men came other merchants, engaged in a multiplicity of trading activities. By the 1840s there were substantial British commercial communities in both Moulmein and Rangoon. Friction between these traders and the Burmese authorities grew from the early 1840s. The Burmese were worried by the voracious overfelling of trees by the British merchants. During the 1840s poor husbandry, short term leases which discouraged planning, and a laissez faire commercial environment resulted in the near exhaustion of the Tenasserim forests, forcing the teak entrepeneurs up country, into Burmese territory.[56] Disagreements with the Burmese followed, especially along the Salween river. The river marked the border between British Tenasserim and Burmese territory, and on occasion logs floated down the river washed up on the Burmese side. The Burmese, eager as ever to maximise state revenues from trade, charged high fees to permit salvage. From 1834, the British placed ropes and chains at strategic points on the river to prevent logs drifting to the Burmese shore, and in 1842 Burmese officials cut these, triggering a major row between the local officials of both sides which was never properly settled.[57] The Burmese had few objections in principle to British merchants engaging in controlled forestry and trade on Burmese territory, provided that full trade duties were paid to the exchequer. The problem was that some British merchants evaded taxes by smuggling teak out of Burma. By the end of the 1840s, both the Burmese government and the Myowuns of Lower Burma had lost patience with this blatant disregard for Burmese law. Burmese officials became heavy handed in their dealings with those British and Asian merchants suspected of misdemeanour. In addition, there was a rash of criminal attacks upon British property in the late 1840s, by dacoits apparently based in Burmese territory. In March 1851, anger erupted in the European mercantile community at the robbery of a local muslim merchant, which led to public accusations that the Burmese authorities were deliberately encouraging and harbouring the culprits.[58] By the late 1840s, these same mercantile interests were pressing the British Commissioner of Tenasserim, and the British administration in Calcutta, to protect their interests.

But in the 1840s the Calcutta authorities were not prepared to go to war in defence of a few British merchants on the imperial frontier.[59] In addition successive Commissioners of Tenasserim, including Major G. Broadfoot and H. M. Durand, were actually quite sympathetic to Burmese attempts to prevent smuggling and deforestation, and tended to see their role as preventing the excesses of British merchants rather than defending them against the Burmese.[60] Why did the British shed this indifference in 1851 to adopt a more aggressive stance, which would lead to war?

The events leading to war were complex. It was in Rangoon that the initial problems arose. Throughout the 1840s British and European merchants had complained about Burmese taxes on trade and their intrusive methods of policing them. In December 1850, the city was all but destroyed by fire, and to meet the costs of reconstruction, the Myowun introduced a special "tide tax" on the use of the shoreline to repair boats and ships.[61] There was an outpouring of rage by the European merchants to both the Bengal administration and the Calcutta press, again with little response. Then in the summer of 1851, there were two Burmese legal cases, affecting British merchants, which became a cause celebre. The intensity of public opinion, in Calcutta, Moulmein and Rangoon was too great for the Bengal administration to ignore. In June, a Captain Robert Sheppard was accused by the Burmese authorities in Rangoon of throwing his pilot overboard, and was fined Rs325. Sheppard claimed that he had incurred losses of Rs1,000 as a result of this action and took his complaint to the Bengal administration. In August, a Captain Lewis of the ship Champion was charged by the Burmese with the murder of one of his crew. Lewis was imprisoned and subsequently fined Rs200. Like Sheppard, Lewis took his complaint to the Indian government. But this time, the Governor General, Lord Dalhousie decided to act, on the grounds that the harsh Burmese treatment of these merchants contravened the spirit if not the letter of the treaty of Yandabo. In mid October 1851, a Royal Navy officer, Commodore Robert Lambert, was despatched to Rangoon with his squadron to seek redress for the "wronged" British merchants from the Myowun. Lambert had been a career officer since 1809. He was familiar with the east, and was in Calcutta in October 1851 en route from Sumatra to the Persian gulf. Nevertheless, for a Royal Naval officer to be sent on a mission normally regarded as East India Company business was unusual, and begs the question why a Company official was not given the assignment. Lambert's instructions were to investigate the matter, and if necessary to make a measured remonstrance to the Rangoon Myowun. He was specifically instructed not to provoke military conflict. Lambert arrived in Rangoon on 26 November 1851, and fell almost immediately under the sway of the European merchants, who persuaded him of the Myowun's vindictiveness. Lambert and his officers decided to teach the Burmese a lesson.[62] A letter from the Bengal administration to the Myowun was delivered, which enclosed additional letters for transmission to the Burmese king. One of these demanded the removal of the Myowun, and requested a response within 35 days. Though Lambert had been instructed to avoid war, the Bengal Council were prepared to allow a blockade of Rangoon, and were also keen to see the permanent establishment of a British Resident at Rangoon. Lambert remained at Rangoon awaiting a reply from the Burmese king. It came on 1 January 1852, and it promised to meet all of the British demands. A new Myowun was appointed, with instructions to negotiate with Lambert, and he arrived in the city on 2 January.

However within a few days relations between Lambert and the new Myowun had soured irretrievably. The disgruntled European merchants circulated rumours that the new Myowun was determined to prevent communications between Lambert's squadron and the European mercantile community. Lambert was also irked at the absence of formal notification of the new Myowun's arrival, which he regarded as a discourtesy. More seriously, when several of Lambert's officers, together with an American missionary, went to see the new Myowun on 6 January, there was an incident in which it was claimed that a British officer was threatened at knifepoint. They were forced to flee without seeing the Myowun. Apparently, the Burmese had been deeply insulted by the manner of the officers, especially their arrival on horseback. The Burmese saw this as a flagrant disregard of diplomatic etiquette. It may even have been deliberately intended by Lambert's men.[63] Relations deteriorated rapidly. Lambert set up a blockade of Rangoon on the following day, offering asylum to Europeans in the city. On the same day a Burmese vessel was seized. Three days later the British squadron was fired on by a coastal battery. It was rapidly destroyed by return fire. The war had effectively begun.

According to his correspondence with Lord Broughton, the President of the Board of Control, Dalhousie was furious. He roundly condemned Lambert's "precipitate act" as "very flamable", and made his famous remark about Naval commodores being "too combustible for negotiations".[64] Lambert himself had returned to Calcutta on 17 January, where due criticism of his conduct was made. Lambert argued that anything less than the strong line he had taken would have invited derision and further aggression from the Burmese. In spite of their condemnation of Lambert's actions, Dalhousie and the Bengal Council entrusted him to carry back an ultimatum to the Myowun, demanding a letter of apology for his treatment of the British officers who visited him on 6 January, compensation for Sheppard and Lewis, and the acceptance of a British Resident at Rangoon. When Lambert approached Rangoon on 31 January, his squadron was fired upon. In response the offending coastal battery was destroyed. The Myowun was prepared to compensate Sheppard and Lewis, but refused the other demands. In reply Dalhousie declared war, demanding complete surrender by the

Burmese authorities on the matters in dispute, and massive compensation of Rs1 million to defray the British costs incurred in military preparation.

These demands were seen as outrageous by Pagan, the Burmese king. Indeed the response of the royal court was one of shock and incomprehension. In their eyes they had acted more than reasonably in replacing the Myowun of Rangoon on the British request, and their assessment of Lambert was not dissimilar to the British opinion of the two successive Rangoon Myowuns whose actions had enraged them so much. The Burmese tried to redirect their diplomatic efforts at the Commissioner of Tenasserim, Bogle, who they saw as much more trustworthy and reliable, but Bogle was forbidden by Dalhousie to respond to the Burmese entreaties. The British invasion fleet, which had been under preparation since the end of January, reached Rangoon on 2 April 1852. British military power was overwhelming. Rangoon and Martaban were in British hands within two weeks, and by the end of May, the town of Bassein was also taken. Initially it was hoped that this would force the Burmese to sue for peace, especially as the onset of the rainy season would provide an opportunity for negotiations.[65] Failing this, the commander of the British forces, Lt General Henry Godwin, was instructed to prepare for a renewal of the offensive in November. In late July, Dalhousie himself visited Burma, and, disappointed at the stubborn refusal of the Burmese to negotiate, decided that the whole of Lower Burma should be annexed. The aim was to punish the Burmese for their intransigence, and provide future security, since it ensured British control of the coastline and the lower stretch of the Irrawaddy. The British advance was resumed in the Autumn, and Prome was taken on 10 October. The British remained there, waiting for a response from the Burmese King. Pegu (Lower Burma) was formally annexed on 20 December 1852. Then events took an unexpected turn. In February 1853, King Pagan was overthrown and replaced by Mindon Min, Pagan's half brother. Mindon sent two Italian priests to the British at Myede to negotiate a peace treaty, releasing European prisoners at the same time as an act of good faith. Although the negotiations with the British were fruitless and no treaty was signed because of the Burmese refusal to accept the annexation of Lower Burma, hostilities were ended at a meeting in Prome in April 1853. It was the second humiliating defeat for the Burmese within a quarter of a century, and it had reduced Mindon's realm to a land locked kingdom, dependent upon British goodwill for access to overseas markets.

Why did the Sheppard and Lewis cases, and Lambert's disastrous mission to Rangoon result in war, while earlier protests from British merchants at Rangoon and Moulmein, and the humiliation of successive Residents at the Burmese capital, had not? Why did Dalhousie and the Bengal Council take such a resolute line, while their predecessors had been prepared to tolerate the most unpalatable humiliations at the hands of the Burmese? When news of the war reached Britain, there was ferocious criticism of the decision to go to war.[66] From this, certain interpretations of events became popular among anti imperialist liberals. Richard Cobden, the Manchester liberal who was deeply opposed to the war, put forward his version of the causes of the war in a controversial pamphlet.[67] Cobden blamed the militarism and aggression of Dalhousie's Indian administration. Interestingly, Cobden was scathing about Dalhousie's decision to send a Royal Navy officer to negotiate with the Rangoon Myowun, arguing that a civilian envoy should have been sent instead. Other contemporaries, notably Lord Ellenborough, a previous Governor General (1842-44) who had carefully avoided conflict with the Burmese, suggested that commercial interests and the press in India influenced Dalhousie, bringing to his attention the enormous wealth of Burma in teak and minerals.[68] However, the emergence of a clear, unified critique of the war was hampered by the remoteness of events, limited knowledge of local conditions, the distorting effects of political intrigue and allegiance, and not least by the deliberate ommission of important documents from the account of events published in the government "blue books".[69]

One view argues that the theory of the "turbulent frontier" is particularly appropriate, that it was events at the frontier of empire, in Burma itself, which were responsible for the war.[70] The eagerness of European merchants in Rangoon and Moulmein to open new vistas for enterprise in Burma, supported by missionaries no less committed in their desire to spread the faith, were the most important forces for expansion on the British side. They displayed consummate skill in winning over Commodore Lambert and his officers, within hours of his arrival, before the Burmese even had a chance to present their case. Lambert thus became "the tool of vested missionary and merchant interests".[71] The cultural gulf between the British and the Burmese exacerbated tensions, causing misunderstandings and offence on both sides. The grotesque confusion between Lambert's officers and the Burmese guards at the residence of the new Rangoon Myowun on 6 January 1852, was only one example in a long history of tragic misapprehension on both sides. The turbulent events in Rangoon between November 1851 and January 1852 convinced Indian administrators that only a resolute and belligerent stance would deter the Burmese, and other powers who would construe a more pacific policy as British weakness. In this, however, the Indian government were led entirely by Lambert and his officers, who were their principal source of intelligence about events and Burmese intentions. Divisions within the Indian administration between Dalhousie and the Bengal Council persuaded the Governor General of the need to demonstrate his qualities of resolution and strength by responding forcefully to Burmese injustice. Dalhousie's resolve was stiffened further when Lambert's account of alleged Burmese misdeeds reached him.[72] The possibility that Calcutta, or other Indian based commercial interests had an influence over the decision to take a firm line in Burma, is considered but largely discounted by this interpretation. It is alleged that the sole source of Ellenborough's accusations to this effect in the House of Lords was H.M. Durand, the former Commissioner of Tenasserim, who was motivated by resentment at past treatment by the Indian administration, and so of questionable reliability.[73]

Other studies have emphasised Dalhousie's character and attitudes, which inclined him towards a tough response to perceived Burmese misdemeanours.[74] Dalhousie tended to respond fiercely to actions by rival powers which undermined British prestige, lest they incite other challenges to British supremacy.[75] But these accounts concede that local mercantile interests and Lambert's failure to follow orders were ultimately the main cause of the Burmese war of 1852.[76] However, one recent account notes the contrast between the attitude of the Dalhousie administration to the Burmese, and that of its predecessors. While earlier Indian administrations had been prepared to tolerate the most grievous insults, including open disregard for the treaty of Yandabo over the question of a British Resident at the capital, Burmese legal indictments against two British merchants had been sufficient in 1851 to elicit the dispatch to Rangoon of a Royal Navy squadron. The protests of merchants at Rangoon and Moulmein, having been consciously ignored throughout the 1840s, were suddenly treated in late 1851 with the utmost seriousness.[77] A change in the circumstances of the Indian administration were responsible for this shift in policy. Whereas earlier administrations, such as that of Lord Auckland at the time of the ending of the British Residency at the Burmese capital, had been confronted with military and political difficulties elsewhere in India, Dalhousie found himself able at the end of 1851 to focus his energies and resources exclusively on Burmese affairs.[78] In this context, the imperialist instincts of the Governor General were given full rein. But the implication is that the impetus for war came as much from Calcutta as Rangoon.

The grounds for locating the initiative for war in Calcutta seem well founded. Dalhousie's sudden resolve against Burmese "injustice" in November 1851, and the decision to send a Royal Navy squadron instead of a Company officer or diplomat, are startling in light of earlier indifference to mercantile pleas for assistance. One explanation, proffered by Lord Ellenborough, that Indian based commercial interests used the Indian press to lobby successfully for war, is generally rejected by historians. However, an examination of the Calcutta press coverage of the Burmese crisis, and correspondence of Dalhousie not previously considered, suggests that Dalhousie was guided by these interests much more than has been assumed. On 3 November 1851, an early stage in the crisis, the Calcutta newspaper "The Englishman" argued that the appearance of "a man of war" in Rangoon would frighten the authorities there "out of their wits".[79] On 13 November, "The Friend of India" roundly condemned the Rangoon authorities' treatment of Sheppard and Lewis, and speculated that a war would be cheaper, easier and vastly more advantageous than the first conflict had been.[80] On 20 January, shortly after Lambert's expedition had set off, the same newspaper, called for the annexation of Pegu, should war break out.[81] On 1 January 1852, when Lambert was awaiting a response from the

Burmese king to the letters to him from Calcutta, "The Bengal Hurkaru" was pressing for the British seizure and annexation of Rangoon, citing the port's commercial value to the British.[82] Throughout the crisis, most of the Calcutta press supported an aggressive stance against the Burmese. Excerpts from letters to Moulmein newspapers from European merchants there, most calling for resolute action, were regularly included in coverage of the Burmese crisis.[83] A central theme was the commercial benefits which would accrue to the British in the wake of war and imperial expansion. On 11 December 1851 "The Friend of India" stressed the enormous value of the teak forests of Pegu and the benefits of acquiring "the magnificent port of Rangoon, evidently destined one day to become the emporium of a large commerce".[84] The press also played upon the possibility that British hesitancy in Burma might tempt other powers to intrude there, particularly the United States.[85] There can be little doubt that the press were reflecting commercial interests in Calcutta, who had an eye on the economic potential of Lower Burma.[86] The vast teak forests were coveted as raw material for the shipbuilding industry, and an additional consideration may have been the demand for wood likely to arise from railway construction in India, which was in its infancy in the early 1850s. Certainly teak was used extensively to make fishplates for the Indian railways later in the century.[87] The existence of commercial contacts between Calcutta firms and merchants in Rangoon, is also evident from the publication of a letter from a Rangoon merchant to an unnamed Calcutta firm late in 1851, which described in detail the damaging effect on trade of deepening political tensions.[88]

The existence of a bellicose press enthusiastic for imperial expansion in Burma is not, of course, evidence that it shaped the judgement of the Governor General and his administration. But there is clear evidence that Dalhousie was influenced by press opinion in India. In a letter dated 3 March 1852 to Sir James Weir Hogg, an MP and East India Company director, Dalhousie emphasised the strength of press and public opinion in India, which had borne down upon him in favour of military action in Burma:

> "No man living can be more deeply mortified and disgusted than I have been of the prospect of another Burmese war. If you will be so good as to read my minutes you will see that no man could have been more adverse to engage in it, or could have laboured harder to avoid it. If you will look to the press you will find that exertions to that end have brought on me reproaches as betraying British interests and lowering British authority. For once that press is unanimous and for once it represents correctly solid public opinion here."[89]

It is unsurprising that Dalhousie should claim to have done everything in his power to avoid war, while resisting demands from the press for a more aggressive line. Dalhousie was mindful of the political hostility likely to erupt in Britain in reaction to the costs of a further extension of empire. Neither did he wish to be depicted as the poodle of the Indian newspapers. Nonetheless, Dalhousie's pronouncements on the unanimity and representative character of press opinion are highly significant, and indicate strongly that Dalhousie felt compelled to take it seriously. Moreover, there is evidence that Dalhousie's own perspective and fears about Burma were led by the press. On 23 February 1852, Dalhousie wrote to the President of the Board of Control, Lord Broughton, alerting him to the danger of American ambitions in Burma.[90] He reported that two American frigates had been seen off the coast of Burma, and he enclosed an extract from a New York newspaper which suggested that "cousin Jonathan" was planning to extend his influence in that country. The source of Dalhousie's information appears to have been "The Friend of India" of the 19 February, which referred not only to the American presence but also to the extract from the New York newspaper mentioned by by Dalhousie.[91] Plainly Dalhousie was using information, argument and opinion presented first in the Indian press, to secure support from the British government for his actions in Burma. The considerable influence of the Indian press is clearly apparent here.

There were other reasons why Dalhousie needed to be mindful of press opinion. The Indian newspapers, particularly in Calcutta, had a long reputation for mischief making, and Dalhousie experienced this at first hand. There were serious differences between Dalhousie and some members of his council, particularly the President, Sir Frederick Currie, about the seniority and authority of their respective positions of Governor General and President of the Council.[92] Currie, with the support of a faction within the Council, claimed that in Dalhousie's absence, the Governor General's full powers were transferred automatically to the President. Since Dalhousie was frequently away from Calcutta, on diplomatic business and military tours of inspection, this would have resulted in a substantial and unwanted delegation of his powers. The Calcutta press soon got wind of these internal squabbles, and not only publicised them, but also criticised Dalhousie for his absences from Calcutta, especially when the crisis in Burma began to deepen.[93] One mysterious correspondent, under the pseudonym "Goliah", mocked Dalhousie for his general handling of the Burmese crisis, and urged the Governor General to curtail his absences from Calcutta.[94]

In this poisonous political climate, Dalhousie needed all the friends he could muster. He could not afford to disregard press opinion, which on the question of Burma was entirely hawkish. Durand was correct when he emphasised the role of Calcutta mercantile interests and their allies in the press. The newspapers truly appear to have been, in Durand's words, "unanimous for the annexation of Burmah".[95] It should also be remembered that by July 1852, Dalhousie was openly supporting a policy demanded by sections of the press right at the beginning of the crisis in 1851, namely the annexation of Pegu.

Durand harboured other suspicions about Dalhousie's initial handling of the crisis, particularly in sending a Royal Navy officer, together with his squadron, to deal with the initial negotiations with the Burmese authorities. Durand believed that Dalhousie was trying to create circumstances in which the relatively minor dispute over the Sheppard and Lewis cases could be blown up into a full scale confrontation. The trivial amounts of compensation demanded by the British were too insignificant to go to war over, but a confrontation involving a vessel of the crown would be an entirely different matter.[96] Dalhousie always maintained that Lambert's handling of the crisis caused him great regret.[97] There is no conclusive evidence that Lambert's appointment was part of a conspiracy to incite war. Yet the choice of appointment was strange, given that the extent of the Governor General's authority over a Naval officer was uncertain. The danger that a full Naval squadron would provoke the Burmese authorities must have been an aspect considered by Dalhousie. Hogg, in London, doubted the wisdom of employing Naval officers in matters of diplomatic sensitivity, because they were "very apt to be saucy without having shewn themselves equally competent".[98] There are at least grounds for suspicion about Dalhousie's motives in appointing Lambert.

The present study locates the main causes and motives behind the second Burmese war in Calcutta rather than at the "frontier" in Rangoon and Moulmein, though no doubt interests there exerted more influence as the crisis in Rangoon deepened. Dalhousie was certainly intent upon maintaining British prestige. Throughout the crisis, he was determined that there should be no loss of face, lest this incite other Indian states to challenge British authority. There is also much in the view that stiffening of British policy towards Burma in 1851 partly reflected the fact that the rest of the Indian empire was relatively quiescent, allowing the British to concentrate their forces. But there was also an economic motive for British belligerence. By the early 1850s there was considerable interest in the commercial potential of Burma, as a possible alternative route to the markets of China, but more particularly as source of raw materials. British merchants in Moulmein and Rangoon were undoubtedly instrumental, from an early stage, in alerting their contacts in Calcutta to the potential benefits of expanded trade and commercial activity in Burma. The rapid development of shipbuilding at Moulmein could not have been ignored in Calcutta. As this process accelerated during the 1830s and 1840s, the traditional regime of monopolies, trade restrictions and tariffs, so important for the fiscal stability of the Burmese state, appeared ever more onerous and tyrannical to British merchants in Calcutta and Burma. Finally, in 1851, the latest "outrages" committed by the Burmese coincided with a strategic opportunity for the Indian government to punish the Burmese for past offences. Commercial interests in Calcutta swung quickly into action, mobilising the press to persuade Dalhousie of the need for expansionist as well as military measures to deal with Burma. The fraught political climate within the Indian administration at the time meant that the Governor General could not disregard this pressure. The tough line adopted by Dalhousie throughout the crisis, and his eventual agreement to the annexation of Pegu, owed much to the insistence of Indian commercial opinion that such measures were necessary.

Ultimately, the second Burmese war is best understood as an episode of "sub imperialism" in which political and economic concerns on the periphery of empire precipitated a new phase of imperial expansion. The principal motivating forces were located in Calcutta rather than the "frontier" interests in Rangoon and Moulmein. The complaints and anxieties of these frontier interests undoubtedly helped to bring the crisis to a head, especially after Lambert's mission to Rangoon in November 1851, but it was essentially the decision in Bengal to adopt a resolute stance which ensured that the crisis would be resolved by war. In this process, the militaristic culture of the Indian administration contributed greatly to the decision to fight, just as it had done in 1824. This time, however, there were also powerful economic interests which lent their weight in favour of war. It was Calcutta based merchants who were the main advocates of expansion for economic reasons. In this the desire to exploit the huge teak forests of Burma for shipbuilding, the railways and other purposes, appears to have been the main incentive. Certainly the annual values of teak imports from Pegu rose consistently in the three years after the war, from Rs306209 in 1851/52 to Rs590220 in 1855/56.[99] In 1855, Dalhousie drew up long term plans for the development and management of the teak forests of Pegu for the benefit of British India.[100]

Just as the development of Asian networks of trade and commerce had shaped the British imperial presence in Malaysia, so the extension of British rule into Lower Burma can be seen as part of a wider process of British and Asian mercantile interests in the east developing regional trade links, and promoting the production of those commodities increasingly in demand in Asian markets. Older considerations of British prestige and security had been very important in precipitating war, but so also had Anglo-Indian commercial interests, and this economic concern with Burma was to become even more important in the decades following the war. The defeat of 1853 and the territorial losses which followed, were to have catastrophic consequences for the Burmese kingdom, which, exacerbated by further British economic expansion and political demands, would make the complete absorption of Burma into the British empire inevitable.

***

While Burma was subjected to the most extreme form of British imperial expansion in the period up to the mid 1850s, the experience of Siam, a close neighbour, was very different. There were no wars of conquest, and few examples of British merchants in Bangkok clamouring for a British invasion. Instead, Anglo-Siamese relations were peaceful and amicable, and had, by the end of the 1850s, been placed upon a stable footing by two treaties, named in British historical accounts after the British officers who negotiated them: the Burney treaty of 1826 and the Bowring treaty of 1855. The contrast between Burma and Siam is even more striking given that in the early nineteenth century, there had been much greater British commercial interest in Siam than in Burma. Siam was valued as a source of rice and a range of luxury produce, especially following the foundation of Singapore. The Burney treaty, which partly addressed the question of Anglo-Siamese relations in the states of the Malay peninsula, was also concerned with commercial relations, and reflected British eagerness to remove any barriers to British commerce. By the mid nineteenth century, British trade with Siam had grown so much that the British merchants and political authorities in the Straits Settlements were determined to further liberalise Siamese trade regulations, in an effort to unlock what they saw as the enormous potential of that state.

The Siamese regime with whom the British had to deal in the nineteenth century, had recently emerged from a period of extreme instability which had destroyed the previous Siamese kingdom based upon the ancient city of Ayudhaya. The immediate cause of the crisis was the successful invasion of Ayudhaya (as Siam was called under the old regime) by the Burmese in the 1760s, which culminated in the complete destruction of the capital in 1767 and the end of the old ruling dynasty. The state disintegrated into regional fiefdoms, governed by local ruling elites. The reconstruction of the state began under Taksin, a former Governor of Tak in north western Siam. In 1782 he was deposed by Chaophraya Chakri, a leading general from an old noble family which had enjoyed prominence under the Ayudhaya regime.[101] The Chakri dynasty was to rule Siam throughout the nineteenth century. Siamese society continued to display the same characteristics which had been evident under Ayudhaya. There were similarities to Burmese society in socio-economic structure. Both countries were Buddhist, hierarchical, rural societies in which rice cultivation and trade were the principal economic activities. There were important differences. Burmese society was not as formally stratified as Siamese society. The Siamese people were rigidly categorised according to the Sakdina system. Under this, each person in society, from the lowliest beggar to the most highly placed minister was accorded a value according to the Sakdina scale, in terms of the number of "rai" to which they were entitled. Originally, a rai was a measure of the land allotted to an individual by the monarchy, approximating to a quarter of an acre, but by the nineteenth century this link between status and land allocation had largely disappeared, and the sakdina rating became an abstract measure of status.[102] The lowest in society might have a rai valuation as low as 5, while a senior minister in charge of a major department of state enjoyed a ranking of 10,000. With a high sakdina rating came power, responsibility and wealth. Generally, those with a ranking of 400 and above were deemed to be "Nai" (patrons), with power and responsibility over those who lived under their authority, and who enjoyed a sakdina rating less than 400. People with a sakdina rating of less than 400 were described as "phrai" (commoners), and were at the bottom of the social pyramid.

The nai, though higher up that pyramid, was answerable to his own superior as defined by the sakdina system, and the ultimate source of all power and authority was the king. The main function of the nai within the state system was to deliver, on demand, those phrai under his authority to provide labour service (corvee) on state lands, usually for work in agriculture or major public initiatives such as irrigation projects. In a relatively sparsely populated country, control over labour power was vital for the state. Within this intensely hierarchical society, royal pomp, ceremony and religion all played a part in ideological justification of the status quo.

All of the Chakri kings, eager to establish the religous legitimacy of their position on the throne, took the name Rama, and the ceremonial trappings of power created an impression of omnipotence. However, the power of this seemingly unchallengeable autocracy was circumscribed in several important ways. Firstly, like Burma, Siam expanded the territory under its control by conquest and the subordination of local rulers, particularly in the frontier regions. One example of this was the consolidation of Siamese power in the Malay peninsula in the early nineteenth century. There were also a series of conflicts in the east which resulted in Siamese territorial expansion. The kingdom resembled a loosely structured empire, in which the Siamese monarch and his administrative machine were heavily dependent upon local, provincial authorities to exercise authority on the centre's behalf. One writer has argued that this devolution of power was so widespread that it is a mistake to see mid nineteenth century Siam as a modern nation state or even a unified political entity.[103] Instead it was a series of autonomous townships, over which the capital, Bangkok exercised only tenuous authority.

The second limitation of central state power stemmed from the dependence of the state upon the nai as administrators of the system of corvee, and as collectors of taxation. Those nai who enjoyed high status were particularly well placed to exploit their positions for personal profit and power. They enjoyed both extensive administrative powers within the state machine, and authority over the extensive lands allocated to them by the crown.[104] These powerful nobles were able to use their enormous powers of patronage to protect those below them from the full demands of the state for corvee or taxes, in exchange for loyalty and payment. Successive Siamese monarchs were conscious of the need to accommodate and placate these powerful noble families. It had always been accepted that not only the nobility, but also the whole official class, were entitled to use their official positions to feather their own nests, taking a share of the revenues they collected. However, in the early nineteenth century Siamese kings came to fear and respect certain powerful families, who had enjoyed high station and influence since the days of Ayudhaya. For example, Rama II (1809-1824) sought connections by marriage with the more powerful noble families to strengthen his position.[105] One result was that by the mid nineteenth century, the major ministries of state were in the hands of these powerful noble families, who used them as instruments to further their own ambition. The ministries themselves were of distant origin, traceable back to the Ayudhaya regime. Over time, these ministries had acquired responsibilities for regional government in addition to their functions within the state administration. There was the Mahatthai (Ministry of Civil Administration), technically responsible for overseeing the state machinery of government, but in practice mainly engaged in superintending the northern provinces of the Siamese empire. The Kalahom, or Ministry of Military Affairs, exercised authority over the southern provinces. The Phraklang, or Ministry of Finance, not only managed the state's financial affairs, it was also the trading agent of the crown, with responsibility for supervising overseas trade. In this capacity it had to deal with foreign traders and powers, a role which gave the department considerable leverage over foreign policy.[106] It also effectively controlled the main coastal ports. There were other departments, but these three were the most important and powerful, exercising extensive territorial as well as administrative authority. In practice they took overarching responsibilty for the collection of taxes and administration of corvee within their territories, supervising local provincial governors. They exercised huge power and patronage. The effect was to limit royal authority and enable the families who ran these ministries to build their own empires within the state machine. In the early nineteenth century, for example, the Phraklang, remained the almost exclusive preserve of the Bunnags, a particularly influential noble family.[107]

International trade also provided a third means by which the nobility could assert their authority at the expense of the crown. The importance of trade monopolies and revenues to the Siamese state has been recently identified by historians.[108] Trade revenues were much more important in the financing of state power under the Chakri dynasty than had been the case in Ayudhaya. Of particular importance was the export of rice, indigo, sugar, pepper, teak and tobacco.[109] Siam in the early nineteenth century was a dual economy, in which a traditional subsistence oriented agriculture was gradually being replaced by an export oriented sector producing for the world market. Siam was being drawn gradually into the global capitalist economic system, a development which has inspired descriptions of Siam in the early nineteenth century as a "peripheral capitalist economy".[110] Exports to China were of particular importance in the first half of the century. The growth of this export trade, while contributing significantly to royal revenues, via state monopolies over certain branches of trade, also enriched and strengthened the nobility, because they controlled the administration of the royal monopolies and the collection of trade revenues. They were therefore well placed to extract for themselves a substantial share of the income generated.[111] The nobility also promoted agricultural production for export, usually with the assistance of Chinese merchants and labour, and they thus benefitted directly from this profitable new sector.[112]

By the mid nineteenth century, this was a society still in the throes of state formation, in which the superficial impression of unassailable autocracy, disguised the reality of a fragile empire dominated by a politically powerful and wealthy nobility. International commerce was well developed, but subject to stringent state control and monopoly. As a consequence, while trade contributed significantly to the wealth and power of the emergent central state, it also strengthened the nobility at the expense of the crown. How did the rise of British power in south east Asia impinge upon this nation-state and its developing social structure?

The first serious diplomatic questions to dominate Anglo-Siamese relations arose from the British presence in the Malay peninsula following the establishment of Pinang in 1786. Growing Siamese power and suspicion of British intentions eventually prompted Siamese aggression against Kedah in 1821. There followed, in the early 1820s, a period of unease between Britain and Siam which was only resolved by the Burney treaty of 1826, which delineated the frontiers of Siamese and British spheres of influence in the Malay peninsula. Although the treaty was mainly concerned with political matters, it also set out regulations governing British trading expeditions to Siam. British commercial interest in Siam had been growing steadily since the beginning of the century, and following the foundation of Singapore in 1819, acquired a new prominence. Burney's visit to Bangkok was by no means the first mission to try to promote trade with Siam. In 1821/22, John Crawfurd had led a mission to Siam to discuss, inter alia, the possibility of improving commercial relations with that state, albeit with little success.[113] The Burney treaty, however, did deliver some limited concessions to British trade. Burney appears to have been successful where Crawfurd failed, largely because of changing geo-political circumstances. When Burney arrived in Bangkok at the end of 1825, the British were winning the first Anglo-Burmese war, and the Siamese were deeply impressed by the formidable military power of the British. Discretion dictated the prudence a diplomatic settlement with the British, which would normalise political and commercial relations. Before the treaty, British traders to Siam had been confronted by a baffling array of regulations, taxes and fees which governed Siamese commerce. The treaty rationalised these, replacing them with a single duty imposed upon British ships calling at Bangkok, determined by the size of the ship. A trader would have to pay 1,700 ticals per Siamese fathom of the ship's beam, if the ship was carrying cargo into port, and 1,500 ticals per fathom if it was unladen.[114] The export of rice and import of opium were forbidden. All trade had to be directed through the organs of the Siamese state, and trade was restricted to the port of Bangkok. British merchants were permitted residence in Bangkok, but only with the express permission of the Siamese government. British merchants were permitted to sell arms only to the Siamese state.

Though still laden with restrictions, British trade with Siam flourished in the wake of the treaty. By 1847/48, some 52,226 piculs of sugar worth $265,453, the most demanded Siamese commodity, were being exported to

Singapore.[115] Some 149 square rigged European vessels arrived at Singapore from Siam between 1829 and 1854.[116] However, the continuing high levels of duty on European vessels made it more economic for European merchants at Singapore to conduct their trade with Siam via the Siamese and Chinese junks which traded between Singapore and other ports of south east Asia. In 1835, some 64.3 per cent of the Siamese trade with Singapore was carried by junk, amounting to \$406,308 in value.[117] Relatively few British merchants established themselves at Bangkok. The leading British commercial firm to do so was Hunter, Hayes and Co., who engaged in the export and import trade through the Siamese state, and conducted agency business for other European traders with interests in the Siamese trade. Hunter had been a member of Burney's 1826 mission to Siam, and he took full advantage of his position, although the firm itself was heavily punished in 1842 for smuggling teak and sugar.[118] The general pattern was a steady growth in the British and European trade with Siam during the thirty years after the 1826 treaty, especially via Singapore. But it was insufficient to satisfy the expectations of British merchants in south east Asia.

Eventually this impatience led in the 1840s to a growing clamour in the Straits Settlements for a revision of the treaty. The 1830s and 1840s had been difficult decades for British commercial interests in the Straits, as a consequence of Dutch protectionism, economic crisis in India and the emergence of a rival port in Hong Kong after 1842. One result was a gradual reorientation of the trade of the Straits Settlements, particularly Singapore towards mainland south east Asia. In this context, the enormous trading potential of Siam for south east Asian British interests was seen as vital. But the Siamese seemed determined to reinforce their monopolistic rights over trade during the 1840s. The punishment of Hunter, Hayes and Co. was one manifestation of this, but even more significant was the restriction in 1840 of sales of sugar to foreign merchants only after the Siamese king's own vessels had been filled.[119] During the 1840s, Singapore merchants pressed for a new treaty with Siam which delivered to them the same liberalisation of trade achieved in China by the Treaty of Nanking of 1842. By 1849, the Singapore Chamber of Commerce was lobbying the British government for a new diplomatic initiative to secure a more favourable trade agreement.[120] Two years earlier, the Straits government had recommended the appointment of a permanent consul at Bangkok to promote trade with Singapore. In 1850 the British government were finally persuaded to seek a new commercial treaty with Siam. The main considerations which prompted this change of heart appear to have been similar to those which led to British acquiescence in the establishment of Brooke rule in Sarawak; namely a desire to promote the trade of Singapore at a time of some economic difficulty for that settlement. Concern with Singapore's commercial interests thus prompted an important change in policy.[121] To this end in 1850, Raja James Brooke of Sarawak was sent to Bangkok to negotiate a new commercial treaty, which would open Siam to British commerce. Before he left for Bangkok in early August 1850,

Brooke consulted with merchants in Singapore, and took with him a draft treaty to present to the Siamese. The document included such proposals as complete freedom for British subjects to reside anywhere in Siam, and the removal of all external duties on all items of commerce, except arms, teak and several other commodities.[122] All commodities except rice, sugar, salt and sapanwood were to be free of all internal trade duties. A permanent British consul was to be established. The mission was a complete failure. Rama III and his advisers rejected the proposals; a response which was expected by most of the merchant community of Singapore. They were resigned to wait for a new monarch to consider their pleas.[123] The negotiations were ill tempered, and privately Brooke urged Calcutta that a show of military force was necessary. But Calcutta ignored this headstrong advice. By October 1850, Brooke had conceded failure and left Bangkok. Prospects for the advancement of British commercial interests appeared bleak.

Yet less than five years later, a new British mission, led by Sir John Bowring, Governor of Hong Kong, successfully negotiated a new commercial treaty with the Siamese which was to transform Anglo-Siamese relations. Bowring negotiated with the full authority of the British Foreign Office behind him. That government department was keen that there should be no repeat of the diplomatic mismanagement which had dragged Britain into the recent war in Burma. Under the treaty, British and Asian vessels were placed on the same footing, removing at a stroke one of the most onerous disadvantages faced by British shipping. The duty based on ship size was abolished and replaced by a single duty of 3 per cent on goods actually landed, refundable if the goods were re-exported. Trade with all Siamese ports was opened, although British rights of residence were still restricted to Bangkok. Finally the bans on the export of rice and the import of opium were lifted, with the provisos that the Siamese government could restrict rice exports in the event of a domestic food shortage, and that opium would only be sold to approved opium farmers.[124] The confinement of arms and munitions sales to the Siamese government was continued. Virtually all of the state's trading monopolies were abolished.[125] Siam had been effectively opened for British trade, and in the years following the treaty there was a dramatic expansion of the volume and value of trade. In 1856/57 alone, some 145 British vessels arrived at Singapore from Siam.[126]

Why did Siamese opposition to a treaty disappear so rapidly? The elevation of Prince Mongkut to the throne in 1851 as Rama IV, was undoubtedly an important factor. Well educated and mindful of the fearsome power of the British, Mongkut was eager to establish friendly relations. The nobility shared this view. They had been shocked and anxious at the threatening demeanour displayed by Brooke in 1850. As in the 1820s, Siamese determination to resist had been severely weakened by witnessing the grim fate of neighbours who had tried to stand up to the British. The defeat of the Burmese in 1853, and the internal crisis which had ensued in that state, dissolved any inclination to thwart the British.

The opening of Siam by the treaty of 1855 has been depicted as the beginning of a new age of British informal empire in that state, opening it up to commercial expansion from Britain as well as south east Asia.[127] In the decades which followed, British as well as Asian manufactures and produce indeed found a lucrative market in Siam. However, it would be a mistake to see the opening of Siam as the work of British industrialists. The main interests which had clamoured for the opening of Siam had been based in south east Asia, mainly in Singapore. Although some British industrial and mercantile pressure groups, disappointed with the growth of trade to China in the wake of the treaty of Nanking, had expressed an interest in opening commercial opportunities elsewhere in Asia, there is no doubt that it was the British interests in Singapore which had played the leading role.[128] To some extent, the focus of Singapore interests on Siam was a logical outcome of the steady shift of the British settlement's trade towards mainland south east Asia. The rapidly expanding Chinese population of the Straits Settlements and the Malay peninsula needed to be fed, and the European merchants there needed new commodities for trade. Siam offered a steady supply of rice and other produce. In this respect, the Bowring treaty was another step in the development of an elaborate trading system within south east Asia, upon which British commercial interests depended. As Chinese entrepeneurship and labour advanced into the Malay peninsula, opening tin mines and pepper plantations, Siam provided a steady supply of food to assist this process. Of course in the long run, Siam was to develop into a supplier of primary and luxury produce for a wider market than just south east Asia, but the economic interests which promoted the expansion of trade with that state in 1855 were firmly entrenched within the region.

From the Siamese point of view, the Bowring treaty created quite serious short term problems. Many sources of revenue arising from trade regulations and monopolies had been swept away at a stroke. It was by no means clear how these lost revenues were to be replaced, and as shown, the state itself enjoyed only a tenuous control over much of its empire. Then there was the question of relations between the crown and the nobility. Both had been heavily dependent upon trade revenues for their wealth and power. How would they fare, and the relationship between them develop, now that this vital source of income had been lost? The looming crisis compelled Mongkut and his nobles to launch a programme of fiscal and economic reform, which was to have a profound influence on their relationship with the British.

NOTES

1. V. Lieberman, "Local Integration and Eurasian Analogies: Studying Southeast Asian History" Modern Asian Studies 27:3, (1993) 475-572, pp475-476.
2. A good brief summary of these developments is to be found in : D.R. SarDesai, South East Asia: Past and Present (London, Macmillan 1989) pp70-74.
3. See also: V. Lieberman, Burmese Administrative Cycles: Anarchy and Conquest, c1580-1760 (Princeton, Princeton University Press 1984), V. Lieberma, "Secular Trends in Burmese Economic History c.1350-1830" Modern Asian Studies 25:1, (1991) 1-31.
4. Thant Myint - U, The Crisis of the Burmese State and the Foundation of British Colonial Rule in Upper Burma 1853-1900 (Unpublished PhD thesis, Trinity College, Cambridge 1995) pp26-27.
5. Lieberman, "Secular Trends in Burmese Economic History" pp22-23.
6. Ibid.: p24.
7. Ibid.: pp8-9.
8. Ibid.: p21.
9. Lieberman, "Local Integration and Eurasian Analogies" p509.
10. O.B. Pollak, Empires in Collision: Anglo-Burmese Relations in the Mid-nineteenth Century (Greenwood, Westport 1979).
11. L. Kitzan, "Lord Amherst and the Declaration of War on Burma, 1824" Journal of Asian History 9:2, (1975) 101-127, p102.
12. Ibid. There were British missions to Burma in 1795 and 1802 (Symes), 1799 (Hill), and 1812 (Canning).
13. C. Bayly, Indian Society and the Making of the British Empire (Cambridge, Cambridge University Press 1988).
14. C. Bayly, Imperial Meridian p134.
15. D.M. Peers, "Between Mars and Mammon; the East India Company and Efforts to Reform its Army, 1796-1832" Historical Journal 33:2, (1990) 385-401, p388.
16. Ibid.: pp388-389.
17. Ibid.: p392.
18. Ibid.: pp393-394.
19. Despatch to the Governor General in Council from J. Nicol, 19 June 1823, (Fort William 11 July 1823) Bengal Secret and Political Consultations, P/BEN/SEC/318, IOR, London.
20. Ibid.: Fendall's minute, 11 July 1823.

21. For example, see Paget to Amherst, 2 October 1823, Amherst Papers, Eur Mss F/140, Vol 7, IOR, London.
22. Ibid.: Paget to Amherst 10 August 1823.
23. Peers, "Between Mars and Mammon" p395.
24. J. Adam to the Court of Directors, 20 July 1823, Home Misc 660, p1, IOR, London.
25. Cpt W. White, A Political History of the Extraordinary Events which led to the Burmese War (London, Hamilton 1827).
26. Ibid.: p123.
27. Amherst to George Canning, 25 March 1824, Harewood Mss 80, Canning Papers, West Yorkshire Archives, Sheepscar, Leeds.
28. Excellent accounts of these events are to be found in Kitzan, "Lord Amherst and the Declaration of War", and G.P. Ramachandra, "The Outbreak of the First Anglo-Burmese War" Journal of the Malaysian Branch of the Royal Asiatic Society 51, (1978) 69-99.
29. Kitzan, "Lord Amherst and the Declaration of War" pp108-111.
30. Ibid.: p112.
31. Ibid.: p115.
32. Ramachandra, "The Outbreak of the First Anglo-Burmese War" pp69-74.
33. Ibid.: p77.
34. G. Bruce, The Burma Wars 1824-1886 (London, Hart-Davis, MacGibbon 1973) pp28-29.
35. Ramachandra, "The Outbreak of the First Anglo-Burmese War" p91.
36. A.T.Q. Stewart, The Pagoda War: Lord Dufferin and the Fall of the Kingdom of Ava 1885-6 (London, Faber and Faber 1972) p37.
37. Bruce, The Burma Wars pp94-95.
38. Stewart, The Pagoda War p38.
39. Tripathi, Trade and Finance in the Bengal Presidency pp161-163.
40. L. Kitzan, "Lord Amherst and Pegu: The Annexation Issue 1824-26" Journal of Southeast Asian Studies 8, (1977) 176-194, p182.
41. Ibid.: pp193-194.
42. D. Peers, "The Duke of Wellington and British India during the Liverpool Administration 1819-27" Journal of Imperial and Commonwealth History 17, (1988) 1-25, pp9-12.
43. Kitzan, "Lord Amherst and Pegu" p182.
44. Bruce, The Burma Wars pp129-130.
45. The Successive residents were:
    John Crawfurd (1826 to 1830)
    Henry Burney 1830 to 1837)
    Richard Benson (1837 to 1838)
    William McLeod (1838 to 1839).
46. Thant Myint-U, The Crisis of the Burmese State pp144-145.
47. Pollak, Empires in Collision p15.
48. Kitzan, "Lord Amherst and the Declaration of War" p103.
49. Ramachandra, "The Outbreak of the First Anglo-Burmese War" p85.
50. SarDesai, British Trade and Expansion pp105-106.
51. Pollak, Empires in Collision p20.
52. Ibid.: 23-24.
53. A. Mukherjee, British Colonial Policy in Burma: An Aspect of Colonialism in South East Asia 1840-1885 (New Delhi, Abhinav Publications 1988) pp46-48.

54. SarDesai, British Trade and Expansion pp105-106.
55. R.L. Bryant, "Shifting the Cultivator: The Politics of Teak Regeneration in Colonial Burma" Modern Asian Studies 28:2, (1994) 225-250, p228.
56. Ibid.: p228.
57. Pollak, Empires in Collision pp45-46.
58. Ibid.: p51.
59. Mukherjee, British Colonial Policy in Burma p85.
60. Pollak, Empires in Collision pp47-50.
61. Ibid.; p56.
62. Ibid.; pp72-73.
63. Ibid.; pp76-77.
64. Dalhousie to John Hobhouse (Lord Broughton), 23 January 1852, Broughton Papers, Add Mss 36477, BL, London.
65. Bruce, The Burma Wars p140.
66. Pollak, Empires in Collision pp87-90.
67. R. Cobden, How Wars are Got up in India: The Origin of the Burmese War (London, W. and F.G. Cash 1853).
68. Pollak, Empires in Collision p89.
69. Ibid.: p90.
70. J.S. Galbraith, "The Turbulent Frontier as a Factor in British Expansion" Comparative Studies in Society and History 2, (1960) 150-168.
71. Pollak, Empires in Collision p82.
72. Ibid.: p68.
73. Ibid.; pp88-89.
74. C.H. Philips, "Dalhousie and the Burmese War of 1852" in C.D. Cowan and O.W. Wolters, Southeast Asian History and Historiography (Ithaca, Cornell University Press 1976) pp51-58.
75. Ibid.; p57.
76. Bayly, Indian Society and the Making of the British Empire p133.
77. Mukherjee, British Colonial Policy in Burma p91.
78. Ibid.; p93.
79. The Englishman and Military Chronicle, 3 November 1851, microfilm, SM49, IOR, London.
80. The Friend of India, 13 November 1851, microfilm, SM141, IOR, London.
81. Ibid. ; 20 November 1851.
82. The Bengal Hurkaru, 1 January 1852, microfilm, SM31, IOR, London.
83. The Englishman and Military Chronicle 3 February 1852.
84. The Friend of India, 11 December 1851.
85. Ibid.: 15 January 1852.
86. The Bengal Hurkaru, 5 February, 1852.
87. SarDesai, British Trade and Expansion p218.
88. The Englishman and Military Chronicle, 31 January 1852.
89. Dalhousie to Hogg, 26 March 1852, Eur Mss E/342/15, IOR, London.
90. Dalhousie to Lord Broughton, 23 February 1852, Broughton Papers, Add Mss 36477, BL, London.
91. The Friend of India, 19 February 1852.
92. Pollak, Empires in Collision p68.
93. The Bengal Hurkaru, 12 January 1852.
94. Ibid.: 23 January 1852.

95. Durand to Lord Ellenborough, 18 June 1852, Ellenborough Papers, PRO/30/12/21/6, London.
96. Ibid.: Durand to Ellenborough, 26 March 1852.
97. Philips, "Dalhousie and the Burmese War" p54.
98. Hogg to Dalhousie, 8 May 1852, Hogg Papers, Eur Mss E/342/2, IOR, London.
99. Bengal Commercial Reports 1851/52, P/174/63, and 1855/56, P/174/67, IOR, London.
100. R.L. Bryant, "Teak Regeneration in Colonial Burma" p230.
101. A concise account of these events may be found in: D.K. Wyatt, Thailand: A Short History (New Haven, Yale University Press 1984) pp139-145.
102. For a brief explanation of the Sakdina system see: B.J. Terwiel, A History of Modern Thailand (London, University of Queensland 1983) pp11-16.
103. C. Rajchagool, The Rise and Fall of the Thai Absolute Monarchy: Foundations of the Modern Thai State from Feudalism to Peripheral Capitalism (Bangkok, White Lotus 1995) p2.
104. Hong Lysa, Thailand in the Nineteenth Century: Evolution of the Economy and Society (Singapore, Institute of South East Asian Studies 1984) pp30-31.
105. Wyatt, Thailand pp161-162.
106. Rajchagool, The Rise and Fall pp4-5.
107. Ibid.: p6.
108. Hans-Dieter Evers, "Trade and State Formation: Siam in the Early Bangkok period" Modern Asian Studies 21:4, (1987) 751-771.
109. Ibid.; p762.
110. Ibid.: p766.
111. Ibid.: p761.
112. Ibid.: p767.
113. J. Crawfurd, Journal of an Embassy from the Governor General of India to the Courts of Siam and Cochin China (London, Henry Colbourn 1828).
114. Wong Lin Ken, "The Trade of Singapore" p139.
115. Ibid.: p151.
116. Ibid. p148.
117. Ibid. pp140-141.
118. SarDesai, British Trade and Expansion pp81-82.
119. Wong Lin Ken, "The Trade of Singapore" p142.
120. SarDesai, British Trade and Expansion p84.
121. Wong Lin Ken, "The Trade of Singapore" p144.
122. Ibid.: p145.
123. Ibid.: p146.
124. Ibid.: pp147-148.
125. Wyatt, Thailand p183.
126. Wong Lin Ken, "The Trade of Singapore" p148.
127. SarDesai, British Trade and Expansion p90.
128. Ibid.: p89.

7. BRITISH IMPERIALISM IN THE MALAY STATES AND BORNEO: 1850-1890

The second half of the nineteenth century saw a rapid expansion of the British empire in south east Asia. By 1900 the Malay peninsula, Burma and northern Borneo had all been subjected to direct rule, while Siam had been drawn into Britain's informal empire. Recent historiography has re-evaluated the reasons for British imperial expansion after 1850. For some historians, the "gentlemanly capitalists" of the City of London, with their enormous wealth, influential social connections and boundless appetite for foreign investment opportunities, were the main driving force behind imperial expansion.[1] To what extent is this explanation applicable to British imperialism in the Malay world in the later nineteenth century?

British expansion into the Malay peninsula has been the source of much contention among historians. Two competing explanations of British expansion have emerged. One identifies rivalry with other imperial powers as the main reason for the establishment in 1873 of British Residents at the courts of the western Malay Sultans to "advise" them, and stop them succumbing to temptations offered by rival imperialists.[2] Against this, another view attributes the abandonment of the British policy of non-intervention to agitation by mercantile interests in London and the Straits Settlements. They convinced the Colonial Secretary, Lord Kimberley that the western Malay states were in a process of political collapse which would do irreparable damage to British commerce in south east Asia.[3] In this account, fear of foreign intervention was used by Kimberley to persuade an anti imperialist Liberal government to permit British intervention, but the real motive was defence of economic interests. Supporters of this interpretation point to the lack of serious consultation by the Colonial Office with the War Office and the Admiralty about military responses to rival imperial adventures in Malaya.[4] They also highlight the absence of any reference to foreign intervention in Kimberley's instructions to Sir Andrew Clarke, the new Governor of the Straits Settlements appointed in 1873.[5] Together these observations are seen as proof that there was no serious expectation of rival imperial adventures in the Malay peninsula. an important task for the present study is to evaluate this debate and suggest a new explanation of these developments.

The period before intervention in 1873 saw dramatic changes in the British presence and economic involvement in the Malay peninsula and Borneo. Some of these changes were already in train by the 1840s. During that decade, Chinese enterprise had developed primary production within the Malay states on an unprecedented scale. From the 1820s, British commercial interests in the Straits Settlements became increasingly dependent upon Chinese middlemen, through whom they conducted their trade with local traders in south east Asia. By the early 1850s, British commercial fortunes rested upon an increasingly complex system of Asian trade in which Indian opium, Malay tin and other local produce all played a vital role. The Chinese were the instrument through which British commercial interests gained access to this system. The point has been made that the fortunes of British merchants in the Straits Settlements, the financial solvency of British governing institutions there, and consequently the security of the whole British position in the region, rested upon this Asian commercial network and the co-operation of the Chinese.

Chinese enterprise in the Malay peninsula continued to flourish between 1850 and 1870, boosting the profits which British and European Straits merchants accrued from their links with the Chinese. The fastest growing and most lucrative branch of local commerce was the tin trade. There was a strengthening or intensification of British dependency upon Chinese enterprise, and upon the Asian trading system which had emerged in the first half of the century. Trade between south east Asia, Europe and the wider global economy began to grow very rapidly, and one consequence of this was an expansion of manufactured exports to south east Asia from Europe. In turn, exports from south east Asia, previously directed mainly towards India, China or other Asian locations, increasingly found markets in the industrialised world. South east Asia was being drawn into an emergent global economic system.

A brief survey of the trade of Singapore provides some indication of the magnitude of these changes. In the 1840s, imports from the United Kingdom were approximately equal in value to imports from Calcutta. For example, imports of merchandise from the UK in 1848/49 were valued at $1,989,536, compared to $2,163,451 from Calcutta.[6] By 1865/66, imports of merchandise from the UK were running at $8,091,017, compared with only $3,103,122 from Calcutta.[7] Whereas in 1845 approximately 22 per cent of Singapore's total trade was with the industrialised west, and 21 per cent with India, by 1865 the respective proportions were 25 and 15 per cent.[8] Without question, trade with Europe, particularly with the UK, played a much more important role in British commerce within south east Asia than had been the case earlier in the century. Imports from the industrialised world grew after 1850, and Malay commodities such as tin began to command markets in the west. In the period 1844-48, of 12,228 tons of tin exported from the Straits

Settlements, 5,171 tons (42 per cent) went to Europe and the USA. Between 1864 and 1868, 35,791 tons out of total exports from the Straits of 50,344 tons (71 per cent) went to Europe and the USA, clearly demonstrating not only the dramatic growth in tin production, but also the increasing importance of the industrialised world as a market for tin.[9] The growth of the tin plate industry in the UK after 1850 ensured that the British market would be in the forefront of these developments.[10]

All of this was accompanied by a significant growth in the total value of trade of Singapore and the Straits Settlements. The total value of Singapore's trade grew from \$25.2 million in 1850 to \$70.8 million in 1870.[11] This was accompanied by a general increase in the volume of shipping arriving at Singapore. In 1850/51 some 56 ships with a total tonnage of 22,286 arrived at Singapore from the UK. In 1865/66 there were 72 arrivals from the UK with a total tonnage of 45,579.[12] One consequence of this growth in European shipping was a gradual displacement of Chinese and Malay shipping from south east Asian waters. The proportion of shipping in Singapore harbour from the Malay archipelago, which were of Malay origin, fell from 43 per cent in 1848 to 27 per cent in 1866.[13] The fall in the proportion of Chinese junks was even greater. Singapore's trade within south east Asia shifted towards the mainland. In 1845, the value of Singapore's trade with mainland south east Asia (Burma, Cambodia, Cochin China and Siam) and the Malay peninsula was approximately \$3,666,000, and constituted about 47 per cent of the Singapore's trade with south east Asian ports. By 1865, the value of Singapore' trade with the mainland had risen to \$15,500,000, and constituted 62 per cent of the port's south east Asia trade.[14]

The reasons for some of these changes are not hard to identify. The accelerating pace of industrialisation in Britain created new markets for south east Asian commodities, and generated new exports to the region. Steam shipping made transport to the east quicker and more reliable, while the development of telegraph made long distance business easier to conduct, plan and predict. In general, technological advances provided the means of a huge expansion in commerce with south east Asia, and western possession of the technologies ensured their growing dominance of shipping and other agencies of trade. It was a process promoted still further by the opening the the Suez canal in 1869.

The impact upon the British communities in the east was quite dramatic. Singapore in particular attracted many Europeans, whose numbers rose from a mere 198 out of a total population of 59,043 in 1850 to 2,445 out of 80,792 in 1860.[15] The dependence of Europeans upon Chinese compradors and intermediaries continued, and the growth of British trade and shipping to the region encouraged speculative enterprises in the states of the Malay peninsula. For example, Guthrie and Co. one of the oldest firms at the port negotiated for mining concessions in Selangor in the late 1860s.[16] Improvements in transport and communications technology, and the increase in British shipping to south east Asia, strengthened commercial links with Britain, especially London. In 1857, the Singapore newspaper "The Free Press", listed nineteen prominent European merchants closely connected with London merchant firms. One prominent British Singaporean noted that these London houses were "very eminent".[17] London banks were also attracted to the Straits. In February 1859, the Chartered Bank of India, Australia and China established a branch in Singapore, and were followed shortly after by the Oriental Bank, the Chartered Mercantile Bank of India, London and China and the Asiatic Banking Corporation.[18] As British trade to the Straits Settlements increased, European Straits merchants, began to see the City of London as a potential source of investment capital. In 1864 a consortium of merchants led by James Guthrie launched the first joint stock company in the Straits, the Tanjong Pagar Dock company. The project, which aimed to massively expand the dock facilities of Singapore, signalled optimism about the long term prospects of the port. When in 1866 the project overran its budget, extra capital was raised by offering the shares in London.[19] There were precedents for looking to London to raise finance. In 1856, James Brooke of Sarawak had decided to fund his commercial activities and the economic development of his territories by floating a company in London. The Borneo Company raised capital of œ60,000 in this way, and inspired similar ambitions among the merchants of the Straits Settlements.[20] In the early 1870s, growing interest in the potential of the Malay peninsula by British Straits merchants also led them to seek financial support in London. The Singapore merchant, W.H. Read, together with his brother in law in London, Seymour Clarke, the general manager of the Great Northern Railway, tried to raise capital for a project to connect Singapore with Siam and Australia by telegraph.[21] Although this was unsuccessful, it did not deter Read and Clarke from trying to entice London investors into other projects. In 1873, together with J.G. Davidson, a prominent Singapore lawyer, they planned to raise finance for the Selangor Tin Mining Company, a concern which was intended to exploit a tin concession granted by the Sultan of Selangor.[22]

Connections between the Straits Settlements and London were political as well as commercial in nature. By the 1850s, an earlier generation of successful Singapore merchants had retired to London, from where many maintained personal and commercial contacts with their erstwhile partners in the east. Over time they came to exercise a considerable voice in the capital on behalf of British merchants in the Straits, defending and promoting their friends' interests. The establishment of Colonial Office authority over the Straits Settlements in 1867 was strongly welcomed by both London and Straits based merchants. Before this, the Straits government had been accountable to the India Office via a chain of command which went through the British authorities in India. It had long been felt that the interests of the Straits were given a low priority in both India and London, because of preoccupation with Indian affairs. After 1867, the Straits government enjoyed a direct channel of communication with the Colonial Office in London.

There was hope that, at last, the voice and needs of British subjects in south east Asia would be heeded. In January 1868, the Straits Settlements Association was set up in London, by such prominent merchants and officials as James Guthrie, John Crawfurd and William Paterson.[23] The Association was to become a defender of Straits interests throughout the rest of the century.

It might be tempting to interpret these developing commercial and political connections with London as the beginning of a phase of financial expansion into the Straits and the Malay peninsula, as London merchants, banks and investors were enticed by Straits entrepeneurs to finance the exploitation of the Malay peninsula. One might expect to see, from the 1860s, a surge of investment into the Straits Settlements and the Malay peninsula. However, developments did not quite follow this pattern. In fact, the export of capital from London into the Straits and the peninsula remained insignificant until at least the 1890s, when tin and rubber finally attracted British investment.[24] Given the enormous expansion of Singapore's trade after 1850, and the presence of tin, a mineral in growing demand in the industrialising world, one might have expected to see an explosion of investment from Britain at an earlier stage. Why then, did it take so long for the export of capital to gather momentum?

Some of the reasons for London's sluggish interest were straightforward enough; after early interest in Malay tin from London financiers in the late 1860s and early 1870s, falling world tin prices during the 1870s, smothered all enthusiasm.[25] But other reasons, connected with the structure of trade and enterprise in south east Asia, also served to discourage London investors. Chinese entrepeneurs, upon whom the British depended so heavily, were able to flourish and expand their commercial and entrepeneurial activities, in spite of the growing incursion of British trade and shipping into the local trade routes of south east Asia. The expansion of British trade and shipping was fatal for some indigenous trading communities in the region. For example, the Buginese traders of Sulawesi were unable to compete with British steam shipping.[26] The demise of the China based junk trade has already been mentioned. But the Chinese merchants of the Straits Settlements adapted to and flourished in this changing and increasingly competitive environment. They successfully adapted their business organisations to met the changing circumstances. Financial, trading and secret society links between Chinese organisations based in the Nanyang, and their counterparts in China, enabled the Straits Chinese to draw upon external reserves of capital and credit. Some Chinese were even able to compete in areas where western enterprise was strongest. By the early twentieth century, for example, several Chinese commercial firms were competing effectively in the European dominated fields of shipping and freight.[27] One successful strategy employed by the Chinese was the establishment of dual status. As western business law became dominant in the Straits Settlements, many Chinese Kongsis recognised the advantages of conforming to such western concepts as the incorporated firm.

By the 1880s therefore, many of them had acquired western style company status for the purpose of securing the protection and advantages bestowed upon such organisations under western law, while at the same time retaining, in their dealings with Chinese and south east Asian traders, the structures of the kongsi form of organisation, as symbolised by the use of the traditional seal, or "chop", on all agreements.[28]

At the heart of continuing Chinese success, at least until the 1880s, were the advantages bestowed upon them by the characteristics of their commercial activities in the Straits described earlier. These included Kongsi-inspired loyalty to the group among Chinese merchants and labourers, the continuing stream of cheap labour from the home country, and the strategic role of opium in enabling Chinese merchants to recoup much of their labour costs by retail of the drug to their own labourers. Opium continued to play a very important role well into the late nineteenth century, especially in the expanding Chinese tin enterprises in the Malay peninsula. Chinese merchants based in the Straits advanced capital to tin mining prospectors and in return received various concessions, including the right to buy a proportion of tin produced at a price lower than the market could dictate, the exclusive right to sell food and other supplies to the tin miners at high prices, and of course the right to sell opium.[29] High profits were generated which enabled the Chinese Straits merchants to fund expansion of their commercial activities. One consequence was that the Straits Settlements remained an important outlet for Indian opium well into the late nineteenth century. In 1872, Pinang imported Indian opium worth $1,129,060, or 8.8 per cent of total imports of merchandise into the settlement for that year.[30] Between the 1850s and the 1890s, Chinese enterprise in tin mining enjoyed a decisive edge over European competitors. In particular, the "tribute system" of organisation enabled Chinese tin prospectors to minimise costs in the early stages of production, or during times of trade depression, when income from tin sales was suppressed. Under this system, debt free Chinese miners were accorded the status of partners in the business. This entitled the labourer to a share of the profits, rather than a wage, based upon the value of their work. The advantages for the Chinese merchant funding the operation, and the prospector leading the enterprise were numerous. They were guaranteed first call on profits because of the large size of their initial investment. Costs of production could also be minimised, if profits were disappointing, because the labourers were the last priority in the distribution of profits, and if no profit was made they received nothing for their work. Because many of the labourers had to purchase stores and opium from the Chinese merchant on credit, it was not unusual for them to incur debts far larger than their share of profits. Thus many coolies found themselves in a vicious circle of indebtedness and low incomes, which served to entrap them in the service of the Chinese entrepeneurs. The steady supply of new indebted coolies from the homeland also helped to keep labour costs low. From the entrepeneurs' point of view, the tribute system delivered flexibility in their cost structures and enabled them to adapt to the most difficult economic circumstances, making it difficult for new European enterprise to break into the market.[31] Chinese mining techniques were also better suited to Malay conditions, at least until the 1890s. The Malay tin lodes were easily accessible to open cast mining, and with simple but cheap technology incorporating the use of water powered drainage pumps, the Chinese adapted to the robust environmental conditions.[32] Western technology, dependent upon steam power, was ill suited to local conditions. Chinese enterprise thrived after 1850, actually prospering from the advance of British trade and shipping into the region, which opened new markets in industrialising Europe.

Chinese tin mining on the peninsula grew rapidly after 1850. The main tin producing areas were the Larut river in Perak, Lukut and Klang in Selangor, and Sungai Ujong in Negri Sembilan, and growth in output was impressive. In the 1830s Sungai Ujong had produced an estimated 7,000 piculs of tin per annum. By the 1860s, this had risen to c.20,000 piculs per annum.[33] By 1861/62, of the total value of imports into Pinang from Perak of $416,249, about 70 per cent was accounted for by tin.[34] The Chinese population of the Malay states also grew rapidly. By 1872, it was estimated that there were perhaps 40,000 Chinese in Larut alone.[35] Competition was fierce to secure the best mining areas, and to control the lucrative trade in stores, tin and opium. There was great rivalry between the various Kongsis, which by the 1860s erupted sporadically into violent feuds between secret societies. By the 1860s, this violence occasionally spilled over into the Straits Settlements. For example, the Ghee Hin and another secret society, the Toa Peh Kong, were involved in violent riots against each other in 1859.[36] There was also sporadic secret society conflict in Singapore over control of the opium farms.[37] Life among the Chinese in the Malay states had an extremely rugged, frontier character. In the absence of clear legal jurisdiction over the Chinese in Malaya (neither the British nor the Malay authorities sought to impose the rule of law over the Chinese mining settlements before the 1870s) disputes over land rights, money or even more trivial matters often degenerated into riots, mass violence and even small wars. Although Chinese society was hierarchical, social advancement was possible through industry, ruthlessness and a great deal of luck. The best example of this was Yap Ah Loy, a Chinese cook who rose from obscurity to become by the 1870s a wealthy entrepeneur, secret society leader and Kapitan China in the Kuala Lumpur region of Selangor.[38] Men like him became crucial, not only as entrepeneurs who organised and directed commercial relations with the Chinese and European merchants in the Straits, but also as leaders of the Chinese mining communities who were responsible for managing relations with the local Malay authorities.

The dramatic growth of Chinese mining communities had serious consequences for the stability of the Malay states, especially Perak, Selangor and Negri Sembilan. These were extremely fragile regimes. Widespread polygamy within ruling families made successions problematic, and often a source of internal strife. The mobility of local populations, recurrent territorial disputes between the Malay states, and constantly shifting alliances between them, rendered politics unpredictable. The local Sultan's power rested upon the co-operation of district chiefs, whose local authority and control of revenues circumscribed royal power. Even in the absence of Chinese involvement, the Malay states were prone to internal and interstate conflict. For example, a succession dispute in Pahang between 1858 and 1863, erupted without the stimulus of a Chinese presence. The two competing princes, Muhatir and Ahmad, eagerly sought allies. Muhatir secured the support of two successive Temmengongs of Johore, Ibrahim and then Abu Bakar, while Ahmad found a potent ally in Sultan Mahmud of Riau. Mahmud had close contacts at the Siamese court, and when Mahmud arrived at Trengganu in 1861 aboard a Siamese ship, there were rumours that he was about to be made Sultan of that state. The British, who till then had kept out of the Pahang dispute, became fearful that there was a plot afoot to re-establish Siamese power in the eastern Malay peninsula. The Straits Governor, O. Cavenagh, ordered the shelling of Kuala Trengganu in November 1862, as a warning against perceived Siamese ambitions. The British government fearing involvement in an expensive imperial war, censured Cavanagh. Thereafter Cavanagh could lend only covert support and encouragement to Muhatir via the successive Temmengongs of Johore, and was unable to prevent the eventual victory of Ahmad.[39]

But the troubles in Perak, Selangor and Negri Sembilan in the 1860s were clearly related to the expansion of the local tin economy by the Chinese. In each of these states there were common developments which demonstrated the destabilising consequences of Chinese enterprise. The rise of tin mining in the 1850s had benefitted those local chiefs whose districts encompassed the tin mines, because of the increased local revenues which were generated. Local chiefs were thus provided with the means of purchasing weapons and attracting supporters for their efforts at self aggrandisement. Inevitably this undermined the authority of the Sultan, as local chiefs lent support to contenders for the throne. There were strong similarities in political developments in the three states. In Selangor, Sultan Muhammed (1826-57) became dependent upon the support of Raja Juma'at of Lukut, as that local chief grew in wealth and power following the growth of Chinese tin mining in the 1850s. Muhammed was forced to grant concessions to Juma'at which, by custom, should have gone to others. The tin rich lands surrounding the Klang river were granted to Juma'at's son, Raja Abdullah. But Muhammed's grandson, Raja Mahdi had been expected to inherit Klang, since his father, Sulaiman, had governed that territory previously.[40] Raja Mahdi's deep jealousy and sense of moral outrage simmered throughout the late 1850s and early 1860s, and he steadily canvassed support, awaiting a suitable opportunity to seize what he considered to be his rightful inheritance. He was assisted by declining royal power, especially under Sultan Abdul Samad (1859-93). Raja Abdullah tried in the late 1850s to appease Mahdi by conceding regular monetary allowances to him, but these only encouraged Mahdi to plot against Abdullah. In 1866, matters came to a head following an agreement between Abdullah and a consortium of Chinese and European merchants, led by W.H. Read of Singapore. Under this, Read's syndicate was granted tax collection rights by Abdullah in return for 20 per cent of the revenues collected.[41] The award demonstrated the growing wealth of Klang to Raja Mahdi. His dignity and status were also affronted when the Read syndicate tax collectors refused to recognise Mahdi's claim to exemption from Klang taxes because of his status as a royal prince.[42] In 1867, Mahdi used a local squabble between immigrant Bugis and Mandeling (from Sumatra) groups to attack Abdullah and his followers, establishing control over Klang by October 1867. Mahdi, in revenge for the injustices meted out to him, refused to pay the revenues due to the crown. Sultan Abdul Samad recruited his son in law, Tunku Kudin of Kedah, to punish Mahdi, and there followed six years of intermittent warfare which disrupted trade.[43] The conflict was compounded by the simultaneous outbreak of war within the Chinese mining community in Selangor. By 1869, the Hai San Chinese secret society, led by Yap Ah Loy, were siding with Tunku Kudin and the Sultan, while the rival Chinese Ghee Hin were fighting alongside Raja Mahdi.

In Perak, there was a similar pattern of local chiefs being strengthened at the expense of the Sultan by Chinese commercial expansion. Long Ja'afar, the local chief of Larut who had grown rich and powerful on revenues from the tin trade, was succeeded in 1858 by his son Ngah Ibrahim. When Sultan Ali died in 1871, Ibrahim became embroiled in the succession dispute, supporting the Bendahara Raja Ismail, against Raja Abdullah.[44] Ibrahim had the assistance of the Chinese Hai San secret society, whom he had supported during a feud with the Ghee Hin in the early 1860s. By 1865, the Ghee Hin had been driven from Larut, largely because of Ngah Ibrahim's support for the Hai San, and so it was no surprise when the Ghee Hin threw in their lot with Raja Abdullah in 1871.

Negri Sembilan had always been the most decentralised political system within the Malay peninsula, with considerable devolution of power into the hands of the local chiefs.[45] The head of state, the Yang Dipertuan Besar, had always represented a much weaker source of authority than his counterparts elsewhere in the Malay states. The authority of the position diminished steadily from the 1830s, to the extent that by the 1850s, Negri Sembilan had all but fragmented into smaller subsidiary states, jealously challenging each other's power. Again, revenues arising from the Chinese tin trade was the key to wealth and power for the local rulers of these subsidiary states. The most prominent of these were the Dato Klana of Sungai Ujong, and the Dato Bandar of the upper Linggi river, who became bitter rivals for the control of the tin trade on the Linggi river. In 1857 the Governor of Singapore sanctioned an expedition to destroy toll stations along the river which were interfering with commerce, and damaging mercantile interests in Melaka.[46] Violence flared again intermittently throughout the following decades.

There was a common pattern in all three western Malay states. Conflict was on a relatively small scale, involving hundreds rather than thousands of men. Warfare was sporadic and consisted of guerilla skirmishes, rather than set piece confrontations. These were wars of stockades and ambushes, in which actual casualties, in true south east Asian tradition, were quite light by contemporary European standards. Nevertheless, the civil wars were particularly disruptive for trade, because the main military targets tended to be the tin mines and the rivers upon which trade depended. The effect was to stimulate British fears that these wars might inflict lasting damage upon the emerging trade with the Malay states. From the mid 1860s, pressure from merchants in the Straits for British intervention to restore order and to defend their interests, began to intensify. Although the Colonial Office was initially firm in its refusal to sanction such a change in policy, by the 1870s this resolve began to weaken.

If the British government firmly set its face against an extension of empire into the Malay peninsula before 1870, this did not prevent James Brooke's private adventure in Sarawak. Brooke, who had been awarded territory in Sarawak by the Sultan of Brunei in the 1840s, was granted additional territory in 1853 and 1861.[47] By 1862 Brooke rule was extended almost as far east as the Tinjar river. The vulnerability of the Sultan of Brunei to challenges to his authority from potential rivals, drove him increasingly to depend upon the military support of James Brooke, who could secure support from the British government. The price was the territorial cessions of 1853 and 1861.[48] Brooke's relations with the British authorities in India and the Straits were erratic. Brooke had been the first governor of Labuan until 1853, and served as British envoy to Siam in the abortive mission of 1850. But the British authorities were nervous of Brooke's aggressive expansionism, which threatened to cause confrontations with both the Dutch and local powers. It was felt that any diminution of Brooke's power or status might have damaging consequences for British prestige throughout the region, possibly encouraging challenges from other quarters. Thus, in spite of their anti expansionist intentions, the British authorities often found themselves reluctantly supporting Brooke. For example, the British treaty with Brunei of 1847 not only confirmed possession by the British government of Labuan, but also prevented the Sultan of Brunei making concessions of territory to other nations. The effect was to reinforce Brooke's dominant position, because it prevented any European moves to counterbalance Brooke, and it marked Brunei as part of the British sphere of influence.[49]

Sarawak had attracted Chinese immigrants seeking to exploit local natural resources. From the early nineteenth century their main economic activity was gold and antimony mining at Pangkalan Tabang and Bau. The Kongsi around which the Chinese were organised, behaved almost like an autonomous state, conducting its own trade within Borneo, exchanging gold and antimony for stores and, of course, opium. The Chinese traded with

Kalimantan and the interior, rather than with the British held port of Kuching on the north coast. From the outset, Brooke was determined to bring the Chinese to heel. To this end opium sales were monopolised by the Brooke government, and a substantial tax in gold was levied on the Chinese kongsi, ostensibly based on their consumption of opium.[50] When opium consumption, and therefore tax revenues fell, Brooke accused the Chinese of smuggling the drug, and substantially increased taxes. The Chinese uprising which followed in 1857 resulted not only in their defeat by the Brooke regime, but also the assertion of Brooke's personal control over the mining industry through the Borneo Company. The defeated Chinese Kongsi were forced to accept Brooke authority, and now had to supply minerals to the company.[51] By 1870, gold, antimony and coal production were all increasing rapidly, and the exports of minerals was worth $38,001.[52] The Borneo Company also asserted a monopoly over trade in agricultural produce, particularly the most lucrative food export, sago. The Chinese traders who had previously dominated the trade were either subordinated or displaced.[53] In addition, the Company made strenuous efforts to control the trade in jungle produce, commodities such as cutch (wood oil) and jelutong (a kind of wild rubber), although it remained heavily dependent upon Chinese traders. This branch of Sarawak's trade in fact proved to be most lucrative. In 1881, the total value of jungle and sea produce exported from Sarawak was $449,840, or 41 per cent of total exports, compared to exports of cultivated produce of $463,978 (44 per cent) and minerals worth $163,010 (15 per cent).[54] In developing this trade, the Company also tapped into indigenous trading networks whose importance, as one historian eloquently demonstrates, has been underestimated.[55]

By 1868 and the succession of Charles Brooke, Sarawak was undergoing extensive economic development, mainly under the auspices of the Borneo Company. It was a unique experiment in imperial expansion, because while the British authorities in the east were unprepared to see the regime toppled by local or European powers, they never extended to it formal protection. In this sense, Sarawak was part of the British informal empire. Ironically this actually delivered considerable autonomy to the Brookes, who could organise the internal affairs of Sarawak as they saw fit. All European competition was excluded from the territory, and economic resources were the near exclusive preserve of the Borneo Company.[56] Straits merchants who coveted these commercial opportunities were resentful. Yet in important respects, the Brooke regime proved a testing ground for methods of government which were to be applied in the Malay states after 1874. Power in the Brooke regime ultimately rested in the hands of the White Raja himself, but beneath him was an elaborate system of administration which incorporated both local chieftains and specially recruited British officers. At the apex of the structure was an advisory Supreme Council which included both senior British officials and some Malay chiefs. Below this were two parallel systems of indigenous and British administration. The local Malay chiefs administered traditional law, collected the White Raja's taxes, and maintained order. They received advice from, and were closely watched by British regional Residents, whose job it was to ensure that the indigenous leaders kept out of mischief. These Residents also took responsibility for the administration of justice, landownership and the control of immigration, through a system of subordinate district officers who took Brooke rule into the villages.[57] The whole concept of the Resident, ostensibly an adviser to the local ruler but in fact a wielder of power in his own right, was one that was applied in the Malay states after 1874. When it was decided in 1873/74 that a system of Residents would be established in the western Malay states, the precise role and duties that the Resident should adopt were by no means clear to the Colonial Office in London. Inevitably it was left to the Residents themselves to define their own role, and in so doing they had to draw upon their own experience or whatever models they could find. Brooke rule in Sarawak was an obvious source of instruction. One of the earliest and most influential of the British Residents in the Malay states, Hugh Low, who was Resident of Perak from 1877 to 1900, modelled his role upon that pioneered by Brooke's Residents in Sarawak.[58] In addition, the tendency to regard different ethnic groups as virtual estates of the body politic, and to attribute to them certain racially defined qualities which determined their socio-economic role, was also transplanted to the peninsula. In Sarawak, the native Ibans were seen as warriors who could defend the regime. The Malay population were categorised as best equipped for farming as smallholders. The Chinese were regarded as miners and merchants, and the best for labour in commercial agriculture. A similar categorisation was to emerge in the Malay states. In this sense, Brooke rule was a prototype of what was to come in the Malay peninsula. As will be seen, the British presence in Borneo as well as in the Malay states, was to grow even more rapidly in the last quarter of the century.

**

Now we must turn to a vexing question for historians: the decision by the Colonial Office in 1873 to intervene in Malay politics by appointing Residents to the courts of each of the Malay Sultans. Within a few years these Residents were effectively running the Malay states. The appearance of Malay authority was continued, in that the Residents exercised power on behalf of their respective Sultans rather than the British government, but this was widely recognised as a fiction. The Pangkor Agreement of 1874, under which the Malay Sultans accepted the appointment of British Residents, began extension of British rule into the states of the Malay peninsula. Why did this reversal of British policy take place?

Two competing explanations of this change of policy have emerged. One is that it was the perceived threat of foreign intervention in the Malay states, prompted by warring factions in the Malay states desperate for allies, which persuaded the Colonial Secretary, Lord Kimberley, to sanction the appointment of Residents. Against this, it has been argued that Kimberley's reference to the danger of foreign intervention as a reason for changing policy, was a ruse to persuade an anti-imperialist government of the need for a more interventionist policy. The real motive was Kimberley's recognition of the needs of British merchants in the Straits whose developing commercial interests in the Malay states, were threatened by the outbreak of civil wars. Which interpretation is more accurate?

The origins of intervention can be traced back into the previous decade. By the time the Straits Settlements were placed under the authority of the Colonial Office in 1867, there was already a growing body of opinion which favoured some degree of British intervention to restore order. In that year, W.H. Read, who was visiting his brother in law, Seymour Clarke, wrote to the Colonial Office, pressing for a redefinition of relations with the Malay states. He argued for arrangements, under which British advisers would provide guidance for local Malay rulers.[59] In the same year, another Straits merchant firm, Paterson, Simons and Company of Singapore, who had suffered confiscation of some of their property during the Pahang civil war, pressed the Colonial Office to intervene on their behalf.[60] Senior Straits officials, most notably Sir Harry Ord, Governor of the Straits Settlements (1867-73), argued in 1868 that the extension of British political influence over the Malay states would have advantages for the Malay rulers as well as the British.[61] All of these pleas for intervention were rejected by the Colonial Secretary, Lord Buckingham. He stuck firmly to the view that intervention would be hard to contain, likely to incur unnecessary costs, would encourage dangerous adventures by officials and merchants in the Straits, and possibly lead to conflict with other European powers. But Buckingham conceded that there might be circumstances in which intervention would be unavoidable. By inference, Buckingham accepted that intervention might prove necessary if disorder in the Malay states threatened the peace and security of the Straits Settlements.[62] It was a small, but ultimately significant qualification. Ord's own predeliction for unapproved diplomatic initiatives in the Malay states brought criticism down upon his head, and made the Colonial Office vigilant of his actions.[63]

However, from about 1870, the pressure upon London to do something about disorder in the Malay states began to intensify, as the situation in Malaya began to deteriorate. In Negri Sembilan, the death of the Yang Di Pertuan in 1869 triggered a serious succession crisis, and was followed by other succession crises within the subsidiary states of Rembau and Sungai Ujong.[64] These separate conflicts became hopelessly intertwined. By September 1873, the conflicts were seriously disrupting trade. Anxiety in Melaka prompted the Neubronner family to make an unsuccessful attempt to mediate between the warring factions. By September 1873, one of the contenders for control of Rembau, Haja Sahil, had erected stockades along the Linggi river, and was detaining tin worth $300,000 owned by British merchants at Melaka.[65] Chinese miners were also killed during the conflicts. The Klang war in Selangor, which had been dragging on since 1867, appeared to be coming to a close in March 1870, when Tunku Kudin's forces managed to drive Raja Mahdi into exile in Pahang. But by July, Mahdi had reassembled his forces and returned to Selangor. At the same time, conflicts among the Chinese factions intensified, and the separate feuds within the Malay ruling elite and among the Chinese secret societies, began to merge as multi-ethnic alliances were formed.[66] The conflict continued through 1871 and 1872, heightening anxiety among British and Chinese merchants in the Straits Settlements. In Perak, the death of Sultan Ali in May 1871, provoked new conflict. The expected heir was Raja Abdullah, but his absence from the funeral, and longstanding disagreements with other Malay chiefs, resulted in Bendahara Ismail being chosen as the new Sultan. The ruling elite split into factions, with the wealthiest chief, Ngah Ibrahim supporting Ismail. By the beginning of 1872, fighting had begun. Matters were further complicated by the outbreak of fighting among the Chinese secret societies in the tin mines of Larut.[67] By 1872 the wars in these three states threatened to merge into one, uncontrollable conflagration, as the various warring factions sought help and alliances from within the neighbouring states. What had started as three separate and localised squabbles for power, were degenerating into a wider conflict which threatened to engulf the whole Malay peninsula.[68]

Anxiety grew rapidly in the Straits Settlements. There was widespread apprehension at the prospect of trade being disrupted. British and Chinese merchants had cultivated commercial partnerships and political alliances with the various contenders for power. In Selangor, Raja Mahdi received help from the Pinang merchant, Edward Bacon in 1870, worth $30,000.[69] He also drew support from two Chinese merchants in the Straits Settlements, Ong Boon Tek of Pinang and Chan Tek Chiang of Melaka.[70] On the other side Kudin ran up massive debts of $400,000 to various merchants in the Straits. Kudin's largest creditor was Lim Tek Hee of Melaka.[71] By the end of the war in Selangor, Kudin also owed J.G. Davidson, the Singapore lawyer $78,400. Davidson was an associate of W.H. Read, and in March 1873, they were granted a substantial portion of the tin mining rights in Selangor by Kudin for the Selangor Tin Mining Company, an enterprise which Read and Seymour Clarke planned to float in London.[72] In Perak, the Ngah Ibrahim/Ismail faction were deeply indebted to the Chinese Pinang merchant, Khoo Thean Teik, head of the Toa Peh Kong secret society, described by one historian as "possibly the most powerful Chinese in Pinang".[73] Other prominent Pinang Chinese, including Ong Boon Tek, supported the Ngah Ibrahim/Ismail faction, and their connections with Chinese mining interests in Larut played a part in developments in that state.[74] Conversely, Raja Abdullah was able to draw support from Khaw Boon Aun, a leading member of the Pinang Ghee Hin, who was promised opium farms in Perak.[75] In Sungai Ujong, The Velge family of Melaka were granted tin concessions in 1872 by one of the contenders for power, and the

Chinese merchant Tan Kim Cheng made substantial sums from the arms trade.[76] From all this, it is plain that the Straits merchants were not mere passive bystanders, suffering innocently as a result of internal squabbles. They were actively engaged in covert factionalism, and there were clear preferences for particular Malay contenders, which led the merchants to try to persuade the Straits authorities to take sides. In this sense, both British and Chinese mercantile interests in the Straits were responsible for exacerbating instability in the western Malay states.

In response, Straits officials asked London to allow them to try to restore order. When Ord returned to Britain on sick leave in 1871, his position was filled temporarily by Colonel Archibald Anson, Lt Governor of Pinang. While Ord tried unsuccessfully to persuade the new Colonial Secretary, Lord Kimberley, that intervention was necessary, in Singapore Anson established a committee to consider relations with the Malay states.[77] In June 1871, it suggested the appointment of British Residents to advise the Sultans on diplomatic and economic matters. The committee noted that a similiar arrangement already existed in Johore. Anson himself favoured an itinerant political agent rather than permanent Residents, but all these suggestions were firmly rejected by the Colonial Office, who were angered by Anson's unauthorised initiative in setting up the committee. But events in Selangor were moving very fast. At the end of June 1871, the crew of a Pinang junk were murdered by feuding Chinese miners. When a police steamer sent by the Pinang authorities to the Selangor river was fired upon by some of Raja Mahdi's men, Anson ordered H.M.S. Rinaldo to the Selangor river to punish the "pirates". The Rinaldo destroyed Raja Mahdi's forts on the river in July 1871.[78] It was an action which involved 400 British troops and considerable loss of life on Mahdi's side. Following this, Anson sent two officials, J.W.W. Birch, Colonial Secretary to the Straits Settlements and C.J. Irving, the Straits Auditor-General, to see Sultan Abdul Samad at Langat to try to re-establish order. A political agreement with the Sultan was reached, which effectively threw British support behind Kudin, who on British insistence was appointed to run the government of Selangor.[79]

The Colonial Office learnt of the Selangor incident in August 1871, just when it was considering its response to the recommendation of the Anson committee. Kimberley rejected the committee's proposals, and expressed his hope that the Langat settlement did not commit the Straits government to intervene on Kudin or the Sultan's behalf. Anson's use of military force was accepted as necessary chastisement of piracy, but Anson was warned to avoid a repetition if possible. Kimberley also let it be known that he could not accept any interpretation of the Langat agreement which precipitated British involvement in the Malay states. The policy of non intervention was to be consistently upheld.

Ord returned to the Straits in March 1872, and he and his officials made numerous visits to the western Malay states in the next two years, in an effort to quell the mounting disorder.[80] At the same time he was inundated with demands from Straits merchants for intervention, particularly W.H. Read, who was most influential in his capacity as Chairman of the Chamber of Commerce.[81] Ord's efforts to secure a lasting peace in the Malay states came to nothing, and he earned only the Colonial Office's contempt, which by 1873 was determined to replace him.[82]

Yet in the summer of 1873, Kimberley changed his mind about intervention. By July of that year, it had been decided that Ord should be replaced by a more competent official, Sir Andrew Clarke. On 22 July, Kimberley suggested that the Foreign Office be asked if it objected to Clarke being instructed to renegotiate existing treaties with the western Malay states to prevent them ceding territory to rival imperial powers.[83] By the time instructions were sent to the new Governor in September, Kimberley wanted Clarke to see if any measures might be taken which could restore "peace and order" in the Malay states, and report back in preparation for further instructions.[84] Kimberley also suggested the appointment of British officers to reside at the courts of the Malay Sultans, whose role would be to maintain peace by advising the local rulers. Clarke ensured that this was incorporated into the Pangkor Treaty of January 1874. The reasons for Kimberley's dramatic change of direction, have stimulated much debate and disagreement among historians. Several factors appear to have shaped the Colonial Office's views during the first half of 1873.

Firstly, the escalation of hostilities in Perak at the end of 1872 was particularly worrying because of the state's extensive trade with the Straits Settlements. The Colonial Office was strongly influenced by a report from a newcomer to the Malay states, George W.R. Campbell, who was temporary Lt Governor of Pinang in 1871, during a period of leave for Anson. Campbell submitted a report on the Perak situation to the Colonial Office at the end of June 1873, while en route to Britain. He had a personal interview with Kimberley in early July.[85] Kimberley was most impressed by the report.[86] It analysed the Larut troubles, identifying the various Chinese and Malay factions involved. Campbell thought the most serious danger was the Chinese conflict, which he feared was likely to spread to Pinang, because of the alliances between rival groups of Pinang merchants and the warring factions.[87] Here was a clear indication that Buckingham's strict preconditions for intervention were beginning to materialise: namely, that the stability of the Straits Settlements was being endangered by unrest in the peninsula. Campbell also mentioned the advantages of Residents to the Malay states, and he may have persuaded the Colonial Office to adopt the idea.[88]

A second factor was the growing volume of protests about the harmful effects of the Malay disorders on the commerce of the Straits Settlements. As early as November 1872, Ord alerted the Colonial Office to the disruption of Straits trade caused by the war in Selangor.[89] Ord enclosed a petition from some 34 Chinese merchants at Melaka, which had been passed to him by W.H. Read, in his capacity as Chairman of the Singapore Chamber of Commerce. The petition was a plea for the British government to restore order in Selangor, where both Chinese and British businessmen had invested heavily in tin mining. They appealed for the British government to intervene on behalf of Tunku Kudin.[90] In response to a restatement of the policy of non-intervention, Read pointed out that the Straits government had encouraged Chinese enterprise in Selangor by its decisive action at the time of the Selangor incident in 1871, and that the Langat agreement which followed stimulated expectation among the Chinese that Tunku Kudin would get British assistance to restore order. Furthermore, the Chinese petitioners had understated the value of Straits commerce with Selangor.[91] Campbell's reference to the impact of trouble in Larut upon the Chinese population of Pinang could only have reinforced this concern about the effect of the Malay troubles upon the Straits Chinese. These warnings were repeated in another petition from over 200 Chinese merchants throughout the Straits Settlements dated 28 March 1873.[92] Ord confirmed to the Colonial Office the extent of Chinese distress, stating that "not ten Chinese are employed where formerly there were a hundred".[93] The petition explained the problems most persuasively. It emphasised the severity of Chinese losses, and the need for British intervention to protect business. It also stressed other causes of difficulty. The petition mentioned the effects of the 1871 treaty between the British and the Dutch, under which the British had effectively recognised Dutch sovereignty over Sumatra, in return for a relaxation of restrictions on British trade with Dutch territories.[94] Problems arose when it became clear that the Acehnese were unprepared to accept their new Dutch overlords. In 1873 the Dutch began to enforce a blockade of Acehnese ports, as a prelude to invasion and annexation. The British Foreign Office had accepted the Dutch right to do this, and had agreed to prevent the export of arms to Aceh from the Straits Settlements. The Chinese petitioners cited the consequent damage to their trade with Sumatra as another cause of their plight.[95] They feared the long term effects of Dutch expansion in Sumatra upon trade. Spanish protectionism in the Sulu archipelago was also identified as a problem. The net effect was that only the Malay peninsula could offer commercial opportunities sufficiently lucrative to compensate them for declining prospects elsewhere. Consequently, the protection of trade and mining in the peninsula was essential for future prosperity. The petition reached the Colonial Office on 21 August 1873.

The third factor stemmed from this wave of mercantile concern about the effects of the Malay unrest. In March 1873 W.H. Read and J.G. Davidson secured an exclusive ten year concession for certain tin mining rights in Selangor. Their intention was to float the Company in London to raise the necessary capital. The consortium was unusually well placed, in that Read's brother in law in London, Seymour Clarke, took a leading role in the project. Clarke was well known in London society; enjoying as he did the prestigious position of General Manager of the Great Northern Railway. Clarke took responsibility for handling the London end of the scheme, supervising the preparations for flotation, and also handling relations with the Colonial Office. Clarke's role was effectively that of the London based "gentlemanly capitalist", at once organising financial support in the City for the enterprise, while securing political support from official circles. But he feared that the disturbances in the Malay states would frighten off potential investors.[96] The ideal solution to this problem would have been an undertaking by the British government to pacify the Malay states by direct intervention, but official resistance to such a policy prompted Clarke to try a different tack. In June 1873, he sought permission from the Colonial Office for the Selangor Tin Company to recruit its own private military force, to defend its concession and property in Selangor.[97] When this was refused, Clarke sent to the Colonial Office a copy of a letter received by one of the promoters of the Selangor Tin Company from Tunku Kudin, which called for the intervention by Britain or "any other government", to quell the troubles in the Sultanate. Clarke warned that some of the rulers of the Malay states were considering placing themselves under the protection of a rival imperial power, probably Germany.[98] Although some of his advisers were sceptical, Kimberley took this very seriously. He suggested consultation with the Foreign Office about the possibility of treaties with the Malay states being renegotiated to prohibit such overtures to Britain's imperial rivals.[99]

Historians have not agreed about the relative importance of these factors. One view places fear of foreign intervention above other considerations, especially in light of recent events. Since the Franco-Prussian war, Germany had been identified a potential threat to British imperial interests. Also, the Dutch assault upon Aceh had been prompted partly by rumours of designs there by other major powers, notably the USA.[100] In these circumstances, Kimberley felt that Clarke's warning should be heeded. Campbell's written and verbal reports, which stressed the seriousness of the disorders in the Malay peninsula, and promoted the concept of Residents to consolidate British influence in the Malay states, also pushed Kimberley towards intervention.[101] The significance of the Chinese petition of March 1873, is downplayed on the grounds that by the time the Colonial Office received it in late August 1873, Kimberley had already made his decision to intervene.[102]

But others have argued that Kimberley's fear of foreign intervention has been much overstated. There was no identification of any specific ambitions on the part of a foreign power among any British official papers, nor did Kimberley consult the War Office or the Admiralty about the alleged threat.[103] It is true that Kimberley asked for a review of existing treaties with the Malay states to see if they excluded foreign interference, and that if they did not, he wanted them renegotiated to include such provisions. But it seems that Kimberley was reassured by his officials that earlier treaties did in fact preclude the cession of territory to rival powers by the Malay states, unless British agreement had been first obtained. Although in September 1873 Kimberley used the possibility of foreign intervention as an argument to convince Gladstone of the necessity of a pre-emptive British initiative in the Malay states, some see this as a ruse by Kimberley to convince his fervently anti-imperialist Prime Minister that there was no alternative to intervention. Other reasons lay behind Kimberley's change of policy. These stemmed from the severity of the economic difficulties confronting the Straits merchants as a result of the Malay disorders, and a genuine concern that they might destabilise the Straits Settlements. For this interpretation, the Straits Chinese merchants' petition of March 1873 was crucial in convincing Kimberley of the need for British intervention.[104] While supporters of the strategic view see the change of policy arising in July 1873, this economic interpretation dates it in late August 1873, after the arrival of the Straits petition.

But this polarisation of opinion between strategic and commercial interpretations obscures rather than reveals the processes which led to the change of policy. The officials of the Colonial Office had a fine grasp of the complexities of the situation in the Straits and the peninsula. It was recognised that British strategic and political security in the Straits was inextricably intertwined with the success of the Chinese and British merchants. Concern about the commercial fortunes of the Chinese merchants was not simply driven by calculations of lost revenues for the Straits government, or lost commercial opportunities in the future, but also recognition of the mayhem that might result if Chinese difficulties and anxieties were not addressed. Rioting and secret society conflicts, already so apparent in the Malay states, could easily spread to the Straits Settlements and render them ungovernable. Chinese riots in Pinang and Singapore during the 1850s and 1860s, were embedded in the memory of both local officers and Colonial Office officials, who dreaded the prospect of a repetition. Such disturbances could easily entice foreign imperial powers to take advantage of perceived British weakness and instability, thus turning economic and internal political crisis into a major international confrontation. In this way, economic difficulties and fear of foreign intervention were closely connected, and explanations which seek to identify either concern as discrete, alternative causes of Kimberley's change of policy, inevitably oversimplify the complex process of policy formation which incorporated and integrated both considerations.

Thus the Straits merchants' protests to London were not simply discounted by the Colonial Office. The argument that the Straits petition of March 1873 arrived after the decision to intervene had been made, is questionable. Although Kimberley was clearly thinking about intervention in July, it is by no means clear that he was committed to it at that stage. His suggestion of treaty revisions to exclude the possibility of foreign intervention in the Malay states was just that: a suggestion. A suggestion, moreover, which was contingent upon a review of existing treaties, that proved to be reassuring. In any case, the March 1873 petition was not the first indication to London of the serious economic and political consequences likely to result within the Straits Chinese community from a continuation of the disorders. The Melaka merchants' petition of July 1872, had alerted the Colonial Office to the severity of the crisis there in the early months of 1873.

Also, Campbell's written report on the situation in Larut, and the likely destabilising effects upon Pinang, was received in late June 1873, before Kimberley's supposed commitment to intervention in July. Thus commercial considerations, arising from the lobbying of Straits Chinese merchants, did play a central role in changing Kimberley's mind on intervention, largely because of the threat to order posed by a deterioration of trade.

But fear of foreign imperialism cannot be dismissed as a factor in the change of policy. Although Kimberley's suggestion of treaty revisions in July 1873 may not have represented a decisive change of policy, the very fact that Kimberley immediately mooted a renegotiation of existing treaties shows that he took Seymour Clarke's warning of foreign interference very seriously indeed. Neither is there any evidence that Kimberley's letter to Gladstone in September 1873, which stressed the dangers of foreign rivals, was intended to manipulate the Prime Minister towards intervention for ulterior motives.[105] It is more likely that Kimberley was expressing sincere fears about the strategic consequences of allowing Malay conflicts to rage unchecked. There is additional evidence that Kimberley was worried by the presence of other powers in south east Asia. For example, the Anglo-Dutch treaty of 1871 in respect of Sumatra caused great concern, not only in the Straits, but also in London. The Straits Settlements Association protested vigorously against the treaty, arguing that it would be detrimental to British trade.[106] Dutch assurances about the preservation of British commerce to Sumatra were simply not believed. In July 1873, British and Chinese Pinang merchants protested to Governor Ord that the Dutch blockade of Aceh was having deleterious effects upon their trade, and their petition was quickly transmitted to London.[107] Even the Straits merchants' petition of March 1873 expressed grave concern about their commercial fortunes in a Dutch-dominated Sumatra.[108] In the Spring of 1873, Kimberley also became concerned about the spread of Spanish power east of Borneo. Like the Dutch, the Spanish adopted protectionist measures to exclude the trade of European rivals, particularly in the Sulu archipelago. Kimberley questioned the wisdom of the Foreign Office in conceding the Spanish right to exclude British commerce.[109]

In this context of foreign intrusion into regions which were traditionally the resort of British trade, any warning of further incursions had to be taken very seriously. Since the 1840s the trade of the Straits Settlements had been gradually reoriented northwards, away from the islands of the archipelago and towards the Malay peninsula and mainland south east Asia. Dutch expansion into Sumatra, and Spanish encroachments in the east in the 1870s represented a marked acceleration of this process. Trade with the Malay peninsula had become vital for the economic wellbeing of the Straits Settlements. Civil wars in the Malay states were a serious enough threat to the future prosperity in themselves, but when it appeared that they would provoke rival imperialist adventures there, the pressure for a change in policy became irresistible.

It is futile to try to pinpoint any one document, piece of correspondence or moment in time when Kimberley decided to adopt a more interventionist strategy. Rather he gradually realised over the summer months of 1873 that the combination of instability in the Malay states and the possibility of foreign intervention, threatened both the commercial viability of the Straits Settlements and the maintenance of peace and order. His awakening to imminent danger was the result of a variety of concerns rather than of any single development. The mercantile petitions alerted London to the economic dangers presented by the situation in the Malay states, Seymour Clarke pointed to the prospect of rival imperial ambitions, and Campbell highlighted the perils of Chinese feuding for the stability of the Straits Settlements. By the time Kimberley issued instructions to Sir Andrew Clarke, on 20 September 1873, the change of policy had been completed.[110] Kimberley's instructions outlined the proposal for the appointment of British officers to the courts of the Malay Sultans to "advise" them, although Clarke was told only to "consider whether it would be advisable" to appoint such Residents. Kimberley used these guarded terms because of his awareness of Gladstone's strong anti-imperialist sentiments, and he wanted to convey an impression of reluctance and caution to the Prime Minister. Nevertheless, Kimberley's intention to intervene is quite clear.

Sir Andrew Clarke followed his instructions with great enthusiasm. When he arrived in Singapore in early November 1873, he quickly recognised the seriousness of the problems in the Malay states, especially Perak. It was here that he made his first move. Through Anson at Pinang and other British officers such as Frank Swettenham, Clarke arranged a conference of the warring Chinese and Malay factions at Pangkor, which began in mid January 1874. The Chinese disputes over mine ownership were resolved within a week, and the respective secret society leaders accepted that British officers would decide between the various claims. The British found in favour of Raja Abdullah's claim to the Sultanate of Perak, though significantly Ngah Ibrahim (who in the 1860s had been given the title of Mentri, one of the great offices of state) was absent from the negotiations. As the Mentri was a prominent supporter of Sultan Ismail, this was bound to create problems for the future. Ismail was allowed to retain the title of "Sultan-Muda", a vaguely defined status which carried no real power. The most significant provision of the Pangkor agreement, signed on 20 January, was the appointment of a Resident and an assistant Resident to advise the new Sultan. The term "advise" was misleading; in practice the Resident would supervise revenue collection and state expenditure, and would effectively dictate policy in all matters of state save those concerning Malay custom and religion. The Resident's salary and expenses would be drawn from state revenues, and would have first call on state resources. There followed similar agreements with Sultan Abdul Samad of Selangor, reached in February 1874, and with the Dato Klana of Sungai Ujong in April 1874.[111] Effectively, by the Spring of 1874, Residents had been established in Perak, Selangor and Negri Sembilan, all with far reaching powers to control revenues, expenditure and state policy. The extension of British imperial rule into the Malay peninsula had begun.

In considering the Colonial Office's change of policy in the Summer of 1873, the role of British commercial interests requires special comment. The Read/Davidson initiative in Selangor, and its connections with Seymour Clarke in London, played a very significant role. Their objective was to secure financial backing in London, preferably via a share flotation, to finance the development of their tin concession. Here was "gentlemanly capitalism" in action; a group of Straits merchants utilising contacts in London to promote their company and raise finance, and also to influence the Colonial Office to optimise political conditions for the whole enterprise. Seymour Clarke, well respected in London business circles and personally related to Read, was the lynchpin of the operation. He raised the spectre of foreign imperial rivalry before the Colonial Office. He also impressed upon Kimberley the great economic potential of the enterprise to the extent that after meeting a deputation from the Selangor Tin Company in early November 1873, the Colonial Secretary instructed Sir Andrew Clarke to report back on the prospects for the firm.[112] But Seymour Clarke's warning of foreign intervention was not the only example of the consortium exercising influence to help change the policy of non-intervention. The Melaka Chinese merchants' petition of 27 July 1872 was channelled to the Colonial Office by the Singapore Chamber of Commerce. Read was the Chairman of this body, and he lent his wholehearted support for the petition.[113] It seems likely that Read may also have had a hand in organising the Straits merchants' petition of March 1873. When Sir Andrew Clarke arrived in Singapore in November 1873, Read dined with him on that very night, and was instrumental in the setting up of the Pangkor conference.[114] Davidson, yet another member of the consortium, was officially appointed by the new Straits Governor as the Resident to the court of Selangor in May 1874.[115] Together these efforts amounted to a co-ordinated strategy of shifting the Colonial Office away from its policy of non-intervention. It involved the mobilisation of commercial opinion in both the Straits and the City of London. The susceptibility of Kimberley and the Colonial Office to this campaign arose not only from the considerable respect that Seymour Clarke could command in the City, but also from the government department's heavy dependence upon Straits merchants such as Read, for intelligence about events in the Malay states. Governing officials in the Straits were also dependent upon them. Through their commercial contacts in the Malay states, the Straits merchants enjoyed access to information about political conditions there which was simply not available to British officials. They were thus ideally placed to shape official perceptions in the Straits and London to their own advantage. As an example of the political mechanics of gentlemanly capitalism, the shift in policy in the summer of 1873 is very instructive, and may provide clues to how City and mercantile interests got their way elsewhere. It was not just that City based interests were well placed socially to influence senior politicians, though this was certainly true of Seymour Clarke. The existence of a network of commercial connections which linked London to the periphery of empire, and upon which officialdom both at home and in the east had to depend for information, ensured that London based gentlemanly capitalists and their allies at the edge of empire, could influence decisively the direction of colonial policy.

Yet in light of the analysis presented earlier, the prominent role accorded to gentlemanly capitalism here may seem contradictory. The efforts of British Straits merchants to raise finance in London for business ventures in the Malay peninsula were stymied at least until the late 1880s. The reasons for this stemmed from the competitiveness of Chinese enterprise based on a durable Asian commercial system and the impact of the world recession of the 1870s. How can this failure be reconciled with the political success of gentlemanly capitalists in precipitating intervention in 1873/74?

In fact the two positions are not contradictory. The low tin price which resulted from the depression, was not expected to last. At the time of the crisis of 1873, the Selangor Tin Company project still appeared to be very promising, if only the difficulties of Malay political instability could be overcome. The organisational advantages of Chinese enterprise were not really recognised by such British merchants as Read, who were convinced of the superiority of western civilisation over Chinese division and barbarism. The assumption was that if only the Malay states could be granted the civilising benefits of British rule, the natural supremacy of western enterprise and the British race would open lucrative opportunities for London investors and Straits merchants alike. The fact that these expectations were to prove far harder to realise than was believed in the early 1870s, in no way diminished the effectiveness of a formidable alliance between prominent Straits merchants such as Read, and leading London businessmen such as Seymour Clarke, in securing policy changes to their advantage. Although the Selangor Tin Company ultimately failed to attract sufficient backing in London and was subsequently abandoned, its promoters managed to get the political changes they required. By the early 1870s the growing political instability of the western Malay states undoubtedly made British intervention more likely, and possibly inevitable. But the political decision to intervene, when it came, was prompted by the efforts of an abortive venture in gentlemanly capitalism. It was the direct result of an attempt to open the peninsula for a partnership between Straits merchants and London investors which, though ultimately unsuccessful from a commercial point of view, nevertheless obtained certain political objectives thought likely to improve the project's prospects. Even in an environment which was to prove difficult for London financed enterprise to thrive, gentlemanly capitalism had nonetheless promoted and prompted imperial expansion.

***

The Pangkor agreement of January 1874 thus marked the beginning of British rule in the western Malay states of Perak, Selangor and Negri Sembilan. British authority was exerted through Residents who were theoretically subject to the authority of their respective Sultans, rather than the Straits authorities or the British government. The precise role of the Resident was not clearly defined either by the Colonial Office's instructions, or Andrew Clarke, who was responsible for the negotiation of the agreements which created the Residency system. The duties and role of the Resident were to evolve through a process of trial, error and changing political circumstances. How did the British administrations in Malaya and Borneo evolve in the last decades of the nineteenth century? What were the economic and social consequences of British rule?

In Britain, Clarke's initiative at Pangkor was readily accepted by Disraeli's new Conservative administration, and the new Colonial Secretary, Lord Carnarvon was quick to defend the new Residents against opposition attacks in the Lords.[116] Privately, he warned Clarke to keep a tight rein on the Residents, lest their actions "lead us further than we now intend to go". [117] In the early years, the Colonial Office and the Straits administration interpreted the role of Resident very differently. In London the Resident was seen as a solitary adviser working in partnership with the Sultan, gently persuading and directing rather than cajoling. But Clarke and his successors were determined that the Residents would become the true wielders of power in the Malay states.[118]

The Malay rulers saw the new arrangements for what they were, an unwelcome intrusion of British imperial power. One of the most naked expressions of British power was the arbitrary replacement of Sultan Ismail of Perak by Raja Abdullah. Ismail's objections, and those of his supporters were simply ignored. The new British Resident, J.W.W. Birch even alienated the new Sultan. Birch made no attempt to disguise his deep contempt for all things Malay. From the moment of his appointment in November 1874 Birch indicated that he would control exclusively all major government functions, particularly revenue collection and state expenditure. When in June 1875 Abdullah objected to the consequent usurpation of traditional Malay authority, the Resident threatened to depose him.[119] Birch further angered the Malays by his open hostility to the practice of debt bondage. He made the Residency at Bandar Bahru a virtual refuge for runaway slaves. Birch found a powerful ally from May 1875 in Clarke's successor as Governor of the Straits Settlements, Sir William Jervois. Jervois' enthusiam for imperial adventure extended initially to advocacy of complete annexation of the western Malay states, until a tour of the peninsula convinced him that moves in this direction would provoke violent resistance. Instead, Jervois aligned himself closely with Birch's authoritarian interpretation of the Residency system. He supported Birch's intimidation of Abdullah in October 1875, which forced the Sultan to openly surrender the reins of government to the Resident. Malay involvement in government was reduced to a small advisory council consisting of the Sultan and a few nobles, which would be consulted only on religious and cultural matters. The consequences of the Birch/Jervois initiative were explosive and tragic. On 2 November, while touring Perak to enforce the new arrangements, Birch was assassinated by disaffected Malays. Jervois had not informed London of his and Birch's initiative in Perak, and his pleas for military assistance provoked suspicion and dismay in the Colonial Office.[120] A British force of 2,000 troops from India and Hong Kong swiftly restored order by the end of the year, but Jervois was a discredited figure. He had resumed his earlier recommendation of annexation, but his advice now carried little weight. Carnarvon bluntly insisted that the Residency system would be made to work.

The Perak war led directly to the consolidation of the Residency system in the form envisaged by Sir Andrew Clarke. The rebellion dispelled any illusion that British "advice" was something the Malays had sought willingly. From now on it was clearly understood that the British would uphold their Residents' authority by force if necessary. The vanquished received stern treatment. Sultan Abdullah was deposed and exiled to the Seychelles. A regency under Raja Yusuf, a Malay chief who had remained loyal to the British, was established in 1877. The Residency system in the western Malay states evolved rapidly into a thinly disguised system of direct rule, under which the Residents effectively ran the state administrations on orders from Singapore or London, while the Sultans were reduced to a cosmetic role of ceremonial heads of state.

The early Residents varied widely in background, ability and experience. Some were remarkably well equipped. Sir Hugh Low, Resident of Perak from 1877 to 1889 brought nearly thirty years of experience as an official in Borneo and Labuan, as well as fluency in Malay and an understanding of Malay customs.[121] Contemporaries credited Low with establishing in Perak the most cordial and successful partnership between British and Malay authorities anywhere in the western Malay states.[122] Another figure, Sir Frank Swettenham, played a prominent role in the events of the mid 1870s, and later rose to become Resident of Selangor (1882 to 1889), Resident of Perak (1889 to 1895), and the first Resident General of the newly created Federated Malay States after 1895. Swettenham earned a reputation for efficiency and as a shrewd promoter of economic development, particularly through the construction of railways.[123] But not all earned such glowing accolades. William Bloomfield Douglas, Resident of Selangor (1876 to 1882) rose quickly in spite of minimal experience of either administration or the Malay world. Circumstance and luck were the main reasons for his success, but his good fortune expired in 1882, when exposure of his involvement in corrupt land sales led to Douglas' resignation in disgrace.[124] Perhaps the only common attribute amongst this diverse group of officials was a shared opinion that the Malays were unfit for self government. A combination of racist assumptions and a firm conviction of the moral benefits of British rule, made all of the Residents reluctant to devolve real power to the Malays.

But dominance over the Malay authorities did not simplify the task of the Resident. Various considerations made his job complex and at times frustrating. The fury of the Colonial Office at the mistakes which led to the Perak war impressed upon the Residents that their careers depended upon the maintenance of order and peaceful relations within their states. Sensitivity to Malay traditions was therefore at a premium. While the Residents exclusively controlled revenue collection, state expenditure and the administration of justice, Malay customs, ceremonies and the traditional status of the Sultan were to be superficially respected. The Sultan occupied centre stage at all major state occasions, such as the opening of new railways, and all public ceremonies emphasised the Sultan's position of theoretical constitutional supremacy over the Resident. The Residents allocated generous allowances to the Sultans - far in excess of their own relatively modest incomes - to fund the lavish lifestyles befitting Malay rulers.[125] But the reality of British rule was laid bare from time to time. The Residents dictated successions to the thrones of the Malay states, ensuring that only those loyal to the British would ascend the thrones. For example, in Perak Raja Yusuf was rewarded for loyal service by his elevation to Sultan in 1887, in preference to Raja Idris, the true successor. Idris became Sultan on Yusuf's death a year later.[126] The personal development of prospective rulers was also carefully monitored, and every effort made to ensure that by education and experience, the Sultans would be well disposed to British authority. Idris of Perak, for example, received an English education in Melaka.

Ethnic diversity further complicated the Resident's job. The growth of the Chinese population necessitated the preservation of order within and between the Chinese and Malay communities. The British regarded the Chinese as more industrious and useful than the Malays, but recognised that Malay sensibilities had to be respected to ameliorate inter communal tensions. Continued recognition of the traditional authority of Malay chiefs and penghulus was seen as necessary to contain Malay resentment of Chinese immigration. The British tried to create a niche for these Malay officials within the colonial administration.[127] The creation of elaborate structures of British authority at the local level, with British District Officers empowered to collect revenues and administer justice, provided the means for careful supervision and control of these local Malay officials. One historian has described the District Officer as a "Resident in miniature".[128] Care was taken to restrict the authority of Malay chiefs and penghulus to religous and customary matters. The strategy for dealing with the Chinese was different. The Chinese also had their own political hierarchies and organisations in the Kongsis and secret societies. They were also isolated geographically from the Malay population by their concentration in the mining regions. It seemed appropriate to the British to keep interference in the Chinese community to a minimum. Until the 1890s, the Residents tended to leave the Chinese to govern themselves, in spite of their suspicion of the Chinese secret societies. Liaison with the Chinese communities was conducted through the Kapitans China, who by the 1870s were usually wealthy merchants or mineowners, and often the head of one of the secret societies. The best example of such a figure was Yap Ah Loy in Selangor during the 1870s. Based in Kuala Lumpur he quickly won the confidence of most British officials, especially Swettenham.[129] When Swettenham became Resident in 1882, he and Yap Ah Loy clashed over municipal planning in Kuala Lumpur and Yap's control of certain revenue farms.[130] Ultimately Swettenham got his way, but he continued to value Yap's co-operation in devising land and mining regulations for the state.

British hesitancy in their dealings with the Chinese stemmed partly from ignorance of Chinese culture and language. A long history of Chinese unrest in the Straits Settlements made Residents reluctant to antagonise them by undue interference in their affairs. Even when legislation was introduced to regulate Chinese commercial practices, the British were tardy in enforcement. For example, in 1877 an ordinance passed by the Straits government seemed to have serious implications for the immigration of Chinese labour into the Malay peninsula. The "Chinese Immigrants Ordinance" created a new office of Protector of Chinese immigrants. New immigrants were required to register at the Protector's office on arrival in the Straits Settlements, and the Protector was empowered to require that all employers furnish their workers with written contracts of employment. In practice however the Ordinance was easily subverted by employers, whose power over new coolies ensured that few immigrants would dare complain of any infringement of their rights.[131]

An important development in the management of ethnic affairs was the emergence during the 1870s of State Councils in each of the western Malay states. It was one of the few innovations of the Jervois governorship which survived. Usually the State Council consisted of the Sultan, the Resident, senior Malay officials and chiefs, and representatives of the Chinese community. Members of the Council were officially appointed for life by the Sultan, but this was subject to approval by the Resident and the Governor of the Straits Settlements. The Councils were not large bodies. The Perak State Council of the early 1890s consisted of twelve members; seven Malays, three Chinese and two British officers.[132] The Councils' role was not clearly defined. Theoretically they enjoyed the full powers of government, circumscribed only by the Sultans and Residents, who were above the authority of the Councils. But in reality, the State Councils exercised little real power, and their authority diminished as time went on. The Resident set the agenda of Council meetings, and he recorded and summarised any decisions made. He also controlled the handsome allowances received by State Council members. In practice, the Resident dictated the course of meetings by "suggesting" policies which were invariably accepted by the Council. The monthly meetings of the Councils were too infrequent for members to get to grips with the complexities of administration. Ultimately the Councils became "rubber stamping" bodies which provided a veneer of traditional legitimacy for British imperial rule.[133] They were useful for pacifying ethnic opinion and securing acceptance of economic and social policies which might otherwise have elicited strong opposition.

As time went on and the British system of administration was comprehensively developed, the Chinese were also brought under direct British control. By 1900, the authority of the Kapitans China had been eroded, and the Chinese were subjected to direct British rule.[134] By then both Malay and Chinese political institutions served only a cosmetic function. They served only to disguise British imperial power as traditional authority. It was as if the structures of Malay and Chinese authority had been dismantled and reconstructed to serve the needs of the British empire. By the early 1890s Perak, Selangor, Negri Sembilan, Johore (which had succumbed to Residential government due to pressure from the Singapore authorities) and Pahang were all subjected to British rule.

The consolidation of the Residency system coincided with accelerating economic growth. Chinese enterprise facilitated a dramatic increase in tin production. Output in Perak, Selangor and Negri Sembilan rose from just under 6,000 tons in 1878 to over 26,000 tons by 1890.[135] British Residents assisted this process by investing state resources in the transport infrastructure. By 1895, Selangor and Perak had 1500 miles of newly constructed roads.[136] State activity promoted growth in numerous other ways. Loans and grants to producers encouraged the development of cash crops such as sugar and coffee.[137] Land reforms in the 1880s provided more secure land tenure.[138] The practice of revenue farming was extended to encourage the opium farming syndicates to invest in mining and related activities, thereby stimulating greater consumption of the commodities which the revenue farmers sold. These state initiatives were funded mainly by a duty on the tin trade, which by 1898 supplied 34 per cent of the revenues of the states.[139] The booming tin industry therefore swelled the states' coffers. In 1876, the total state revenues of Perak, Selangor and Negri Sembilan were $560,000, but had risen to $3.6 million by 1888.[140] Residents displayed little preference for British enterprise, and actively encouraged entrepeneurs regardless of ethnic origin. In fact some Colonial Office advisers were suspicious of Europeans, regarding them as unruly adventurers likely to clamour for further imperial expansion. Shortly after the establishment of the Residency system, Robert Herbert, the permanent under secretary, advised the Colonial Secretary, Lord Carnarvon that Malaya was "unsuitable for European colonisation". [141]

The Straits Settlements benefitted from economic growth on the peninsula. The value of Singapore's trade rose from $89.7 million in 1873 to $232.5 million in 1893.[142] By 1885, 30 per cent of Singapore's trade was with the industrialised world.[143] The Indian trade declined in importance for the port, falling from 11 per cent of Singapore's trade in 1875 to 65 per cent in

1895.[144] Commerce with mainland south east Asia also flourished, especially with Siam. British manufactured exports to the region via the Straits Settlements were boosted by improvements in steam navigation and the opening of the Suez canal. Expansion of dock facilities and shipping services transformed Singapore into a port of considerable international standing.[145]

In spite of this impressive growth, European commercial firms in Singapore changed little before the end of the century. They remained small underfunded partnerships dependent upon credit from British based export firms and the activities of Chinese compradors.[146] Trade and finance, rather than production, continued to be the main activities of the Straits agency houses. Efforts to break into the near Chinese monopoly of tin mining met with little success before the mid 1890s. Even when international demand for tin flourished in the 1880s, European entrepeneurs made little headway in the Malay peninsula. At first the omens seemed promising. Recovery in the price of tin from the low levels of the 1870s, and the British conquest of Burma in 1885 stimulated enthusiasm for tin in both the Straits and London. In June 1886, the London financial journal, "Stocks and Shares" heralded new opportunities in south east Asia in the wake of the annexation of Burma.[147] The "Mining Journal and Railway Gazette" stressed the greater security afforded to British entrepeneurs in the region by dominion over Burma.[148] Company promoters met in London to discuss the potential of the region for investment.[149] Meanwhile in the east, the establishment in 1886 of the Straits Trading Company launched a new wave of local European interest in tin. The founders of the company, Herman Muhlinghaus of Brandt and Co., and James Sword of Gilfillan, Wood and Co., intended that their main business would be the purchase and smelting of tin.[150] The company secured extensive preferential rights to buy and smelt tin in Selangor and Sungai Ujong, but Chinese protests blocked similar concessions elsewhere. Nevertheless, the advantage of economies of scale which the company acquired through its large smelting works ensured that by the mid 1890s it was the largest smelter of tin on the peninsula.[151] Optimism about the prospects for the Malay tin mines set off a feverish wave of company flotations in London during the mid 1880s.[152] But achievements did not live up to expectations, for a number of reasons.

Firstly, the Chinese mining interests on the peninsula were too well placed to be challenged by the Europeans. Skilled tin miners were almost exclusively Chinese, and the taukehs and Kongsis used their control of labour to stifle European recruitment of Chinese workers.[153] European entrepeneurs also lacked knowledge of local conditions, and by the mid 1890s most firms still in business had resorted to franchising out their concessions to Chinese enterprise. Even with the backing of London finance, the Europeans failed to dislodge Chinese enterprise from its dominant position in the western Malay states, at least before 1895.

But those Malay states yet to attract Chinese immigration offered better prospects. Pahang attracted intense interest from London backed mining companies in the late 1880s. Since 1881, the Straits government had exerted a growing influence in Pahang, in an effort to secure the eastern flank of the western Malay states. The Bendahara of Pahang also wished to emulate the economic success of Perak and Selangor, and he began to encourage European interest in his country. From 1884, concessions were offered to British mining companies, particularly in Kuantan district, where the most promising tin lodes were located. In 1886, a large concession there was purchased by a consortium of London investors.[154] By early 1887, they were ready to float the Pahang Mining Company Ltd. Since 1885, the Straits government had been seeking to negotiate a treaty with Pahang similar to one agreed with Johore in the same year. The British wanted a Consul at the court of Pahang who could control the foreign policy of the state, and would be empowered to veto undesirable concessions to entrepeneurs. British mining interests would have welcomed this initiative, had it not been for the Straits government's policy, declared in February 1885, of discouraging the granting of concessions to European enterprise by the unprotected Malay states. Behind this policy lay the fear that unrestricted commercial grants to competing Europeans might precipitate conflict between them, and provoke the long dreaded foreign intervention in the peninsula. Because of this, Straits based entrepeneurs interested in Pahang initially opposed the establishment of British political influence in the state. Within a few years, however, worries about the security of the mines eventually persuaded them and their London backers that a treaty would bring more benefits than disadvantages, provided that it allowed for the appropriate development of the country's resources.

During 1887, the Sultan of Johore acted as intermediary between the British and the Bendahara in the treaty negotiations. In anticipation of a treaty which might prohibit or restrict the granting of concessions, there was a rush of concession applications. By the time the treaty was signed, about 80 per cent of the land area of Pahang had been granted in 39 separate concessions.[155] In the event entrepeneurs' fears proved groundless. European and Chinese concessionaires persuaded the Bendahara to refuse surrender of control of the concessions to the British Consul, thereby paving the way for the treaty of October 1887, which enjoyed the full confidence of the business community.[156] In December, the Pahang Tin Mining Company Ltd was floated in London as the Pahang Tin Corporation Ltd, and the future of western enterprise in Pahang seemed assured.

But for various reasons, results were to prove disappointing. The Bendahara did not prove to be the understanding patron of tin mining promised in the early 1880s. Under the concessions he was entitled to royalties of 10 per cent on all mineral output, and other payments related to the associated importation of opium. Naturally, he wanted mining to commence as soon as possible. But a legal dispute between the Pahang Corporation and the Resident of Sungai Ujong over the territorial limits of the concession, delayed commencement of production. William Fraser, the

Pahang Corporation's local representative, feared the Bendahara's impatience, and so in July 1887 he secured the Pahang ruler's agreement to a two year postponement of commencement of mining, in return for compensation of $30,000, payable within three months. But Fraser neglected to clear this with London, and following the company's refusal to pay the agreed sum, the Bendahara cancelled the concession in March 1888.[157] Although intercession by the Colonial Office secured a new and improved concession for the Corporation from the Bendahara, the crisis dampened enthusiasm in London. When the tin mining companies subsequently discovered that dense forest, poor transport facilities and labour shortages all demanded greater inputs of capital than originally estimated, it proved very difficult to persuade London investors to furnish them with the necessary funds. The resulting capital shortages further delayed commencement of production in many of the concessions. By the mid 1890s general disillusionment had set in. In December 1893, the now British dominated Pahang government cancelled 21 European concessions which had yet to be brought into production, and redistributed the land to tried and tested Chinese mining enterprises.[158] By the end of 1895, only six of the original European concessions were operating, and all had been substantially reduced in size.[159] As in the western Malay states, European enterprise had failed to establish itself in tin mining, in spite of backing from London based gentlemanly capitalists.

The commercial failure of European enterprise was in sharp contrast to their political success in securing the protection and promotion of their interests. The influence of the tin mining concessionaires in shaping the Pahang Treaty of 1887 has been described. When the Bendahara cancelled the Pahang Corporation's concession in 1888, the full armoury of gentlemanly capitalist influence was employed to reverse the decision. Nevil Story Maskelyne MP, a director of the Corporation lobbied the Colonial Office persistently.[160] The Colonial Office persuaded the Bendahara to issue a new concession, and also supported the extension of the Residency system into Pahang in August 1888.[161] European commercial failure should not obscure the potency of gentlemanly capitalists in shaping imperial policy.

The disappointing performance of European capital in Pahang prompted further political change. Between 1888 and 1892, the British invested large sums in Pahang's infrastructure, on the assumption that rapid growth there would generate ample revenues to repay the large borrowings incurred to fund the investment. But economic disappointment created anxiety about the prospects of repayment. By 1892, the Pahang administration had borrowed over $800,000 from the administrations of Perak, Selangor and the Straits Settlements.[162] Trade depression in the early 1890s made it clear that the existing system of loans and subsidies could not continue indefinitely. Moreover, Pahang was not the only problem state. By the end of 1891, the administration of Sungai Ujong also owed the Straits Settlements $199,000. The deepening fiscal crisis now threatened to undermine the whole structure of British administration in the Straits Settlements and the Malay peninsula.

The most attractive solution appeared to be a centralised financial and administrative structure for all the protected Malay states, which could utilise the revenue surpluses of the wealthier states to meet the burgeoning costs of the poorer ones. It was also felt that centralisation of administration would rationalise and reduce the state bureaucracies, saving funds for more productive uses. By 1893, reform had become inevitable.

Reform was stimulated by administrative as well as financial concerns. The unplanned evolution of Residential governments had led to considerable diversity across the Malay states in law, property rights and in provision for judicial administration. It was feared that further divergence would create legal and administrative complexities which might obstruct further commercial development. As early as 1889, Swettenham had advocated the appointment of a "Resident-General" empowered to enforce greater uniformity in law and judicial administration throughout the protected Malay states.[163] Commercial interests in the Straits supported the idea of reform, arguing that the existing patchwork of administrative provision caused confusion and uncertainty, and deterred inward investment.[164] By 1893, the pressure for reform was irresistible.

Under the reforms implemented in 1896, the four states of Perak, Selangor, Negri Sembilan and Pahang were designated as the Federated Malay States (FMS). Local rulers and their Residents continued in office, but were now subject to the supervisory authority of a Resident General based in Kuala Lumpur. The Resident General was answerable to the Straits Governor, who now also carried the title of High Commissioner to the FMS. From him the chain of command led directly to the British government in London via the Colonial Office. The various administrative departments of the Malay states, such as police, public works, telegraph and railways were now placed under the central authority of FMS directors, who could ensure uniformity and monitor efficiency. A central treasury was created, and subsequently the separate legal codes and judicial systems of the states were harmonised to accommodate the needs of European capital.

Although hitherto Chinese enterprise had stymied the best efforts of European business to conquer tin mining, after 1895 there was a sea change in fortunes. The administrative reforms boosted European confidence, just as Chinese enterprise ran into difficulties. Increased demand for labour in China and French Indo-China curbed the flow of Chinese coolies into the Malay peninsula.[165] A brief depression in world demand for tin in the late 1890s also hit the Chinese hard.[166] A serious long term problem was the gradual exhaustion of easily mined surface deposits and the growing prevalence of deep mining in which western technology enjoyed a decisive edge. Between 1900 and 1914 the western tin mining companies began to overtake their Chinese rivals. Chinese problems were compounded by the declining importance of opium farming as a source of revenue for the British in the Malay states, as tin duties and taxes arising from rubber cultivation provided more funds. From the early 1890s it was easier for the British authorities to indulge newly found moral objections to the drug, curtailing its retail and use, although opium farms remained important to the Straits Settlements for several more decades.[167] These difficulties were not insurmountable, and Chinese enterprise survived in this more competitive environment. Chinese banking and insurance corporations were established, some even competing successfully with their western counterparts. Chinese capitalism was assisted by a network of connections throughout the east, which enabled entrepeneurs to mobilise capital and adapt quickly to changing economic circumstances. For example, the Sze Hai Tong Bank had branches in Hong Kong and Bangkok.[168] The formation of the Singapore Chinese Chamber of Commerce symbolised this durability. But there were also weaknesses. The centrality of family relationships in the management of Chinese firms was not always advantageous. Financial decisions were too frequently dictated by family loyalties rather than dispassionate commercial considerations. Capital tended to be dispersed widely among family members rather than concentrated in the hands of the most able individuals or enterprises. During the twentieth century, as western firms drew upon the resources of London, and became more sophisticated in organisation and management, Chinese enterprise fell behind.[169]

But the era of European dominance really began with the development of rubber cultivation in the early twentieth century. Land under rubber expanded from just 20,000 acres in 1903, to 2,260,000 acres by the early 1920s.[170] British capital financed this development. Between 1903 and 1905, eighteen rubber companies were floated in London, of which eight paid a dividend within two years. Returns were high, usually between 5 and 10 per cent, stimulating great enthusiasm in the City.[171] By 1907, there were 60 companies, mostly financed by London flotations, and 34 individuals involved in rubber cultivation.[172] By 1910 there were nearly 30,000 British investors in Malay rubber, led and advised mainly by those London based mercantile firms with longstanding connections in south east Asia.[173] New opportunities opened for the British agency houses based in the Straits Settlements. Often it was one of these firms which first informed London of the potential of a particular tract of land, via their contacts in the City. Once the process of company formation was under way, the Straits agency house usually became the principal managing agency, overseeing the development of production, and providing day to day manangement. In some cases managing agency of rubber plantations replaced the traditional trading activities of the houses, establishing connections with the City which were stronger than ever. Some Straits agency houses were even incorporated and floated in London, most notably Guthrie and Co. (1903), Harrisons and Crosfield (1908), and Paterson, Simons and Co (1907).[174] By 1914, British Malaya exported 47,000 tons of rubber, or 37.8 per cent of world exports.[175] The impact upon Malay society was profound. Racist disdain for the Malays, and shortages of Chinese labour, led the British to promote Indian immigration to provide workers for the rubber plantations. By 1911 there were some 172,500 Indians in the FMS. The census of that year also revealed that the population of the FMS had swelled to just over a million, with the immigrant communities outnumbering the Malays, with 41.8 per cent of the population of Chinese origin, and 16.6 per cent Indian.[176] The FMS had become an ethnically segregated economy, in which the Malay population continued their traditional activities as semi-subsistence farmers, the Indians provided labour for plantation agriculture, and the Chinese continued as a mixture of entrepeneurs and labour. The persistence of this social structure into the post colonial period illustrates the formative influence which British rule has had upon recent Malaysian history.

In Borneo, the frontiers of Brooke rule in Sarawak continued to expand at the expense of Brunei. The official British attitude to the Brooke regime remained ambiguous, because while it excluded rival European powers from northern Borneo, it occasionally threatened to embroil the British in local quarrels. In 1868, the latter consideration prompted the British government to block cession of the Baram district to Brooke.[177] James Brooke's son, Charles, sought to develop the export of forest produce such as jelutong ("jungle rubber"), camphor, gutta percha and ivory. These commodities, gathered by indigenous tribes living deep in the forests and passed to the British via a complex trading network of local and Chinese merchants, were crucial for the nineteenth century British regimes in northern Borneo, even more than mining and plantation agriculture.[178] They also stimulated further expansion of Brooke rule. In spite of misgivings, British governments eventually agreed to expansion in Sarawak, and also the creation of an entirely new and separate British regime in northern Borneo. By the late 1870s the British were worried that rival powers might threaten the sea route between Australia and China, which passed between Sulu and Northern Borneo. The Spanish in the Phillipines, the French in Indo China, the Dutch in southern Borneo, and the appearance of the United States as a possible imperial rival in the 1870s, all made the British government willing to permit extensions of British territorial control.

The new British possession was the work of a member of Dent and Co., one of the oldest British agency houses in China. In 1877 the Austrian Consul in Hong Kong, Baron Von Overbeck had acquired an unexploited concession in northern Borneo. Overbeck, a former employee of Dent and Co., sought financial support from Alfred Dent, a partner in the firm.[179] The concession consisted of 17,252,000 hectares of land, in return for annual payment of $15,000 to the Sultan of Brunei. Dent bought out Overbeck's share and used his contacts in the City to charter the British North Borneo Company, with a remit to develop the concession. The project was approved by the British government, which at the same time maintained an official distance from what was ostensibly a "private" venture. In fact official involvement was substantial. The Governor of Labuan, William Treacher had been involved in the original negotiations to secure the concession, and Dent used influential contacts in the Foreign Office to full advantage.[180]

Following the establishment of the company, Treacher was seconded to become the first governor of North Borneo. Between 1885 and 1891 treaties and conventions were agreed by the British government with Spain, Germany and the Netherlands, which confirmed the legitimacy of the British North Borneo Company's regime, and defined its territorial limits. Here was the measure of official British support for this "independent" experiment in British rule. Having permitted the creation of a rival private British "empire" in Borneo, the British government felt obliged to allow yet further expansion of Brooke rule in Sarawak, at the expense of Brunei. In 1888, to curb the expansionism of the two private British "colonies", they were incorporated into the Protectorate system which governed the western Malay states. The Governor of the Straits Settlements adopted the additional title of Consul-General for the Borneo states, and the foreign policies of the two British regimes were now subject to official control.

Economic progress was slow, and depended mainly upon the exploitation of forest produce. Mining and plantation agriculture only became significant in the twentieth century. The North Borneo Company faced many problems, particularly in collecting sufficient revenues to cover administrative costs. The small European administration depended upon local intermediaries to collect revenue and conduct trade. Ethnic conflict proved a major difficulty, especially following the influx of Malays, Chinese and Indians who followed British rule. In the 1890s, local resentment of the heavy taxation demands of the company flared into open resistance, most notably in the Malingkote revolt of 1891, and the more serious Mat Salleh rebellion of 1895, which dragged on for ten years.[181]

By the turn of the century, settled boundaries of British rule in the Malay peninsula and northern Borneo were becoming clear, although absorption of the states of the Northern Malay peninsula was only completed in 1909. Brunei, though rescued from conquest by the independent British regimes, was by 1906 clearly part of informal empire. In spite of early disappointments, economic development of the British territories in Borneo gathered pace in the twentieth century. A Chinese merchant class emerged as intermediaries between the British and the local population. It maintained close links with Chinese commercial interests in Singapore. But the role of London based gentlemanly capitalists in providing financial and political backing for both the Brooke regime and the North Borneo Company was crucial. Without supporters in London, it is questionable whether Alfred Dent's ambitious project would ever have materialised. As in the Malay states, London gentlemanly capitalists had contributed significant political support for the expansion of British rule.

NOTES

1. Cain and Hopkins, British Imperialism Vol. 1, p131.
2. This view is particularly well articulated in: C.D. Cowan, Nineteenth Century Malaya: The Origins of British Political Control (London 1961) p165. It is largely supported by: W.D. McIntyre, The Imperial Frontier in the Tropics 1865-75 (London, Macmillan 1967) pp204-205.
3. SarDesai, British Trade and Expansion pp162-163.
4. Ibid.: p164.
5. Ibid.: p165.
6. Wong Lin Ken, "The Trade of Singapore" p209 and p213.
7. Ibid.: p210 and 214.
8. Wong Lin Ken, "Singapore: Its Growth as an Entrepot" p53.
9. Wong Lin Ken, The Malayan Tin Industry to 1914 (Tucson, University of Arizona 1965) p12.
10. Ibid.: p6 and p13.
11. Wong Lin Ken, "Singapore: Its Growth as an Entrepot" p57 and p63.
12. Wong Lin Ken, "The Trade of Singapore" p277.
13. Wong Lin Ken, "Singapore" p61.
14. Ibid.: p54.
15. Buckley, An Anecdotal History p533 and p683.
16. Drabble and Drake, "The British Agency Houses" p305.
17. Buckley, An Anecdotal History p647.
18. Ibid.: p673 and p711.
19. Khoo Kay Kim, The Western Malay States p97.
20. Kaur, "The Babbling Brookes" p75.
21. Khoo Kay Kim, The Western Malay States pp104-105. Also, S. Clarke to Lord Carnarvon, 8 July 1874, CO/273/78, PRO, London.
22. Lord Kimberley to A. Clarke, 22 November 1873, and enclosed correspondence, CO/273/74, pp231-233, PRO, London.
23. Straits Settlements Association to the Duke of Buckingham, Secretary of State for the Colonies, 7 February 1868, CO/273/24, pp185-189, PRO, London.
24. Drabble and Drake, "The British Agency Houses" pp301-302.
25. The Economist Monthly Trade Supplement, 10 April 1886, p5.
26. Ray, "Asian Capital in the Age of European Domination" pp481-482.
27. Ibid.: p512.
28. Ibid.: p518.

29. Wong Lin Ken, The Malayan Tin Industry pp60-61.
30. Lt Governor of Pinang, George R. Campbell's report on the "Blue book" statistics for Pinang in 1872. CO/273/74, p164, PRO, London.
31. Wong Lin Ken, The Malayan Tin Industry pp61-62.
32. Ibid.: p56.
33. Khoo Kay Kim, The Western Malay States p78.
34. Ibid. p71.
35. Campbell's Report on Pinang "Blue book" 1872, CO/273/74, p180, PRO, London.
36. Khoo Kay Kim, The Western Malay States pp112-113.
37. Trocki, Opium and Empire pp86-116.
38. See Middlebrook, "Yap Ah Loy".
39. Andaya and Andaya, A History of Malaysia pp144-145.
40. Khoo Kay Kim, The Western Malay States pp152-153.
41. Mohd Amin Hassan (1985), "The Klang War 1867-1873" Malaysia in History 28, (1985) 55-93, pp59-60.
42. Ibid.: p60.
43. For Details of Tunku Kudin's role in Selangor Affairs see: J.M. Gullick (1986), "Tunku Kudin in Selangor 1868-1878" Journal of the Malaysian Branch of the Royal Asiatic Society 59:2, (1986) 5-50.
44. Khoo Kay Kim, The Western Malay States pp160-175.
45. Ibid.: p21.
46. Andaya and Andaya, A History of Malaysia p146.
47. Kaur, "The Babbling Brookes" pp70-71.
48. A particularly useful summary of these developments is to be found in: G. Saunders, A History of Brunei (Kuala Lumpur, Oxford University Press 1994) pp80-83.
49. Ibid. pp78-79.
50. Kaur, "The Babbling Brookes" pp74-75.
51. Ibid.: p75.
52. Ibid.: p78.
53. Ibid.: p83.
54. M.C. Cleary, "Indigenous Trade and European Economic Intervention in North West Borneo c1860-1930" Modern Asian Studies 30:2, (1996) 301-324, p313.
55. Ibid.: p320.
56. Andaya and Andaya, A History of Malaysia p126.
57. Ibid.: p128.
58. E. Sadka, The Protected Malay States 1874-1895 pp106-109.
59. McIntyre, The Imperial Frontier pp160-161.
60. Ibid.: p161.
61. Ibid.: p163.
62. Ibid. pp163-164.
63. W.D. McIntyre, "Britain's Intervention in Malaya: The Origin of Lord Kimberley's Instructions to Sir Andrew Clarke in 1873" Journal of Southeast Asian History 2:3, (1961) 47-69, pp52-54.
64. Khoo Kay Kim, The Western Malay States pp148-150.
65. Ibid.: p150.
66. Ibid. pp156-159.
67. Ibid.: pp160-168.
68. Ibid.: p184.

69. Gullick, "Tunku Kudin in Selangor" p16.
70. Khoo Kay Kim, The Western Malay States p205.
71. Gullick, "Tunku Kudin in Selangor" p26.
72. Ibid.: p28.
73. Khoo Kay Kim, The Western Malay States p209.
74. Ibid.: p210.
75. Ibid.; pp211-214.
76. Ibid.; pp221-222.
77. McIntyre, The Imperial Frontier p185.
78. Ibid.: pp188-189.
79. Ibid.: p190.
80. Ibid.: p192.
81. Ibid.: p195.
82. McIntyre, "Britain's Intervention in Malaya" p61.
83. Kimberley's memorandum, 22 July 1873, CO/273/74, p188, PRO, London.
84. Kimberley to A. Clarke, 20 September 1873, CO/273/67, pp338-342, PRO, London.
85. McIntyre, The Imperial Frontier p200.
86. Kimberley's note, dated July 1873, CO/273/74, p155, PRO, London.
87. Campbell's Report, CO/273/74, pp180-181, PRO, London.
88. McIntyre, The Imperial Frontier p200.
89. Ord to Kimberley, 6 November 1872, CO/273/61, p154, PRO, London.
90. Petition of the Melaka merchants to the Singapore Chamber of Commerce, 27 July 1872, CO/273/61, pp177-183, PRO, London.
91. Birch to Read, 21 August 1872, and Read's reply dated 17 September 1872, CO/273/61, pp184-191, PRO, London.
92. Translation of Chinese merchants' petition, 28 March 1873, CO/273/67, pp316-337, PRO, London.
93. Ord to Colonial Office, 10 July 1873, CO/273/67, pp306-315, quotation is from p308.
94. M. Kuitenbrouwer, The Netherlands and the Rise of Modern Imperialism: Colonies and Foreign Policy 1870-1902 (Oxford, Berg 1991) pp60-61.
95. Ibid.; pp106-107.
96. Wong Lin Ken, The Malayan Tin Industry p36.
97. McIntyre, The Imperial Frontier p201.
98. S. Clarke to Herbert, 18 July 1873, CO/273/74, pp191-192, PRO, London.
99. Kimberley's memorandum, 22 July 1873, pp188-189, and Macdonald to Meade, 19 July 1873, p187, CO/273/74, PRO, London.
100. Cowan, Nineteenth Century Malaya pp170-171.
101. McIntyre, "Britain's Intervention in Malaya" pp170-171.
102. Ibid.: p67.
103. SarDesai, British Trade and Expansion p164.
104. Ibid.; p165, and C.N. Parkinson, British Intervention in Malaya 1867-1877 (Singapore, University of Malaya 1960) pp109-110.
105. McIntyre, "British Intervention in Malaya" p67.
106. Pope-Hennessy to Kimberley, 12 December 1871, enclosing an extract from the London and China Telegraph, referring to the Straits Settlements Association's objection to the treaty, Kimberley Papers, 4107, New Library, Bodleian, Oxford.
107. Petition from Pinang merchants to Ord, 12 July 1873, CO/273/69, pp21-25, PRO, London.

108. Petition of Straits merchants, 28 March 1873, CO/273/67, p321, PRO, London.
109. Kimberley to Granville, 15 May 1873, Granville Papers, PRO 30/29/55, London.
110. Kimberley to Clarke, 20 September 1873, CO/273/67, pp338-342, PRO, London.
111. McIntyre, The Imperial Frontier pp295-300.
112. See Herbert's memorandum, 7 November 1873, setting up meeting of the deputation with Kimberley for Friday, 14 November 1873, CO/273/74, p226, and Kimberley to A. Clarke, 22 November 1873, CO/273/74, p230, PRO, London.
113. Read's reply to Birch concerning the Melaka petition, 17 September 1872, CO/273/61, pp188-190, PRO, London.
114. McIntyre, The Imperial Frontier p292.
115. Ibid.: pp296-297.
116. Ibid.; p298.
117. Carnarvon to A. Clarke, 29 May 1824, Carnarvon Papers, PRO 30/6/40, London.
118. Sadka, The Protected Malay States pp51-55.
119. Ibid.: pp83-84.
120. McIntyre, The Imperial Frontier pp310-311.
121. J.M. Gullick, Rulers and Residents: Influence and Power in the Malay States 1870-1920 (Singapore, Oxford University Press 1992) p366.
122. Sadka, The Protected Malay States p109.
123. Gullick, Rulers and Residents p369.
124. Sadka, The Protected Malay States p129.
125. Ibid.: p175.
126. Ibid.: pp162-164.
127. Ibid.: pp279-282.
128. Ibid.: p215.
129. The shifting and volatile relationship between the two men is explored fully in: E. Chew, "Frank Swettenham and Yap Ah Loy: The Increase of British Political Influence in Kuala Lumpur, 1871-1885" Journal of the Malaysian Branch of the Royal Asiatic Society 57:1, (1984) 70-87.
130. Ibid.: pp79-80.
131. K. Viviane Frings, "The Turbulent but Commercially Viable Chinese: A Comparison of French and British Policies Towards the Chinese in South East Asia" Itinerario 19;1, (1995) 48-68, pp49-50.
132. Sadka, The Protected Malay States p178.
133. Ibid.: 194, Gullick, Rulers and Residents p34.
134. Viviane Frings, "The Turbulent but Commercially Valuable Chinese" p53.
135. Wong Lin Ken, The Malayan Tin Industry p249.
136. Sadka, The Protected Malay States pp338-339.
137. P.J. Drake, "The Economic Development of British Malaya to 1914: An Essay in Historiography with some Questions for Historians" Journal of Southeast Asian Studies 10:2, (1979) 262-290, pp272-279.
138. Sadka, The Protected Malay States pp342-343.
139. Drake, "The Economic Development of British Malaya to 1914" p277.
140. Ibid.: p273 and p277.
141. Herbert to Carnarvon, 3 January 1876, Carnarvon Papers, Add Mss 60792, p186, BL, London.

142. Wong Lin Ken, "Commercial Growth Before the Second World War" in E.C.T. Chew and E. Lee, eds, A History of Singapore (Singapore, Oxford University Press 1991) 41-65, p51.
143. Ibid.: p50.
144. Ibid.
145. G. Bogaars, "The Effect of the Opening of the Suez Canal on the Trade and Development of Singapore" Journal of the Malaysian Branch of the Royal Asiatic Society 28:1, (1955) 97-143, pp128-131.
146. Drake and Drabble, "British Agency Houses in Malaysia" pp305-306.
147. Stocks and Shares: An Independent Weekly Journal for the Investing Classes 12 June 1886, p4, Colindale, London.
148. The Mining Journal, Railway and Commercial Gazette 5 June 1886, Letter from Dan Grove Junior of 10 Austin Friars, London, dated 1 June 1886, Colindale, London.
149. Wong Lin Ken, The Malayan Tin Industry p123.
150. Ibid.: p163.
151. By 1895, the Straits Trading Company smelted 30 per cent of the tin output of Perak and Selangor, and 54 per cent of Negri Sembilan, Ibid.: p165.
152. Ibid.: pp124-125.
153. Ibid.: p149.
154. Ibid.: p129.
155. Ibid.: p131.
156. Ibid.; p133.
157. Ibid.; pp133-134.
158. Ibid.: p144.
159. Ibid.
160. See: Maskelyne to Lord Knutsford 19 April 1888, 2 May 1888, 16 August 1888, 9 October 1888, CO/273/157, pp340-375, p383, p425 and pp449-450 respectively, PRO, London.
161. Wong Lin Ken, The Malayan Tin Industry p136.
162. Sadka, The Protected Malay States p366.
163. Ibid.: pp369-370.
164. Ibid.: pp257-258.
165. Wong Lin Ken, The Malayan Tin Industry p172.
166. Chai Hon-Chan, The Development of British Malaya 1896-1909 (Kuala Lumpur, Oxford University Press 1964) p176.
167. Trocki, Opium and Empire p184.
168. Ray, "Asian Capital in the Age of European Domination" p521.
169. These arguments are vividly outlined in R.A. Brown, Capital and Entrepeneurship in South-East Asia (Basingstoke, Macmillan 1994) pp251-257; see also: C.F. Yong, Chinese Leadership and Power in Colonial Singapore (Singapore, Times Academic Press 1992).
170. J.H. Drabble, "Investment in the Rubber Industry in Malaya c.1900-1922" Journal of Southeast Asian Studies 3:2, (1972) 247-261, pp247-248.
171. J.H. Drabble, Rubber in Malaya 1876-1922 (Kuala Lumpur, Oxford University Press 1973) p35.
172. Ibid.: p53.
173. Ibid.: p63.
174. Drake and Drabble, "British Agency Houses in Malaysia" pp307-309.

175. M. Havinden and D. Meredith, Colonialism and Development: Britain and its Tropical Colonies 1850-1960 (London, Routledge 1993) p109.
176. Ibid.: pp110-111.
177. Andaya and Andaya, A History of Malaysia p184.
178. This is the central argument of Cleary, "Indigenous Trade and European Economic Intervention in North-West Borneo".
179. Saunders, A History of Brunei p87.
180 Andaya and Andaya, A History of Malaysia p185.
181. Ibid.: pp190-191.

8. BURMA AND SIAM 1850-1900: CONQUEST AND COLLABORATION

As in maritime south east Asia, British expansion on the mainland took a variety of forms. By 1890, all of Burma had been incorporated into the British empire. In contrast Siam, though free from direct rule, survived only by accommodating British economic and political demands. The kingdom had become part of informal empire. The contrasting fates of these two states is even more striking in light of their similarities in social and political structure. Both regimes were rural, feudal autocracies which had emerged from the instability of the eighteenth century. In the nineteenth century, accommodating British economic and military might was a problem faced by both states. Why and how did Siam avoid the humiliating tragedy which destroyed the Burmese kingdom?

The complexity of developments dictates that Burma should be examined first. The end of the second Burmese war in April 1853 was unsatisfactory for the British, in spite of their resounding victory. In spite of lengthy negotiations, the British Commissioner of newly annexed Pegu was unable to secure a satisfactory treaty from Magwe Wingyi, King Mindon's wily chief minister. Crucially, the Burmese refused to accept the British annexation of Pegu, and this question threatened to poison future relations between the two sides. Mindon, as a new and insecure monarch, could not afford to demonstrate weakness by conceding openly such a massive surrender of Burmese territory. In the unstable political environment which prevailed, such a course could only encourage fresh challengers for the crown. In the end no treaty was signed, and the two sides agreed to differ on the the future of Lower Burma. But the fact of British military superiority was recognised by Mindon, who signalled his desire to accept the reality of British possession of the region in practice if not in law. Above all a period of peace and stability was now essential if his Kingdom was to survive. However, just as Yandabo had failed to establish a peace acceptable to both sides, the uncertain cessation of hostilities in 1853 left a dangerous legacy of bitterness and unresolved questions.

The problems facing Mindon were formidable. The king's fragile hold on power rendered him heavily dependent upon Prince Kanaung, his younger brother, whose military prowess had placed Mindon on the throne.[1] Mindon and Kanaung's revolt against King Pagan had originated in their opposition to war with the British. Pious and well educated, Mindon was a persuasive leader of the peace faction. When Pagan moved to arrest his opponents in November 1852, Mindon fled the capital and the revolt began in earnest. British successes helped to deliver victory to Mindon, and by Spring 1853, Amarapura was in rebel hands. Nevertheless, such was the severity of social and political upheaval that Mindon did not feel sufficiently safe to enter the capital until December 1853.[2] Consolidation of his position remained a priority for Mindon in the following years. Marriage was one way of securing support from rival families. In 1853, Mindon took eight new wives, each of them related to either Tharrawaddy or Bagyidaw. By the time of his death, Mindon had acquired fifty five wives.[3]

In addition to these immediate political difficulties, the loss of Pegu was a severe blow. The territory encompassed the kingdom's only remaining coastline, produced most of the country's rice, and generated vital revenues for the state coffers. The loss of these assets made reform of the Burmese state and economy imperative for the regime's survival. Defeat by the British for the second time in thirty years lent greater urgency to calls for reform. Mindon was only too aware of hawkish elements in the British administration and commercial community in Lower Burma, who nurtured ambitions for still further annexations of Burmese territory. Modernisation of the Burmese state and its army was vital to discourage these tendencies. Mindon and Kanaung set out with the aim of "transforming the traditional Burmese state into a viable, nineteenth century nation".[4]

Reforms were judicial, military and economic. Reform of the system of justice entailed the tightening of central state control over the system of provincial courts. State action was in response to misuse of power by local judges, either to line their own pockets or those of allies among the local village headmen (Myothugyi and Taikthugyi). Such widespread corruption undermined confidence in the authority of the crown at a time when its restoration was crucial following war and revolution. Mindon subjected judges to a battery of strict regulations, covering the conduct of trials and fees charged by the courts.[5] In 1865, further reforms removed criminal cases to higher district courts, whose judges were subject to even stricter state scrutiny.

Military reform set out to change the existing economic and social structure of the army. Traditionally, officers and their units (ahmudan) were allocated land to farm, from which they were required to surrender a quarter of their produce to the state. It was a skeleton army expanded in wartime by conscription of men between seventeen and sixty. Training was minimal, desertion and corruption were endemic, and discipline lax. The army had been no match for the British, and Mindon wanted to transform it into a modern fighting force. The land allocation system was virtually abolished, and the officer corps turned into a modern, salaried, professional service.[6] Senior officers were sent to Europe for training, and efforts were made to procure modern weaponry. When the British prohibited the flow of arms into Burma later in the 1850s, Mindon tried, with limited success, to develop an indigenous armaments industry. Dependence on foreign arms supplies proved impossible to break, and the British ensured that the Burmese could never achieve military parity. During the negotiations leading to the treaty of 1867, Calcutta vetoed a proposal that restrictions on the export of arms to Burma be relaxed.[7] But while ambitions to match the British remained unfulfilled, the reforms did give the Burmese a decisive edge when confronted by internal rebellions, an advantage which alone justified Mindon's initiatives.[8]

Economic reforms began in the 1850s with an extension of state irrigation works to increase rice production in Upper Burma. The aim was not only to replace food supplies formerly provided by Pegu, it was also to prevent the wholesale migration of Burmese peasants to British Burma, where large food surpluses ensured lower prices.[9] But the rivers were too low and the land insufficiently fertile for the scheme to compensate for the loss of Lower Burma. By the 1870s, Upper Burma was heavily dependent upon rice imports from British Burma. Imports rose from 26,655 tons in 1872/73 to 71,444 tons in 1877/78.[10] The price of rice rose by more than a third between 1855 and 1875, and combined with the depreciation of the silver based Burmese currency, this quintupled the cost of rice imports into Upper Burma.[11] The state irrigation schemes at best could only delay an impending food and balance of payments crisis.

Heavy state expenditure on reform, and the deteriorating balance of payments made fiscal reform imperative to sustain the modernisation programme. Export trades had to earn sufficient foreign exchange to finance food imports. Burmese teak, cotton, earth oil and precious stones all seemed promising. Mindon exploited existing state monopolies over the production or trade in these commodities to maximise earnings. The monopolies were either run by the state or by private individuals to whom the monopolies had been leased at a high price. They delivered handsome revenues. In 1885 alone, the state monopolies for cotton, cutch, lead, timber and rubies yielded 1.8 million Kyats (£227,500).[12] This strategy was probably Mindon's best option to cover the costs of reform and minimise balance of payments difficulties. It exploited the main consumers of Burmese exports, the British and Chinese, and shielded the Burmese population from punitive and politically dangerous levels of taxation. But there was a price for shifting the revenue burden onto international trade. The state monopolies excluded many Burmese entrepeneurs from the most lucrative branches of commerce, thereby stifling the private sector of the economy. State income from international trade was also highly vulnerable to the vagaries of the international economy and foreign political events. For example, Burmese revenues were hit severely by the Panthay rebellion in China after 1857, which suppressed Chinese demand for Burmese exports.[13] Moreover, the state monopolies exacerbated tensions with the British, whose commitment to free trade was in direct conflict with Mindon's strategy.

The annexation of Pegu stimulated British enterprise in Lower Burma, because it removed at a stroke the Burmese trade restrictions so irksome to the British merchants of Rangoon and Moulmein. As in the Straits Settlements, an Asian mercantile community emerged as partners for the British in the expansion of production and commerce. The Nattukottai Chettiars of south India, wealthy bankers with widespread Asian connections provided credit for Burmese cultivators, enabling them to increase the rice exports which proved so profitable for British merchants.[14] The economic potential of the Burmese teak forests had long been recognised, and as early as 1851, Dalhousie had expressed concern at the wasteful methods employed by British timber merchants in Tenasserim.[15] In 1856 a Superintendent of Forests was appointed for British Burma, with instructions to prevent the earlier exhaustive forestry practices of the past. The first Superintendent, Dr Dietrich Brandis, has been credited with the introduction of the Taungya system, which combined forestry with subsistence and cash cropping, and replaced trees felled by seedlings.[16] First introduced in the hill region of the Pegu Yoma, the local Karen population were coerced or persuaded to adopt the system by a mixture of financial incentives, punitive taxes or even imprisonment.[17] By the 1860s the system was well established, although in the long run, most British forestry in Burma was undertaken on large European managed plantations. The Taungya system was notable because it secured first compliance with, and later support for, the colonial regime among the Karens.[18] They were to prove invaluable as scouts, guards and rangers, giving notable service during the third Anglo-Burmese war.

During the 1860s, as the teak firms of Lower Burma expanded operations, some flowered into multinational businesses with connections in London. The most important of these was established by William Wallace, originally a partner in the family firm of Wallace and Co. in Bombay.[19] So successful was he following his arrival in Burma in the early 1850s, that in 1862 he accompanied his friend, Chief Commissioner Arthur Phayre to Mandalay to help negotiate the treaty signed in that year. During the early 1860s, William's success in Burmese teak, and Wallace and Co.'s success in Indian cotton, enabled the family to establish the London sister firm of Wallace Brothers and Co., which was incorporated as a limited company in 1862.[20] The motive was to secure City finance to fund commercial expansion.[21] At the same time, William and his younger brother Alexander set up the Bombay Burmah Trading Corporation (BBTC), which was subsequently floated in London.[22] The BBTC expanded operations in Burma dramatically. It immediately negotiated teak concessions in Upper Burma from Mindon's government.[23] The company facilitated a massive expansion of teak exports from Burma. Average annual exports rose from 85,000 tons in the period 1857 to 1864, to 275,000 tons in 1883-84.[24]

The 1860s saw rapid British commercial expansion in Burma. Excited by the prospect of new opportunities in Upper Burma, British merchants became impatient with the trade protectionism of Mindon's regime. The Indian government's decision in 1862 to rationalise the administration of British Burma stemmed partly from the need to formalise and improve relations with Mindon, and to contain the demands of the more belligerent British merchants. Arakan, Tenasserim and Pegu, previously governed by separate officers as discrete commands, were united under the authority of Arthur Phayre, the first Chief Commissioner of British Burma.[25] Commercial interest was not confined to Upper Burma. There had been enthusiasm for a land route to China through Burma since the 1830s.[26] In the late 1850s the explorations of a retired army officer, Captain Richard Sprye, caught the imagination of businessmen in Britain and Burma. At the time there was boundless optimism about the potential of China as a market for British exports. In 1860, the Chambers of Commerce of Manchester, Liverpool, Huddersfield and Leeds lobbied government for a railway to China.[27] Other expeditions followed. In the late 1860s, the British representative at Mandalay, Dr Clement Williams, travelled to Bhamo in an effort to identify a practical route.[28] Later in the decade, Major E.B. Sladen, British Political Agent at Bhamo, led an expedition into south western China.[29] Then in 1874 there was a two pronged expedition to identify a land route to the east coast of China. Colonel Horace Browne's expedition entered China from Bhamo, while a party led by the diplomat, Augustus Margary, advanced from Shanghai towards Yunnan, to meet up with Browne.[30] The failure of the mission, with Margary's tragic death at the hands of some Chinese soldiers, did not diminish enthusiasm in commercial circles. On the eve of British conquest in October 1885, the explorer Archibald Colquhoun regaled the London Chamber of Commerce with the lucrative markets which an extended eastern rail network would open.[31] The emergence of a French presence in south east Asia from the late 1850s also promoted official interest in a viable route to China, from fear that Britain's traditional European rival might be first to exploit the potential for overland access. But in the end, aspirations for a "golden" overland route were never fulfilled. The potential of China as a market had been grossly overestimated, as had Burmese willingness to tolerate any route which traversed their territory. Mindon recognised that such a project would increase the British presence in his diminished kingdom, encouraging demands for yet further territorial expansion at Burma's expense. The Burmese used every opportunity to obstruct British attempts to establish a trans-Burmese trade route. The Imperial Chinese government were equally unwilling to co-operate. Then there were the difficulties of terrain and climate, which threatened to inflate construction costs so much, that the Sprye plan for a rail link was quietly abandoned. Later plans for a trade route relied upon utilisation of the Irrawaddy and Salween river systems, especially after the establishment of the Irrawaddy Flotilla Company, a subsidiary of the Henderson Line which operated between Glasgow and Rangoon.[32] But even here, problems meant that high expectations were never realised.

In spite of these disappointments, commercial pressure altered official British attitudes towards Burmese modernisation. Mindon's trade restrictions and monopolies had been reluctantly tolerated in the 1850s when the British were eager to normalise relations following the war. But in the early 1860s, burgeoning commercial growth convinced the Indian government that Mindon should be pressed to relax taxes and restrictions on trade.[33] The result was Phayre's mission to Mandalay in 1862.[34] As ever, Mindon was suspicious and fearful of British intentions, but he was pressured into accepting a new commercial treaty.[35] Reluctantly Mindon agreed to the eventual removal of all duties on trade between his kingdom and British Burma. The treaty stipulated that the British would comply immediately, with Burma following suit four years later.[36] It is doubtful whether Mindon had any real intention of meeting this deadline, and within a few years it became clear that it would not be met. The abolition was to apply also to the transit trade between British Burma and China, and British traders were to be granted free movement up the Irrawaddy and royal protection of their persons and property in Burma.

Burmese sloth in implementing the treaty was greeted with growing impatience among British merchants and officials. Successive British agents in Mandalay nagged Mindon to keep to the timetable of reform. Tensions were exacerbated by squabbles at the frontier of Lower and Upper Burma between British merchants and Burmese border guards.[37] By 1866, the British were convinced that a fresh treaty was necessary to secure their objectives. Phayre arranged to visit Mandalay again in September 1866, but he was delayed by a rebellion against the Burmese king. When the Chief Commissioner eventually arrived in the capital in November, he found Mindon initially resistant to pressure. The king refused to accept Phayre's demands for the termination of various royal monopolies as stipulated in the 1862 treaty, and the appointment of a British officer to monitor Burmese compliance with that agreement.[38] Phayre left Mandalay empty handed, but friction in the negotiations and problems in Upper Burma had softened Mindon's resistance. The rebellion of 1866, led by the king's son Prince Myingun, had resulted in the assassination of Kanaung, and a close brush with death for Mindon himself.[39] Though defeated, Myingun had fled to the Shan states, where he continued to encourage revolt. Mindon suspected the British of complicity in the rebellion, although he was unable to uncover proof. Myingun was eventually interned by the British, and Mindon feared that his son might be used by them to foment further rebellions. The fragility of his position was thus very clear to the Burmese king. In this context, when Phayre's successor, Albert Fytche led a new delegation to Mandalay in October 1867, Mindon was compliant. The new treaty immediately reduced all duties on trade between Upper and Lower Burma to 5 per cent. Most royal trade monopolies were abolished, except those for earth oil, timber and precious stones.[40] A British Political agent at Mandalay was also to be appointed with legal jurisdiction over disputes between British subjects. He was also to sit with a Burmese judge in jurisdiction over disputes between British and Burmese individuals. There was to be an Assistant British Resident at Bhamo, on the route to China, and the Irrawaddy Flotilla Company was permitted to navigate the river freely. In return, Fytche promised informally that Mindon would be allowed greater freedom to import arms, although the Calcutta authorities vetoed the formal inclusion of this in the treaty.[41]

The treaty of 1867 proved to be a turning point, not only in Anglo-Burmese relations, but also in the fate of the Burmese kingdom. Fytche's promise of increased arms supplies was never fulfilled, souring relations with the Burmese. One recent historian argues that the treaties of 1862 and 1867 are best understood as a British attempt to assert informal imperial control over the Burmese, compelling Mandalay to accommodate British economic requirements.[42] Certainly the tone of British diplomacy in the 1870s displayed slight regard for what was now seen as a satellite state. Two issues emerged which exemplified this assumption, and poisoned diplomatic relations. The first was the refusal of the British to extend to Burma the etiquette normally displayed to states of equal stature. The British insisted upon conducting relations with the Burmese through the India Office rather than the Foreign Office, implying that Burma was a vassal state of the British empire in India. The humiliation was at times cruel and blatant. In 1872, a Burmese delegation to Britain was only permitted an audience with Queen Victoria in the presence of the Secretary of State for India, and were required to prostrate themselves before the British monarch.[43] Little wonder that the Burmese began to seek closer relations with the French, in an effort to reassert their independence from British power.

The other issue became known as the "shoe question". According to Burmese tradition, foreign representatives were required to remove their shoes, disarm themselves, and kneel before the king. In spite of the fact that they had previously observed the custom, the British decided in 1876 to object to it on the grounds that the ritual was demeaning to British prestige. Anglo-Burmese relations never recovered from this surreal diplomatic episode. Although the British maintained their Resident at Mandalay, he no longer attended audiences with the king, preferring to conduct business indirectly through royal officials rather than suffer the "humiliation" of removing his footwear. British motives were nakedly imperialist. They wanted to impress upon Mindon that he was a subordinate whose position depended upon British goodwill. For the king and his officials the British attitude was unbearable. It insulted the most sacred Burmese religous beliefs, and encouraged minorities within the remnants of the Burmese empire to adopt an equally contemptuous posture. The effect was to harden Burmese determination to resist British imperialism.

But the treaties of 1862 and 1867 had even more serious consequences. Mindon had looked to the state monopolies and taxes on trade to raise the monies required to pay for modernisation. The treaties severely restricted the scope for raising funds from this source, and compelled Mindon to increase revenue collections from his subjects. In the 1850s, the Thathameda, a tax in kind on cultivator households, had been introduced, taking approximately 10 per cent of produce.[44] In 1866, Mindon directed that in future the thathameda would be collected in cash. For many poor cultivators this was a grievous blow. A general tightening of fiscal policy ensued. Traditionally, the remuneration of central state officials had depended upon their right to keep a share of the revenues they collected for the state. In the tightening financial environment of the mid 1860s such leakage of state income was no longer acceptable. In 1866, the practice of self remuneration was replaced by salaries paid directly from the state treasury. Inevitably this meant a drastic reduction in the incomes of officials, provoking a deep sense of grievance among the country's administrative elite.[45] There was also fury in the villages as tax demands on the population escalated steadily from the late 1860s. The effect was to undermine the systems of local rule and patronage which had long been the bedrock of royal authority. Increasing taxation also triggered rebellion among the ethnic minorities. When economic conditions deteriorated severely in the early 1880s, the weakened state structures collapsed under an avalanche of popular discontent and revolt.

To make matters worse, new economic problems emerged in the 1870s. At the root of these was the loss of Lower Burma and the growing dependence upon imported rice. To meet spiralling import bills, a thriving export economy was needed. A motive for turning the thathameda into a monetary tax had been to compel subsistence cultivators to produce for the market by confronting them with steep cash tax liabilities. But deterioration in the terms of trade during the 1870s made import costs impossible to offset. A major factor in this was the steady depreciation of silver based currencies (such as the Burmese currency) against gold based ones. The outcome was high inflation, especially for rice and other imported foodstuffs. Between 1865 and 1885, the price of rice in Upper Burma more than doubled.[46] Of Burmese exports, only teak held its own during the 1870s, as falling world prices hit Burmese cotton exports hard. Rice shortages in Upper Burma had to be met increasingly by large scale state purchases on the international market, which the Burmese state could neither afford nor sustain. The escalating cost of food fuelled popular discontent among a Burmese population already deeply resentful of increasing state revenue exactions.

Growing British political power had undermined the economic base of the Burmese regime. Mindon was increasingly forced to finance his modernisation strategy by imposing deeply unpopular levels of taxation on his people, and administrative reforms which alienated most of the country's elite. The effect was to destabilise the already fragile relationship between central government and an ethnically diverse population. Coupled with the intractable problem of food price inflation, itself a consequence of the earlier British annexation of the kingdom's main food producing region, these difficulties made collapse of the Burmese state inevitable. The only questions were how long the collapse could be postponed, and the form it would take when delay was no longer possible.

The last years of Mindon's reign saw increasingly desperate attempts to shore up Burmese independence by seeking assistance from rival European powers. The same Burmese delegation so cruelly humiliated before Queen Victoria, managed to secure a provisional commercial treaty with France in 1873.[47] In fact, disagreements over detail prevented ratification of the treaty, and in the end served only to inject still more poison into Anglo-Burmese relations. The British engaged in diplomatic mischief during the 1870s, by encouraging Burmese vassal states to flout Mandalay's authority. One historian has described the British residency at Mandalay as a "magnet for would be conspirators and various rival factions".[48] In 1875, the British bullied Mindon into abrogating all Burmese claims of sovereignty over western Karenni, a territory which the British believed might provide the elusive route into China.[49] At the end of his life in 1878, Mindon was a broken king trying to rule a broken country. As he lay dying, there were already voices in London urging yet further intrusion into his decaying kingdom.[50] The stage was set for the final act in the British conquest of Burma.

**

Mindon's death precipitated a serious crisis. Fearful that any prospective successor might meet the same fate as Kanaung, Mindon had appointed no prospective heir (einshemin). Polygamy had ensured that there was no shortage of contenders. In addition to the exiled Myingun, there were numerous princes, but all of them were sons of queens of modest status. None of them could lay an unchallengeable claim to the throne.[51] In these circumstances, the task of selecting a new king fell to the senior legal and governing assembly, the Hluttaw.

Senior ministers and members of the royal family now jostled for influence and position. One of Mindon's lesser queens, Sinpyumashin, manoeuvred to secure a higher status among the dead king's wives.[52] Even before Mindon's death she had been pressing the candidacy of Thibaw, a young prince of low status, who was betrothed to her two daughters, Supayalat and Supayagi. Following the election of Thibaw, both Sinpyumashin and Supayalat came to exercise considerable political influence over the new king. Thibaw also won the support of Kinwun Mingye, Mindon's senior minister. Kinwun Mingye had been alarmed by the drift of Anglo-Burmese relations under Mindon. The desperate condition of state finances in the last years of his reign had compelled Mindon to reintroduce certain state trade monopolies in contravention of the 1867 treaty.[53] There had also been numerous clashes between Burmese officials and British traders on the Irrawaddy.[54] Kinwun Mingye feared the possibility of war if friendly relations could not be re-established. He wanted a pliable new king who could be guided in this direction, and also towards a continuation of internal reforms to stabilise the kingdom.[55] At the tender age of twenty, Thibaw was made einshemin in September 1878. He became king on Mindon's death a few weeks later.

The context of the succession contributed greatly to the tragic events which followed. Spiralling food prices and discontent within the state bureaucracy were accompanied by a wave of social disorder. Traders and villages became targets for banditry (dacoity). The new king and his advisers were fearful that if a challenge to Thibaw's kingship arose, the country would be plunged into chaos and civil war. On 17 February 1879, the British Resident in Mandalay, Robert Shaw, noted in his diary rumours of the murder of several members of the royal family.[56] It soon became clear that there had indeed been a massacre of princes and their families by the king's personal bodyguard, led by Thibaw's childhood friend, the Lord of Yanaung.[57] Although a few princes escaped to British Burma, Thibaw had swept away most of his potential rivals at a stroke. Historians disagree about the the reasons for the massacre. One established view identifies Yanaung and Supayalat as the principal culprits.[58] A more recent and convincing explanation locates the cause in the battle for power between Thibaw's main supporters, Kinwun Mingye, Sinpyumashin and Supayalat. Shortly after Thibaw's accession, the chief minister secured a major restructuring of the Hluttaw which enhanced his own power and prestige at the expense of the crown.[59] These changes improved the prospects of continuing administrative reform. But as members of the royal family, Sinpyumashin and Supayalat were determined to defend the crown's authority. According to this interpretation, they ordered the killing of some forty members of the royal family to demonstrate the extent of their power to Kinwun Mingye, and to remove any possible contenders he might promote when Thibaw's rejection of his reforms became obvious. The strategy worked, because the chief minister displayed little resistance when the Hluttaw reforms were subsequently reversed by the king.[60] Thereafter, Kinwun Mingye's influence steadily declined, to be replaced by that of another Hluttaw official, Taingda. An arch conservative and traditionalist, Taingda was deeply hostile to both reform and appeasement of the British. Together with Supayalat and a strong traditionalist faction at court, he set Thibaw on course for confrontation with the British.

In many ways, Resident Shaw's reaction to the royal massacre came to epitomise the British view of Thibaw. Shaw's lingering descriptions of the atrocities encapsulated the moral outrage and contempt felt by most British officials and observers.[61] There was growing concern for the safety of the British Resident. Although Colonel Horace Brown was appointed Resident on Shaw's death in June 1879, within three months the Residency had been withdrawn from Mandalay. Alarm at Thibaw's belligerence, and the outbreak of colonial wars in Afghanistan and southern Africa, persuaded the British government that withdrawal was prudent. An assault on the British Resident would undoubtedly mean war, and a third colonial conflict might stimulate opposition at home. Besides, it had been the murder of the British Resident in Kabul which had sparked off the conflict in Afghanistan.[62] The end of the Residency proved a severe handicap for Anglo-Burmese diplomacy. Even though the shoe question had already impaired communications between the two sides, the Resident could at least be trusted, as a British official loyal only to his government, to report events in Mandalay accurately. Following withdrawal, the British government had to depend for intelligence upon the agents of British commercial firms in Mandalay. Events were to throw their impartiality into doubt.

In spite of his hawkish advisers, Thibaw was dismayed by the end of the Residency, and he at once sent a delegation to British Burma to seek an audience with the Viceroy in India. C.U. Aitchison, the Chief Commissioner, was instructed not to to co-operate. The Burmese delegation was detained at the border town of Thayetmyo. In response to Burmese protestations of a desire for a new treaty and the normalisation of Anglo-Burmese relations, Aitchison stressed that negotiations could only begin after a Burmese apology for past mistreatment of British Residents, and the resumption of the Mandalay Residency on British terms.[63] Discussions were soured by a squabble between an IFC steamer captain and Burmese officials at Mingyan in November 1879.[64] An impasse was reached, and in May 1880 the Burmese mission retreated to Mandalay empty handed.

British anger at the massacres and past treatment of Residents were the reasons for their intransigence. But it was clear that matters could not be allowed to drift indefinitely. Certain articles of the 1867 treaty were subject to time limitation clauses which had expired in 1877. Thibaw was now entitled to increase the duties on trade between his kingdom and British Burma from 5 to 10 per cent.[65] The deepening fiscal crisis of the Burmese state made this move irresistible. The Indian government, led by Lord Lytton, now considered draconian measures which ran contrary to the previous British commitment to free trade. It was suggested that a complete abrogation of the 1862 and 1867 treaties by the British might have a sobering effect on Thibaw. British duties on trade could then be increased dramatically, permitting the British to shift the burden of taxation from the population of British Burma onto trade.[66] The Burmese kingdom, which was heavily dependent upon food imports from British Burma, would be coerced into recognition of their dependence upon British goodwill, and Anglo-Burmese relations renegotiated on British terms.[67] Had such a policy been pursued, the Burmese state might have collapsed several years earlier than it eventually did, and British conquest might have been completed in 1880. Lytton believed that Disraeli's Conservative government could be persuaded to support an invasion, should military action prove necessary. Higher

British duties on trade would have had a devastating impact on Burma, which was already unable to cope with the long term shift against it in the terms of trade. The final crisis might have come in 1880 instead of 1885.

But the election of a Liberal government in 1880 replaced the hawkish elements within the Indian administration. The new Secretary of State for India was the anti-imperialist Lord Hartington, while Lord Ripon, the new Viceroy of India, and Charles Bernard, the new Chief Commissioner of British Burma, clearly understood the antipathy towards imperial adventure which prevailed in Gladstone's cabinet. The new team set out to reconstruct Anglo-Burmese relations on an amicable basis. Events made this almost impossible to achieve. Desperate for new revenues, Thibaw took advantage of the expiry clauses of the 1867 treaty to re-establish certain state monopolies, most notably over the export of cotton.[68] Leases permitting the BBTC to fell timber in the Toungoo forests of Ningyan in Upper Burma were renegotiated between 1880 and 1883, and it was clear that higher fees would be demanded from the company.[69] To stave off financial collapse, Thibaw also borrowed heavily from wealthy Burmese merchants such as Moola Ismail.[70]

In January 1882, Ripon instructed Bernard to press Thibaw to negotiate a new political and commercial treaty. Ripon proposed a tough stance to drag Thibaw back to the table. Bernard was empowered to threaten Thibaw with British abandonment of all previous treaties and punitive retaliatory tariffs in reply to Thibaw's recent protectionist measures, if the Burmese king refused to negotiate. Intimidated, Thibaw abolished the renewed state monopoly of cotton exports and agreed to talks. A Burmese delegation reached Simla in April 1882, and at first the discussions promised to be fruitful. But even as the talks proceeded, Taingda was busy convincing Thibaw that he could not afford to make concessions on the question of the Burmese trade monopolies. Any surrender of these would deny the Burmese state the resources essential for it to cope with the deepening internal economic and social crisis. On instructions from Mandalay, the Burmese negotiators in Simla became increasingly intransigent.[71] After a few months, they were recalled to Mandalay without any agreement being reached. Ripon was disappointed, but unprepared to implement the earlier threats of retaliatory tariffs, lest this precipitate the war he was so eager to avert. Instead, he opted for a policy of persuasion and quiet diplomacy, in the forlorn hope of improving relations.

By 1882, the problems of dacoity and disorder in Upper Burma were becoming very severe. It has even been suggested that senior members of Thibaw's court were connected with the dacoit gangs who now terrorised the villages around the capital.[72] Financial difficulties made it difficult for the government to send sufficient troops to quell this lawlessness. Worsening shortages and accelerating price rises fuelled popular discontent. Having rejected the latest British moves for a treaty, Thibaw now worried that Ripon might give British support to one of the numerous potential pretenders to the throne currently in exile in British territory. In desperation, Thibaw turned to the French, in the hope that the abortive commercial treaty of 1873 could be revived.[73] In 1883, a Burmese mission was sent to Paris, ostensibly for scientific and cultural purposes, but in reality to exhume the earlier project of a Franco-Burmese treaty. Thibaw wanted to involve the French in Burmese commercial enterprise, eliciting in the process a French commitment to check British influence in Burma. At the very least, he wanted a French undertaking to supply arms. At most, Thibaw wanted the French to become a counterweight to British influence, which would help preserve Burmese independence.

The French were intrigued by the Burmese overtures. In 1882, they were at war in Tonkin with the Chinese, and in the following February, Jules Ferry formed an imperialist administration in France which was committed to expansion in south east Asia. Ferry was particularly concerned about the security of French possessions in Cambodia and Cochin China, and their sensitive western border with Siam. Ferry suspected the British of using their considerable influence in Bangkok to encourage Siamese expansion eastwards into territory coveted by the French. Ferry anticipated enormous advantages in establishing a political presence in Mandalay as a counterpoise to British influence in Bangkok.[74] In the long run, a French position in Burma might become a useful bargaining chip to persuade the British not to oppose French initiatives on the eastern frontier of Siam. But there were dangers. To openly embrace Thibaw's invitation into his kingdom might inflame Anglo-French relations. The consequences for France might be disastrous, given British military superiority in the east. Too eager a French response to Thibaw might even precipitate immediate British annexation of Upper Burma, sweeping away the opportunity offered by the Burmese king. In November 1883, when the British got wind of Franco-Burmese discussions, Lord Lyons, the British ambassador in Paris, bluntly warned Ferry that London regarded Upper Burma as part of the British sphere of influence and that they would tolerate nothing stronger than a purely commercial agreement between Thibaw and the French.[75] As a result, Franco-Burmese discussions moved at a snail's pace. Ferry would countenance no agreement which might provoke British action, or at least he wanted such agreements kept secret until they could be openly employed in a general Anglo-French renegotiation of relations in the east. A sticking point was the provision of arms by the French for the Burmese. Negotiations dragged on for nearly eighteen months before a treaty was finally signed in January 1885. Superficially a commercial treaty, it did establish a French Consul at Mandalay. Ferry reassured the British that French interests were purely commercial, but he made clear that he expected to be consulted in future about any intended British military action against Burma.[76] Unknown to the British, Ferry had made a secret promise to supply arms to the Burmese.[77] It was to cause much friction when it was subsequently exposed.

The Burmese crisis, which had been looming for several years, came to a head in 1885. It culminated in the British conquest of the kingdom, and a prolonged guerilla war which cost thousands of lives, and drew in tens of thousands of British imperial troops. Several main developments brought matters to a climax. Firstly, the social and economic breakdown of Upper Burma gathered pace. Widespread dacoity threatened the safety of British commerce, and there were several serious rebellions among the ethnic minorities. There were also border raids by Chinese bandits, who sacked Bhamo.[78] As order broke down, there was an exodus of Burmese refugees into British Burma. J.A. Bryce, the BBTC's manager in Burma warned his superiors that "the condition of Upper Burma is wretched in the extreme".[79] One historian has argued that severe deforestation in Upper Burma by the BBTC contributed to an ecological crisis which severely undermined the rice harvests between 1883 and 1885.[80] By 1885, the British feared that the Upper Burmese crisis would spill over into British territory. In these circumstances, British intervention in Upper Burma began to seem inevitable.

Secondly, Ferry's promise to supply Thibaw with arms was dramatically exposed in July 1885. Giuseppe Andreino, the Italian Consul at Mandalay, and agent there for several British companies, including the BBTC and IFC, acquired a copy of the secret letter from Ferry promising to furnish the Burmese with arms. Andreino's source has never been identified conclusively, but it seems that he had close ties with one of Kinwun Mingye's secretaries.[81] Ferry's letter was sent to the British government, together with further revelations. The French Consul, Frederic Haas, who arrived in Mandalay in May 1885, was accused by Andreino of negotiating a new secret treaty which delivered far more to the French than the vaguely worded agreement of January 1885. Under this new agreement, the French were to build a railway from Mandalay to Toungoo, funded partly by a loan of £2.5 million from the French government. Thibaw agreed to consign management of the royal monopolies to the French, who would also take 7.5 per cent interest for their loan from river duties, which they would now collect on behalf of the Burmese government. The French agreed to to help establish a Burmese national bank, which would lend to the Burmese government at preferential rates. The French would receive the Burmese ruby mines as security, although profits from mining would be shared equally between the French and Burmese governments.[82] Andreino described the establishment of a French commercial and political influence in Upper Burma which was most threatening to British political and commercial interests.

Historians have disagreed fiercely about the authenticity of Andreino's documents pertaining to this alleged Franco-Burmese agreement, and also about the reliability of the Italian Consul as a servant of the British.[83] But it does seem that Andreino's accusations had substance. In October 1885, a British diplomat in Paris, John Walsham, was approached by a Mr Farman, a British journalist resident in Paris. Farman revealed his involvement in a private French enterprise seeking to secure the right to build a railway between Mandalay and Toungoo. His partner was the Comte de Trevelac, and when the Burmese mission had visited Paris in 1883/84, secret talks had been held with the Burmese delegates. Although no agreement had been completed at that time, Farman believed that De Trevelac was still pursuing negotiations at the time of Farman's meeting with Walsham. De Trevelac was in Mandalay as part of the French diplomatic team. Farman revealed that discussions with the Burmese in Paris had also explored the possibility of establishing a bank at Mandalay. It had been anticipated that the French syndicate would meet the costs of railway construction by being granted the right to collect customs duties at the frontier with British Burma. Should receipts from these prove inadequate to meet French costs, it had been suggested that Burmese receipts from the BBTC forest concessions in Upper Burma be paid directly to the French consortium.[84] Walsham made it plain that Farman's involvement in the project was unacceptable, and the chastened journalist promised to desist immediately.[85] Ultimately, events overtook the plan when the British invaded Upper Burma later in the year; but the scheme described by Farman was similar if not identical to the one outlined by Andreino in July. The few differences might be accounted for by misunderstanding of the details on Andreino's part, or by the negotiation in Burma of new clauses which were unknown to Farman. Andreino may also, of course, have exaggerated the concessions granted to the French to elicit a firmer response from the British authorities. Whichever was the case, Andreino's claims were not groundless.

The eruption of a major legal dispute between the BBTC and the Burmese government was the third factor contributing to British intervention. In April 1885, the company was accused of extracting timber without paying the due royalties. They were also accused of witholding wages owed to some of their Burmese foresters.[86] Again historians have disagreed over which side was at fault.[87] It does seem that Thibaw's increasingly desperate need for funds drove him towards confrontation with the BBTC.[88] The outcome of the dispute convinced the British finally that action was necessary. On 12 August 1885 the Hluttaw ordered the BBTC to pay £33,333 to the foresters and £36,666 to the king in undeclared royalties. In addition a fine was imposed equal to the unpaid taxes, bringing the BBTC's total liabilities to over £100,000. Coming just after Andreino's revelations, the BBTC case convinced commercial opinion in Britain and Burma that Thibaw could be tolerated no longer. Chambers of Commerce in both countries began to lobby the India Office for annexation.[89] The BBTC case was the final straw for Anglo-Burmese relations.

The fourth factor contributing to the crisis was the replacement of the Gladstone government by Salisbury and the Conservatives in June 1885. Lord Randolph Churchill, the new Secretary of State for India was an enthusiatic imperialist. As a minority administration in office only because of Liberal divisions over Irish Home Rule, the Conservatives faced an election within months, and the electorate's perception of the new government's handling of events would be critical for the party's fortunes. For this reason, the Burmese crisis demanded a decisive response from Churchill. The new

Secretary of State recognised that a resolute stance in Burma, even going as far as military conquest, could yield significant electoral dividends.[90] Churchill's instincts were confirmed by the welter of petitions for intervention from commercial interests. Officials in the India Office were also supportive. Sir Owen Burne, the departmental Under Secretary was determined that the crisis would be resolved by British annexation of Upper Burma, and he promised Churchill that he would concoct "a Bill of indictment against him [Thibaw] that would make every old woman in London weep!".[91] Enthusiastically, Churchill replied: "I should like to see this indictment got ready".[92] In fact, Churchill's belligerence exceeded that of British officials in the east. The Viceroy, Lord Dufferin, had been appointed in the previous year by Lord Kimberley, Churchill's Liberal predecessor at the India Office. Dufferin regarded aggression against Burma as a risky strategy.[93] He was opposed to annexation because of the destabilising effect it might have on British relations with the Indian princes, who might fear that they were the next target for annexation.[94] As a Liberal sympathiser, Dufferin's instincts were anti expansionist, and he ascribed the economic problems of British Burma to international depression, rather than the crisis in Upper Burma.[95] But for personal reasons, Dufferin was eager to keep his job, and he followed Churchill's line without much resistance.[96] In 1885, the mounting evidence of French involvement in Upper Burma made it easier for the Viceroy to accept that conquest might, after all, be the best option.[97]

War became inevitable when in late October 1885 Churchill decided to issue an ultimatum to the Burmese king. Churchill demanded resolution of the BBTC dispute by arbitration, Burmese acceptance of a British Resident at Mandalay without submission to "any humiliating ceremony", and Burmese acquiescence to British regulation of the country's foreign relations. Thibaw was prepared reluctantly to accept the first two demands, but not the third, which amounted to a final surrender of Burmese sovereignty.[98] A belated offer by Farman in Paris to act as intermediary between British and Burmese representatives in that city, in an effort to secure peace, came to nothing.[99] Thibaw rejected the ultimatum at the end of October, and the British, who had been preparing for months, launched their invasion on 11 November. The British force of 10,000 men and a flotilla of armed river steamers was led by General Prendergast, and it took Minhla on 17 November.[100] At the end of the month, following the Burmese army's rout at Myingyau, Thibaw surrendered. The king was exiled to India, and the British went on to formally annex Burma. But the dacoity and disorder which had plagued the kingdom persisted. A bitter guerilla war against the British continued, which tied down tens of thousands of British troops. Only by 1890 were the British fully in control, and a substantial military presence had to be maintained indefinitely. Nevertheless, the formal annexation of Burma on 1 January 1886 ended both the Konbaung dynasty and the Burmese kingdom. A new phase of British colonial rule had begun.

***

Historical explanations of the third Anglo-Burmese war have divided broadly into two main camps. Their positions are similar to those held by the opposing sides in the debate about intervention in Malaya during the 1870s.[101] One view attributes British conquest to strategic fears arising from the growth of a French diplomatic presence in Upper Burma, which represented an unacceptable incursion into the British sphere of influence. According to this interpretation, the BBTC case was merely a pretext for actions really motivated by strategic considerations.[102] The other position in the debate locates motives for conquest primarily in the growth of British commercial interest in Upper Burma, and the economic benefits which annexation would bring.[103] The contention is that the French threat was not as great as has been suggested, and that it receded rapidly following the fall of Ferry's imperialist administration in the summer of 1885.[104] For this "commercial" explanation of conquest, it was the trumped up French threat which was the pretext for action actually motivated by economic aims. The threat to the BBTC forestry interests in Upper Burma are seen as a genuine and major reason for British intervention. Recent research also points to the emergence of interest in the Burmese ruby mines by wealthy gentleman capitalists in the City, notably Lord Rothschild.[105] Eager to secure the mines, Rothschild used his enormous wealth, political influence and his friendship with Churchill to achieve his aim.[106] To date, these conflicting strategic and commercial interpretations remain unreconciled. What is the view of the present study?

Firstly, it is clear that until recently, insufficient weight has been attached to developments within Upper Burma itself. New research shows that by 1885, Burmese society was teetering on the brink of collapse, as a result of territorial losses, the deteriorating international terms of trade and unsuccessful and counterproductive attempts to reform the Burmese state.[107] It is clear that by 1885, Burmese society was in the throes of a catastrophic breakdown of order, which would have inevitably precipitated British intervention at some point. As the crisis in Upper Burma had deepened, the British feared that trade disruption and population migration into British Burma would spread disorder into their own territories. Burmese problems undoubtedly heightened British fears for the security of their commercial interests, and the desperate search for resources to bolster state authority helped stimulate Thibaw's unacceptable courtship with the French. All of these considerations contributed to the political crisis which culminated in the British invasion.

But when the British decision to invade was made, Burmese collapse was not identified as the main reason for British action by any of the British politicians or officials involved. Strategic worries about the French, and economic concerns centring upon the BBTC case, were the most frequently cited reasons for intervention. While this takes us back to the preceding debate between strategic and commercial explanations of expansion, it is the view here that a new evaluation of the balance between these motives is long overdue. As in the debate over British expansion into Malaya, excessive and simplistic polarisation of positions has tended to obscure the complex interaction between strategic and economic considerations. Yet it is possible to reconcile these apparently conflicting explanations of events.

Let us first consider the strategic interpretation. It seems clear that British fears of French involvement in Upper Burma during 1885 were real and well founded. Farman's confession to Walsham is persuasive evidence that Andreino's accusations were not fabrications. Even after the fall of Ferry's government, the British were not convinced by spurious French disavowals of imperial designs in south east Asia. The brief but volatile history of the Third Republic bore testimony to the unpredictability of French politics. The British suspected that French imperial enthusiasm could be rekindled as quickly as it had been dampened.

But the importance of strategic considerations in promoting British intervention does not imply that commercial interests played no part in the decision to invade. In fact, in several ways they were instrumental in persuading the British government that conquest was necessary. The termination of the British Residency in 1879 had left the British authorities entirely dependent upon private commercial channels of intelligence in Mandalay. Andreino was the main source of information, and his dire warnings were taken very seriously by the India Office. But what is interesting is how private commercial interests exploited this dependence to shape the British government's view of events. Wallace Brothers became an essential source of information for the India Office.[108] In fact, J.A. Bryce, a senior figure in the company maintained regular contact with Churchill throughout the crisis months of July and August 1885. It enabled Wallace Brothers to exert a powerful influence over the official view of events in a way reminiscent of the Singapore merchants and their London allies in the 1870s, leading to British intervention and the establishment of the Residency system in Malaya. Churchill's officials appear to have trusted the word of Wallace Brothers. In late August 1885, when Bryce informed Churchill's secretary, A.W. Moore that copies of the Burmese concessions to the French were being circulated in London, Moore wondered privately if Bryce could supply a copy.[109] Farman's revelations to Walsham served to confirm the reliability of Wallace brothers. Of course, it would be naive not to suspect Andreino and Wallace Brothers of exaggerating the scale and progress of French ambitions, but their warnings clearly had substance. British fears about the French were thus fuelled and manipulated by the commercial interests upon whom the government depended for intelligence. The simplistic division between strategic and commercial considerations obscures this dependence of strategic calculation upon the commercial channels of information and influence, which shaped government policy. In this way, private, commercial control of the main sources of intelligence gave connected commercial interests in Burma and Britain leverage, and enabled them to encourage invasion and annexation.

Moreover, government sensitivity to commercial pressure was heightened by the striking effectiveness of Anglo-Burmese commercial interests in stimulating wider mercantile and public support for their cause. Again, Wallace Brothers were major players. The firm adopted a central role in co-ordinating a wave of protests by Chambers of Commerce all over Britain, which demanded decisive government action in Burma. By the 1880s, Wallace Brothers had become a leading finance house in the City, with an extensive network of contacts in London, Scotland and the provinces.[110] The firm epitomised gentlemanly capitalism, especially in its multifarious commercial and financial activities, great wealth and formidable commercial and political influence. The BBTC case and the Burmese crisis were serious threats to the firm's prosperity, and it used all of its considerable means to enlist the protection of the British state. In November 1884, Wallace brothers were already moving to defend their Burmese interests. In that month they persuaded allies in the Manchester Chamber of Commerce to highlight the crisis in Upper Burma in discussions with the new Viceroy of India, Lord Dufferin.[111] Following the Hluttaw's ruling in the BBTC case in August 1885, there was a barrage of petitions from Chambers of Commerce across Britain, demanding resolute action by the British government. At the head of this movement was the London Chamber of Commerce. Established in 1882, it became the principal mouthpiece of the gentlemanly capitalists of the City.[112] The London Chamber's call for the annexation of Burma was made almost at the same time as Churchill's ultimatum to Thibaw.[113] There is evidence which suggests that Wallace Brothers co-ordinated this mercantile pressure for British intervention. On 13 August 1885, the day after the Hluttaw's decision on the BBTC case, the company's Rangoon office telegraphed Wallace Brothers, imploring them to mobilise public opinion behind British intervention:

> "If annexation clearly or probable best policy and the English
> government unwilling to act without following popular opinion
> act according to your discretion bring all we know before
> newspapers chambers through trusted third parties"[114]

Wallace Brothers responded enthusiastically to this appeal.

The political environment was certainly favourable for the lobbyists. The Irish question had opened divisions within both parties, and had made parliamentary politics extremely volatile. The split in the Liberal party over Ireland, the presence of a substantial Irish Home Rule party in the Commons, the precarious position of Salisbury's minority government, and the new franchise arrangements of the 1884 Reform Act, all served to make the forthcoming general election the most unpredictable for many years. In these circumstances, the Conservative government was acutely sensitive to any strong expressions of public opinion, such as the clamour by British business for intervention in Burma. Churchill was quick to recognise the electoral advantages which a decisive response to Thibaw might bring. In this way the domestic political conditions of Autumn 1885 provided the most congenial climate possible for commercial pressure group activity.

As in Malaya in the 1870s, the British conquest of Burma in 1885 was promoted by prominent gentlemanly capitalists. The leading protagonists were Wallace Brothers, who used their intimate contacts with the India Office, their control of vital sources of intelligence in Burma upon which the British government depended, and their wide influence in commercial circles in London and the provinces, to secure annexation. But they were not alone in their efforts. Even more prominent gentlemen capitalists were also active. Lord Rothschild exploited his personal friendship with Randolph Churchill to pursue opportunities in Burma. Shortly after Churchill became Secretary of State in 1885, Rothschild offered £400,000 for exclusive mining rights in Burma. Also, there followed further proposals for railway construction projects.[115] Although Churchill left office before these were realised, it is plain from Rothschild's subsequent involvement in the scramble for the Burmese ruby mine concessions that this eminent and influential gentleman capitalist was keenly interested in Burma. Rothschild's covert involvement undoubtedly helped to maximise the political impact of the City's clamour for annexation. Another firm interested in Burmese rubies, the Indian based firm of Gillanders, Arbuthnot and Co., was connected with the City house of Ogilvy Gillanders and Co., whose family connections with W.E. Gladstone lent it considerable political influence.[116] The Rangoon Oil Company, shortly to be incorporated as the Burma Oil Company, also lobbied for annexation in Summer 1885 when Thibaw put the oil monopoly up for sale, threatening in the process to terminate the British company's arrangement with Moola Ismail, the existing royal contractor.[117] All this commercial pressure on government in favour of intervention propelled it towards war.

Thus the final conquest of Burma is best understood as the product of the political and economic collapse of the kingdom, caused largely by the effects of earlier conflicts with the British, combined with the efforts of powerful gentlemanly capitalist interests in London, who skillfully exploited the British government's strategic worries about the French to secure annexation. The expectation was that direct British rule would provide a more stable and peaceful environment in which business could thrive. It proved to be a forlorn hope. The social and economic collapse of the Burmese kingdom, with its accompanying problems of disorder and dacoity, left a legacy of bitter and violent resistance against British rule. War against Burmese insurgents dragged on for years, resulting in the deployment of 35,000 British and imperial troops to impose order. When an uneasy peace was established by the early 1890s it became clear that the social and political institutions of the former Burmese state had completely disintegrated. With it had gone most of the old governing class. As a consequence, there was no local elite through whom British governance could be administered, no class of collaborators who could pacify the local population and minimise the costs of imperial rule. The result was the imposition by the British of possibly the most intrusive system of formal rule in the empire. Right down to the level of the local village, the new system of imperial government came to depend upon the presence of British officials who enjoyed far reaching and draconian powers.[118] As a system it was not conducive to the development of institutions and personnel capable of supervising a resumption of self rule. As a result of the absence of local elites educated, trained and placed socially to inherit the reins of power from the British, the new Burmese state which emerged after independence in 1948, struggled in vain to reconcile the ethnic and social divisions which wracked the country. In spite of its democratic constitution, the new state simply lacked the social and political elites necessary for stable government and effective leadership. Ultimately, to prevent fragmentation of the state into warring ethnic factions, Burma's post colonial governments resorted to authoritarian military rule, the methods of which resembled those of the preceding British colonial regime. In this sense the origins of the crisis of modern Burma, with its post independence legacy of political disorder, authoritarian government and crippling poverty, can be traced back to the fateful events of the 1880s.

****

Finally there is the question of the British presence in Siam in the second half of the nineteenth century, arguably one of the most controversial areas of British imperialism in south east Asia. Unlike Burma, Malaya and northern Borneo, Siam was never subjected to formal British colonial rule. The kingdom also reaped the benefits of a programme of modernisation which strengthened central government and helped it survive the aggressive ambitions of European colonial powers. But there has been much debate among historians about the extent of British political influence and power in Siam. The central question for many writers is whether or not the British presence was sufficiently intrusive and domineering to merit application of Robinson and Gallagher's term, "informal empire".[119] How far could the British effectively enforce their will in Bangkok? How much independence were successive Siamese kings able to salvage in face of French and British military power? Some historians have contended that informal influence has been much overstated, claiming considerable Siamese success in their efforts to resist the Europeans.[120]

Thus even if one accepts the applicability of informal empire in the case of Anglo-Siamese relations - and the present study does, broadly - numerous additional questions and issues arise. What were the British economic or strategic interests which lay behind their presence in the kingdom? To what extent did gentlemanly capitalists influence British policy? How was British influence exerted and how effective was it? What measures enabled the Siamese monarchy to preserve their formal independence in the face of predatory European imperialists? Given the economic, social and political similarities between the two countries, how did Siam avoid the tragic fate of Burma?

The Bowring treaty of 1855 opened the floodgates for British commerce in Siam. The removal by the treaty of most of the tariffs, monopolies and trade restrictions facilitated a massive expansion of trade. The total value of Siamese overseas trade rose dramatically from 5.6 million baht (c. œ700,000) in 1850 to 10 million baht (c,œ1,250,000) in 1868.[121] By 1884, British trade with Siam accounted for almost 68 per cent of Siam's total trade by value, a proportion which grew to 93 per cent by 1892.[122] Singapore was crucial in the British trade connexion, and Siam became an important supplier of rice for British India, the Straits Settlements and the Malay states. British ships dominated the harbour at Bangkok, with 87 per cent of the total tonnage of shipping at Bangkok in 1892.[123] By then, British shipping companies, such as the Holt Line and the Scottish Oriental Steamship Company linked Bangkok with Singapore and other Asian ports. Siam emerged as a lucrative market for British exports, notably cotton textiles, almost wiping out Siamese village craft industries in the process. But British commercial involvement was not restricted merely to the export and import trades. Siam's bountiful resources attracted direct British investment. During the 1880s, the forests of northern Siam attracted interest from large British teak forestry companies, most notably the BBTC, supported by Wallace Brothers.[124] By 1895, Siam exported 61,800 tons of teak, virtually all of it felled and transported by British companies.[125] In that year, total investment in the Siamese teak forests came to £900,000, most of it British.[126] The City of London was the main source of this investment.[127] The presence of gentlemanly capitalist interests in Siam from the 1880s is scarcely surprising, given their role in promoting the annexation of Burma, and the benefits which they accrued from that development. The consolidation of their position in Burma provided a springboard for new initiatives in Malaya and Siam. Up to 1894, all of the banks in Siam were British owned, and London based insurance companies were the main providers of insurance throughout the kingdom.[128]

But British interest was not just commercial.[129] A longstanding British preoccupation had been the security of their imperial possessions in India and its adjoining territories. Financial parsimony dictated that this was to be achieved with a minimum commitment of military force. In the first half of the nineteenth century, the major British preoccupation on the eastern frontier had been the perceived Burmese threat, which led to wars in 1824 and 1851. Friendly relations with Siam had been convenient in these circumstances, because as a longstanding adversary of the Burmese, a potential threat from Siam in the east could help exert a restraining influence over Burma. Siamese sovereignty over the Malay states also necessitated cordial relations with Bangkok, lest the spread there of British trade and influence precipitate conflict. Such was the background to the signing of the Burney treaty in 1826. In the second half of the century, a major British objective in south east Asia was to avoid the contiguity of British territories with those of other European imperial powers. Western advances in the technologies of warfare and transport made the British confident that they could defeat any Asiatic military power. But other European powers were a different proposition, and required the deployment of more expensive British troops. The British preference was to surround their territories with stable, independent Asian states able, with British diplomatic support, to resist the influence of other European imperial powers. With the emergence of France as a major power in Vietnam and Cambodia after the 1860s, the British needed an independent Siam free of French control or influence. Before the annexation of Burma in 1885, the British feared French ambitions in mainland south east Asia, which might threaten the eastern frontiers of their Indian empire. Even after the annexation of Burma, French influence in Siam would compel the British to maintain indefinitely a large and expensive British army in Burma. Thus the essence of British policy in Siam was to sustain a continuous diplomatic and economic influence, which would provide cheap security for British Burma and the eastern frontier of India, and ensure that British interests in the Malay peninsula would remain free of Siamese resistance or interference. It would also allow British commercial and financial interests to pursue their objectives in Siam under the most congenial conditions, thereby furthering national economic prosperity and strengthening the economies of other British colonial possessions, through the provision of cheap food (rice) and raw materials (teak). The British aim was therefore always the maintenance of influence rather than direct control - informal rather than formal empire.

The problem of the French became increasingly acute in the 1880s and 1890s, initially in respect of Burma, and later in Siam. French concerns in Vietnam and Cambodia brought them into conflict with Siam. The border territories between Siam and the French colonies to the east had never been subjected completely to the authority of Bangkok, because local provincial governors enjoyed a high degree of autonomy. The Siamese kingdom was a highly decentralised political entity, in which regions distant from the capital were almost independent of Bangkok's control. As French power spread from the east, the eastern periphery of Siam became increasingly vulnerable to French expansionism. The potentially contested territories included Laos and most of the lands to the west of the Mekong river, regions which had traditionally been disputed between the Siamese and the Vietnamese empires, but which in the first half of the century had been successfully claimed by the Siamese. Matters were complicated by periodic incursions into these lands by Chinese bandits from the north. It was opportune for the French to revive pre-existing Vietnamese claims to these lands. During the 1880s, the Siamese king, Chulalongkorn, aimed to consolidate Bangkok's authority over the eastern border territories. By the late 1880s, the French were frustrated by their failure to develop a presence in eastern Siam.[130] The British invasion of Burma in 1885 ended the French plan to use their Burmese presence to persuade the British to tolerate French influence in Siam. Following this, Chulalongkorn's Royal Commissioners in Luang Prabang, Nong Khai and Ubon Ratchathani strengthened Bangkok's control over Laos, just as the French were nurturing ambitions for these territories, exacerbating tensions between the French and the Siamese towards the end of the 1880s.

Eventually these tensions erupted in the confrontation of 1893. At the heart of the crisis was August Pavie, a French adventurer and explorer who was made French Vice Consul in Luang Prabang in 1886. Pavie was an idealistic imperialist who saw French colonialism as a great civilising force. Pavie believed that the French had a moral obligation to rescue the peoples of Laos and Cambodia from Siamese "tyranny". Moreover, the apparent weakness of the Siamese convinced Pavie that a resolute line with Bangkok would yield great dividends. In the late 1880s, Pavie went home to France, where he promoted French imperial expansion in the eastern regions of the Siamese empire. On his return to south east Asia in 1890, he was placed in charge of the Mission Pavie, ostensibly a scientific and commercial expedition, whose real purpose was to spread French political influence throughout the lands adjacent to the Mekong river. The Mission sought to persuade local rulers of the benefits of French influence and ease Siamese officials from their positions of tenuous authority.[131] The Mission covered vast tracts of territory in 1890 and 1891, but with little real success. Chulalongkorn's policy of establishing Royal Commissioners to strengthen Bangkok's control had entrenched Siamese authority. The consolidation of Siamese power in Laos and along the western shores of the Mekong had the effect of strengthening the hand of the Parti Colonial, a loose political alliance in France of politicians, businessmen and other public figures, dedicated to French colonialism.[132] They skillfully exploited the turbulent political climate of the Third Republic to whip up imperial sentiment and ambition. In the early 1890s, French bitterness at being thwarted in Burma and Laos, was bolstered by a new French confidence in international diplomacy. By 1892, a Franco-Russian rapprochement was developing into a full, formal military alliance. Now the French considered they had powerful friends who could be called upon in confrontations with the British. The French government became committed to seizing control of Laos and most of the west bank of the Mekong. In 1892 there were acrimonious clashes between the Siamese authorities and the French, involving the arrest by the Siamese of two French officials posing as commercial agents. There had also been seizure of territories and outposts by both sides. By early 1893, a serious crisis seemed unavoidable. In March, negotiations to settle differences had failed, and relations took a turn for the worse. In April, French forces were sent into Laos, where they met Siamese resistance. A French officer was killed, and the French escalated the conflict. French gunboats were sent to the mouth of the Chaophraya, and when the Siamese refused to allow them to proceed up the river to Bangkok, the French commander fired upon the Siamese defences at Paknam, at the mouth of the river. The French force pressed on to Bangkok, and in spite of a Siamese agreement to evacuate certain areas on the eastern shore of the Mekong, the French refused to leave matters there. In October they compelled the Siamese to sign a costly and humiliating treaty. Under this, a demilitarised zone twenty five kilometres wide, running the whole length of the west bank of the Mekong was created, from which the Siamese were required to withdraw all garrisons and officials. They also had to pay an indemnity of three million francs.

The Siamese were bitterly disappointed by a British refusal to defend Siamese interests. The British had allowed the French to pressurise the Siamese into the treaty of 1893. But it would be a mistake to believe that this demonstrated either British weakness, or reluctance to protect their vital interests in Siam. The British response to Franco-Siamese skirmishes and disagreements over Laos and the Mekong in the early 1890s had been largely one of indifference; they saw them as minor frontier disputes which threatened no British commercial or political interests. There were few British commercial interests in the territories coveted by the French, and so the initial British response to French incursions was muted. But when French naval power was used against the Siamese capital, the British became deeply alarmed. Here were located very significant British commercial interests which required protection. The British Foreign Office had not expected such aggression from the French, and within days British businesses in Siam sprang into action to protect themselves from what they saw as a bid for French hegemony in Siam. In July some eighteen petitions from British merchants in Siam, the Straits Settlements and Britain were submitted to the Foreign Office demanding protection for British business in Siam.[133] Chambers of Commerce in Britain were among the signatories, both as separate entities, and collectively in the form of a joint memorial from the Associated Chambers of Commerce representing some seventy nine Chambers across the United Kingdom.[134] The general concern of the petitions was the perceived threat posed to British commercial interests in Siam by French expansion. The petitioners feared that once established as masters in Siam, the French would exclude British capital by protectionist measures. As with Burma, Wallace Brothers were active lobbyists, writing to the Foreign Secretary in July 1893.[135]

The British government responded to these pleas. A French threat to Bangkok and those regions of the country in which there were substantial British commercial interests could not be tolerated. At the height of the crisis at the end of July 1893, the Foreign Secretary Lord Rosebery warned the French that exploitation of the crisis to extend French power over Siam would not be tolerated. This included any annexations or impositions which undermined the viability of the Siamese state.[136] A British gunboat was kept at Bangkok throughout the crisis.[137]

Once the Franco-Siamese treaty was signed, the British were determined to ensure that there would be no repeat of the instability and tensions which had so nearly triggered a Franco-British war in the far east. An understanding had to be reached between the British and the French in Siam, which would not only delineate their respective spheres of influence, but also minimise the possibility of border confrontations. There had already been preliminary discussions about the possibility of creating a "buffer zone" between the two powers as early as 1889.[138] The crisis of 1893 emphasised the need for such a settlement. After the crisis had been resolved there were new talks on how to establish a stable frontier between the two European empires in mainland south east Asia. They were conducted in 1895 by Lord Salisbury, the new Tory Prime Minister and Foreign Secretary. The outcome was the Joint Anglo-French declaration of January 1896.[139] Central to the agreement was a guarantee that the heartland territories of the Siamese state - the Menam Basin, including the Chaophraya and most of its tributaries and adjoining territories - would not be invaded by either power. Neither side would seek or obtain advantages in this heartland region without the express permission of the other side. This part of the agreement was couched in terms of preserving the independence of Siam, although in fact only the Menam basin and the central provinces were identified as being protected by the declaration. Eastern regions of Siam, notably Battambang and Siem Reap, were excluded from this clause, as were the northern territories of the Malay peninsula. Both of these were regions in which the French and British had ambitions for the expansion of their influence. To the north of Siam, up to the Chinese border, the Mekong was identified as the frontier between the British and French empires, a decision which involved the transfer by the British to the French of the territory of Muong Sing, a remote province of little commercial value to the British. In total, the declaration went a considerable way to alleviating Anglo-British tensions in mainland south east Asia, in a way which protected both the eastern borders of the Indian empire, and British commercial interests in Siam (concentrated principally in the Menam basin expressly protected by the declaration) at minimum cost.

The deliberate exclusion of eastern Siam and the northern Malay peninsula from the guarantee, led to suspicion that the French and British had earmarked these secretly for their own expansionist intentions.[140] Evidence of this was not long in emerging. In 1907 the British signed a secret convention with Siam, under which the Siamese, in return for British recognition of their sovereignty over the northern Malay states, agreed not to surrender any concessions or territories to rival European powers. In the following decades both the British and French extended dominion into the territories excluded from the declaration of 1896. In 1904, French rule was extended into southern Laos, and by agreement in 1907, Bangkok ceded Battambang, Siem Reap and Sisophon to the French.[141] Under the treaty of 1909, the steady advance of British commerce in the Malay states of Kelantan, Trengganu, Kedah and Perlis, was recognised by the transfer of suzerainty over these territories by the Siamese to the British, in return for the submission of British subjects in Siam to the jurisdiction of the Siamese courts. A total of 176,000 square miles of Siamese territory was surrendered after 1906, all of it to prevent aggressive action by one or other European power.[142] Thus, recognition by the British and French of Siamese independence in 1896, as a "buffer state", in no way implied equal status for Siam. Rather the declaration was an expression of European hegemony over the kingdom, arranging its territorial frontiers to suit the needs of the French and British. As such, it was a flexible arrangement which could be amended to accommodate further European imperial expansion in those regions of the Kingdom not "neutralised" by the declaration. The declaration also served to protect British political and commercial interests in Siam, which were largely concentrated in the neutralised regions. The British were effectively given a veto over any French military, political or commercial initiative into the heartland of the Siamese state. While the French theoretically enjoyed the same veto over British incursions, the fact was that the British were already well established in Bangkok and Siam proper. They already commanded a huge proportion of the kingdom's trade, and were already represented substantially at the royal court. In this respect the effect of the declaration was to define the geographical limits of British informal empire in Siam, and insulate it from threats from rival European powers. For this reason some historians reject entirely use of the term "buffer state", because it disguises the extent of Siam's absorption into Britain's informal empire.[143]

In this way the declaration of 1896 reconciled Anglo-French imperial aspirations and protected British informal dominion over Siam. Three additional questions arise from this, however. What were the means by which the British asserted their dominance in Siam? Why and how did Siam avoid the catastrophic economic and political collapse which made formal colonial rule necessary in Burma? What were the defining characteristics of the emerging Siamese state in the last decades of the nineteenth century, and how successfully did it address the political and economic problems which confronted it?

The most potent source of British political influence in Bangkok was also the oldest. From the earliest decades of the century, the Siamese elite had been in awe of British military might. Fear of British power had persuaded the Siamese to sign the Burney treaty of 1826 and the Bowring treaty of 1855. British actions in Burma and Malaya reinforced Siamese fears. When in 1862 the Siamese supported a candidate for the throne of Pahang unacceptable to the British, a British warship shelled Kuala Trengganu, where the candidate and his Siamese escort were located.[144] The Siamese promptly desisted from interference in Pahang's affairs. Of course, British military power offered advantages as well as disadvantages. British military strength was seen as a source of protection against French ambitions. The effect was to reinforce Bangkok's subordination to the British.

Another source of British influence arose from administrative reform in Siam. Both Mongkut and Chulalongkorn appointed large numbers of European advisers, mostly British. British advisers were especially important in those government departments dealing with financial and economic affairs. By 1891, there were 102 European advisers in the Siamese state bureaucracy, of whom 46 were British.[145] British officials occupied some of the most senior positions. For example, in the early 1890s it was decided that a senior European financial adviser was needed to assist the Siamese government in managing the state's increasingly complex international commercial and financial relations. Siam had become a major rice exporting economy by the last decade of the century, and the state had embarked upon an extensive programme of infrastructure modernisation (railway construction and irrigation schemes) which necessitated large European loans.[146] The first major appointment was Alfred Mitchell Innes, who served as senior financial adviser from 1896 to 1899. He was succeeded by Charles James Rivett-Carnac (1899-1904) and Walter Williamson (1904-1925), all of them British colonial officials with considerable financial experience. They each exerted great influence in the development of Siamese economic policy, especially in international trade and finance. Rivett-Carnac and Williamson were instrumental in shifting Siamese policy towards the gold standard between 1900 and 1908.[147] Some historians have seen these advisers as a simple conduit for British political influence at the Siamese court, implying that they were directed by instructions from the British Foreign Office.[148] In fact there is little evidence of this and the advisers usually adopted a fiercely independent line, even if this meant contradicting the designs of the British government.[149] But British financial advice was not neutral in effect. In seeking to placate the British, the Siamese had to provide an economic and political environment congenial to the needs of business. Economic and administrative modernisation was required to accommodate the demands of British informal imperialism. British financial advisers provided indispensable assistance in enabling Chulalongkorn's government to implement the necessary reforms required to achieve this objective. In this sense, the role of British financial advice and advisers was to facilitate Siamese adaptation to the demands of informal empire.

There is little doubt that British capitalists with interests in Siam constituted a third source of political influence. The economic changes which followed the Bowring treaty enhanced the political influence of British business in Siam. The principal reason was the growing importance of the export economy (particularly rice and teak) in generating the wealth and revenues upon which the state came to depend. Inevitably, British and other European merchants in Bangkok became significant in the economic life of the country. Furthermore, from the 1880s, when Chulalongkorn's modernisation programme began to gather momentum, the Siamese came to see London as a vital source of loan finance to sustain reform. The transition from the silver to the gold standard between 1902 and 1908 was motivated partly by the state's need to raise credit in London.[150] The slump in the value of silver in the last decades of the nineteenth century threatened to push up the costs of servicing and repaying debts owed by silver currency states like Siam to countries on the gold standard such as Britain. In this way the Siamese state accommodated the needs of British capital to secure the funds necessary for government and modernisation. An inevitable consequence was that British merchants and bankers came to wield considerable political influence in Bangkok. It was an ability which rarely needed to be used. But on one occasion the Siamese government was stopped in its tracks by protests from British business interests. When in November 1902 the Baht was taken off the silver standard and revalued upwards from 21 baht to œ1 to 17 baht: œ1, there were ferocious protests from the three major European banks in Bangkok, the Hong Kong and Shanghai Bank, the Chartered Bank and the French Banque de L'Indo-Chine. Their problem was that they held their funds in dollars in Hong Kong and Singapore, and any upward revaluation of the baht would cost them dearly when they reimported their dollars and converted them into baht to finance their Siamese commercial activities.[151] What happened next illustrated dramatically the enormous political clout of British capital. The two British banks refused to purchase the baht at the new rate, in effect terminating all exchange business. So serious was the threat to the Siamese economy, which was heavily dependent upon the European banks' financial services to fund the export of rice, that the Siamese government climbed down and revalued the baht at 20: œ1. Although new arrangements were devised subsequently which permitted an upward revaluation of the baht, and the eventual introduction of the gold standard, the government were careful to work with the banks, enabling them to adjust to the changing arrangements. The shift to gold itself drew the Siamese closer to the British, strengthening the financial ties between Bangkok and the City of London. A gold backed baht made it easier for the Siamese state to raise capital in London, because it removed the danger that depreciation of the baht would inflate the costs of servicing debts to creditors in gold standard economies. In addition, the new arrangements involved the maintenance of an exchange reserve fund by the Siamese government in London, with the National Provincial Bank.[152] The overall effect was to tie the Siamese into the City's international system of currency management and credit, subordinating Siamese economic policy to the strictures of London based gentlemanly capitalism.

Also central to the maintenance of informal dominion was a Siamese state which was willing and able to deliver the economic and political conditions necessary for British interests to thrive. The Siamese were conspicuously successful in providing these for the British, and this was a major factor which enabled Bangkok to maintain formal independence. Two questions immediately spring to mind. How did the Siamese adapt their social and political system to accommodate the British? Why were they so successful in comparison to the Burmese?

The emergence of a Siamese state and economy congenial to British needs was the result of market-driven economic change throughout society, and ambitious reforms imposed by the state. These changes occurred over the half century following the Bowring treaty of 1855. It is worth recapping some of the defining features of Siamese society at the time the treaty was signed. Siam was a hierarchical society, in which a dominant nobility (nai), who enjoyed administrative position and authority, held sway over a peasant population (phrai), and was answerable only to a king with theoretically autocratic power. In spite of the mainly agrarian and subsistence character of the economy, there was a thriving export sector in teak, sugar and rice, which was monopolised and controlled by the state and its noble servants. The hierarchical character of social relations was illustrated by the enforcement upon the peasants of labour duties to the state and the local nobility (corvee), and the importance of vertical social relations of deference and patronage. In spite of pretensions of omnipotence, the monarchy's power was circumscribed in numerous ways. The king's authority was strong only in Bangkok and the Menam basin. Away from the capital, the crown depended heavily upon the co-operation of local provincial rulers, who ruled their territories almost as independent autocrats. Siam was a loosely structured empire rather than a unified nation state. In addition, the nobility, who controlled the state apparatus, including revenue collection and enforcing corvee, wielded great political power which limited the king's authority. The central state bureaucracy was subject to the competing self interests and machinations of several noble families. These noble dynasties exploited their entrenched power to feather their own nests at the expense of the crown. State policy was often distorted by competing private interests, and the crown's rights to revenues and income from trade monopolies were often infringed by the avarice of those powerful noble families who controlled revenue collection.

The Bowring treaty threatened this fragile social and political order in a number of ways. Firstly, the treaty diminished drastically what had been a vital source of revenue for both the crown and the nobility: taxes and other state incomes arising from Siam's international trade. The strict limits imposed upon the Siamese trade duties reduced the incomes of the Siamese state and the nobility. The crown had found it difficult to assert its authority even before this blow to its fiscal resources, and prospects seemed bleak after 1855. There was also the question of how the powerful noble families would respond to Mongkut's (Rama 4th) surrender to British demands. Would they tolerate a king who had dealt them so grievous a blow? A second potential source of danger was the influx of British merchants and capital which the Bowring treaty made possible. British merchants flooded mainly into Bangkok and its environs, but they were also tempted by the teak forests of northern Siam and the tin mines of the northern Malay peninsula. British merchants had been vociferous and successful supporters of British imperial aggression in Burma. Would they not pursue a similar course in Siam? It was not simply a problem of how the crown should conduct relations with British merchants. The "federal" character of the Siamese empire meant that some British merchants would be dealing not with Bangkok but with provincial rulers on the north west frontier with Burma, or in the northern states of the Malay peninsula. Relations with the British would be out of Bangkok's control, with potentially dangerous consequences. Peripheral regions might fall prey to British imperialism because of the intemperate actions of provincial rulers. If this happened, Siamese power would be diminished, and Bangkok itself might wet the appetite of British imperialists. Burma illustrated clearly the dangers posed by British economic expansion.

Yet Siam did manage to avoid the fate of Burma, even though territorial concessions on the periphery had to be made to both the British and French. Siam's survival depended upon processes of fortuitous economic change and skillful adaptation by the Siamese state to its altered circumstances. The Siamese economy adjusted rapidly to its incorporation into the international economy. Siam proved to be a thriving market for imported British manufactures, but the negative consequences, such as the elimination of traditional village craft industries, were offset by the expansion of agricultural production for export, particularly rice. Exports grew from 60,000 tons of rice in 1857 to 152,000 tons in 1870 and 475,100 tons by 1890.[153] The huge expansion of teak exports has already been noted. The opening of the Siamese economy brought massive changes in economic and social relations. There was a marked shift away from subsistence agriculture by the peasantry towards market oriented production for export. With the rise of market economic relations came the growing importance of money. Many taxes previously collected by the state and nobility in the form of goods or corvee were converted into monetary payments. Free labour and the abolition of compulsory labour dues had been virtually achieved by the end of the nineteenth century.[154] From the 1860s, property rights in land were gradually recognised, although not until the early twentieth century did land tenure resemble the pattern in western capitalist societies.[155] The nobility and the crown were, however, able to increase their rental income as the rice export sector grew.

The late nineteenth century thus saw the transformation of Siam from a traditional Asiatic society into a peripheral capitalist one, in which social and political structures were adjusted to permit the expansion of export oriented primary production demanded by the British. There has been much debate about these socio-economic changes. Some Marxist interpretations regard this process as traumatic and revolutionary.[156] Siam in the mid nineteenth century is seen as a feudal society approaching transition to capitalism. But even as capitalist economic relations developed, the feudal elite preserved its dominance by recruiting the support of Chinese immigrants who were instrumental in creating the new market economy. Chinese merchants emerged under the new capitalist system as the principal entrepeneurs and merchant middlemen who facilitated the growth of the export trades and relations with the international economy. They constituted the main element of the emergent capitalist class (bourgeoisie). But as an unpopular and vulnerable ethnic minority, the Chinese depended upon the protection of the Siamese feudal elite. Consequently, this alien bourgeoisie became committed to sustaining rather than challenging the traditional political structure. Siamese society was therefore never able to progress to mature capitalism, in which bourgeois political dominance would create the conditions for industrialisation. Instead the nobility retained its wealth and political dominance of the state, parasitically draining the wealth of the capitalist economy. The price was the stifling of Siamese economic development.

But more recent analyses are sceptical of this characterisation of traditional Siam as a western-style feudal society, in which the state and landed elite extracted most of their resources from a compliant peasantry. In fact, the state and elite had always depended heavily upon revenues derived from trade, long before the liberalisation of trade in the late nineteenth century. Siam had been a developing peripheral capitalist economy even before the Bowring treaty. Long before then, the regime had relied upon Chinese merchants, through whom most international trade was conducted, to raise revenues.[157] These arrangements made it easier for the Siamese to adapt to the economic changes imposed upon them by the British in 1855. The Sakdina oligarchy had always derived much of its wealth from trade, and did not really resemble the Marxist concept of an anti-capitalist feudal elite whose wealth was based solely upon the extraction of agricultural surplus. In fact, this predominantly urban ruling class displayed some of the characteristics of a capitalist elite.[158] One recent Marxist analysis has even conceded that by the end of the nineteenth century the Sakdina nobility had "transformed itself into the class of capitalist expropriation".[159] As such, it had become a political and social elite equipped to manage the Siamese state in its peripheral capitalist relationship with the world economy. The central point in this revisionist assessment is that the Siamese political elite of the early nineteenth century was more attuned than has been recognised to the demands of international commerce, and therefore better able to manage the international pressures upon Siam following the Bowring treaty. This accounts for the adaptation of the Sakdina nobility to their changed financial circumstances after 1855, and their eventual acceptance of the modernisation programme of Chulalongkorn's reign. The reforms enabled the regime to accommodate British demands while preserving Siamese independence, and contrasts starkly with the tragic course of events in Burma.

Probably the most serious difficulty confronting the Siamese regime in the immediate aftermath of the Bowring treaty was the loss of tax revenues from trade. The treaty replaced the complex system of trade duties and monopolies by a simplified system of reduced tariffs, and opened the regime fully to international commerce. Yet trade duties had furnished both the crown and the nobility with a substantial portion of their incomes. The duties were collected for the crown by the nobles who ran the state bureaucracy, and they extracted a substantial share of the revenues raised as lawful remuneration for their tax gathering services. The sudden termination of the system threatened both the crown and the nobility, and might have triggered an internal political crisis similar to those which beset Burma on several occasions in the nineteenth century. But Siam avoided the fiscal crisis which proved so intractable in Burma during the 1860s and 1870s, because the longstanding orientation of Siam towards international commerce provided alternative sources of revenue not available in Burma. The presence of a sizeable Chinese immigrant population was the key to Siamese survival. Taxes were raised from the Chinese through opium, liquor and gambling duties, and also from a national lottery. These discriminatory and regressive taxes fell disproportionately upon the heads of the growing Chinese population, and filled the hole in state finances left by the Bowring treaty. As the Siamese export economy in rice, teak and tin expanded, so did the Chinese immigrant population who came to trade, mine and work in the fields. By 1894, 46 per cent of total state revenues came from opium, gambling, liquor and the lottery.[160] While these taxes were insufficient to fund adequately the modernisation programmes pursued by Chulalongkorn, they at least enabled the Siamese state to avoid the disastrous fiscal crisis which helped destroy the Burmese regime.

Financial pressure also prodded the Siamese state towards administrative reform. Under Mongkut relatively slow progress was made in this direction, principally because Mongkut was reluctant to antagonise the powerful noble families who dominated the major departments of state. In spite of this there were symbolic changes. A government gazette was launched, publishing state legislation for the first time, and the first foreign advisers were introduced into the state bureaucracy. Mongkut also tried to offset British power over his kingdom by signing treaties similar in content to the Bowring treaty with the United States and France.[161] These had little effect in practice, because of the overwhelming dominance which British commerce enjoyed in Siam.

The real age of reform began when Chulalongkorn took the throne in November 1873. His reign did not enjoy an auspicious beginning. On the death of Mongkut in 1868, the Bunnag family, headed by Suriyawong, the head of the Kalahom, moved to assert themselves in the question of the succession. Chulalongkorn, then only fifteen years old, was confirmed as Mongkut's heir, but his full accession to power was delayed until 1873. Suriyawong was designated as Regent, and he moved swiftly to establish Prince Wichaichan, the son of a former second king, as the heir assumptive after Chulalongkorn. Suriyawong's intentions were to entrench further his influence and power, and to circumscribe the power of the new king. But upon his accession in 1873, Chulalongkorn emerged quickly as a radical reformer. Shortly before assuming full royal power, the new king made public his intention to implement dramatic changes in the state bureaucracy. Provision was made for the abolition of slavery, the creation of a special court to clear the backlog of legal cases awaiting attention in the ministerial courts dominated by the nobility, and the creation of a Privy Council and Council of State with far reaching powers, to be manned by the new king's friends and family.[162] In total, the reforms threatened to strengthen the crown and modernise the state bureaucracy at the expense of the nobility. Inevitably they provoked resistance.

In 1874, some of Chulalongkorn's radical allies in the Privy Council began to criticise Prince Wichaichan's appointment as heir apparent by Suriyawong on the grounds that traditionally this had been the exclusive right of the king. In the last months of 1874, Wichaichan, who occupied the prestigious Front Palace in Bangkok, decided to retaliate. His troops were ordered to drill publicly in the palace grounds. Alarmed at this thinly disguised threat of military action, Chulalongkorn responded in similar fashion. A royal "cold war" ensued. Eventually this tense situation culminated in the confused events of 28 December 1874. On that night, the outbreak of a fire in Chulalongkorn's palace provided Wichaichan with an excuse to send his armed guard to the young king's palace, where they confronted Chulalongkorn's forces who refused them entry into the king's palace. A terrifying stalemate followed. Over the next few days, there was an atmosphere of fear and hostility in the capital, as expectations of civil war grew. But in the end confrontation was averted. Wichaichan fled to the British Consul when it became apparent that Chulalongkorn was intent upon reducing his status and power, but all his protests were of no avail. He eventually returned to the Front Palace and his previous station, much diminished in authority and status.

But the "Front Palace Crisis" as it became known also had a chastening effect upon Chulalongkorn, who was forced to rein in the more radical elements in his administration. The crisis had impressed upon the king the vulnerability of his position in face of concerted opposition from the traditional noble families who still occupied key positions in the state administration. Many of the reforms already implemented were abandoned or watered down, and his most zealous supporters demoted. Chulalongkorn settled down for a long, protracted war of attrition, introducing his reforms gradually and in piecemeal fashion, as opportunity allowed. In fact it proved to be a successful strategy which helped him to avoid the disastrous confrontations which so undermined his contemporaries in Burma.

Chulalongkorn waited until the older generation of nobles who occupied key positions of power died or retired, replacing them one by one with men more sympathetic to the king's reformist aspirations. The deaths of Suriyawong in 1883 and Wichaichan in 1886 were particularly important. Chulalongkorn involved his brothers in the arduous task of reform. In the late 1870s the king's secretariat was transformed into an engine of reform, while the creation of a Royal Audit Office brought in men with new skills in accountancy and book-keeping. Gradually the royal finances improved. Mongkut's practice of recruiting European advisers, was continued and extended. The king took full advantage of administrative positions which fell vacant to advance those sympathetic to reform, appointing Prince Phuttharet as Minister for the Capital in 1876, and Prince Prachaksinlapakhom as Minister for the Palace in 1882. But the major push for reform began in 1885, with a dramatic reorganisation of the Phraklang, following the retirement of its head. Henceforth the Phraklang was replaced by two ministries, one for Foreign Affairs and a separate Treasury. Two of Chulalongkorn's brothers were appointed to run these new departments, Prince Devawongse taking the post of Foreign Minister and Prince Chakkraphat at the head of the new Ministry of Finance. In the years which followed, other royal princes were appointed to senior positions in the army, the judicial system and other key areas of the administration. By 1892, these new appointees had been welded into a functioning cabinet government, answerable to the king.[163]

But the reform programme went further than a mere change of personnel and structures at the apex of the state. There were major changes in the structure of administration at lower levels and in the regions. Just as significant was a shift in the culture of government, with the adoption of western administrative skills and practices, record keeping and correspondence, even down to the maintenance of western style office hours! The general thrust of reform was to strengthen the authority of the central state and the crown at the expense of the nobility and to extend and consolidate Bangkok's rule on the geographical periphery of Siam. A state revenue collection service gradually replaced farming tax collection out to members of the nobility and wealthy Chinese intermediaries. In the long run this enriched the state by curbing leakages of tax revenues into private pockets, but it was a process notable for its pragmatism. Where existing tax arrangements appeared to be the best means of maximising revenues, or their abolition threatened political crisis or confrontation, they were left in place until such time as reform was more easily achieved.[164] Care was taken not to push the traditional Sakdina elite to the point of rebellion. In any case, by the end of the century they shared in the fruits of the thriving export economy through the increased rents which accrued to them. Such caution and political sensitivity contrasted sharply with Mindon's disastrous tax reforms of the late 1860s and 1870s in Burma.

Of particular significance were Chulalongkorn's efforts to assert Bangkok's authority in the geographical periphery of Siam, transforming it from a loose affiliation of self governing townships and regions into a more centralised nation state. Early moves in this direction were made in the Anglo-Siamese treaty of 1874, which gave Bangkok responsibility for adjudicating in any disputes between the local governor of Chiengmai in the north east of Siam, and the British timber interests which were moving into the region.[165] A Siamese police force was established under Bangkok's control, and a British Vice Consul was appointed in Chiengmai. Then in 1883, Bangkok's control was tightened further by the Treaty of Chiengmai. Under this, one of Chulalongkorn's brothers was appointed as Commissioner with far reaching powers over the local ruler. It effectively began the subordination of the region to Bangkok's control. The Chiengmai experiment became a blueprint for a more systematic attempt in the 1890s to impose greater control generally from Bangkok. In 1893, Prince Damrong, the new Minister for the Interior, established what became known as the Thesaphiban system. Under this tracts of the various outlying provinces in Siam were designated as distinct administrative units known as Monthons. A Royal Commissioner, answerable and loyal to the crown, was appointed to each Monthon, with far reaching powers over revenue collection, legal administration and policing. Effectively this represented an assertion of central state power over the noble families who had previously dominated these territories. The Ministry of the Interior thus became the agent of royal authority throughout the kingdom.[166]

Crucially, Chulalongkorn's reforms created a state administrative machine capable of satisfying the demands of British informal empire. The assertion of central state control over truculent provincial governors and semi-independent rulers, removed potential flashpoints of confrontation which might have precipitated British aggression and imperial expansion. The epitomy of this strategy was the new arrangements in Chiengmai after 1883, which were prompted mainly by Siamese fears that friction between the local ruler and the British might trigger conflict. The overhaul of the state revenue and administrative systems were designed to establish strong government, and a stable regime within which British commercial enterprise could function profitably, to the mutual benefit of both the British and the Siamese. It was broadly successful, as illustrated by the British satisfaction with their agreement with the French in 1896 to designate central Siam as a neutral zone free from European incursion or interference. The British were confident that the Siamese regime was sufficiently stable, strong and compliant to meet their economic and strategic requirements without the need for formal intervention.

Thus Siam, by dint of cautious reform and diplomacy, managed to ensure its survival as a distinct political entity, preserving in the process much of its traditional political and social structure, albeit adapted to meet the demands imposed by the country's absorption into the world economic system. The price was surrender to the dictates of British informal economic imperialism, which insisted upon the defence of British commercial interests in the country and the fulfilment of Siam's desired role as a source of essential foodstuffs, raw materials and a market for British manufactures. In Siam, the British managed to establish the relationship of informal dominance to which they had aspired unsuccessfully in Burma between 1852 and 1884. The project had met with greater success in Siam for a number of reasons. The country's economic and social structure had always been oriented towards external trade and political relations, helping to produce a social and political elite which was more sensitive to external economic and political pressures, and better equipped to adapt to changing external circumstances. The best illustration of this was the successful exploitation of the country's immigrant

Chinese population to replace sources of revenue lost as a result of the Bowring treaty of 1855. The skill and political acumen of Mongkut, Chulalongkorn and their advisers also played no small part in the regime's survival. However, probably the most important difference between Burma and Siam was distance from British India. It had been the contiguity of Burma to British India which had been such an important factor in the British decisions to fight in 1824 and 1851, and in the annexations of territory which followed both wars. These annexations, particularly of Pegu in the wake of the second war, destroyed the economic viability of the Burmese kingdom, removing from it the country's major supply of food and creating a dependency upon overseas supplies of rice, the cost of which proved impossible to meet as the century progressed. Siam never suffered such a catastrophic loss of essential economic resources, and export earnings from rice exports, together with the tax revenues which they generated indirectly, contributed significantly to the stability and survival of the regime. As a result, Siam had emerged by the end of the century as a client state of the British, firmly ensnared in London's informal empire, but retaining its formally independent political status.

NOTES

1. Pollak, Empires in Collision p105.
2. Ibid.
3. Ibid.: p106.
4. Ibid.: p114.
5. Ibid.: pp115-116; Thant Myint U, The Crisis of the Burmese State and the Foundations of British Colonial Rule in Upper Burma 1853-1900 (PhD thesis, Trinity College, Cambridge 1979) p79.
6. Thant Myint U, The Crisis of the Burmese State p80.
7. Pollak, Empires in Collision p120.
8. Maung Htin Aung, Lord Randolph Churchill and the Dancing Peacock: British Conquest of Burma 1885 (New Delhi, Manohar 1990) p14.
9. Pollak, Empires in Collision p123.
10. Thant Myint U, The Crisis of the Burmese State p112.
11. Ibid. The price of rice was 45 Rupees per basket in 1855, and 65 Rs in 1875.
12. Ibid.: p84.
13. Ibid.: p86.
14. Ray, "Asian Capital in the Age of European Domination" pp528-529; P.A. Coclanis, "Southeast Asia's Incorporation into the World Rice Market" Journal of Southeast Asian Studies 24:2, (1993) 251-267, pp261-263.
15. Dr Falconer, "Report on the Teak Forests of the Tenasserim Provinces" quoted in: R.L. Bryant, "Shifting the Cultivator: The Politics of Teak Regeneration in Colonial Burma" Modern Asian Studies 28:2, (1994) 225-250, p230.
16. Ibid.: p231. The article provides a description and explanation of both the economic and political benefits which the British derived from Taungya forestry.
17. Ibid.: pp234-235.
18. Ibid.: pp241-242.
19. A useful account of the early history of Wallace Brothers is: A.C. Pointon, The Bombay Burmah Trading Corporation Ltd 1863-1963 (Southampton, Millbrook Press Ltd 1964). See pp1-5 for details of the early careers of the family.
20. S. Chapman, The Rise of Merchant Banking (London, Unwin Hyman Ltd 1984) p55.
21. D. Kynaston, The City of London, Volume One: A World of Its Own 1815-1890 (London, Pimlico 1995) pp225-226.
22. Pointon, The Bombay Burmah Trading Corporation p5.
23. Maung Htin Aung, Lord Randolph Churchill p144.

24. Pointon, The Bombay Burmah Trading Corporation p12.
25. Mukherjee, British Colonial Policy in Burma p215.
26. SarDesai, British Trade and Expansion in Southeast Asia p105.
27. Ibid.; p120.
28. The expedition is described in detail in: C. Williams, Through Burma to Western China (London, W. Blackwood 1868).
29. SarDesai, British Trade and Expansion in Southeast Asia p179.
30. Ibid.: pp185-186.
31. The text of Colquhoun's speech is found in Supplement to the Chamber of Commerce Journal 5 October 1885, and in the India Office Home Correspondence L/P & S/3/215, pp795-798, India Office Records, London.
32. Maung Htin Aung, Lord Randolph Churchill p31.
33. Pollak, Empires in Collision p159.
34. Ibid.: p161.
35. Ibid.: p162.
36. A useful summary of the main provisions of the 1862 and 1867 treaties is to be found in: Dharm Pal, "British Relations with Burma 1864-1868" Indian Historical Quarterly 21:4, (1945) 271-283.
37. Pollak, Empires in Collision p165.
38. Ibid.: p166.
39. Maung Htin Aung, Lord Randolph Churchill p14.
40. Dharm Pal, "British Relations with Burma" pp276-277.
41. Pollak, Empires in Collision p171.
42. Thant Myint U, The Crisis of the Burmese State p98.
43. Maung Htin Aung, Lord Randolph Churchill pp24-25.
44. Pollak, Empires in Collision p117.
45. Thant Myint U, The Crisis of the Burmese State p123.
46. Ibid.: p112.
47. Maung Htin Aung, Lord Randolph Churchill pp76-77.
48. Thant Myint U, The Crisis of the Burmese State p101.
49. SarDesai, British Trade and Expansion in Southeast Asia p190.
50. Ibid.: p190.
51. Foreign Department of the Government of India: Memorandum to Lord Cranbrook, Secretary of State for India, 7 March 1879, Parliamentary Papers, Burmah 1886 L.269, c.4614, p18.
52. Maung Htin Aung, Lord Randolph Churchill p37.
53. Foreign Department's memo, 7 March 1879, p14.
54. These continued after Mindon's death. See for example the complaints of G.J. Swann, Manager of the Irawaddy Flotilla Company to G.U. Aithcheson, Chief Commissioner of British Burma, 8 November 1878, Parliamentary Papers, Burmah 1886 p9.
55. Thant Myint U, The Crisis of the Burmese State p125.
56. Shaw's confidential diary, 17 February 1879, Enclosure no. 5 in Lytton to Cranbrook, 20 March 1879, Parliamentary Papers, Burmah 1886 p20.
57. Maung Htin Aung, Lord Randolph Churchill pp47-48.
58. Ibid.: pp47-50.
59. Thant Myint U, The Crisis of the Burmese State pp125-126.
60. Ibid.: pp128-130.
61. See, for example, Shaw's diary, 20 February 1879, Parliamentary Papers, Burmah 1886 p21.

62. A.T.Q. Stewart, The Pagoda War pp62-63.

63. Government of India to Aitcheson, 18 November 1879, Parliamentary Papers, Burmah 1886 p63.

64. Viceroy to Secretary of State for India, 9 December 1879, Parliamentary Papers, Burmah 1886 p65.

65. Government of India to Lord Cranbrook, Secretary of State for India, 14 January 1880, Parliamentary Papers, Burmah 1886 p67.

66. Ibid.: pp67-68.

67. Ibid.: p68.

68. SarDesai, British Trade and Expansion in Southeast Asia p195.

69. Pointon, The Bombay Burmah Trading Corporation pp18-19.

70. Thant Myint U, The Crisis of the Burmese State p135.

71. SarDesai, British Trade and Expansion p196.

72. Stewart, The Pagoda War p64.

73. For a fuller explanation of why these negotiations yielded so little, see: Maung Htin Aung, Lord Randolph Churchill pp77-79.

74. P.Tuck, The French Wolf and the Siamese Lamb: The French Threat to Siamese Independence 1858-1907 (Bangkok, White Lotus 1995) pp71-77.

75. Ibid.: pp73-74.

76. Ibid.: p76.

77. Ibid.

78. Stewart, The Pagoda War p64.

79. Memorandum on the Affairs of Burma and Siam, by J.A. Bryce, enclosed in Alexander F. Wallace to Richardson, 4 November 1884, Indian Letters commencing 25 January 1884, p330, Papers of Wallace Brothers, Guildhall Library, London.

80. C.L. Keeton, King Thebaw and the Ecological Rape of Burma; The Political and Commercial Struggle between British India and French Indo-China in Burma 1878-1886 (Delhi, Manohar 1974) p12.

81. Ibid.: pp173-174; and Maung Htin Aung, Lord Randolph Churchill pp123-125.

82. Bryce of Wallace Brothers to R. Churchill, Secretary of State for India, 25 July 1885, Home Correspondence of the India Office, L/P & S/3/263, pp427-433, India Office Records, London.

83. Stewart, The Pagoda War pp70-71; SarDesai, British Trade and Expansion p201; Maung Htin Aung, Lord Randolph Churchill pp79-80 and p128; See also R. Foster, Lord Randolph Churchill: A Political Life (Oxford, Oxford University Press 1988) p207; Tuck, The French Wolf pp76-78.

84. Walsham to Lord Salisbury, Foreign Secretary, 6 October 1885, Home Correspondence of the India Office, L/P & S/3/265, pp579-581, India Office Records, London.

85. Walsham to Lord Lyons, 12 October 1885, Home Correspondence of the India Office, L/P & S/3/266, pp135-146, India Office Records, London.

86. Maung Htin Aung, Lord Randolph Churchill p142.

87. Stewart, The Pagoda War p73; Keeton, King Thebaw and the Ecological Rape of Burma p199; D.G.E. Hall, A History of South East Asia (London, Hutchinson 1950) p553; Maung Htin Aung, Lord Randolph Churchill p158; SarDesai, British Trade and Expansion p205.

88. W. Churchill, Lord Randolph Churchill (London, Macmillan 1906) Volume 1, p521; Thant Myint U, The Crisis of the Burmese State pp159-160.

89. For example, see the London Chamber of Commerce petition to Churchill of 23 October 1885, Home Correspondence of the India Office, L/P & S/3/265, pp1361-1367, India Office Records, London.

90. Foster, Lord Randolph Churchill p208.

91. O.S. Burne to Moore, India Office, 3 October 1885, Home Correspondence of the India Office, L/P & S/3/265, pp763-767, India Office Records, London.

92. Ibid.

93. Stewart, The Pagoda War p27.

94. Lord Kimberley to Dufferin, 26 March 1885, Kimberley Papers, Ms D. 2456, p99, Bodleian Library, Oxford.

95. R.V. Turrell (1988), "Conquest and Concession: The Case of the Burma Ruby Mines" Modern Asian Studies 22:1, (1988) 141-163, pp145-146.

96. Maung Htin Aung, Lord Randolph Churchill p99.

97. Turrell, "Conquest and Concession" p147.

98. Stewart, The Pagoda War pp73-74.

99. Lord Lyons to Salisbury, 3 November 1885, enclosing a memorandum by G. Bonham on his meeting with Farman on 2 November 1885, Home Correspondence of the India Office, L/P & S/3/266, pp643-664, India Office Records, London.

100. Bruce, The Burma Wars pp156-157.

101. Still the best summary of the debate is: E. Chew (1979), "The Fall of the Burmese Kingdom in 1885: Review and Reconsideration" Journal of Southeast Asian Studies 10:2, (1979) 372-380.

102. This view is held by the following historians: J. Furnivall, Colonial Policy and Practice: A Comparative Study of Burma and Netherlands India (Cambridge, Cambridge University Press 1948) pp70-71; D.G.E. Hall, Burma (London, Hutchinson 1950) p130; J.F. Cady, A History of Modern Burma (New York, Ithaca 1958) pp116-121; Chew, "The Fall of the Burmese Kingdom" pp376-377.

103. D.P. Singhal, The Annexation of Upper Burma (Singapore, Eastern Universities Press 1960); D. Woodman, The Making of Burma (London, Cresset 1962); Maung Htin Aung, The Stricken Peacock: Anglo-Burmese Relations 1752-1948 (The Hague, Nijhoff 1965); Maung Htin Aung Lord Randolph Churchill.

104. Woodman, The Making of Burma pp226-227.

105. Turrell, "Conquest and Concession".

106. Ibid.: p160.

107. This is the central argument of a brilliant PhD thesis: Thant Myint U, The Crisis of the Burmese State.

108. Bryce to Churchill and enclosures, 25 July 1885, Home Correspondence of the India Office, L/P & S/3/263, pp425-433, India Office Records, London.

109. Bryce to Moore, 26 August 1885, Home Correspondence of the India Office, L/P & S/3/264, p497, India Office Records, London.

110. Chapman, The Rise of Merchant Banking p143.

111. A.F. Wallace to Richardson, 4 November 1884, Indian Letters, Wallace Brothers Papers, Guildhall Library, London.

112. Kynaston, The City of London pp377-378.

113. London Chamber of Commerce to Churchill, 23 October 1885, Home Correspondence of the India Office, L/P & S/3/265, p1361, India Office Records, London.

114. Telegram from BBTC in Rangoon to Wallace Brothers, London, 13 August 1885, Wallace Brothers Papers, Private BBTC letters and telegrams, Guildhall Library, London.
115. Turrell, "Conquest and Concession" p157.
116. Kynaston, The City of London p378.
117. Turrell, "Conquest and Concession" p146.
118. Thant Myint U, The Crisis of the Burmese State p167.
119. SarDesai, British Trade and Expansion p270.
120. D.J.M. Tate, The Making of Modern South-East Asia, Volume 1: The European Conquest (Kuala Lumpur, Oxford University Press 1971) p519.
121. Wyatt, Thailand: A Short History pp185-186.
122. Tuck, The French Wolf p9.
123. SarDesai, British Trade and Expansion p92.
124. Ibid.: pp92-93.
125. Paper by Mr J. Homan Van Der Heide to the Siam Society, "The Economical Development of Siam during the last half century", 22 November 1906, published in: C. Nartsupha and S. Prasartset, The Political Economy of Siam, 1851-1910: Volume 1 (Bangkok, Social Science Association of Thailand 1981) 73-112, see p84, and introduction by Nartsupha and Prasartset p12.
126. SarDesai, British Trade and Expansion p93.
127. C.S. Leckie (1894), "The Commerce of Siam in Relation to the Trade of the British Empire" Journal of the Royal Society of Arts 42, 649-660, published in: Nartsupha and Prasartset, The Political Economy of Siam 1851-1910 115-152, p128.
128. SarDesai, British Trade and Expansion p94; and Wallace Brothers to the Earl of Rosebery, 19 June 1893, F.O. Siam 422/35, p121, PRO, London.
129. Tuck, The French Wolf pp8-12.
130. Ibid.: p68.
131. Ibid.: p93.
132. Ibid.: pp100-103.
133. F.O. Siam 422/36; SarDesai, British Trade and Expansion p241.
134. SarDesai, British Trade and Expansion p242.
135. Wallace Brothers to Rosebery, 19 June and 27 July 1893, F.O. Siam 422/35 PRO, London.
136. C. Jesharun, The Contest for Siam 1889-1902: A Study in Diplomatic Rivalry (Kuala Lumpur, Penerbiti Universiti Kebangsaan Malaysia 1977) p70.
137. Ibid.: p78.
138. SarDesai, British Trade and Expansion pp236-237.
139. Probably the most thorough analysis of the negotiations and the declaration is to be found in Jesharun, The Contest for Siam pp153-230.
140. SarDesai, British Trade and Expansion p247.
141. Wyatt, Thailand: A Short History p206.
142. Ibid.: p208.
143. C. Rajchagool, The Rise and Fall of the Thai Absolute Monarchy: Foundations of the Modern Thai State from Feudalism to Peripheral Capitalism (Bangkok, White Lotus 1995) pp34-40.
144. Andaya and Andaya, A History of Malaysia pp144-145.
145. SarDesai, British Trade and Expansion p97.
146. These developments are well explained in: I.G. Brown, The Elite and the Economy in Siam c.1890-1920 (Singapore, Oxford University Press 1988).

147. See I.G. Brown, "Siam and the Gold Standard 1902-1908" Journal of Southeast Asian Studies 10:2, (1979) 381-399.
148. A view held by Sardesai and Ingram: SarDesai, British Trade and Expansion p96; J.C. Ingram, Economic Change in Thailand since 1850 (California, Stanford University Press 1971) p173.
149. I.G. Brown, "British Financial Advisers in the Reign of King Chulalongkorn" Modern Asian Studies 12:2, (1978) 193-215, pp213-214.
150. Brown, "Siam and the Gold Standard" p381.
151. Ibid.: p384.
152. Ibid.: p395.
153. Figure is from Homan Van Der Heide's papers to the Siam Society, 22 November 1906, Nartsupha and Prasartset, The Political Economy of Siam p84.
154. Rajchagool, The Rise and Fall of the Thai Absolute Monarchy p66.
155. Ibid.: pp67-69.
156. Nartsupha and Prasartset, The Political Economy of Siam 1851-1910. This is the main theme running through the editors' introduction.
157. Evers, "Trade and State Formation in Siam" p760.
158. Ibid.: p767.
159. Rajchagool, The Rise and Fall p171.
160. Hong Lysa, Thailand in the Nineteenth Century p128.
161. Wyatt, Thailand p184.
162. Ibid.: p192.
163. Hong Lysa, Thailand in the Nineteenth Century p113.
164. Ibid.: pp120-121.
165. Rajchagool, The Rise and Fall p19.
166. Wyatt, Thailand pp209-210.

9. CONCLUSION

Thus, by 1900 the territorial limits of the British empire in south east Asia had been defined. Burma had been annexed, while the Malay states of Johore, Pahang, Negri Sembilan, Selangor and Perak were all governed by the new Federal administration based in the Straits Settlements. The northern Malay states were to be gradually absorbed into the British empire in the following decades. Siam, though formally independent, was compelled to pursue foreign and domestic policies congenial to British interests. British shipping dominated the seas from Calcutta to Hong Kong, and Singapore was the main commercial centre in south east Asia. British naval and economic strength had diminished fears of foreign imperial rivalry, and this was assisted by various diplomatic settlements, particularly with the French and the Dutch. Malay tin, Burmese and Siamese teak and rice were flooding onto the world market, enriching British merchant houses and financiers in the process. By 1920 Malay rubber would prove to be a spectacular success, although early hopes for Burmese oil and precious stones were never to fulfill expectations. As elsewhere, the most significant economic effect of British imperialism was to draw the territories of south east Asia into the rapidly expanding global network of production, trade and finance. Of course, south east Asia had been no stranger to global commerce, even before European incursion into the region. But British imperialism opened the societies of the region to the world economy to an extent unparallelled even in the "Age of Commerce". Burma, Malaya and Siam were transformed from societies based upon subsistence agriculture and state regulated commerce, into informal satellites and colonies specialising in large scale production of food and raw materials for export.

In the process, local political structures had been either destroyed or refashioned to accommodate the relentless demands of British commerce. Local societies had been radically transformed, most dramatically in Malaya, where a large Chinese immigrant population was instrumental in the development of the export economy. By 1900 British imperialism had irrevocably changed those societies over which it held sway, and had set in train a pattern of socio-economic development which is still unfolding today.

How are we to assess the significance of British expansion in south east Asia in the "long nineteenth century"? It should be clear that some of the accepted explanations of British expansion in the region are open to challenge. Explanations of British imperialism which emphasise the importance of the region as a market for British industrial produce particularly require revision. These interpretations have defined Britain as a predominantly industrial society, in which industrialists and merchants engaged in the export of manufactures were the main economic interests promoting colonial expansion. But this conception of Britain has been challenged by new perspectives which redefine British society as one in which financial and pre-industrial aristocratic interest groups tended to outweigh Manchester cotton men and Liverpool merchants. Certainly British manufacturing interests were far less influential in triggering expansion in the cases of Singapore, Burma and Siam than has been asserted. In fact British mercantile interests based in the region itself tended to be the most vociferous advocates of imperial adventure. The agency houses of Singapore, and their role in the establishment of the Malay Residency system in the 1870s spring to mind here, as do the teak merchants of Moulmein, Rangoon and Calcutta in the second Burmese war in the early 1850s. Even where British merchants did enjoy close connections with British based economic interests, these were with London financiers or traders rather than provincial industrialists. The pivotal role of Wallace brothers in the final annexation of Burma of 1885 is a case in point. Some earlier accounts of British imperialism in south east Asia have also been rather vague in their characterisation of British business interests, submerging industrial, mercantile and financial organisations with quite separate and sometimes conflicting objectives, under the general category of "British commerce". At times British business is presented as a monolithic entity, united in its pursuit of markets, raw materials and imperial aggrandisement. Sectional divisions are rarely identified clearly. It is here that recent historiography, which has emphasised divisions within British capitalism between London based financial and mercantile interests on the one hand, and provincial industrial capital on the other, has much to offer.

A second feature of the existing body of scholarship has been the conflict between economic and strategic explanations of expansion in respect of British colonial acquisitions in the last quarter of the nineteenth century. To some extent this reflects the debate, current in the 1960s and 1970s, between adherents of the early liberal/Marxist economic explanations of European imperialism posed by Hobson and Lenin, and those who supported the Gallagher and Robinson thesis of the transition from informal to formal empire as a response to imperial rivalry from other emergent European powers. Probably the best illustrations of this polarisation of opinion are the disagreements about the establishment of the Residency system in Malaya in

1874, and the British annexation of Burma in 1885. But in both cases, the interaction between commercial interests and strategic considerations by the British state has been oversimplified, underestimating the extent to which government depended for information and intelligence of distant events upon private commercial interests on the periphery of empire. Furthermore the central role played by London gentlemanly capitalist organisations as a channel of communication between merchants at the periphery and government ministers in London, has been underestimated as a factor in the formation of imperial policy.

Gentlemanly capitalist interests were instrumental in consolidating British possession of Singapore, stimulating later expansion into the Malay peninsula in the 1870s and 1880s, and in the final conquest of Burma in 1885. These cases demonstrate much about how gentlemanly capitalists secured the policy changes they required. Networks of commercial and personal connections between south east Asia and London helped bring concerted pressure to bear on government at moments of crisis. The skillful manipulation of Chinese opinion in the Straits Settlements by W.H. Read in the early 1870s, and the co-ordinated efforts of Seymour Clarke to raise strategic concerns in London, spring to mind here, as does the activity of Wallace Brothers in mobilising London and provincial opinion behind the annexation of Burma. Earlier, during the Anglo-Dutch negotiations of 1820 to 1824, London based East India Agency houses had helped to ensure that Singapore would remain a British port. These cases illustrate that it was not just the personal and social relationships between prominent gentlemanly capitalists and senior politicians which gave the former so much political clout, though these were unquestionably helpful - witness Lord Rothschild's connections with Churchill in respect of Burma in the 1880s. It was also the dependence of the British government upon gentlemanly capitalists and their associates for intelligence of developments at the periphery of empire. London mercantile and financial firms enjoyed extensive connections across the globe, often, as in the case of Burma after 1879, in remote locations where there was no official diplomatic representation for the British government. The City, with its complex web of international contacts, provided an essential if unofficial supplement to the formal channels of diplomatic and colonial intelligence gathering.

City interests also brought together diverse commercial interests at the periphery of empire and in Britain, to lobby for specific government actions. Wallace Brothers' central role in mobilising opinion for action in Burma involved rallying not only Burmese based and London business to the cause through the Rangoon and London Chambers of Commerce, but also persuading provincial merchants to join in the campaign. The wide range of commercial activities in which some London firms were engaged, equipped them to play this leading role. For example, Wallace Brothers were involved in such a wide range of commercial activities, including export agency for northern manufacturers and financial links with the National Bank of

Scotland, that they were able to lead a broad based campaign on the Burmese question. Sometimes what appeared to be provincial industrial political campaigns were actually organised by London based gentlemanly capitalists with their own agenda in mind. The consolidation of informal influence in Siam in the 1890s and 1900s also owed much to gentlemanly capitalist influence, especially the adoption of the gold standard and the placing of the country's reserves with a London bank.

But it would be a mistake to regard the British presence in south east Asia solely as the product of the schemes of City bankers. British interest had originally arisen out of the strategic and economic needs of the East India Company in India, and well into the nineteenth century, the requirements of British India dominated British policy in south east Asia. From south east Asia British merchants also exercised a major influence over British imperial policy, particularly the agency houses of the Straits Settlements, and the teak merchants of Moulmein and Rangoon in Burma. Of course, later in the nineteenth century, these merchants established and developed connections with London, but for much of the first half of the century they were essentially local interests. In the early nineteenth century, the main dynamic behind British expansion came from India or within the British community in south east Asia. For example, the first Burmese war was a product of Anglo-Indian militarism and concern about the security of the eastern borders of the Indian empire. Similar concerns also shaped British objectives in the second war in the early 1850s, but this time British merchants in Calcutta and Burma also pressed for war in pursuit of their own commercial objectives. In Siam, British merchants in the Straits Settlements were instrumental in opening that country to British trade and political influence through the treaties of 1826 and 1855. Sarawak was brought under British rule by a local adventurer, James Brooke, with the support of British merchants in Singapore.

In spite of the importance of events in south east Asia, developments in Britain also promoted expansion. Socio-political and economic changes in Britain itself shaped British policy in south east Asia. The emergence in the eighteenth century of an alliance between the aristocratic elite and the merchants and bankers of the City, provided the state and the aristocracy with financial support in return for mercantilist trading regulations which favoured the large commercial organisations of London. One example of this was the East India Company's monopoly of trade between Britain and the far east, which ensured high profits for that organisation. British expansion into south east Asia in the late eighteenth century took place within the context of this monopoly, and the British commercial firms based in India and south east Asia operated within it and expected it to continue. However, the rise of industrialism, and social instability, especially during the Napoleonic wars, prompted a shift away from protectionism, a process which culminated in the establishment of free trade by the middle of the nineteenth century. The abolition of the East India Company monopoly of trade with India in 1813, and the China monopoly in 1833, were examples of this liberalisation of commerce, and both caused serious problems for commercial interests in India and south east Asia. The undermining of the old mercantilist structures which governed the trade to India and commercial activity in the east, had devastating consequences for local private capital and British rule. Probably the most serious crisis was the economic collapse of 1833, which swept away the Calcutta agency houses. These commercial bodies were vital for the smooth functioning of the Anglo-Indian colonial economy, and were an essential source of finance for the East India Company administration in India. After their demise, it took several years for new firms to emerge which could perform effectively in the open and competitive commercial environment which now prevailed in the east, and for several decades the Company's Indian administrations were subject to severe financial parsimony. But the effects of trade liberalisation were felt particularly acutely by British merchants in the Straits Settlements, especially in the recently acquired port of Singapore. Many of the British merchants who came to Singapore in the 1820s had close links with the Indian agency houses, and all anticipated that their commercial activities would be conducted within the context of a continuing Company monopoly of trade to China. The existing monopoly and economic and structures offered invaluable opportunities for Straits merchants, notably the transhipment trade and the financial resources of the Indian agency houses upon which many merchants depended for the expansion of their activities. The crisis of 1833 destroyed these advantages, and as a consequence the 1830s and 1840s saw much hardship in the Straits Settlements, with a high rate of business failures.

But the crisis compelled the Straits mercantile community to seek new stategies for commercial survival. Probably the most important of these was the increasing dependence of British merchant firms on Chinese middlemen, whose expertise in local trade and markets was tapped to maximise profits. Although links with merchant firms in Britain were also important, the Chinese connections proved to be the key to the survival of British agency firms in the Straits. Chinese capital and labour also began the development of the Malay states as a source of raw materials for the expanding world market. Sugar, pepper, gambier and of course tin production were the almost exclusive preserve of Chinese enterprise, which supplied these commodities for export by the British merchants of the Straits. The growing Chinese population of the Straits settlements and the Malay states, provided a lucrative market for Indian opium. Opium farms also became a vital source of revenue for the Straits administration, largely paying for the costs of government. But it was the role opium played in maximising the profitability of Chinese enterprise which proved especially valuable for British economic interests in the long run. The ruthless exploitation of Chinese labour which opium facilitated, promoted the rapid expansion of commodity production. Opium was thus a key article of imperial commerce, which generated profits for British merchants and revenues for British administration, but assisted

Chinese development of the economies of the Straits Settlements and the neighbouring Malay states.

By the 1850s, economic and administrative structures in the Straits Settlements had emerged which enabled local British commercial interests to prosper in the more liberal commercial environment imposed from Britain. The rapid expansion of the port facilities of Singapore in the 1860s is evidence of this success. By then, Singapore merchants required new sources of capital, and so increasingly they began to turn to the City of London to raise funds through bank loans and share flotations. London finance began to be enticed to the Malay peninsula by the potential of Malay tin. But the local structures of commerce which had been created during the austere decades of the first half of the century proved remarkably durable and resistant to change. Efforts by British entrepeneurs, funded by monies raised in the City, to break into tin mining produced disappointing results, mainly because Chinese enterprise proved too competitive for inexperienced European businessmen. Not until the early twentieth century did Europeans make headway in tin mining, and by then the development of rubber cultivation provided new opportunities in which London based companies were able to excel. Before the late 1890s, gentlemanly capitalists were more effective in shaping British imperial policy in Malaya than they were in exploiting commercial opportunities there. Chinese entrepeneurs were therefore allowed an opportunity to adapt to the changing economic circumstances in which they had to operate. Chinese firms developed a dual status, adopting western legal forms to allow them to function in the increasingly western dominated system of international trade. The more successful ones became part of the emerging system of international trade and finance which gentlemanly capitalism was creating. Although traditional Chinese social structures and activities, such as the secret societies, the sale of opium and even tin mining were either abandoned or altered radically, the Chinese commercial communities adapted to the global economy created by western imperialism and economic expansion.

But successful adaptation did not amount to parity with their western counterparts. Organisational improvements by western firms, coupled with longstanding flaws in the financial structure of Chinese enterprises, which placed family values above commercial considerations, ensured that British capital would dominate the eastern business world in the first half of the twentieth century. One is struck however, by the cosmopolitan character of capitalist development in south east Asia, which displayed numerous examples of profitable cross fertilisation between western and Chinese enterprise. The startling success of Singapore owed much to local Chinese commercial elites, who successfully adapted to the international economy, adding western commercial practices to their own traditional structures, and developing their own international linkages between Chinese firms in south east Asia and China. This network of Chinese finance and enterprise existed from the late nineteenth century, and blossomed spectacularly after decolonisation in the 1950s and 1960s. In promoting Chinese enterprise, British imperialism in Malaysia and the Straits during the first half of the nineteenth century laid the foundations of later economic success.

Imperial expansion was also encouraged by the impact of British commerce upon local social and political structures. The British imperial presence was shaped by the ability of local political structures to weather the demands made upon them by the British. A general problem was the basic incompatibility between the needs of local rulers and the requirements of private British commerce. An ability to raise finance by controlling international trade was essential for state formation and survival. The powerful south east Asian states of the "Age of Commerce" had depended upon state monopolies over the most lucrative branches of commerce, and heavy taxation on trade to raise resources for government. But in the eighteenth century, merchants from Britain wanted free trade, without the heavy exactions demanded by local states. British traders from the mid eighteenth century grew intolerant of what they saw as arbitrary impositions made by local rulers of dubious legitimacy. British military power prevented many local rulers insisting upon their traditional rights in respect of trade.

Some states fared better than others. Siam was most successful in preserving a sufficient revenue base to maintain internal stability and political independence. The surrender of revenue rights under the Bowring treaty was compensated by shifting the burden of taxation onto the growing Chinese population. This enabled the Siamese state to establish a client relationship with the British empire, in which the state's political independence was guaranteed in return for compliance with the needs of British commerce and strategic interests. It was a difficult relationship, sustained by careful diplomacy and by the modernisation of the Siamese state, which enabled it to provide the internal stability and environment required by the British. At the other extreme was Burma. Located on the eastern fringe of the Indian empire, this state had always worried the British, who regarded it as a potential threat to the security of India. The first war of 1824-26 resulted in a serious loss of territory, and a legacy of sour relations which made further conflict more than likely. In 1851, the refusal of the Burmese to comply with British demands to remove trade restrictions, and the avarice and imperial zeal of Calcutta and Rangoon commercial interests, triggered a second conflict whose long term consequences were to prove fatal for the Burmese state. The loss of Lower Burma, with its essential capacity for food production, was a blow from which it proved impossible to recover. Destabilisation of the kingdom, and deepening internal strife eventually provoked invasion and conquest in 1885. There followed a bloody guerilla war and the assertion of possibly the most intrusive form of formal colonial rule in the British empire. Efforts to establish the Burmese kingdom as a compliant client state had failed miserably.

In Malaya between 1786 and 1874, and including up to 1819, Aceh, the pattern of British relations with local states was more complex. There were the same tensions between central states seeking to enforce traditional rights over trade, and British merchants and administrators determined to obtain free access to local markets. But the severity of political collapse in the seventeenth century meant that the Sultans had never been able to reassert the degree of authority enjoyed in the "Age of Commerce". In practice, much power had devolved to district chiefs and village headmen, who collected trade revenues on behalf of the Sultan, The eighteenth century saw attempts by some rulers, notably in Aceh, to re-establish traditional monopolies over trade, and to centralise the collection of revenues in the hands of officials of the central state. With the economic recovery and expansion of European trade to the region in the late eighteenth century, the resurrection of traditional royal powers over trade seemed to promise a return to the high point of state formation several hundred years earlier. But in practice, local chiefs prevented restoration of royal authority, and throughout the Malay states the late eighteenth and nineteenth centuries saw deepening tensions between central state authority and the district chiefs. British merchants preferred dealing with local chiefs, whose limited military power and territorial scope of authority, curbed their revenue exactions on European traders. It was far better than having to deal with formidable Sultans whose demands would be greater. Consequently, there was a tendency for British traders to simply ignore the Sultans' regulations and monopolies, and to deal with local chiefs or village headmen. Sultans tried to negotiate agreements with the British authorities in the Straits Settlements which would stop freebooting British merchants ignoring their authority. But such agreements were notoriously difficult to enforce, not least because of a lack of commitment by British administrators. In practice, private British merchants traded with whoever they wished. The result was a shift of wealth and power from the Sultans to the local chiefs throughout the Malay states, who secured for themselves a larger share of the revenues arising from trade. There was widespread internal strife, as the Sultans attempted to reassert their traditional rights and authority. An example of these trends was the Acehnese civil war of 1814 to 1819. From the 1850s, the western Malay states were wracked by similar internal power struggles, as rival contenders for the thrones of Perak, Selangor and Negri Sembilan, canvassed support from powerful local chiefs, who had been strengthened by the huge revenues arising from Chinese tin mining. By the early 1870s the conflicts were raging out of control, and were compounded by parallel conflicts between rival Chinese secret societies, battling for control of the tin mines. These chaotic conditions threatened the security of British commerce in the peninsula, particularly the valuable tin trade, and there was a real fear that the disorders might spill into the Straits Settlements.

Here lay a major reason for the assertion of British control over the western Malay states under the Pangkor Agreement of 1874. The weakness of central state authority, and internal conflicts, eventually threatened the security of British possessions. Informal influence, the cheaper and preferred

British political stategy for dealing with the Malay states, was no longer sufficient to protect British interests. The Residency arrangements were an imposed settlement of the various internal conflicts, and evolved quickly into de facto formal rule. But the structures of traditional Malay authority were preserved superficially, with the Sultans continuing to enjoy enormous wealth and ceremonial prestige, to pacify Malay opinion. In practice, the British controlled revenue, public expenditure, defence and even the various royal successions. It was formal rule masquerading as advice, and Colonial Office officials made no effort to disguise the fact in their communications with each other. Federation in 1895 underlined the reality of British formal rule.

What is interesting in these various examples of British rule in the region, is the extent to which they were shaped by local conditions and the varying ability of local regimes to accommodate British economic and political demands. Gallagher and Robinson, and other historians such as Fieldhouse, have argued convincingly that British governments in the nineteenth century were reluctant to allow the extension of formal colonial rule on grounds of cost. However, they have tended to see the shift to formal empire late in the nineteenth century as a product of European imperial rivalry. There is no doubt that this played a part in stimulating extensions of formal empire, but the internal condition of local states, and their ability to accommodate British requirements, was probably much more important in prompting the assertion of formal imperial rule in south east Asia. Local conditions were also the main determinant of the nature and structures of formal empire.

Indeed, in concluding this study of British imperial expansion in south east Asia, it is worth emphasising the diversity of British imperial rule in the region. The rigid and oppressive colonial regime in Burma contrasts sharply with the subtleties of informal persuasion in Siam. The thin facade of direct rule through Resident advisers in the Malay states was an example of formal empire camouflaged as local sovereignty, while the semi-independent status of the White Rajas of Sarawak has no parallel anywhere. In reflecting upon the varied experiences of the modern states of south east Asia since decolonisation, it seems that colonial rule still casts a long shadow. The legacy of British rule appears bleakest in Burma, where the destruction of local political structures and elites in 1885 wreaked devastating consequences from which the post colonial state has yet to recover. The difficulties which beset the modern state of Myanmar are to an uncomfortable degree the result of British imperialism. At the other extreme, it is difficult not to attribute the stunning economic success of Singapore at least partly to the effects of British colonialism. The emergence of a Chinese commercial and financial elite there, attuned to the demands of the world economy, was a direct consequence of the British colonial economic system which developed in the nineteenth century. Singapore remains the main regional centre of trade it was in the nineteenth century, and indeed some of the agency houses of British origin still thrive. If a case were to be made for the beneficial consequences of

British imperial rule, it would probably be based on the experience of this city state. Elsewhere the effects of British imperium are more difficult to assess. Malaysia has experienced much turbulence since independence, and it is more difficult to see any clear connection between recent economic buoyancy and the experience of British rule. In Thailand, the tenuous and informal nature of the British presence makes it difficult to attribute the principal developments in that society to British imperialism. In all of these cases, assessments of the long term effects of British imperialism are likely to be amended as events unfold.

Arguably the most significant and lasting effects of British imperialism have been felt in Britain itself. Imperialism has been instrumental in shaping the British sense of national identity. The less savoury aspects of this have included xenophobia and racism, but perhaps an antidote to atavistic notions of national greatness and racial superiority is to be surpassed by those countries once subject to imperial rule. In spite of the financial crises of the late 1990s, the breathtaking success of the "eastern tigers" has left a particularly strong impression in Britain, where memories of imperial dominance of the far east and south east Asia are still potent. For many in Britain, the economic success of Singapore serves to throw recent British decline into sharp relief, and has stimulated wide interest in the reasons for eastern success. The recent spate of studies concerned with the eastern "economic miracle", some of which express openly a desire for imitation, is evidence of this trend. Perhaps for Britain and her former colonies in south east Asia this is the beginning of the very last phase of decolonisation: the liberation of British minds from imperialistic illusions of British superiority.

BIBLIOGRAPHY

PRIMARY SOURCES

NEWSPAPERS

The Economist (1886), The British Library, Newspaper Library, Colindale, London.
The Englishman and Military Chronicle (!851/52), SM49, British Library India Office Records, London.
The Friend of India (1851/52), SM141, BL, IOR, London.
The Bengal Hurkaru (1851/52), SM31, BL, IOR, London.
The Manchester Chronicle (1820/21), Manchester Central Lbrary.
The Manchester Mercury (1820/21), Manchester Central Library.
The Mining Journal, Railway and Commercial Gazette (1886), BL, Colindale, London.
The Prince of Wales Island Gazette, (1805-1811) BL, IOR, London.
Stocks and Shares: An Independent Weekly Journal for the Investing Classes (1886), BL, Colindale.

OFFICIAL RECORDS

The Bengal Commercial Reports, Range 174, BL, IOR, London.
The Bengal Public Consultations, Range 4, BL, IOR, London.
The Bengal Secret Consultations, BL, IOR, London.
The Bengal Secret and Political Consultations, (P/BEN/SEC), BL, IOR, London.
The Bengal Board of Trade Proceedings, West Bengal Archives, Calcutta, India.
The Board of Control Collections, F/4, BL, IOR, London.
The Board of Control Drafts of Secret Letters to India, BL, IOR, London.
Records of the Supreme Court, Calcutta High Court Archives, Calcutta, India.
Colonial Office Papers and Correspondence Relating to the Straits Settlements and Malaya, CO/273, PRO, London.
The Dutch Records, BL, IOR, London.
Foreign Office Papers Relating to Siam, FO/422, PRO, London.
Home Correspondence of the India Office, L/P & S/3, BL, IOR, London.
Home Miscellaneous Series 660, BL, IOR, London.
Liverpool Parliamentary Office Papers, PAR/328, Central Libraries, Liverpool.
The Straits Settlements Records, G/34, BL, IOR, London.

PARLIAMENTARY PAPERS

Burmah (1886) L.269, c4614.
Select Committee of the House of Commons on the Affairs of the East India Company c 735 (II).
Select Committee of the House of Commons on trade to the East Indies and China (1821/2) c746.
Select Committee of the House of Lords on trade to the East Indies and China (1821/2) c476.

PERSONAL PAPERS

Papers of John Adam, EUR MSS F109, BL, IOR, London.
Papers of Lord Amherst, EUR MSS F140, BL, IOR, London.
Papers of Lord Wellesley, ADD MSS13870, BL, London.
Papers of Lord Broughton, ADD MSS36477, BL, London.
Papers of David Brown, Royal Commonwealth Society Library, London.
Papers of Lord Carnarvon, ADD MSS60792, BL, London.
Papers of Lord Carnarvon, PRO30/6/40, PRO, London.
Papers of Lord Ellenborough, PRO30/12/21, PRO, London.
Papers of George Canning, Harewood and Stapleton Manuscripts, West Yorkshire Archives, Leeds.
Papers of Charles Weir Hogg, EUR MSS E342, BL, IOR, London.
Papers of Lord Kimberley, New Library, Bodleian, Oxford.
Papers of John Palmer, Bodleian, Oxford.
Personal Memoirs of William Prinsep, EUR MSS D1160/1-3, BL, IOR, London.
Papers of Thomas Stamford Raffles, EUR MSS D742, BL, IOR, London.
Papers of Wallace Brothers, Guildhall Library, London.

SECONDARY SOURCES

BOOKS

B.W. Andaya and L.Y. Andaya, A History of Malaysia (Basingstoke, Macmillan 1982).
C.A. Bayly, Indian Society and the Making of the British Empire (Cambridge, Cambridge University Press 1988).
C.A. Bayly, Imperial Meridian: The British Empire and the World 1780-1830 (London, Longman 1988).
R. Bonney, Kedah 1771-1821: The Search for Security and Independence (Kuala Lumpur, Oxford University Press 1971).
I.G. Brown, The Elite and the Economy in Siam 1890-1920 (Singapore, Oxford University Press 1988).
R.A. Brown, Capital and Entrepeneurship in South-East Asia (Basingstoke, Macmillan 1994).
G. Bruce, The Burma Wars 1824-1886 (London, Hart-Davis, MacGibbon 1973).
G. Buckley, An Anecdotal History of Old Times in Singapore 2 vols; (Singapore, Fraser and Neave Ltd 1902).

J.F.H. Cady, A History of Modern Burma (New York, Ithaca 1958).

P.J. Cain and A.G. Hopkins, British Imperialism: Innovation and Expansion 1688-1914 Vol 1; (London, Longman 1993).

J. Cameron, Our Tropical Possessions in Malayan India, being a Descriptive Account of Singapore, Province Wellesley and Malacca: Their People, Products and Government (London, Elder & Co. 1865).

Chai Hon-Chan, The Development of British Malaya 1896-1909 (Kuala Lumpur, Oxford University Press 1964).

S. Chapman, The Rise of Merchant Banking (London, Unwin Hyman 1984).

K.N. Chaudhuri, The Trading World of Asia and the English East India Company 1660-1760 (Cambridge, Cambridge University Press 1978).

W. Churchill, Lord Randolph Churchill 2 vols; (London, Macmillan 1906).

J.C.D. Clark, English Society 1688-1832 (Cambridge, Cambridge University Press 1985).

H.P. Clodd, Malaya's First Pioneer: The Life of Francis Light (London, Luzac & Co. 1948).

R. Cobden, How Wars are Got up in India: The Origin of the Burmese War (London, W & F.G. Cash 1853).

Sir R. Coupland, The British Empire after the American Revolution (London, Longmans, Green & Co. 1930).

C.D. Cowan, Nineteenth Century Malaya: The Origins of British Political Control (London, Oxford University Press 1961).

N. Crafts, British Economic Growth during the Industrial Revolution (Oxford, Clarendon 1985).

J. Crawfurd, Journal of an Embassy from the Governor General of India to the Courts of Siam and Cochin China (London, Henry Colburn 1828).

J.H. Drabble, Rubber in Malaya 1876-1922 (Kuala Lumpur, Oxford University Press 1973).

A.T. Embree, Charles Grant and British Rule in India (London, Allen & Unwin 1962).

D.K. Fieldhouse, Economics and Empire 1880-1914 (Ithaca NY, Cornell University Press 1973).

R. Foster, Lord Randolph Churchill: A Political Life (Oxford, Oxford University Press 1988).

H. Furber, John Company at Work (Cambridge, Mass., Harvard University Press 1948).

J. Furnivall, Colonial Policy and Practice: A Comparative Study of Burma and Netherlands India (Cambridge, Cambridge University Press 1948).

J. Gallagher and R. Robinson, Africa and the Victorians: The Official Mind of Imperialism (London, Macmillan 1961).

M. Greenberg, British Trade and the Opening of China 1800-42 (Cambridge, Cambridge University Press 1951).

J.M. Gullick, Rulers and Residents: Influence and Power in the Malay States 1870-1920 (Singapore, Oxford University Press 1992).

A. Gunder Frank, Capitalism and Underdevelment in Latin America (Hamondsworth, Penguin 1971).

D.G.E. Hall, A History of Southeast Asia (London, Macmillan 1955).

V.T. Harlow, The Founding of the Second British Empire 2 vols; (London, Longman 1952 and 1964).

M. Havinden and D. Meredith, Colonialism and Development: Britain and its Tropical Colonies 1850-1960 (London, Routledge 1993).

B. Hilton, Corn, Cash and Commerce: The Economic Policies of the Tory Governments 1815-1830 (Oxford, Oxford University Press 1977).

J. Hobson, Imperialism: A Study (London, Unwin Hyam 1902).

J. Holland Rose, A.P. Newton and E.A. Benians (eds), The Old Empire from Beginnings to 1783 (Cambridge, Cambridge University Press 1930)

Hong Lysa, Thailand in the Nineteenth Century: Evolution of the Economy and Society (Singapore, Institute of South East Asian Studies 1984).

J.C. Ingram, Economic Change in Thailand since 1850 (California, Stanford University Press 1955).

L. Jenks, The Migration of British Capital to 1875 (New York, A.A. Knopf 1927).

C. Jesharun, The Contest For Siam 1889-1902: A Study in Diplomatic Rivalry (Kuala Lumpur, University of Malaya 1977).

C.L. Keeton, King Thebaw and the Ecological Rape of Burma: The Political and Commercial Struggle between British India and French Indo-China in Burma 1878-1886 (Delhi, Manohar 1974).

Khoo Kay Kim, The Western Malay States 1850-1873: The Effects of Commercial Development on Malay Politics (Kuala Lumpur, Oxford University Press 1972).

M. Kuitenbrouwer (1991), The Netherlands and the Rise of Modern Imperialism: Colonies and Foreign Policy 1870-1902 (Oxford, Berg, English trans 1991).

D. Kumar and M. Desai (eds), The Cambridge Economic History of India vol 2; (Cambridge, Cambridge University Press 1983).

D. Kynaston, The City of London Volume 1: A World of Its Own 1815-1890 (London, Pimlico 1995).

P. Lawson, The East India Company: A History (London, Longman 1993).

Lee Kam Hing, The Sultanate of Aceh: Relations with the British 1760-1824 (Kuala Lumpur, Oxford University Press 1995).

Lee Poh Ping, Chinese Society in Nineteenth Century Singapore: A Socio-Economic Analysis (Kuala Lumpur, Oxford University Press 1978).

V.I. Lenin (1916), Imperialism: The Highest Stage of Capitalism (Moscow, Progress Publishers).

V. Lieberman, Burmese Administrative Cycles: Anarchy and Conquest c.1580-1760 (Princeton, Princeton University Press 1984).

H. Marks, The First Contest for Singapore 1819-24 (Gravenhage, Nijhoff 1959).

P.J. Marshall, East Indian Fortunes: The British in Bengal in the Eighteenth Century (Oxford, Clarendon 1976).

P.J. Marshall, Bengal: The British Bridgehead, Eastern India 1740-1820 (Cambridge, Cambridge University Press 1987).

Maung Htin Aung, The Stricken Peacock: Anglo-Burmese Relations 1752-1948 (The Hague, Nijhoff 1965).

Maung Htin Aung, Lord Randolph Churchill and the Dancing Peacock: British Conquest of Burma 1885 (New Delhi, Manohar 1990).

D. McIntyre, The Imperial Frontier in the Tropics 1865-75 (London, Macmillan 1967).

A. Mukherjee, British Colonial Policy in Burma: An Aspect of Colonialism in South East Asia 1840-1885 (New Delhi, Abhinav Publications 1988).

C. Nartsupha and S. Prasartset, The Political Economy of Siam 1851-1910 vol 1; (Bangkok, Social Science Association of Thailand 1981).

C.N. Parkinson, British Intervention in Malaya 1867-1877 (Singapore, University of Malaya 1960).

C.H. Philips, The East India Company 1784 to 1834 (Manchester, Manchester University Press 1961).

C.H. Philips (ed), The Correspondence of David Scott, Director and Chairman of the East India Company, relating to Indian Affairs 2 vols; (London Camden Third Series 1951).

A.C. Pointon, The Bombay Burmah Trading Corporation (Southampton, Millbrook Press 1964).

O.B. Pollak, Empires in Collision: Anglo-Burmese Relations in the mid nineteenth Century (Greenwood, Westport 1979).

C. Rajchagool, The Rise and Fall of the Thai Absolute Monarchy (Bangkok, White Lotus 1995).

A. Redford, Manchester Merchants and Foreign Trade (Manchester, Manchester University Press 1934).

A. Reid, Southeast Asia in the Age of Commerce 1450-1680, Volume One: The Land below the Winds (New Haven, Yale University Press 1988).

A. Reid, Southeast Asia in the Age of Commerce 1450-1680, Volume Two: Expansion and Crisis (New Haven, Yale University Press 1993).

W.D. Rubinstein, Capitalism, Culture and Decline in Britain 1750-1990 (London, Routledge 1993).

E. Sadka, The Protected Malay States 1874-1895 (Kuala Lumpur, University of Malaya 1968).

D.R. SarDesai, British Trade and Expansion in Southeast Asia 1830-1914 (New Delhi, Allied Publishers 1977).

D.R. SarDesai, South East Asia: Past and Present (Basingstoke, Macmillan 1989).

G. Saunders, A History of Brunei (Kuala Lumpur, Oxford University Press 1994).

D.P. Singhal, The Annexation of Upper Burma (Singapore, South Asian Publishers 1960 and 1981 2nd ed).

S.B. Singh, European Agency Houses in Bengal 1783-1833 (Calcutta, Firma K.L. Mukhopadhyay 1966).

M.F. Somers Heidhues, Bangka Tin and Mentok Pepper: Chinese Settlement on an Indonesian Island (Singapore, Institute of South East Asian Studies 1992).

A.T.Q. Stewart, The Pagoda War: Lord Dufferin and the Fall of the Kingdom of Ava 1885-6 (London, Faber & Faber 1972).

N. Tarling, Anglo-Dutch Rivalry in the Malay World 1780-1824 (Queensland, University of Queensland Press 1962).

N.Tarling, The Fall of Imperial Britain in Southeast Asia (Singapore, Oxford University Press 1993).

D.J.M. Tate, The Making of Modern South East Asia, Volume One: The European Conquest (Kuala Lumpur, Oxford University Press 1971).

B.J. Terwiel, A History of Modern Thailand 1767-1942 (London, University of Queensland 1983).

A. Tripathi, Trade and Finance in the Bengal Presidency 1793-1833 (Calcutta, Oxford University Press 1978 2nd ed).

C. Trocki, Opium and Empire: Chinese Society in Colonial Singapore 1800-1910 (Ithaca, Cornell University Press 1990).

P. Tuck, The French Wolf and the Siamese Lamb: The French Threat to Siamese Independence 1858-1907 (Bangkok, White Lotus 1995).

C.M. Turnbull, A History of Singapore 1819 to 1975 (Oxford, Oxford University Press 1977).

P.H. Van Der Kemp, De Singapoorsche Papierlog (The Hague 1898).

Captain W. White, A Political History of the Extraordinary Events which led to the Burmese War (London, Hamilton 1827).

C. Williams, Through Burma to Western China (London, Blackwood 1868).

D. Woodman, The Making of Burma (London, Cresset 1962).

Wong Lin Ken, The Malayan Tin Industry to 1914 (Tucson, University of Arizona 1965).

H.R.C. Wright, East Indian Economic Problems of the Age of Cornwallis and Raffles (London, Luzac & Co. 1961).

C.E. Wurtzburg, Raffles of the Eastern Isles (London, Hodder & Stoughton 1954).

D.K. Wyatt, Thailand: A Short History (New Haven & London, Yale University Press 1984).

C.F. Yong, Chinese Leadership and Power in Colonial Singapore (Singapore, Times Academic Press 1992).

ARTICLES

D.K. Bassett (1961), "The Surrender of Dutch Malacca 1795" in D.K. Bassett, British Trade and Policy in Indonesia and Malaysia in the Late Eighteenth Century (Centre for South-East Asian Studies, University of Hull 1971) 108-123.

D.K. Bassett (1964), "British Trade and Policy in Indonesia 1760-1772" in Bassett, British Trade and Policy 1-29.

D.K. Bassett (1965), "Anglo-Malay Relations 1786-1795" in Bassett, British Trade and Policy 72-107.

D.K. Bassett (1964), "British Commercial and Strategic Interest in the Malay Peninsula during the Late Eighteenth Century" in Bassett, British Trade and Policy 50-71.

D.K. Bassett, "British Country Trade and Local Trade Networks in the Thai and Malay States c.1680-1770" Modern Asian Studies 23:4 (1989) 625-643.

J. Bastin, "Raffles and British Policy in the Indian Archipelago" Journal of the Malaysian Branch of the Royal Asiatic Society 27:1 (1954) 84-119.

L. Blusse, "No Boats to China. the Dutch East India Company and the Changing Pattern of the China Sea Trade, 1635-1690" Modern Asian Studies 30:1 (1996) 51-76.

G. Bogaars, "The Effect of the Opening of the Suez Canal on the Trade and Development of Singapore" Journal of the Malaysian Branch of the Royal Asiatic Society 28:1 (1955) 97-143.

T. Braddell, "Notices of Pinang" Journal of the Indian Archipelago and Eastern Asia (1851).

I.G. Brown, "British Financial Advisers in the Reign of King Chulalongkorn" Modern Asian Studies 12:2 (1978) 193-215.

I.G. Brown, "Siam and the Gold Standard 1902-1908" Journal of Southeast Asian Studies 10:2 (1979) 381-399.

R.L. Bryant, "Shifting the Cultivator: The Politics of Teak Regeneration in Colonial Burma" Modern Asian Studies 28:2 (1994) 225-250.

P.J. Cain and A.G. Hopkins, "The Political Economy of British Expansion Overseas 1750 to 1914" Economic History Review 33:4 (1980) 463-490.

S.D. Chapman, "Business Marketing Enterprise: The Changing Roles of Merchants, Manufacturers and Financiers 1700 to 1860" Business History Review 53 (1979) 205-233.

S.D. Chapman, "Financial restraints on the Growth of Firms in the Cotton Industry 1790-1850" Economic History Review 32:1 (1979) 50-69.

BIBLIOGRAPHY

E. Chew, "The Fall of the Burmese Kingdom in 1885: Review and Reconsideration" Journal of Southeast Asian Studies 10:2 (1979) 372-380.

E. Chew, "Frank Swettenham and Yap Ah Loy: The Increase of British political Influence in Kuala Lumpur 1871-1885" Journal of the Malaysian Branch of the Royal Asiatic Society 57:1 (1984) 70-87.

E. Chew, "The Naning War, 1831-1832: Colonial Authority and Malay Resistance in the Early Period of British Expansion" Modern Asian Studies 32:2 (1998) pp351-387.

M.C. Cleary, "Indigenous Trade and European Economic Intervention in North West Borneo c.1860-1930" Modern Asian Studies 30:2 (1996) 301-324.

J.E. Cookson, "British Society and the French Wars 1793-1815" Australian Journal of Politics and History 31 (1985) 192-203.

C.D. Cowan, "Early Penang and the Rise of Singapore 1805 to 1832" Journal of the Malaysian Branch of the Royal Asiatic Society 23:2 (1950) 1-210.

C.D. Cowan, "Governor Bannerman and the Penang Tin Scheme 1818-1819" Journal of the Malaysian Branch of the Royal Asiatic Society 23:1 (1950) 52-84.

J. Crawfurd (1837), "A Sketch of the Monetary and Mercantile System of British india with Suggestions for their Improvement by Means of Banking Establishments" in K.N. Chaudhuri, The Economic Development of India under the East India Company 1814-1858 (Cambridge, Cambridge University Press 1971) 217-316.

Dharm Pal, "British Relations with Burma 1864-1868" Indian Historical Quarterly 21:4 (1945) 271-283.

J.H. Drabble, "Investment in the Rubber Industry in Malaya c.1900-1922" Journal of Southeast Asian Studies 3:2 (1972) 247-261.

J.H. Drabble and P.J. Drake, "The British Agency Houses in Malaysia: Survival in a Changing World" Journal of Southeast Asian Studies 12:2 (1981) 297-328.

P.J. Drake, "The Economic Development of British Malaya to 1914: An Essay in Historiography with some questions for Historians" Journal of Southeast Asian Studies 10:2 (1979) 262-290.

H.D. Evers, "Trade and State Formation: Siam in the Early Bangkok Period" Modern Asian Studies 21:4 (1987) 751-771.

J.S. Galbraith, "The Turbulent Frontier as a Factor in British Expansion" Comparative Studies in Society and History 2 (1960) 150-168.

J. Gallagher and R. Robinson, "The Imperialism of Free Trade" Economic History Review 6 (1953) 1-13.

C.A. Gibson-Hill, "Raffles, Acheen and the Order of the Golden Sword" Journal of the Malaysian Branch of the Royal Asiatic Society 29:1 (1956) 1-20.

M.F. Goldman, "Franco-British Rivalry over Siam 1896-1904" Journal of Southeast Asian Studies 3:2 (1972) 210-228.

J.M. Gullick, "Tunku Kudin in Selangor 1868-1878" Journal of the Malaysian Branch of the Royal Asiatic Society 59:2 (1986) 5-50.

M.A. Hassan, "The Klang War 1867-1873" Malaysia in History 28 (1985) 55-93.

J. Hobson, "Capitalism and Imperialism in South Africa" Contemporary Review 63 (1890).

G.W. Irwin, "Governor Couperus and the Surrender of Malacca 1795" Journal of the Malaysian Branch of the Royal Asiatic Society 29:3 (1956) 86-134.

A. Kaur, "The Babbling Brookes: Economic Change in Sarawak" Modern Asian Studies 29:1 (1995) 65-109.

B.E. Kennedy, "Anglo-French Rivalry in South East Asia 1763-1793" Journal of Southeast Asian History 4:2 (1973) 199-213.

L. Kitzan, "Lord Amherst and the Declaration of War on Burma 1824" Journal of Asian History 9:2 (1975) 101-127.

L. Kitzan, "Lord Amherst and Pegu: The Annexation Issue 1824-26" Journal of Southeast Asian Studies 8 (1977) 176-194.

G.R. Knight, "John Palmer and Plantation Development in Western Java in the Early Nineteenth Century" Bijdragen 131:2/3 (1975) 309-337.

M. Lee (Stubbs Brown), "Trade and Shipping in Early Pinang" Malaysia in History 21 (1978) 17-35.

D. Lewis, "The Growth of the Country Trade to the Straits of Malacca 1760-1777" Journal of the Malaysian Branch of the Royal Asiatic Society 43:2 (1970) 114-129.

V. Lieberman, "Secular Trends in Burmese Economic History, c.1350-1830, and their Implications for State Formation" Modern Asian Studies 25:1 (1991) 1-31.

V. Lieberman, "Local Integration and Eurasian Analogies: Structuring Southeast Asian History 1350-1830" Modern Asian Studies 27:3 (1993) 475-572.

J.R. Logan, "Notes on the Chinese in the Straits" Journal of the Indian Archipelago and Eastern Asia 9 (1855) 109-124.

D. McIntyre, "British Intervention in Malaya: The Origin of Lord Kimberley's Instructions to Sir Andrew Clarke in 1873" Journal of Southeast Asian History 11:3 (1961) 47-69.

S.M. Middlebrook, "Yap Ah Loy 1837-1885" Journal of the Malaysian Branch of the Royal Asiatic Society 24:2 (1951) 1-119.

W.G. Miller, "Robert Farquhar in the Malay World" Journal of the Malaysian Branch of the Royal Asiatic Society 51:2 (1978) 123-138.

D.J. Moss, "Birmingham and the Campaigns against the Orders in Council and the East India Company Charter 1812-13" Canadian Journal of History 2 (1976) 172-188.

I. Nish, "British Mercantile Co-operation in the Indo-China Trade from the End of the East India Company's Trading Monopoly" Journal of Southeast Asian History 3:2 (1962) 74-91.

D. Peers, "The Duke of Wellington and British India during the Liverpool Administration, 1819-27" Journal of Imperial and Commonwealth History 17:1 (1988) 1-25.

D. Peers, "Between Mars and Mammon: The East India Company and Efforts to Reform its Army 1796-1832" Historical Journal 33:2 (1990) 385-401.

Sir C. Philips, "Dalhousie and the Burma War of 1852" in C.D. Cowan and O.W. Wolters (1976), Southeast Asia and Historiography (Ithaca, Cornell University Press 1976).

O. Prakash, "Opium Monopoly in India and Indonesia in the Eighteenth Century" Indian Economic and Social History Review 24:1 (1987) 63-80.

G.P. Ramachandra, "The Outbreak of the First Anglo-Burmese War" Journal of the Malaysian Branch of the Royal Asiatic Society 51 (1978) 69-100.

R.K. Ray, "Asian Capital in the Age of European Domination: The Rise of the Bazaar 1800-1914" Modern Asian Studies 29:3 (1995) 449-554.

A. Reid, "The Seventeenth Century Crisis in Southeast Asia" Modern Asian Studies 24:4 (1990) 639-659.

A. Reid and C. Trocki, "The Last Stand of Autonomous States in Southeast Asia and Korea 1750-1870: Problems, Possibilities, and a Project" Asian Studies Review 17:2 (1993) 103-120.

J.F. Richards, "The Indian Empire and Peasant Production of Opium in the Nineteenth Century" Modern Asian Studies 15 (1981) 59-83.

R. Robinson, "Non European Foundations of European Imperialism: A Skatch for a Theory of Collaboration" in R. Owen and R. Sutcliffe (eds), Studies in the Theory of Imperialism (London 1972).

J. Schumpeter (1919), "The Sociology of Imperialism" in J. Schumpeter, Imperialism and Social Classes (New York, Augustus M. Kelley 1951).

A. C. Staples, "Memoirs of William Prinsep: Calcutta Years 1817-1842" Indian Economic and Social History Review 26:1 (1989) 61-79.

F.G. Stevens, "A Contribution to the Early History of Prince of Wales Island" Journal of the Malaysian Branch of the Royal Asiatic Society 7:2 (1929) 377-414.

Tan Chung, "The Britain-China-India Trade Triangle 1771-1840" Indian Economic and Social History Review 11:4 (1974) 411-431.

Tan Kim Heng, "Chinese Sugar Planting and Social Mobility in Nineteenth Century Province Wellesley" Malaysia in History 24 (1981) 24-38.

N. Tarling, "Intervention and Non Intervention in Malaya" Journal of Asian Studies 11:4 (1962) 523-527,

N. Tarling, "The Palmer Loans" Bijdragen 119:2 (1963) 161-168.

N. Tarling, "The Prince of Merchants and the Lions City" Journal of the Malaysian Branch of the Royal Asiatic Society 37:1 (1964) 20-40.

J.S. Tay, "The Attempts of Raffles to Establish a Base in South East Asia" Journal of Southeast Asian History 1:2 (1960) 30-46.

C. Trocki, "The Origins of the Kangchu System 1740-1860" Journal of the Malaysian Branch of the Royal Asiatic Society 49:2 (1976) 132-155.

C. Trocki, "The Rise of Singapore's Great Opium Syndicate 1840-86" Journal of Southeast Asian Studies 18:1 (1987) 58-80.

R.V. Turrell, "Conquest and Concession: The Case of the Burma Ruby Mines" Modern Asian Studies 22:1 (1988) 141-163.

K. Viviane Frings, "The Turbulent but Commercially Valuable Chinese: A Comparison of French and Chinese Colonial Policies towards the Chinese in Southeast Asia" Itinerario 19:1 (1995) 48-68.

J.R. Ward, "The Industrial Revolution and British Imperialism 1750-1850" Economic History Review 47:1 (1994) 44-65.

J. Warren, "Balambangan and the Rise of the Sulu Sultanate 1772-1775" Journal of the Malaysian Branch of the Royal Asiatic Society 50:1 (1977) 73-93.

A. Webster, "British Export Interests in Bengal and Imperial Expansion into South East Asia: The Origins of the Straits Settlements" in B. Ingham and C. Simmons, Development Studies and Colonial Policy (London, Frank Cass 1987).

A. Webster, "The Political Economy of Trade Liberalisation: The East india Company Charter act of 1813" Economic History Review 43:3 (1990) 404-419.

A. Webster, "British Expansion in South East Asia and the Role of Robert farquhar, Lt Governor of Penang 1804-5" Journal of Imperial and Commonwealth History 23:1 (1995) 1-25.

Wong Lin Ken, "The Trade of Singapore 1819-69" Journal of the Malaysian Branch of the Royal Asiatic Society 33:4 (1960) 11-301.

Wong Lin Ken, "Singapore: Its Growth as an Entrepot Port 1819-1941" Journal of Southeast Asian Studies 9:1 (1978) 50-84.

Wong Lin Ken, "Commercial Growth before the Second World war" in E.C.T. Chew and E. Lee (eds), A History of Singapore (Singapore, Oxford University Press 1991).

H.R.C. Wright, "The Anglo-Dutch Dispute in the East 1814-24" Economic History Review 3:2 (1950/51) 229-239.

Yen Ching Hwang, "Class Structure and Social Mobility in the Chinese Community in Singapore and Malaya 1800-1911" Modern Asian Studies 21:3 (1987) 417-445.

UNPUBLISHED PHD THESES

I.G. Brown, The Ministry of Finance and the Early Development of Modern Financial Administration in Siam 1885-1910 (University of London 1975).
Thant Myint U, The Crisis of the Burmese State and the Foundation of British Colonial Rule in Upper Burma 1853-1900 (Trinity College, Cambridge 1995).
A. Webster, The Origins of the Straits Settlements: British Trade and Policy in the Malay Archipelago 1786-1824 (University of Birmingham 1984).

INDEX